D0038663

THE NATIONAL
GEOGRAPHIC TRAVELER

LOS
ANGELES

THE NATIONAL
GEOGRAPHIC TRAVELER

LOS
ANGELES

Marael Johnson

Contents

How to use this guide 6–7   About the author 8
Areas of Los Angeles 45–224   Excursions 225–234   Travelwise 235–264
Index 265–69   Credits 270–71

History & culture 9
Los Angeles today 10–17
History of Los Angeles
  18–33
The arts 34–44

**Downtown &
vicinity 45**
Introduction & map 46–47
Underground art tour
  60–63

Midtown 75
Introduction & map 76–77
Feature: Car culture 90–91
Walk: Melrose Avenue
  shopping 96–97

**Hollywood & West
Hollywood 99**
Introduction & map
  100–101
Hollywood 102–129
Walk: Along Hollywood
  Boulevard 110–11
Feature: Putting the tinsel
  into town 118–19
Feature: Altars & egos
  124–25
West Hollywood 130–37
Walk: Sunset Strip 132–35

**Griffith Park &
vicinity 139**
Introduction & map 140–41

**Beverly Hills &
vicinity 151**
Introduction & map 152–53
Walk: Shop till you drop
  along Rodeo Drive
  156–57
Feature: Fads, food, fat, &
  faces 158–59

The Westside 169
Introduction & map 170–71
Walk: UCLA walking tour
  174–75

**Santa Monica,
Venice, & Malibu
187**
Introduction & map 188–89
Drive: Along beaches &
  through canyons 198–99
Feature: Calamities & car
  crashes 200–201

**San Fernando &
San Gabriel
Valleys 203**
Introduction & map
  204–205
Walk: Old Pasadena to the
  Playhouse District 218–19

Excursions 225
Introduction & map 226–27

Travelwise 235
Planning your trip 236
How to get to Los
  Angeles 236–37
Getting around 237–39
Practical advice 239–42
Emergencies 242–43
Activities 243
Hotels & restaurants by
  area 244–57
Shopping 258–61
Entertainment 262–64

Index 265–69
Credits 270–71

Page 1: Sunset casts a
romantic light over L.A.'s
skyline.
Pages 2–3: Following the
"Walk of Fame"
Left: Ever busy freeways
laden with myriad vehicles
provide much of the city's
evening lights.

How to use this guide

See back flap for keys to text and map symbols

The *National Geographic Traveler* brings you the best of Los Angeles in text, pictures, and maps. Divided into three main sections, the guide begins with an overview of history and culture. Following are eight area chapters with featured sites selected by the author for their particular interest. Each chapter opens with its own contents list for easy reference. A final chapter suggests excursions from Los Angeles.

A map introduces each area of the city, highlighting the featured sites and locating other places of interest. Walks and drives, plotted on their own maps, suggest routes for discovering the most about an area. Features and sidebars offer intriguing details on history, culture, or contemporary life. A More Places to Visit page generally rounds off the chapters.

The final section, Travelwise, lists essential information for the traveler—pre-trip planning, getting around, communications, emergencies, and activities—plus a selection of hotels and restaurants arranged by chapter area, shops, and entertainment.

To the best of our knowledge, all information is accurate as of the press date. However, it's always advisable to call ahead.

Color coding

206

Each area of the city is color coded for easy reference. Find the area you want on the map on the front flap, and look for the color flash at the top of the pages of the relevant chapter. Hotel and restaurant listings in **Travelwise** are also color coded to each area.

Visitor information

Schindler House

- 🅰 Map pp. 100–101
- ✉ 835 N. Kings Rd.
- ☎ 323/651-1510
- 🕐 Closed Mon.–Tues.
- 💲 $$

Practical information is given in the side column (see key to symbols on back flap). The map reference gives the page number of the map. Further details include the site's address, telephone number, days closed, and entrance charge in a range from $ (under $4) to $$$$$ (over $25). Visitor information for smaller sites appears in italics and parentheses in the text.

TRAVELWISE

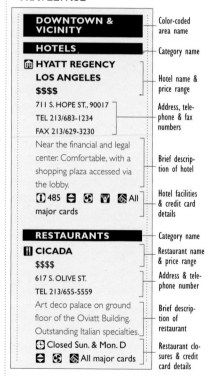

Color-coded area name

Category name

Hotel name & price range

Address, telephone & fax numbers

Brief description of hotel

Hotel facilities & credit card details

Category name

Restaurant name & price range

Address & telephone number

Brief description of restaurant

Restaurant closures & credit card details

Hotel & restaurant prices

An explanation of the price bands used in entries is given in the Hotels & Restaurants section (beginning on p. 244).

AREA MAPS

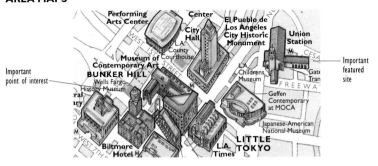

Important point of interest

Important featured site

- A locator map accompanies each area map and shows the location of that area in the city.

WALKING TOURS

Point of interest not on walk route

Starting point

Red numbered bullets link site on map to descriptions in the text

Direction of walk route

Walk route

Featured site (in bold) on walk route

Building outline

- An information box gives the starting and ending points, time and length of walk, and places not to be missed along the route.

EXCURSION MAP

Important featured town

Point of interest

Road number

- Towns and sites described in the Excursions chapter (pp. 225–34) are highlighted in yellow on the map. Other suggested places to visit are also highlighted and are shown with a red diamond symbol.

THE NATIONAL GEOGRAPHIC TRAVELER

LOS ANGELES

About the author

Marael Johnson is a travel writer and editor who has lived in Southern California for most of her life. She has written for many prominent print and online publishers on regions as diverse as Outback Australia, Europe's Basque region, remote South Pacific islands, and Louisiana's Cajun country. The author grew up in Los Angeles and is a bona fide graduate of Hollywood High School.

History & culture

Los Angeles today 10–17
History of Los Angeles 18–33
The arts 34–44

Reminders of L.A.'s earliest inhabitants share the midtown turf.

Los Angeles today

LOS ANGELES IS NOT JUST ANOTHER CITY: IT'S ANOTHER PLANET. IMAGINE you are gazing down at Greater Los Angeles from space. You peer through the heavenly mist and fiery spirits of the atmosphere (okay, perhaps it's a layer of smog), and you are struck not by some tediously recognizable architectural or geographical feature, but spread out before you, like a phantasmagoric vision, by an enormous, colorful, vibrant, and rollicking movie set.

There is no other place on Earth like L.A. Millions of people—including Americans hailing from almost every other U.S. town and city, immigrants from Albania to Zambia, and a smattering of "real natives"—presently call this city and its environs home. The locals ascribe to a diverse range of religious persuasions, from the more familiar Judeo-Christian and Islamic brands to any Eastern sect that ever burned a stick of incense and every New Age philosophy ever espoused. And their socioeconomic scale begins with the homeless and bottom-of-the-barrel poor, skyrockets its way through the middle- and upper-middle class "regular" folk, and goes off the charts when it reaches the rarefied air of seven-figure-income tycoons and celebrities.

Like the population, the living areas run a broad spectrum. Residents inhabit modern apartments, high-rise condominiums, 1960s "sitcom-style" homes, cloned tract houses, planned communities, converted warehouse lofts, rundown dwellings with barred windows, old cardboard boxes beneath bridges or alongside the railroad tracks, and palatial gated estates down by the beach or high in the hills. Each section of town is like a city within a city, and some are even countries within cities. Koreatown, Chinatown, Little Tokyo, Little Saigon, Little India, and the Eastern European and African communities are cultural microcosms where immigrants speak their native languages, eat the dishes handed down through generations, and continue life as though they were still back in the old country.

As befitting a city built around films and glamour, L.A. is pure drama, besieged by a

plethora of multiple personalities. It all comes down to sets and costumes, with frequently changing scenes and endless mood switches, to lighting and action, and to time warps and futuristic concepts. Everyone is playing to some camera, real or imagined.

Like the stills of a film, image after image assails the curious onlooker. Thousands of cars join the jams of rush-hour traffic or at one of the sadistic freeway merges, the drivers narrowly missing one another while gesturing explicitly. Meanwhile, golf carts career across manicured championship courses in other parts of town, and cyclists and in-line skaters easily maneuver their wheels at the beach. Joggers (who have their own special "traffic" lane in many areas) go it on foot, often running all the way to the office, where they left the BMW the day before. The limo riders, oblivious to it all, sit back, buff their nails, watch TV, chat on their cell phones, and check the mirror for evidence of new wrinkles. And don't forget those glorified car chases! Life practically stops as motorists caught in the melee try to veer out of the way, and everyone from housemaids to high-level executives bee-lines for the nearest TV to watch, riveted, until the escapade is over, veiling disappointment at the mostly nonviolent endings.

At the beach, the surf crowd hangs ten, bikini-clad natural blondes work hard to darken their fair skin, and musclemen and women pump iron on the glistening sand. Over in Hollywood, ambitious performers practice their craft, sweat over auditions, and spend hours of every day rehearsing drama, dance, music, and theatrical productions. All the while they check every inch of their bodies for cellulite, and perfect flaw-covering and youth-endowing makeup techniques. The city's visual artists are probably ensconced in their studios—from the downtown

Just another ordinary fellow dining on a burger and milk shake in one of the many eateries on Melrose Avenue.

warehouse district all the way to Venice Beach—working on cutting-edge contemporary projects. Or they may be literally underground, polishing up subway installations for one of the country's most impressive and aggressive public art projects.

In the evenings, the too-trendy-for-words Cocktail Nation patriots dress in their best basic black, purchased at the city's most expensive boutiques, for the chance to swill overpriced martinis in chic supper-club ambience. Older, less-affluent, down-to-their-last-paycheck couples wash their faces after work, change into T-shirts and jeans, and enjoy the same cocktails—minus the swizzle sticks and double-digit tabs—at a neighborhood bar. And then there's the Muscatel-in-a-paper-bag crowd, leaned against darkened downtown doorways. The yup-and-comings are also highly visible, sipping Chardonnay or Merlot in Westside bistro gardens or in posh hotel lobbies, although, thanks to

The car is king in L.A., and cruising Hollywood Boulevard has long been a favorite pastime.

Starbucks, café society has also seduced the L.A. cool. The city's blue-collar workers, meanwhile, chill out by grabbing a Bud from an ice chest seconds after the final punch of the day's timecard.

In L.A. everyone does their own thing, be they gang members brazening the streets over in the South Central jungle, or movie moguls and their protégés bonding in some genteel and discreet location. Women with ticking biological clocks and men unwilling to make commitments flood the city's clubs, cafés, gyms, and Starbucks' counters. The streets are teeming with every type of performance imaginable, some of which are dangerous (though certainly no worse than in any other densely populated region) while the majority are just laughably and phenomenally unique.

Most frames merely flash by, with the odd still and tedious instant replay. Oil wells pump as regularly and fervently as Angelenos' biceps and pecs. Women line up for breast implants, men for hair transplants, and both sexes are in a face-lift frenzy. Cosmetic surgeons are revered as saints in this town, as are maître d's, hairstylists, and personal trainers. Day spas are as commonplace today as dime stores once were. Hey, what's life without a regular cucumber and walnut body peel? Judges, lawyers, and the occasional high-profile madam, john, prostitute, or criminal are also granted celebrity status—at least until the trials are over and the tabloids have grown bored.

L.A. is a land of macho men and drag queens, people in touch with their feelings, and those too numb even to feel a touch. This is a town of swaying palms and staggering bums, rude stars and classy acts, the hopefuls and the hopeless. You'll glimpse plenty of shallow types, just burning to become rich

Christmastime on Rodeo Drive: Although the shops are for the rich, there is plenty of entertainment for everyone.

and famous, and who would sell their bodies and souls for the chance. Yet they are juxtaposed by deep-thinking New Agers who burn candles, chant mantras, and have their chakras aligned, hoping for complete attunement of body and soul. Aside from the colors—and the neighborhood—it's not all that easy to tell hardened gang members from highly paid celebrities. All seem to have tattoos, and you'd have to look pretty closely (which you probably don't want to do) to differentiate between some death symbol and an artsy stylized design. Anyway, you still might not be on the mark. Was that some nasty skinhead who just passed by, or was it Demi Moore gone Buddhist? Tough call.

L.A. was at the forefront of California cuisine, where food lovers became the

hippest crowd in town, and where celebrity chefs such as Wolfgang Puck and Joachim Splichal are revered (and rich), spreading their talents into more and more branch restaurants (don't ever call them chains!). Directors, agents, scouts, stars, star wanna-bes, fans, paparazzi, and ladies who lunch can all be tracked down at a multitude of exclusive foodie havens, most of them to be found in West Hollywood, Beverly Hills, on the Westside, or at the beaches.

Somehow it all works, like a succession of perfectly directed movies featuring drama, comedy, action, romance, tragedy, and disaster titles, all set against the backdrop of beaches, mountains, valleys, concrete jungle, and shopping malls.

And don't let the hyped-up media fool you; most Angelenos really do get along (no one loves gangs, but they come with the territory —and pretty much stay in their own). There is an inherent respect for one another's life-styles,

An actress dangles on a wire in front of the Hollywood sign.

the kinkier and more offbeat the better. It's commonplace for strangers to smile at one another in passing or to hug after a brief encounter, and that goes for both sexes. Perhaps it's down to the mild climate, or the sea air, the exhaust fumes, or the smog. Or perhaps it's even the magic of Hollywood and all that it created shining through.

Los Angeles goes by many names, including the City of Angels, the Cocktail Nation, LaLaLand, Tinseltown, Glitter Gulch, Surf City, Hell A, and Hollyweird. If these don't suit then make up your own—it's sure to fit perfectly somewhere in the sphere. And for all its oddities, frailties, and occasionally lousy P.R., the undeniable fact is that Los Angeles is fun, and visiting the city is as exciting as discovering a mysterious and wondrous new planet. ∎

History of Los Angeles

UNLIKE OTHER STALWART CITIES OF THE WORLD, L.A. HAS A HISTORY AND culture that are ever changing and fluid, regularly reinventing themselves much like an improvised script. Missionaries and Spanish colonization were headliners one day, the birth of Tinseltown and movie-star glamour another. Then boom, the city was gripped by an animated mouse and the Barbie doll, followed by surfers, rock stars, and flower children. A nod and a blink later, and wood-fired pizzas and a street named Melrose entered the spotlight; then just as quickly Melrose was passé and everyone began drooling over the macaroni and cheese that mom used to make. L.A. history also embodies an array of riots and disasters, peppered with the opening of monumental museums and cultural institutions, and criminal trials that double as miniseries. It all adds up to a historical timeline befitting a larger-than-life movie, and it could only happen in the City of Angels.

FROM OUT OF THE TAR

L.A. has been a strange place since the Ice Age, about 10,000–40,000 years ago. In those early days the region harbored a plethora of Pleistocene-epoch creatures, which in the distant future would become the model stars for movies that would delight LaLaLand's kids. More than 600 species used to roam the region, and their remains can still be viewed at La Brea Tar Pits in midtown. Among the earliest inhabitants were saber-toothed cats (the official state fossil), dire wolves, mammoths, mastodons, horses, bison, and birds galore. Believing the tar pits (which are not tar, but asphalt) to be watering holes, the creatures met a sticky death; hundreds of fossils continue to be uncovered here each year.

FIRST PEOPLE

Although many Angelenos equate the term hunters and gatherers with the somewhat tawdry dealings of showbiz, these were in fact the activities of the early inhabitants who cruised Greater L.A. long before the streets were paved in glitter (or paved in anything, for that matter). The primary inhabitants were the Hokan-speaking Chumash peoples, who occupied the western San Fernando Valley and portions of the southern shoreline, and the Tongva people, who put down stakes in the interior basin and along the coastline from the Chumash border south to the present Orange County line. The far-older Chumash group may well have lived in the area as far back as 11,000 B.C., while the Tongva (later referred to as the Gabrieliño or Fernandeño, according to which mission they ended up near), members

of the Uto-Aztecan linguistic family and descendants of the Shoshone, didn't arrive in the golden state until 2000 B.C.–A.D. 700. Various sources peg their combined population somewhere between 5,000 and 30,000, and—unlike Native Americans in other states—they did not live in tribes, but in single-family villages of a few hundred people or so.

The living was easy for these peoples, and their dealings with one another were amicable. They existed by hunting birds, game, and fish (the Chumash, in particular, were known for their fishing prowess), and collecting berries, acorns, nuts, seeds, and edible plants. Dwellings were simple cone-shaped huts, built from local reeds, grasses, and rushes. The Tongva were the primary artists and craftspeople, forging utensils and implements out of soapstone and steatite, and creating baskets from plant material and natural dyes (these were waterproofed with the asphalt from the local tar pits). The Chumash and Tongva freely traded with one another and with other tribes, using seashells for currency. The Chumash even traveled all the way to the Channel Islands in their handcrafted plank canoes to deal with the native peoples there. Ritual healing, mythology, a deep respect for nature, and impeccable hygiene were all part of everyday life, as were the other dictates of Chengiichngech (a chief god with a strict behavioral code). Archival

Introduced by the mission padres, religious processions incorporated music, candles, and the carrying of crosses and banners.

storytelling and intermarriage between the kindred peoples were not only tolerated but encouraged. It was only natural, therefore, that these peace-loving people welcomed the Spanish explorers, many of whom repaid the friendly gestures by abusing Native American women, by introducing alcohol and disease, and by decrying the "heathen" religion.

Celebrating L.A.'s Mexican heritage: September 16th's Mexican Independence Day festival on Heritage Square

EARLY EXPLORATION

A few European explorers had already wandered this way before the Spanish began their serious occupation in 1769. Juan Cabrillo had sighted San Diego harbor back in 1542 and sailed along the coast up to Santa Barbara, naming some of his stops along the way (including San Pedro Bay). Various others followed, including Sir Francis Drake, who in 1579 was the first to set foot on California soil (near San Francisco), and Sebastián Vizcaíno, who entered Monterey Bay in 1602 (five years before John Smith and company settled

Jamestown on the East Coast). And then nothing—at least not for another 167 years, the length of time it took for the Spanish to realize they'd hit upon something important.

SPANISH COLONIZATION

California had been left to languish, viewed by the Spanish as a wild frontier region, although they did use the harbors as shelters and restocking points on their trade voyages between Europe and the Orient, hauling cargoes of silks, sandalwood, spices, and other riches. But then Spain caught wind that some other European countries (notably England and France) might be interested in the region. To top it off, the Russians were heading south from Alaska, hot on the trail of sea-otter pelts. The Spaniards realized it was time to colonize and claim California, and their simple formula for such occasions was to create presidios, pueblos, ranchos, and missions. And so California was "hispanized."

Under orders of the king of Spain, Alta California was soon occupied, leaving little doubt to the rest of the world that this region was firmly controlled by the Spanish Crown. In 1769 the Franciscans—under the leadership of Father Junípero Serra and backed by Gaspar de Portolá—established a chain of 21 missions along the El Camino Real (Royal Road). In 1771, Mission San Gabriel Arcángel was founded northeast of what is now downtown Los Angeles, followed 26 years later by Mission San Fernando Rey de España at the eastern edge of the San Fernando Valley.

MISSION ACCOMPLISHED

Various theories exist as to why many Native Americans opted to jump right into mission life. One notion is that they were attracted to the greater stability of agricultural society, with the additional incentives of such perks as soapmaking and olive-oil production. Of course, in some cases they were given no choice, and were simply herded out of their villages and indoctrinated into the Christian life. For the Native Americans, however, this rarely meant brotherhood for all and angels around every corner; rather, their conversion had to be earned through slave-type labor and assorted God-fearing punishments. Once baptism had taken place, the Native American was irretrievably locked into the often harsh sys-tem—a hard religion indeed for peoples who had previously lived at one with the Earth. If a Native American ran away (which often occurred), he would be hunted by soldiers and flogged back into Christian conversion. Father Serra himself, often touted as a benevolent priest, has been viewed by some historians as a

EL PUEBLO

In 1781—shortly before the British surren-dered to George Washington in Virginia—Felipe de Neve, then governor of Spanish California, established El Pueblo de Los Angeles slightly northwest of its present site. The governor and his aides then recruited a group of 44 *pobladores* (settlers) from Sonora,

slave driver in collusion with the repressive colonial forces.

Despite such brutality, life at the mission went on, and, somewhat surprisingly, both San Gabriel and San Fernando Missions each numbered about 1,000 neophytes (new con-verts) at a time when the population at the nearby El Pueblo settlement was still in triple digits. In time, the Franciscans were endowed with an enviable Native American workforce, skilled at farming, weaving, and carpentry. After the missions were secularized in the 1830s, the Native Americans drifted to towns or ranchos, living mainly in poverty and falling victim to smallpox epidemics. As a result, by World War I about 95 percent of the original population had been obliterated.

L.A. in the 1860s was a small spacious town, a far cry from the bustling city it is today.

Mexico, who committed themselves to march-ing through the burning desert to build the plaza that would one day mark the center of downtown L.A. These early settlers were an intriguing multicultural conglomeration of blacks, mestizos, mulattos, Native Americans, and Mexican Españoles, with the number of adults and children almost equally divided. The pobladores got off to a slow start, partly because a smallpox epidemic forced them into quarantine, and also because the population merely trickled into town rather than flocking in droves as had been the plan.

Growth began in spurts—much of it dependent upon the Zanja Madre (L.A.'s original irrigation ditch), which brought water to the pueblo—and a smattering of streets, houses, and corrals were built. However, in 1786 a law empowered the governor to give land grants and 2,000 head of cattle to retired soldiers and government servants, thereby instigating the creation of huge ranchos. The pueblo itself was considered a land grant, and so the hard-working settlers were given smallish plots in the village along with no more than 50 cows, horses, or sheep each.

At the turn of the 19th century, the City of Angels boasted a population of 315 humans and 12,500 cows. The ranchos more or less followed the pattern of the missions, putting the Native Americans to work tending the homes and herds, although presumably the rodeos were more fun than sermons. Floods in the early 1800s finally spawned some large-scale development and a move to slightly

higher ground not far from the original settlement. Construction began in earnest on the present plaza, on Avila Adobe, and on the Church of Our Lady the Queen of the Angels.

UNITED STATES OF MEXICO

After gaining independence in 1821, it was inevitable that Mexico would push the Spanish out of the action. However, mestizo families such as the Sepulvedas, Verdugos, Olveras, Picos, and Felizes (names you still see

Battles such as that at Palo Alto in 1846 eventually wrested California from the Mexicans for the United States of America.

around the city) had held a fairly tight rein on the region, and they weren't about to release it. By this time L.A. was Alta California's largest population center, making it the entire region's economic, cultural, political, and religious hub. Independence also saw the secularization of the missions, and the Spanish priests were expelled. Although Mexico had declared itself a republic, it not only abided by the previous land grants but also doled out some of its own, albeit in smaller plots than had the Spaniards. Mission land comprising millions of acres was broken up into parcels by the new Mexican government, and eventually a couple of dozen families were ensconced on

In the early beginnings, downtown was the place for a shopping spree.

land that had once belonged to the San Gabriel and San Fernando Missions. In effect, suburbia had been created. The converted Native Americans, who by right should have received land grants, considered themselves lucky to find work with the rich land barons. Meanwhile, Governor Pío Pico established Los Angeles as the capital of Alta California.

UNITED STATES OF AMERICA

Ultimately, the United States decided it was necessary for its people to occupy all of the land between East and West coasts, and so began the Mexican-American War. Although the war mostly took place in Texas, the Battle of San Pasqual was fought near San Diego. The Californios resisted, but eventually America won the grand prize. In 1846 the U.S. military landed in San Pedro and captured the pueblo (not a shot was fired), and a truce was signed, followed by the final peace treaty in January 1847. The Treaty of Guadalupe, signed one year later, fixed the disputed borders, and in 1850 California was admitted to the United States as the 31st state.

Los Angeles made an easy adjustment from Mexican to American rule. By 1850 the city had become the county seat, a mayor had been installed, and the Protestants had come to town. The Americans lost no time in passing the 1851 Land Act, which basically challenged the rancheros to their property rights, keeping them entangled in a money-draining legal web until ultimately many of the Mexican elite were replaced by Americans.

BOOM & BUST

The 1849 Gold Rush at Sutter's Mill up in Coloma spilled south into L.A. with effects that were both good and bad. Although gold had been discovered first near Mission San Fernando, the Sutter's Mill bonanza made the Southern California find seem insignificant. Still, the region benefited in other ways because it had plenty of cattle and other food to sell to the hungry miners, and prices rose accordingly. By the mid-1850s, however, the boom had gone bust. Disgruntled miners came down to L.A. to take out their frustrations on the burgeoning city. The influx did increase L.A.'s population, but it wasn't the sort of settlers the city had been hoping for. As a result, L.A. became known as "Hell Town" and was the epitome of the lawless Wild West even before the notion of a Wild West had truly emerged. Saloons, brothels, and gambling halls were crawling with bad-tempered lowlifes, and the murder rate soared to as high as one per day. As for the Native Americans, naturally they incurred the worst wrath.

Vigilante groups, meanwhile, were driving away hordes of Mexican miners (with Anglo lawyers and merchants only too happy to pitch in), and it wasn't long before the Mexicans lost their Spanish land grants thanks to "real" American lawyers and creditors. The Latinos didn't take well to this displacement, which inspired groups of *banditos* to ambush stage-coaches (they were particularly fond of the treasure-laden Wells Fargo coaches). And adding to the ethnic melting pot was a growing Chinese settlement. Basically, this was not a town for more genteel citizens until after the Civil War and the arrival of the railroads.

THE BIG ORANGE

Juicy oranges from Los Angeles—and equally juicy tales of the city—had begun to circulate around the United States. Many Easterners and Midwesterners, in particular, had partaken of the sweet fruit and gained a taste for it that gave way to fantasies and cravings. Oranges had actually been planted at the San Gabriel Mission back around 1800, and in the early 1840s on a 70-acre orchard in what is now downtown L.A. Then along came the prized navel orange, a seedless variety that heralded from the wilds of Brazil. As they bit into these perfect round fruits, the cold Midwesterners and Easterners must have imagined a land of perpetual sunshine, with posies in winter, healthy air, and those phenomenal and ubiquitous oranges dangling at arm's reach. Groves were planted by the thousands (including most of the land between the Los Angeles River and Alameda Street), and Greater L.A. was lauded as an agricultural paradise.

In 1876, Southern Pacific Railroad extended its line to Los Angeles, and the resulting price war with the Santa Fe Railroad brought the cost of a St. Louis–L.A. ticket down to a single greenback. The throngs descended on the City of Angels in their hundreds of thousands—immigrants, vacationers, dreamers, and Midwestern Protestants. By the late 1880s the Los Angeles Chamber of Commerce had been formed, and a major campaign that proclaimed the area a semitropical paradise was launched to lure immigrants to the golden state. Many warmth-seeking passengers fell for the promises and boarded the transcontinental trains, only to be met at the LaLaLand end by sharklike realtors thrusting juicy oranges-on-a-stick in their pale faces.

The city was booming (at least for the time being), depending on your point of view. The Midwesterners pretty well shunned the

Hispanics, and the growing Chinese population wasn't having a particularly good time of it either. The death of a Caucasian man in a Chinese shop in 1871 had led to random attacks on Chinese residents, with almost two dozen killed, although practically none of the perpetrators were jailed. The developers, meanwhile, were overjoyed with things. Grand

Fragrant orchards of juicy oranges seduced early immigrants from the Midwest and East Coast.

hotels went up, real-estate developments flourished, land barons were in hog (or orange) heaven, and fortunes were being made overnight.

One of L.A.'s earliest and most dynamic entrepreneurs was whiz kid Phineas Banning, developer of San Pedro Harbor. Barely into his twenties, the farsighted and ambitious Banning was instrumental in the city's growth. Among his more illustrious "hobbies" were shipping, transportation, ranching, and property and railroad development. Making history along with young Phineas Banning were such eclectic heavyweights as Henry

Huntington, who established the city's electric Red Car transit system, and Edward Doheny, who just happened to strike oil. The city also drew creative types such as writer Charles Fletcher Lummis, who came to L.A. from Cincinnati on foot and became a staunch supporter of Native American rights and history. (Hispanic architecture was also being rediscovered by new immigrants, who appropriated mission-style homes for their own.) In 1902 the first Rose Bowl game and parade took place in Pasadena. There were still some rough spots here and there, but basically, L.A. was the hottest city in the U.S., just as it is today.

THE WATER DILEMMA

Cities—especially the hottest ones—need water, and in L.A. around the turn of the 20th century this became a big problem indeed. At that time the population numbered around 100,000, and the water supply was simply drying up. This was a big drawback for luring

Farmers Market, still a hometown favorite, offered local growers an easy and delightful spot to sell their produce and flowers.

settlers to build on the land, not to mention the fact that all those groves and fields of crops needed watering.

The first settlers of El Pueblo had constructed a crude system of open ditches called *zanjas,* which diverted water from the L.A. River (formerly known as El Río de Porciúncula). By 1860 the privately owned Los Angeles Water Works, later under the leadership of infamous former L.A. mayor Fred Eaton, constructed the city's first reservoir and inaugurated a more modern method of transporting water through hollow wooden pipes. But it was going to take plenty more resources and know-how than that to quench the thirst of the ever increasing population, especially in light of the parching turn-of-the-century drought.

Enter William Mulholland, an uneducated Irish immigrant who was soon immortalized as the City of Angels' guardian water bearer. Mulholland had held assorted jobs as he made his way westward. After arriving in L.A., he became intrigued with the zanjas and went to work as a ditch digger, eventually becoming the first superintendent of the new municipal water department. When the workday was over, Mulholland spent his free time studying engineering and mathematics. By the time the water crisis was at a boiling point and drought was settling in (making the outlook rather dismal in terms of city expansion), Mulholland had devised a brilliant engineering plan. In 1904, along with partner Fred Eaton, he set out in search of more water, with the intention of siphoning it from the Owens Valley, in the eastern Sierra Nevada. Mulholland took one look at the brilliantly clear Owens River and immediately calculated that he could get that water to L.A. (about 250 miles/400km south) using the simple force of gravity. The outcome? The Los Angeles Aqueduct, a quickly constructed project that incorporated an eye-popping structure of tunnels, canals, and inverted steel siphons. At first, however, the water only made it as far as the San Fernando Valley and not to L.A. proper. Here property values soared and eventually the San Fernando Valley became the penultimate American suburb and Valley Girl prototype.

When the water began flowing into the parched San Fernando Valley, Mulholland is reputed to have said, "There it is. Take it." He'd pulled off an astonishing engineering feat, and

Marilyn Monroe and Clark Gable star in the 1961 film *The Misfits*.

agricultural community. The plan had been to name their Utopia "Figwood." On the train ride out from Topeka, however, Daeida snapped up the name Hollywood after hearing it roll off a fellow passenger's lips. Little did prim and proper Harvey and Daeida realize what that word would come to symbolize.

The youthful Hollywood was soon awash both in citrus groves and Protestantism. Alcohol and saloons were banned, and puritanical values and church construction were encouraged. In 1910 Hollywood merged with Los Angeles and, a year later, director David Wark (D.W.) Griffith, the head honcho at New York's Biograph film company, came to town for a winter film shoot. For nearly three months the troupe holed up in the Hollywood Inn (whose sign once proclaimed "No Dogs or Actors") on Hollywood Boulevard. By the time the East Coast was starting its spring thaw, more than 20 films had been produced out West. A year later, director Mack Sennett followed and formed his Keystone Company. Within five years about 35 more companies had settled in town, bringing with them a myriad of badly behaved show-biz types and all the glitter and debauchery they could muster. It was goodbye temperance and morals, hello Hollywood. (Also see pp. 118–19.)

FROM BOOM TO BOOM BOOM

Thanks to the new gush of water, L.A. was again lush with flowers, orchards, palm trees, and all the other trappings of Eden. More liquid success ensued when Edward Doheny discovered oil near MacArthur Park. Before long, thousands of derricks were pumping away in the Greater Los Angeles area, and California soon became one of the U.S.'s top three oil-producing states. Life in L.A. was becoming quite interesting: The military and moviemaking industries had arrived, and the newspapers covering all the hullabaloo were flourishing as never before. Organized labor emerged neck and neck with the factories and production facilities, and by around 1910 the first strikes had already taken place. Real-estate developers were in a feeding frenzy, reeling in the cash from subdivisions and growth-related construction. Everyone, it seemed, was involved in real estate in one way or another.

By 1920 over 700 Pacific Red Cars carried

was hailed a hero by the citizenry (particularly the real-estate developers). Later, the Owens Valley supply became insufficient and Mulholland built another aqueduct from the Colorado River. Eventually, the exploding city was able to add more and more communities, particularly those with unproductive wells.

HERE COMES HOLLYWOOD

The film industry was easily seduced into setting up shop in L.A. Pre-Tinseltown Hollywood had been established in 1903 by Harvey Henderson Wilcox and his wife Daeida, staunch Midwesterners who came out to the coast to form a religion-based

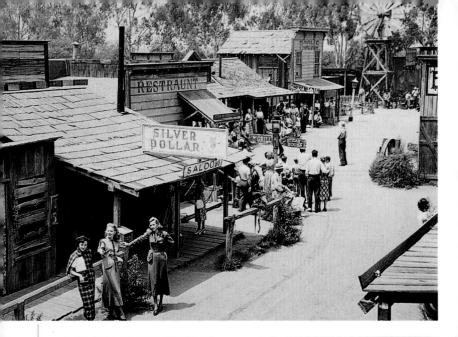

The Knott family created a "wild west" backdrop for their jams, jellies, berries, and chicken dinners.

more than 200,000 passengers per day in and out of the city to more than 40 towns (a ride between downtown and Venice Beach took just under 40 minutes). In addition, the horseless carriage had hit the streets, starting what would become the city's lifelong love affair—and total obsession—with these four-wheeled beasts and the freeways and fuel they require. L.A. also soon became as popular for airborne vehicles as for those on the ground. The aviation industry had descended upon the region: The Lockheed Brothers relocated their company from Santa Barbara; Donald Douglas fabricated his first transport plane on the site of the present Santa Monica Airport; and Northrup started up his own company, as did Howard Hughes. All became major players in the country's military-industrial complex, now headquartered in L.A.

By 1930, the strange and wondrous L.A. City Hall had been built, the Los Angeles Stock Exchange (now Pacific Stock Exchange) had turned downtown's Spring Street into the Wall Street of the West, almost all of the world's films were being produced in the city (making it the country's fifth-largest industry), and not even World War II kept the tourists and new-

comers away. Sights such as Abbot Kinney's Venice, Santa Monica's Ocean Park, the Pike at Long Beach, and Santa Catalina Island replaced ugly war thoughts with the L.A. specialties of fun, frolics, and escapism. Prohibition had, for the most part, been ignored.

Unfortunately, it was difficult for L.A. to ignore the Great Depression completely. Aside from the collapsed banks and businesses, the region had to cope with the influx of a new wave of immigrants. No longer just a haven for wealthy Easterners, pious Midwesterners, and glamorous stars, L.A. took in a conglomeration of poorer and simpler folk. Dust-bowl Okies and Texans, hobos, African Americans, and Mexican Americans all came calling, along with pioneering political movements, alternative religions, and assorted eccentrics.

World War II hardly did much to cheer the populace, although the aviation and industrial sectors thrived, and the military bases had also become a major growth industry. Racial tension, however, was rampant in its wake. Japanese-American citizens and immigrants had been rounded up and interned in camps, a mob, including many servicemen, took their anger out on Hispanics in a hideous affair known as the Zoot Suit Riots, and the increasing waves of African-American incomers were also greeted with discrimination. Jewish

people—especially those in the film industry—had almost always been discriminated against. (Later they would be joined by other rich and powerful folks in the Hollywood film scene who'd been blacklisted for alleged "left wing" leanings by the House Un-American Activities Committee, see pp. 118–19.)

AFTER THE WARS

The postwar era was a time of astounding change for L.A. The population explosion created both the numerous rewards of industrialization and expansion, and the pitfalls and challenges of differing socioeconomic and racial groups trying to live in harmony. Government contracts were poured into the defense industries by the billions of dollars, while housing, schools, libraries, police and fire departments, and shopping facilities were changing the cityscape dramatically, especially as the citrus orchards gave way to tract housing and asphalt sidewalks.

Somehow, most groups found (or were placed into) their own niche neighborhoods: The Hispanics went to East L.A., the African Americans settled South Central L.A., and low-income Jewish residents set up shop around Fairfax Avenue in midtown. The Chinese and Japanese also had their own towns-within-the-city. Some wealthy whites stayed put in Pasadena, Hancock Park, Beverly

Oil derricks have been pumping into the L.A. landscape since the early 1900s.

Hills, and the Hollywood Hills, while many others relocated to prime Westside enclaves such as Westwood, Brentwood, Bel Air, Pacific Palisades, and Malibu. The San Fernando Valley became synonymous with a suburbia of low-lying ranch homes offering lanais and swimming pools, lush landscaping, and simple living. Many political conservatives put down roots in Orange County, the birthplace of right-wing idol and future President Richard M. Nixon.

The Cold War and House Un-American Activities Committee were countered by happier events such as the births of both Mickey Mouse (and Disneyland, the ultimate escape from reality) and Barbie, the perfect, blond babe. But for car-crazy L.A., perhaps the greatest moment was the construction of the freeway system, beginning with the Pasadena Freeway in the late 1930s and networking the entire city and environs by 1970.

SWINGING SIXTIES

The press made much of the 1965 Watts Riots, which were triggered by the arrest of a speeding African-American motorist, and which involved almost a week of rioting, resulting in

millions of dollars in damage and about 34 deaths. Little mention was made of the oppressive heat wave at the time, a natural element that often precedes city violence. In comparison, very few non-Angelenos ever heard about an earlier riot at Hollywood High School, when the L.A. cops were called out in full force to break up a mass protest. The trigger again was a heat wave that had made the mostly well-off, mostly white kids moody and irritable. And while Watts was seemingly burning, in the rest of the city—including other ethnic areas—it was business as usual.

LaLaLand was becoming a very exciting place indeed. Surf culture had permeated the sand and waves from Malibu to Huntington Beach, romanticized in song by the Beach Boys and Jan and Dean, and in films such as

Gidget and the Frankie and Annette beach party flicks. Actor Ronald Reagan, a city resident, was elected governor of California in 1966, and conservative mayor Sam Yorty was replaced in 1973 by Tom Bradley, L.A.'s first black leader. Senator Bobby Kennedy was assassinated at the Ambassador Hotel in 1968, about the same time as the Jacuzzi brothers were introducing their whirlpool bath at the Orange County Fair. Vietnam War protests were heating up, the Beatles created chaos at the Hollywood Bowl, flower children took to the streets of Hollywood and West Hollywood, and the Whisky A Go Go and other Sunset Strip clubs became world renowned for head-liner rock groups and caged go-go girls in boots and tassels. "Make love, not war" became the favorite line of both flower

ment and frustration, which then dominoed into the retail sector. Gangs—with their graffiti, tattoos, colors, and violence—claimed turf in East and South Central L.A., eventually jumping into portions of the San Fernando Valley and Venice, and, in one isolated episode, even making their way into peaceful Westwood Village. Hard knocks aside, the 20-year tenure of Mayor Bradley was no doubt a major factor in keeping tensions from getting completely out of hand. Bradley, who was pushed into office by the Hispanic and Jewish communities, as well as by African Americans, lent a sort of calm and healing aspect to the bursting-with-angst city. And the influx of foreign investment in the 1980s, particularly in the downtown area, lent a much-needed boost as well.

The Internet was born at UCLA, while Caltech was think-tanking voyages to the moon and beyond, not to mention measuring every shaky quake, particularly the damaging 1971 and 1991 episodes. The videotaped beating of Rodney King by the L.A.P.D. in 1994, and the subsequent acquittal of the officers involved, resulted in riots that made world news. Again the media taunted L.A., showing that tape over and over and over. And then there was the media circus that surrounded O.J. Simpson, who was charged with the brutal murder of his wife and her friend. Yet, lest any forget, the flashbulbs also popped on the 1984 Summer Olympic games, the expanded Los Angeles Convention Center, the opening of both the Museum of Contemporary Art and the Getty Center, and the 1994 Soccer World Cup.

As L.A. enters the new millennium, it is full of economic and social resurgence, pumped by a fresh burst of optimism. Wealthy Mayor Richard Riordan, who took over from Bradley, has quite capably seen the city move into an upswing and has taken the helm for such spirit-raising events as the 1999 Women's Soccer Grand Final Championships. Jaded and faded Hollywood is being reglitzed, and older neighborhoods have been revamped and titivated. Meanwhile, the latest influx of immigrants—from Asia and the former Soviet Union—have joined the rest of the diverse eight-digit population who make their home in this sweet, crazy, lovable, fickle, show-off town. ■

L.A.'s long shoreline and the Pacific waves attracted surfers looking for the romantic ideal portrayed in the Beach Boys' songs.

children and exploiting cruisers trying to cash in on the seemingly endless supply of free love. Long hair, bell-bottom pants, incense burners, marijuana, and Eastern religion had all winged their way to the City of Angels.

INTO THE NEW MILLENNIUM
From the 1970s through the '90s, L.A.—like most cities—has seen some ups and downs, along with plenty of yuppies and down-and-outs. Things were tense for a while. The dissolution of many manufacturing plants, combined with the decline in the aerospace industry, resulted in widespread unemploy-

The arts

EVERYTHING ABOUT LOS ANGELES BESPEAKS ART: THE ECLECTIC ARCHITEC-
ture, magnificent museums, world-class public arts program, and noir literature, not to
mention the ever famous movie and music scenes. The pervasive and vibrant circuslike
atmosphere celebrates the creative side of everything, from car chases and catastrophes to
death and religion. And recognition, be it from passersby or talent scouts, is what most of
the population clamors for.

LITERATURE

As the center of the entertainment industry,
L.A. has been bequeathed a number of tantalizing literary figures. Some were here to write
specifically for the films or to turn their
published tomes into scripts; others penned
the city as their main character. This tradition
continues in the same way as acting, drawing
successful talents, talents who never quite
make it, and plenty of wanna-bes. There are
no reclusive J.D. Salinger types in this egoma-
niac city though; the goal here is to get as
much P.R. as possible.

Golden Age

Hollywood boasted the cream of *provocateur*
writers during its glory years, from the 1920s
into the '40s, including the likes of F. Scott
Fitzgerald, Ernest Hemingway, William
Faulkner, Dorothy Parker, Robert Benchley,
John Fante, Nathanael West, Dashiell
Hammett, James M. Cain, and, of course,
Raymond Chandler. Some, like Hemingway
and Fitzgerald, took to running back and forth
between LaLaLand and Paris, and they could
be found (on either continent) espousing their
works and various political grievances at a
string of literati bars and cafés. When in the
L.A. area, most hung out at the Cinegrill (in
the Hollywood Roosevelt Hotel) and the
Musso & Frank Grill, both still in business on
Hollywood Boulevard. During the 1930s and
'40s, Sunset Boulevard's Garden of Allah Hotel
was a favorite soiree spot, and scandal upon
scandal was created within those pink
Moorish walls—even spilling out onto the

street at times, to the delight of passersby and waiting fans. There was plenty of broken glass, screaming and yelling, suicide attempts, and although most of it didn't make the printed page it did reach the gossip columns. Some writers threw their energies into the political arena, most notably Upton Sinclair, who founded the End Poverty in California movement and was defeated in a gubernatorial bid.

Noir literature

Raymond Chandler was in a separate class from the rest of the Golden Age writers. For one, he emerged on the scene much earlier, in 1912, a few years before even the opening of the Musso & Frank Grill, which would become his favorite hangout. And for another, he made an unparalleled contribution to L.A.'s noir culture, a trend that has continued in books and films from Chandler's time to the present day.

Chandler changed residences around the city numerous times, and this restlessness was also reflected in his paper creation, the cynical, yet cushy-hearted detective Philip Marlowe. Through his wise-cracking Marlowe, Chandler explored L.A.'s darker side, both in locations and plot lines. This "noir" stylization, assisted

David Hockney's "Mulholland Drive"—the mountain road that snakes above the city.

by the World Wars and Great Depression, was characterized by shadowy figures and foreboding angst, unforgettable topics of the times (along with the debunking of the "L.A. as Heaven on Earth" campaign). Chandler's works soon became the darling of the film industry, which snapped up such titles as *The Big Sleep* (starring Chandler's favorite Marlowe, Humphrey Bogart), *The Long Goodbye,* *Farewell My Lovely,* and *The Lady in the Lake.* Joining Chandler in the genre was James M. Cain, who penned *The Postman Always Rings Twice, Mildred Pierce,* and *Double Indemnity.*

Many writers have not only settled in L.A., but, like Chandler, star it in their works. The city is a writer's dream, with locales that leap from sandy beaches to gritty streets, backdropped by movie stars, rock musicians, and a multitude of ethnic groups.

From beatniks to barflies

Although perhaps not as fabulous as that of San Francisco, L.A.'s beat scene was a scintillating time for writers. The beatniks wore black, read Ayn Rand, chain-smoked in underground coffeehouses that sported black-painted walls and makeshift tables topped with chess sets, and spewed existentialist poetry to the accompaniment of a stand-up bass. The beats were later replaced by the flower children, who still hung out in the coffeehouses but who wrote song lyrics instead, to a background of acoustic guitars. Local literature of the time was of the drug-inspired or spiritual bent. Among the prominent works were Carlos Castaneda's trippy *Teachings of Don Juan* (Castaneda was supposedly a UCLA teaching assistant at the time) and Paramahansa Yogananda's *Auto-biography of a Yogi* (Yogananda had founded his Eastern religion-based Self-Realization Fellowship in Pacific Palisades in 1950). Meanwhile, Ray Bradbury and Harlan Ellison were wooing sci-fi fans, and San Pedro-based poet Charles Bukowski was idolized by the fringe crowd and university literati alike.

The contemporary scene

Nearly everyone is a writer in L.A., even if only in their dreams and through the fantasies inspired by ubiquitous self-therapy journals. Depending on which part of town you're in, cafés are rampant with dreamy-eyed espresso drinkers, pens poised over empty pages, perhaps working away on a film treatment or television plot, or even that great American novel. Contemporary L.A. writers include Mike Davis, Carrie Fisher, and countless self-improvement and New Age gurus. Crime novelist James Ellroy, author of *The Black Dahlia* and other whodunits, has done a grand job of continuing Chandler's noir tradition.

A multitude of bookstores host signings by prominent authors, along with up-and-coming talents. Other literary events are hosted by museums, libraries, universities, and local colleges. And for those heeding the call of the muse, L.A. offers workshops on everything from iambic pentameter and journal writing to screenplays and bilingual revolutionary treatises.

ART

Almost everything in L.A. can be considered art, including graffiti, cuisine, calamities, death, and even the masterpieces that hang on museum walls. Like the city, the art scene is diverse and vibrant.

Art museums & galleries

City museums contain some of the most important collections in the country, be they of old masters or abstract contemporaries, sculpture, or decorative arts. Galleries, meanwhile, show an enviable range of international and local talents, and traveling exhibits.

For some of the finest artwork in the country, seek out L.A.'s esteemed museums: Los Angeles County Museum of Art, the Museum of Contemporary Art, Geffen Contemporary at MOCA, Norton Simon Museum, Huntington Art Gallery, and the knock-your-socks-off Getty Center. L.A. even has a Museum of Neon Art, with a neon "Mona Lisa" as its mascot.

Galleries also run the range, from the museum-quality to small, alternative spaces. More than 100 private galleries are spread throughout the city, clustered in West Hollywood, Santa Monica, Brentwood, Hancock Park, and Beverly Hills, although almost every neighborhood harbors at least

one. Bergamot Station in Santa Monica is one of the favorite venues in the city, housing a variety of galleries under one roof as well as the Santa Monica Museum of Art.

Downtown's Brewery Arts Complex, an industrial work/live space, offers a peek into the rarefied world of L.A.'s working artists.

The "Calendar" section of the *Sunday L.A. Times* features listings of galleries and their shows, while the "ArtScene" pamphlet (detailing the local exhibits) is available at most galleries. Almost every gallery is open to the public during regular hours, and most offer artists' receptions to herald new shows.

Public art

Los Angeles features one of the most dynamic public arts programs in the country, and even in the world. The city is rife with paintings, murals, mosaics, graffiti, sculpture, and

Russell Crowe and Kim Basinger star in *L.A. Confidential* (1997).

assemblages. Some are anonymous impromptu creations, but much is funded by the city or other government agencies.

L.A.'s car-crazed populace is finally being lured onto the public transportation system of subways and the light rail network via the city's favorite medium—art, of the showy, quirky, inventive, imaginative variety that appeals to the eclectic and ethnic masses. Since its inception in 1989, Metro Art (a department of the Metropolitan Transit Authority) has commissioned more than 175 well-known and emerging artists to create permanent and temporary projects at each of 50 subway stations along its three crisscrossing lines. Unlike other city subway stations, where each looks pretty much the same, L.A.'s present individual galleries with unique works of art, some thought-provoking, others fanciful, and much of it reeling riders right into the exhibit. For example, you might well ponder the "people's art" at Slauson Station, smile at the metaphorical journey at Transit Mall Station, or plunk your

A graffiti artist immersed in this unique, highly detailed "street art"

body right down onto the art-as-seating at Vernon or Union station. Even the MTA buses have jumped onto the creative bandwagon, exhibiting poetry placards to entertain riders instead of dreary ads for cheap dentures and contact lenses.

Murals

Perhaps the city's most noticeable public art is its magnificent murals (there are more than 1,000 of them), painted throughout the Greater L.A. area. Although murals have been part of the cityscape since the early 1900s, the real frenzy began in the 1960s, and (as in the early days) L.A. can credit the Hispanic community with inspiring the movement. The city's earliest wall paintings were created by famed Mexican muralists David Alfaro Siqueiros, Diego Rivera, and José Clemente Orozco. The controversial "Tropical America," painted by Siqueiros in 1932, on the south wall of El Pueblo's Italian Hall, so upset city officials with its scathing sociopolitical message that it was whitewashed over and has only recently been restored by the Getty Conservation Institute.

By the 1960s, the artists-as-activists Chicanos (Americans of Mexican descent) were again hitting the streets, paint buckets in hand. Spurred by Cesar Chavez and the United Farm Workers movement, they spread their messages—social commentaries that variously reflected rage, injustice, pride, and accomplishment—along the walls and freeways of the city barrios. The Chicano artists were soon joined by African Americans and hippies, who had their own stories to paint, and by the mid-1980s murals had popped up all over the concrete jungle, stretching from the barrios to the beaches. The corporate and government sector finally jumped in with sponsorships (many of the freeway murals were commissioned by the 1984 Olympic Committee), and this support continues to the present day, eliciting unexpected surprises along the walls and roadways of America's most colorful city.

The mix is dazzling, as are the artists, who range from amateurs to pros, and who hail from assorted ethnic and educational backgrounds. Subject matter encompasses a dizzying range of ancient ceremonies, religious and social statements, fine art, sarcasm, and humor noir, and a couple of the works are already record-breakers. "The Great Wall of Los Angeles," a collaborative effort by more than 200 young Angelenos, relates the city's illustrious history. Spread across 2,500 feet of concrete in a San Fernando Valley flood-control channel, this ranks as the world's longest mural. "Hog Heaven," artist Les Grimes's sardonic tribute to pigs that become sausages, painted on the walls of the Farmer John Packing Plant in Vernon, is considered the world's longest commercial mural. Visitors will spy such visions as ancient Roman and Greek structures entwined with the L.A. skyline, a five-story-tall Anthony Quinn doing his Zorba thing, and Oprah Winfrey flanked by Josephine Baker and Sarah Vaughan. Present-day master muralist Kent Twitchell—known for his meticulously executed works—has bequeathed the city many of his masterpieces and is proud to be relegated to L.A.'s inimitable (and well-trafficked) freeway system.

ARCHITECTURE

L.A.'s rich architectural heritage is symbolic of all the wonderful wackiness and highbrow artistry that the city embraces, be it early Spanish Mission, Modernist masterpieces, art deco buildings, kitsch Googie-style diners, the finely crafted Gamble House, or, yes, even the mini-mall. The city sprawl boasts numerous treasures designed by a star-studded cast of world-class architects, including Myron Hunt, Charles and Henry Greene, Robert Derrah, Julia Morgan, Bertram Goodhue, Frank Lloyd Wright, Rudolf Schindler, Richard Neutra, George H. Wyman, Arata Isozaki, Frank Gehry, and Richard Meier. Many standout structures and residences are interspersed with ordinary neighborhoods and unremarkable shopping strips, while in some cases entire streets or districts are designated architectural enclaves.

Spanish influence

Visitors can view the city's first buildings at both San Gabriel Arcángel and San Fernando del Rey Missions. In addition, several early adobes and a piece of the Zanja Madre (original irrigation ditch) still stand at the 44-acre El Pueblo de Los Angeles Historic Monument. Aside from the original structures, the Spanish Mission influence can be seen throughout the Greater L.A. area. This mimicry was not an attempt to emulate the Franciscan friars, but rather a resurgence in popularity of the style spearheaded by Helen

Simon Rodia's incomparable "Watts Towers" rank as penultimate examples of folk art.

Hunt Jackson's *A Century of Dishonor,* a scathing 1880s saga that unveiled the plight of the Native Americans who had been coerced into slave labor. Reclaiming the Hispanic architectural styles, turn-of-the-century residents romanticized the era (albeit with plenty of money), incorporating within their own homes architectural and design elements attributed to the region's historic missions and pueblos. Writer Charles Fletcher Lummis, whose arroyo home serves as the headquarters of the Historical Society of Southern California, was the leading proponent of the effort to rekindle the early design.

Victorian & Craftsman

The turn of the 20th century was heralded not only by Spanish Revival structures but also by glorious Victorian homes and buildings, and by exquisite Craftsman-style bungalows (not forgetting that Venice, Italy, was being re-created at the beach at this time). Most of the Victorian dwellings, unfortunately, did not survive the onslaught of city growth. Some have been preserved in residential districts between midtown and downtown, and a grouping of buildings moved to Highland

Park comprises the Heritage Square Museum. One of the more sublime Victorian-era commercial edifices is downtown's Bradbury Building, a blast from the past that was featured in the futuristic sci-fi film *Blade Runner*.

Happily, numerous examples remain of the Craftsman era, which also flourished around this period. Distinguished by the use of exposed wooden beams, cobblestones, large fireplaces, overhanging roofs, and rustic styling, the "bungalow" became an expression of the Arts and Crafts movement of the time. Architect brothers Charles S. and Henry M. Greene left their mark throughout Pasadena, most notably on the exquisite Gamble House, with its impeccable woodwork and breath-taking art glass.

From deco to modernism

Although L.A.'s Golden Age is often thought of in terms of films and celebrities, it was also a time of some of the city's most celebrated architecture; after all, those films had to be shown somewhere, and the stars needed homes and services. Two of L.A.'s most illustrious buildings were constructed at this time in downtown—City Hall and the Central Library. In addition, downtown's (now) Historic Theater District went up, as did the movie palaces along Hollywood Boulevard. The City of Angels dazzled with art deco, beaux arts, and fantasy monuments such as Robert Derrah's Coca-Cola Building and the Crossroads of the World, and Meyer and Holler's Chinese and Egyptian theaters.

Meanwhile, Frank Lloyd Wright had come to town, bringing his renowned modern designs to Hollyhock House, the Ennis-Brown House, and a number of other residences. Wright was followed by protégés Rudolph Schindler, Richard Neutra, and Lloyd Wright (his son), all of whom made their mark on the cityscape. Schindler House, in particular, continues to inspire architects who revere organic modern styling.

Postwar to new millennium

An even stranger conglomeration of architecture emerged in post-World War II L.A., then bursting with new arrivals. Suburbs took the place of citrus groves, and office buildings

supplanted old Victorians. Architect Cliff May created the ranch house, popularized throughout the country right around the same time as John Lautner designed his "googie" coffee shop. Googie's was an actual Sunset Strip coffee shop, but it became the tag name for those space age-looking glass, formica, and neon-lit diners. The Capitol Records Tower stack of 45s came to life, as did slicked-out Century City and the Pacific Design Center. This was also the dawn of the mini-malls.

Pasadena's Gamble House exemplifies exquisite Craftsman-era architecture and design.

Architect Frank O. Gehry hit the scene in the 1970s with almost the same impact as Frank Lloyd Wright. He has designed such freethinking, trendsetting buildings as the Geffen Contemporary at MOCA, Loyola Law School, the Aerospace Hall of the California Science Center, and Chiat/Day Advertising Agency, and he is currently working on the L.A. Performing Arts Center's masterful Walt Disney Concert Hall. Gehry's own abode is also a sight to see, although many of his neighbors view it as an eyesore. Interestingly, however, it is the monumental Getty Center, designed by Richard Meier (also architect of the Museum of Radio and Television in Beverly Hills) and filled with European paintings, that is poised to move the City of Angels into the next millennium.

PERFORMING ARTS

Cinema, theater, music, and dance have been the lifeblood of this city since D.W. Griffith and troupe hit town in the early 1900s, and much of it is entwined with the history and attractions covered in this guide.

Cinema

Angelenos are natural moviegoers, and (after the star-studded premieres) usually get the first peek at new blockbusters and often the only peek at independent and experimental films. Showings take place in restored movie palaces, a mega-assortment of multiplexes, and a few distinctive vintage filmhouses. The American Film Institute, UCLA, USC, and other universities and colleges often present student works, art films, and film series.

Theater

Although New York's Broadway and London's West End boast higher marks in the theater

**The many buildings that make up the
Getty Center are reflected in one another.**

department, L.A. still flaunts an enviable
assortment of live productions—more than
1,000 per year, in fact, including major crowd-
pleasers as well as little theater, experimental
works, and performance art (not to mention
the impromptu acts in the city streets). The
landmark Pasadena Playhouse, opened in
1925, has been a launching stage for many

well-known actors, and it still grabs the old-
money (and conservative) crowd with its non-
controversial productions. The Sondheim/
Webber-type spectacles reign at the
Ahmanson, Pantages, and Shubert theaters,
while the Geffen Playhouse and Mark Taper
Forum offer a wealth of interesting and well-
directed productions. Smaller theaters that
present classical, contemporary, and avant-
garde works include the award-winning
Matrix Theater Company (L.A.'s equivalent of

Lights, camera, action! are everyday events in the studios and streets of L.A.

off-Broadway), Actors' Gang Theater, Henry Fonda Theater, and the intimate Coronet Theater. L.A.'s universities and colleges also present eclectic offerings.

The music scene

L.A.'s music scene—as well as its venues—is as prestigious and notorious as the film industry. Landmarks and icons bespeak the successes of many musicians, particularly 1960s rock groups. Sounds waft from the record companies, music videos are filmed all around town, and musicians perform in such diverse arenas as the L.A. Music Center and Hollywood Bowl, and at the Whisky and the Viper Room. The Grammy Awards, moving from the Shrine Auditorium to the new Staples Center, pay annual tribute to the best in the business.

The L.A. Philharmonic Orchestra makes its home at the Music Center's acoustically excellent Dorothy Chandler Pavilion, with summer performances at the hometown favorite, the Hollywood Bowl. The Hollywood Bowl and Greek Theater both present renowned under-the-stars summer performances, ranging from baroque and jazz series to the hottest rock bands, while the Universal Amphitheater (now sporting a lid) is one of the city's largest indoor venues.

Visitors can take their pick of musical styles, such as classical, jazz, blues, heavy metal, world music, and rock 'n' roll. Settings range from supper clubs to museum auditoriums, crowded bars, and legendary night spots, and they can be black-tie or blue-jean casual. Thanks to the climate, outdoor concerts are held at public parks and beaches throughout the year, and many are free.

Dance & opera

Choose from the greatest international names or the excellent local talent—often one and the same. After the Philharmonic moves over to the Hollywood Bowl for the summer, the Los Angeles Opera takes to the Dorothy Chandler Pavilion stage, hosting crème de la crème operatic superstars that have included Placido Domingo and Maria Ewing.

Touring companies such as the American Ballet Theater and the Joffrey Ballet are also hosted at the Chandler Pavilion, while the Shrine Auditorium presents the foremost visiting dance companies—the Bolshoi and the Kirov. Contemporary dance troupes include L.A.'s own Pasadena Dance Theater, while the visiting companies of Martha Graham, Paul Taylor, and others bring their creative bodies to stages such as UCLA's Royce Hall. ■

Surprisingly compact for such an enormous city—so much so, in fact, that it is often passed over—L.A.'s downtown has gone from relative decay and dowdiness to a snazzy redeveloped central core with futuristic overtones.

Downtown & vicinity

Introduction & map 46–47
El Pueblo de Los Angeles City
    Historic Monument 48–49
Union Station 50
Chinatown 51
Civic Center & City Hall 52
Performing Arts Center 53
Los Angeles Times Building 54
Little Tokyo 55–56
Bunker Hill 57
Museum of Contemporary Art
    58–59
Underground art tour 60–63
Central Library 64
Biltmore Hotel 65
Bradbury Building 65
Grand Central Market 66
Historic Theater District 67
Museum of Neon Art 68
University of Southern California
    69
Shrine Auditorium 69
Exposition Park 70–73
More places to visit in
    downtown & vicinity 74
Hotels & restaurants 244–46

The gleaming Westin Bonaventure Hotel

Downtown & vicinity

DOWNTOWN USED TO BE ONE OF THE SLEAZIEST PARTS OF THE CITY, AND indeed portions still lean toward the seedy side, albeit in a lovable and devil-may-care sort of way. You'll catch film noir nuances, vibrant ethnic images, and sassy street life reflecting off slick high rises and cultural institutions, concert halls, and the convention center.

Amazing though it may seem, until the 1970s and '80s, when an influx of investors and developers coaxed sleek high rises to blossom forth from the trash-laden sod, the area's most majestic skyscraper was the diminutive 27-story City Hall—small in size, perhaps, but pretty hefty in stature (after all, Superman used to dangle from this building). City Hall anchors a relatively staid Civic Center and the tedium of government, while the nearby Music Center and its three theaters fairly tremble with the vibrations of world-class performances.

You'll see plenty of reminders of the humble little pueblo that used to be L.A. along the river (although if you mention the L.A. River to locals you'll be greeted with a smirk, for the "river" is a dingy trickle almost narrow enough to hop across). El Pueblo's boundary begins just across the street from Union Station, where the Old Plaza, scattered adobes, and famed Olvera Street have long been mainstays on the visitor's must-see agenda. L.A.'s Chinatown, just a fortune cookie's toss from Olvera Street, is the historic enclave of the city's Chinese community.

Bunker Hill (reached via Angel's Flight Railway) and environs is home to the financial district, the Museum of Contemporary Art, and a variety of ever expanding residential and commercial complexes. The grand Los Angeles Central Library—complete with trendy café—sits nearby, as does the landmark Biltmore Hotel and the regally renewed Pershing Square, downtown's only park and former no-man's-land. Broadway is a conglomeration of its New York namesake and several Latin-American countries. The indoor Grand Central Market is the place to soak up atmosphere and fortify yourself before exploring the beautiful historic theater district and other architectural treasures.

Little Tokyo, southeast of the Civic Center, shelters the Japanese cultural and commercial hub. The Geffen Contemporary, a cutting-edge branch of the Museum of Contemporary Art, is almost side by side with Little Tokyo and its age-old traditions. The hip Museum of Neon Art is slightly off the beaten path.

Exposition Park (adjacent to USC campus, southwest of downtown) dates from the late 1800s and is home to such dynamic sports and cultural venues as the Memorial Coliseum and Sports Arena (although for the time being both of these have been supplanted by the Staples Center, adjacent to the Convention Center). It is also the setting for museums of natural history, science and industry, and African-American achievement.

You can easily do most of downtown in a day, either on foot, on the DASH shuttle, or on the Metro (don't miss the MTA's "art gallery" stations—see pp. 60–63). Most of the area is best explored during the day; otherwise, you might find yourself sharing the streets with shady characters and neo-noir film crews. ∎

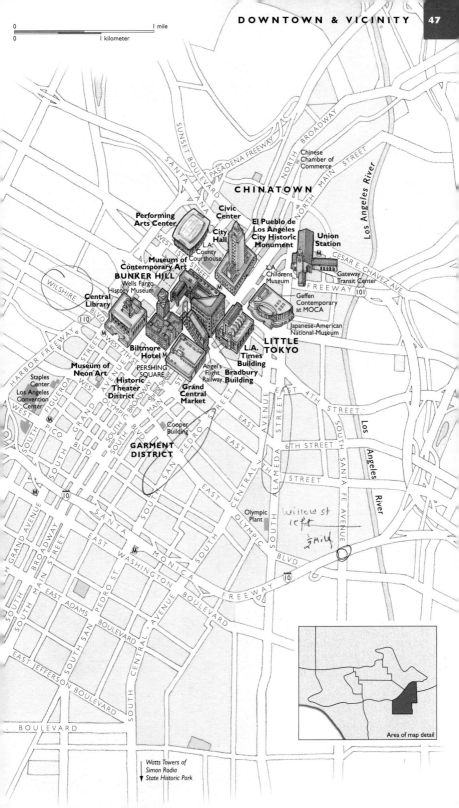

0   1 mile
0   1 kilometer

CHINATOWN

Chinese Chamber of Commerce

Performing Arts Center

Civic Center

El Pueblo de Los Angeles City Historic Monument

City Hall

Union Station

Museum of Contemporary Art

BUNKER HILL

L.A. County Courthouse

L.A. Childrens Museum

Gateway Transit Center

Central Library

Wells Fargo History Museum

Geffen Contemporary at MOCA

WILSHIRE BLVD

Japanese-American National Museum

LITTLE TOKYO

Biltmore Hotel

PERSHING SQUARE

L.A. Times Building

Museum of Neon Art

Angel's Flight Railway

Bradbury Building

Staples Center

Los Angeles Convention Center

Historic Theater District

Grand Central Market

Cooper Building

GARMENT DISTRICT

Olympic Plant

SUNSET BOULEVARD

SANTA ANA

PASADENA FREEWAY

NORTH BROADWAY

NORTH MAIN STREET

Los Angeles River

CESAR E. CHAVEZ AVE

FREEWAY 101

WEST 1ST STREET

HARBOR FREEWAY

WEST 2ND STREET

WEST 3RD STREET

GRAND AVENUE

WEST 4TH STREET

WEST 5TH STREET

WEST 6TH STREET

WEST 7TH STREET

FIGUEROA

SOUTH BROADWAY

SOUTH HILL STREET

SOUTH MAIN

SPRING STREET

EAST 3RD STREET

EAST 4TH STREET

EAST 5TH STREET

EAST 6TH STREET

SOUTH SAN PEDRO STREET

SOUTH ALAMEDA STREET

SOUTH SANTA FE AVENUE

Los Angeles River

EAST 6TH STREET

EAST 7TH STREET

WEST PICO BLVD

WEST OLYMPIC BLVD

SOUTH GRAND AVENUE

SANTA MONICA BOULEVARD

EAST WASHINGTON BOULEVARD

SOUTH BROADWAY

SOUTH MAIN STREET

EAST ADAMS BOULEVARD

SOUTH SAN PEDRO STREET

SOUTH CENTRAL AVENUE

EAST JEFFERSON BOULEVARD

BOULEVARD

Watts Towers of Simon Rodia State Historic Park

Area of map detail

willow st left 5 mile

El Pueblo de Los Angeles
City Historic Monument

El Pueblo de Los Angeles

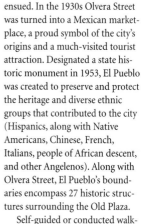

🅰 Map pp. 46–47

✉ 125 Paseo de la Plaza

☎ 213/485-6885

Sepulveda House Visitor Center

✉ 662 N. Main St.

☎ 213/628-1274

🕐 Closed Sun.

Olvera Street woos shoppers with its Mexican flare and flavors.

THIS 44-ACRE SITE, BOUNDED BY CESAR CHAVEZ AVENUE and Alameda, Arcadia, and Spring Streets, encompasses the city's oldest dwellings and gives a thought-provoking glimpse into L.A.'s humble beginnings. Imagine, L.A. was once a small community!

The community was founded in 1781 by 44 settlers of mixed heritage from northern Mexico, although the mud huts have long gone. However, once the Stars and Stripes was raised after the 1846 Mexican-American War, more and more immigrants started relocating to L.A. By the turn of the century, and with the encouragement of fare-war incentives from competing railways, the city was booming. The old pueblo area deteriorated as the city developed and more affluent residents spread southward.

By the 1920s, the former heart of L.A. was in dire need of resuscitation. An urban-renewal campaign ensued. In the 1930s Olvera Street was turned into a Mexican marketplace, a proud symbol of the city's origins and a much-visited tourist attraction. Designated a state historic monument in 1953, El Pueblo was created to preserve and protect the heritage and diverse ethnic groups that contributed to the city (Hispanics, along with Native Americans, Chinese, French, Italians, people of African descent, and other Angelenos). Along with Olvera Street, El Pueblo's boundaries encompass 27 historic structures surrounding the Old Plaza.

Self-guided or conducted walking tours (from Sepulveda House) point out early commercial buildings and residences, L.A.'s oldest Catholic church, the first water system and first firehouse, and commemorative statues and murals. Well-known Mexican artist David Alfaro Siqueiros' 18-by-80-foot "Tropical America" mural, painted in 1932, is on the south wall of the **Italian Hall** (*650 N. Main St.*). Whitewashed over, Mother Nature and arts preservationists have partially uncovered it.

OLD PLAZA
Hispanic social and cultural life has always revolved around its plazas, be they tiny patches of dusty earth or tropical oases. El Pueblo's former town square, at the beginning of Olvera Street, is no exception. It may be set in the center of downtown L.A., but you'll probably feel like you're south of the border. The

plaza was made circular and landscaped in the 1870s, when the shade-bequeathing Moreton Bay figs were planted. Folkloric dance groups and mariachis often take to the central bandstand on weekends and holidays—try to visit the area during a festival, when El Pueblo commemorates its Hispanic beginnings in real *olé* style. The nightly pre-Christmas Las Posadas processions are dazzling but don't hold a candle to the Blessing of the Animals (Saturday before Easter), when locals bring every type of pet imaginable for priestly prayers. The statue near the bandstand depicts El Pueblo's founder, Spanish Governor Felipe de Neve (governed 1775–1782).

OLVERA STREET

Although it is just one block long, brick-paved, and pedestrian-only, Olvera Street is a lively mix of festive Mexican marketplace and significant architectural landmarks. Souvenir stands instantly woo you with bright piñatas, puppets, sombreros, serapes, and an array of handicrafts, while the food stalls tempt with fresh tortillas, tropical fruits, and *pandulces* (sugary Mexican sweets). A number of restaurants offer indoor or patio dining and Mexican specialties, while the bars pour de rigueur cervezas and margaritas.

Redbrick **Sepulveda House,** an 1887 former boarding house between Main and Olvera Streets, houses the visitor information center, as well as a gift shop and gallery. One of the most noteworthy structures along Olvera Street is **Avila Adobe** *(No. 10),* L.A.'s oldest adobe (1818). **Pelanconi House** *(No. 17),* one of the city's first brick buildings (1855), is still a private residence and also houses La Golondrina Café, one of the street's earliest businesses. You can still spot a fragment of **Zanja Madre,** L.A.'s original irrigation ditch (dating from 1781), in front of Pelanconi House; it is marked by diagonal bricking on the street. Walking-tour maps are available at Sepulveda House, and free docent-guided tours take place several times daily, Tuesday to Saturday. ■

Often filled with fiestas and families, El Pueblo's plaza is surrounded by some of the city's oldest buildings.

Union Station
combines the
romance of rail
travel with
genteel Spanish
architecture.

Union Station

ALTHOUGH MOST MODERN VISITORS TO L.A. JET INTO LOS
Angeles International Airport, the city's Union Station offers a superb
entry point, a reminder of days when train travel was wreathed in
glamour, and when redcaps toted steamer trunks and hatboxes for
fur-coated ladies and their dapper escorts. As one of the last grand
railway stations to be built in the United States, Union Station provided a theatrical entrance most suitable for a star's arrival during
Hollywood's glory days, or as the setting for a film-noir classic.

Union Station
- Map pp. 46–47
- 800 N. Alameda St.
- 213/683-6875

Built in 1939 as a joint venture of
the Union Pacific, Southern Pacific,
and Santa Fe railroad companies,
the Spanish Mission-style terminal
was hailed as an architectural landmark and became an instant hit.
The station is a stunning compilation of early California Mission,
Streamline Moderne, and Moorish
elements. Though some changes
have been made over the years,
much of the building remains
intact. Exterior standouts include
the Spanish-tile roof and high bell
tower, and the two patios with scal-
loped archways connecting to the
main structure. The grandiose 52-
foot-tall lobby was and still is a
great place to people-watch, though

you're more likely to be casting
your eyes over commuters and regular folk than the Greta Garbos and
Sam Spades of yore. Sink deep into
those built-for-real-bodies heavy
wooden chairs with their cracked
leather seats, and gaze at the massive wood beams above your head
and the marble floors beneath your
feet. Extensive tilework throughout
ranges from art deco motifs to
earth-tone Navajo knockoffs.
The trendy restaurant **Traxx** has
replaced the original coffee shop
and soda fountain, while, at the east
side of the building, the Gateway
Transit Center affords access to the
bus and subway, plus a trove of
public artwork (see pp. 60–63). ■

Chinatown

L.A.'S CHINATOWN HARDLY MEASURES UP TO ITS COUNTER-part in San Francisco, but nonetheless it remains a vital cultural center for the Chinese community.

If Chinatown seems small today, back in 1850, the only Chinese residents were two male servants. Within 20 years, however, the population had multiplied to a whopping 172 people! Housing restrictions and anti-Chinese hostilities in the 1870s resulted in the tiny community being relegated to one of downtown's most run-down areas. Thus began "old Chinatown." Families evolved, independent farmers grew and sold produce to Angeleno residents. Following the displacement caused by the development of Union Station in the 1930s, many Chinese moved either closer to the produce area or to what is still referred to as "new Chinatown."

Bordered roughly by Cesar Chavez, Spring, Yale, and Bernard Streets, present-day Chinatown is home to around 15,000 residents and serves as the cultural center for more than 400,000 Chinese Americans from the Greater Los Angeles area, as well as recent Chinese immigrants from Southeast Asia. The main thoroughfare is North Broadway (the 700–1000 blocks), where you'll find embellished roofs, ornamental facades, fabulous restaurants, and herbalists. **Gin Ling Way** (Street of the Golden Palace), between Broadway and Hill Street, is a pedestrian thoroughfare lined with touristy shops and restaurants. The 600 block of Spring Street is a commercial district geared towards the Chinese community and so affords a much more authentic feel. Celebrations, especially Chinese New Year (late February or early March), are festive occasions. For information on walking tours, contact the Chinese Chamber of Commerce. ∎

Embellished roofs and ornamental facades mixed with L.A.'s characteristic neon signs give Chinatown a unique ambience.

Chinese Chamber of Commerce
🅐 Map pp. 46–47
✉ 977 N. Broadway
☎ 213/617-0396

Civic Center & City Hall

L.A.'S CIVIC CENTER COMPRISES ONE OF THE LARGEST government complexes outside of Washington, D.C. Although most of its buildings are rather lackluster, visual boredom is alleviated by the monumental and somewhat peculiar-looking City Hall next door.

Some of the world's most celebrated (and televised) trials have taken place within these courthouse walls.

Civic Center
Ⓜ Map pp. 46–47

City Hall
Ⓜ Map pp. 46–47
✉ 200 N. Spring St.
☎ 213/485-2121
🕐 Currently closed for renovation until 2001. Generally closed Sat.–Sun.

CIVIC CENTER

The Civic Center, which is bounded by San Pedro, Figueroa, and First Streets, and by the Hollywood Freeway, is the administrative and political center for most of the city and county, as well as for an array of federal agencies. The landscaping helps to soften its drab image—subtropical foliage is planted around the Arthur Will Memorial Fountain, and from fall through spring L.A.'s official flower, the bird of paradise, parades its striking orange plumes. Visit at any time and you might find yourself in the middle of some real-life drama—the rather drab **L.A. County Courthouse** was the scene of the lengthy O.J. Simpson trial.

CITY HALL

Almost every TV and movie buff will recognize City Hall, even if it was moved from its looming position above the Civic Center—the place has been filmed as often as Fabio. Its most notable appearances were in the old *Dragnet* series, as a symbol of law and order, and in the original *Superman* series, where it masqueraded as the *Daily Planet* newspaper offices.

Built in 1928, the 27-story pyramid-topped edifice broke the city's height regulations, which, until the late 1950s, had been set at a squat 13 stories. This simply wasn't quite prestigious enough for a boomtown like L.A., so a special ordinance was passed allowing architects to go all out (or, in this case, up) with the new city monument. The best architects and designers in the area put their heads and styles together to create a masterpiece of eclectic design, from the classical temple base to the pyramid tower. Inside, the public areas are rich in marble columns, inlaid tile, and painted ceilings. More than 4,000 pieces of marble in the rotunda floor depict a historic Spanish caravel (a popular ship of early days), while the mosaic-tiled dome represents various facets of city government.

Seal of the City

L.A.'s seal is a representation of the city's history: The lion of León and the castle of Castile depict Spanish sovereignty, the eagle holding a serpent bespeaks Mexican rule, a bear flag heralds the California Republic. Add the American stars and stripes, and L.A.-as-garden olive, orange, and grape sprays—the whole shebang encircled in rosary-like beading, paying tribute to the mission padres. ∎

Performing Arts Center

FORMERLY KNOWN AS THE MUSIC CENTER, THE CITY'S major performing arts center is, surprisingly, not located in Hollywood or Beverly Hills, but smack in the center of downtown L.A. just across from the Civic Center.

The Performing Arts Center of Los Angeles County, along with the John F. Kennedy Center for the Performing Arts and the Lincoln Center, is among the largest performing arts centers in the country, and it is the leading cultural center in the West. Opened in 1964 with a performance by the Los Angeles Philharmonic Orchestra at the new Dorothy Chandler Pavilion, the center became an instant success. Popularity inspired more growth, with the addition of the Mark Taper Forum and the Ahmanson Theater, and prestigious national and international touring companies and artists continue to clamor its stages. Resident companies include the orchestra that inaugurated the center, the L.A. Philharmonic, as well as the Los Angeles Opera, the Los Angeles Master Chorale, and the Center Theater Group. Each year the center draws more than four million people.

The L.A. Philharmonic, which debuted in 1919, continues to perform at the 3,197-seat **Dorothy Chandler Pavilion,** October to May, under the direction of dynamic, young Esa-Pekka Salonen. The orchestra presents an exciting variety of concerts and has an impressive roster of internationally acclaimed guest conductors and artists. The L.A. Opera, established in 1986, also takes to the Pavilion stage with glorious, gorgeous, and varied productions. Placido Domingo, the opera's principal guest conductor, took over as artistic director in June 2000. Also crowding into the Pavilion is the L.A. Master Chorale, founded in 1962 by Roger Wagner. Lauded as America's premier professional chorus, the chorale presents programs ranging from traditional classics to Broadway hits, and it regularly performs with the L.A. Philharmonic. In the 2,000-seat **Ahmanson Theater** you'll see original Broadway and London dramas, comedies, and full-blown musicals, complete with star-studded casts, while the 750-seat **Mark Taper Forum** presents a more intimate setting suitable to innovative works.

Watch for major changes sometime in 2002, the anticipated completion date of the new Frank Gehry-designed **Disney Concert Hall.** Besides a 2,300-seat concert hall (which will be the next home of the L.A. Philharmonic), there will be a 2,200-car garage, an outdoor park with public gardens, a restaurant, and a café. ■

Angelenos from all over the city flock downtown to experience the Performing Arts Center's world-class presentations.

Performing Arts Center
- 🅰 Map pp. 46–47
- ✉ 135 N. Grand Ave.
- ☎ 213/972-7211
- 💲 $–$$$$$

Los Angeles Times Building

CONVENIENTLY LOCATED ACROSS THE STREET FROM THE Civic Center and catty-corner to the ever busy City Hall, the Los Angeles Times Building, crowned with a distinctive clocktower, is where the newspaper that so many Angelenos depend on for their world view is cranked out every day of the year.

Los Angeles Times Building

- Map pp. 46–47
- 202 W. 1st St.
- 213/237-5000
- No tours Sat.–Sun.

The original Los Angeles Times Building, designed in 1935 by architect Gordon Kaufmann, was constructed in the Moderne style of the time, a sort of toned-down version of the more decorative pre-Depression buildings nearby. However, the headquarters, with its ever increasing journalist, advertising, and editorial staff, soon became as crammed as the Sunday classified section. In 1973, William Pereira and Associates completed the long-awaited steel and glass addition.

The circular lobby features two large murals, a revolving globe, and a display of headline-making news during the paper's first century (1881–1981). Free 45-minute guided tours (reservations required a week in advance, children must be age ten or over) enable visitors to peek into a day in the life of a major newspaper. You'll be led through the editorial offices, as informative guides explain the various processes and answer questions about the paper's history up through its present production. Some of the corners you'll get to peer into include the newspaper morgue, the photography department, the prepress and page make-up areas, and the test kitchen, where recipes are tested for the Food Section. You'll also need to make advance reservations to tour (about one hour) the **Olympic Plant.** Opened in 1990 at Alameda and Eighth streets it is the site of the *Times'* current production facility. Here each high-speed printing press cranks out about 70,000 96-page editions per hour. ∎

Little Tokyo

"Garden in the Sky," an escape from the city bustle

ALTHOUGH RELATIVELY FEW JAPANESE ACTUALLY LIVE IN or around Little Tokyo, the district nonetheless is a vital cultural, economic, and social center for Southern California's Japanese community, as well as for many visitors and business executives.

Established in 1903, the area thrived after World War I, but it didn't fare so well during World War II, when some 30,000 residents were forcibly booted out of their community and into internment camps—including U.S. citizens and legal residents. Decades later, more than 200,000 Japanese Americans have reclaimed this territory, now a flourishing enclave thanks to money from L.A.'s Community Redevelopment Agency and by successful business entrepreneurs.

Bounded by Alameda, Los Angeles, First, and Third Streets, Little Tokyo—with its mix of 19th-century commercial buildings and contemporary styles—gives visitors a glimpse into Japan's bustling city life without ever leaving L.A. On First Street, "Omoide no Shotokyo" ("Remembering Old Little Tokyo"), a 1,000-foot public art installation, literally walks you through more than six decades of Japanese-American life, using text and quotations etched in front of 13 historic buildings.

Within the **Japanese Cultural and Community Center** are the Japan America Theater, which presents everything from Grand Kabuki to contemporary performances and puppet theater, and George J. Doizaki Gallery, which exhibits historical and new works as well as calligraphy. If you're an avid Japanese history buff, make an appointment to peruse the collection at the Franklin D. Murphy Library. The James Irvine Garden, also known as Seiryu-en (Garden of the Clear Stream) and again in the Japanese Cultural and Community Center, is

Japanese Cultural and Community Center
- Map pp. 46–47
- 244 S. San Pedro St.
- ☎ 213/628-2725

Japan America Theater
- Japanese Cultural & Community Center
- ☎ 213/680-3700

George J. Doizaki Gallery
- Japanese Cultural & Community Center
- ☎ 213/628-2725
- Closed Mon.

Franklin D. Murphy Library
- Japanese Cultural & Community Center
- ☎ 213/628-2725
- Open Sat. by appointment

**Japanese-American
National Museum**

▲ Map pp. 46–47
✉ 369 E. 1st St.
☎ 213/625-0414
🕐 Closed Mon.
💲 $$

**Geffen
Contemporary at
MOCA**

▲ Map pp. 46–47
✉ 152 N. Central Ave.
☎ 213/621-2766
🕐 Closed Mon.
💲 $$. Free Thurs. 5–8
p.m. Admission
allows entry to the
Museum of
Contemporary Art
(see pp. 58–59)

an East-meets-West sunken oasis, perfect for a little Zen contemplation. Better still is the New Otani Hotel's Garden in the Sky *(120 S. Los Angeles St.),* a 0.5-acre strolling garden that uniquely incorporates the city skyline.

Since 1979, Little Tokyo's center of commerce has been **Japanese Village Plaza,** an outdoor mall with distinctive white stucco, blue-tile roofs, and a traditional fire-tower. Shops in the complex offer upscale goods such as silk kimonos, and a number of sushi bars are also located here. Three newer shopping centers within Little Tokyo's boundaries contain even more Japanese cultural and culinary experiences. And after dark, oil up your vocal chords and head for the karaoke bars. Major community events include Nisei Week (August), with a parade, food stalls, dancing, demos of traditional arts and crafts, and, of course, the tea ceremony.

JAPANESE-AMERICAN NATIONAL MUSEUM

The former Nishi Hongwanji Buddhist Temple, built in 1925, was remodeled in 1992 into a private museum that pays homage to Japanese Americans and their experiences. Frequently changing exhibits portray the lives and genealogies of early *issei* (first-generation) pioneers, with particular emphasis placed on that unpleasant period of forced incarceration during World War II. "America's Concentration Camps," one of the museum's first exhibits, provides an in-your-face depiction of the intense material hardships endured by the many Japanese-American internees. Other displays pay tribute to heroic Japanese Americans who served in the U.S. armed forces, contributions made by Japanese Americans to the agriculture of both Hawaii and

California, and Sumo wrestling as well as American pop culture.

The museum focuses on Japanese immigration and assimilation in the United States, using both permanent and changing exhibitions. Enlightening displays include photographs, artifacts, family photo albums, and *Moving Memories,* a 15-minute home-movie video. A new 85,000-square-foot pavilion not only provides plenty of additional exhibition space, but houses a National Resource Center where visitors can access family internment files and other information via computer.

GEFFEN CONTEMPORARY AT MOCA

This "other" branch of the Museum of Contemporary Art was actually its original location. Opened in 1983 as a temporary exhibition space while Arata Isozaki constructed the main facility over on Bunker Hill, the Temporary Contemporary (as it was dubbed then) became just too well loved to fade away. The challenge of converting this former hardware store/warehouse/service garage, secreted in a dead end in Little Tokyo, was left in the capable hands of renowned California architect Frank Gehry. Gehry's knockout renovation concentrated on the building's original and historical elements—massive overhead doors, a redwood ceiling, industrial hardware, existing skylights, steel columns, trusses, and beams. The subtle, unpretentious renovation, combined with the building's open plan and vast spaces, wowed visitors and critics alike, prompting the museum board and the City of Los Angeles to keep it open—at least until the lease expires in 2038. The intriguing building is now used primarily for MOCA's more sprawling and avant-garde exhibitions. ■

Bunker Hill

FROM THE 1870s UNTIL AFTER THE TURN OF THE 20th century, downtown's Bunker Hill, then covered in glorious mansions, was one of the most beautiful residential areas in town. By the 1940s, however, most of the middle- and upper-class dwellers had floated westward into the more prestigious suburbs, leaving the once stately gingerbread Victorians to crumble. The neighborhood took on a sleazy ambience until around 1960, when the Community Redevelopment Agency decided to plow down the houses, lop the top off Bunker Hill, and turn it into the new financial district.

Bunker Hill
Map pp. 46–47

Angel's Flight Railway
Map pp. 46–47
351 Hill St.
213/626-1901
$ (25¢)

The "new and improved" Bunker Hill—bounded by I-110, First, Eighth, and Hill streets—has far less character than its predecessor, but it did bring an influx of money. With Flower Street as its nucleus, L.A.'s financial center includes several of the largest banks in the country, rendering it the U.S. capital of the Pacific Rim money machine. Surrounding real estate and slick high rises mushroomed. The Museum of Contemporary Art (see pp. 58–59) is one saving grace, as are the two interesting methods of ascending Bunker Hill. You can climb the behemoth **Bunker Hill Steps,** designed in 1990 by Lawrence Halprin as landscape art *(5th St., between Grand Ave. & Flower St.),* or hop a ride on the historic Angel's Flight Railway.

ANGEL'S FLIGHT RAILWAY
Who could resist a ride on the "world's shortest railway?" An L.A. landmark since 1901, the funicular system's two original orange and black cable cars once transported the city's early trendies between their mansions and the business district. Moved from its original site in 1969, the railway remained out of action for almost 30 years. Meanwhile, the cable cars and beaux arts station were impeccably refurbished and reconstructed a short distance away. Operation was

reinstated in 1996, giving a 70-second ride up a 298-foot incline at a whopping 3.5 mph, between the Pershing Square subway station and Watercourt Garden at California Plaza, adjacent to the MOCA. ∎

Angel's Flight was built nearly a century ago to transport passengers up Bunker Hill.

Museum of Contemporary Art

IT WON'T TAKE LONG BEFORE VISITORS TO L.A. REALIZE what a difficult task it must be to contain art within the walls of a museum, especially contemporary art. Artists have flocked to anything-goes L.A. for decades, unleashing their spirits and expressing creativity along bridges, barriers, warehouses, sidewalks, and fire hydrants. And that was even before the inception of L.A.'s world-famous public arts program.

Thought-provoking exhibitions draw visitors to the slick Museum of Contemporary Art.

Museum of Contemporary Art

- Map pp. 46–47
- 250 S. Grand Ave.
- 213/621-2766
- Closed Mon.
- $$. Free Thurs. 5–8 p.m. Admission allows entry to Geffen Contemporary at MOCA (see p. 56)

The Museum of Contemporary Art (MOCA), situated at California Plaza on Bunker Hill, is devoted exclusively to works dating from 1940 to the present day. Although it was founded in 1979 by a partnership of public agencies and private enterprise, the museum didn't actually open until 1986. In 1983, while MOCA was under construction, the Temporary Contemporary was installed in a renovated warehouse near Little Tokyo, taking up the slack for eager contemporary art enthusiasts. The "TC" (now called the Geffen Contemporary at MOCA—see p. 56) became so popular that, even after MOCA's opening, the facility has become a permanent and vital link to the main site on Bunker Hill.

THE BUILDING

MOCA's December 1986 grand opening signaled the first major U.S. building designed by celebrated Japanese architect Arata Isozaki. He created an exquisite jewel-like structure, utilizing Japanese spiritual traditions combined with the logic of Western geometric forms. Although more than half of the building's seven stories are below street level, the view of pyramids, cubes, and cylinders poking up presents a striking profile against the neighboring skyscrapers.

Two gallery wings are faced in rough red Indian sandstone, with a massive copper-sheathed barrel vault (which houses the library) providing a symbolic gateway to the museum. The pyramidal skylights above the exterior walls flood the galleries with natural light. Other elegant and imaginative materials used by Isozaki include sleek sheets of white crystallized glass on interior lobby walls, perforated stainless-steel panels atop the lobby ceiling, travertine concrete in various spaces, and an arched window of delicately veined onyx in the library. The cube-shaped information booth, along with portions of the office wing, are encased in green aluminum panels outlined in a bright pink diamond pattern, while the luminous galleries are accessed off the sunken courtyard.

THE EXHIBITIONS

MOCA leans heavily toward traveling exhibitions, rather than repetitive displays of its permanent collection. More than 20 exhibitions are presented annually, including one-person retrospectives, newly commissioned projects, and works by both new and established artists. Media include not only painting, drawing, sculpture, and photography, but also incorporate video, architecture, film, music, dance performance, design, and new forms.

The permanent collection is a stellar compilation of more than 4,600 works of abstract expressionist and pop art by an esteemed A-list of internationally renowned artists such as Diane Arbus, John Baldessari, Willem de Kooning, Sam Francis, Arshile Gorky, Robert Irwin, Jasper Johns, Ellsworth Kelly, Roy Lichtenstein, Joan Miró, Louise Nevelson, Claes Oldenburg, Jackson Pollock, Robert Rauschenberg, Mark Rothko, Richard Serra, Cindy Sherman, and Andy Warhol.

Major collectors and benefactors, as well as a number of artists, have made substantial contributions to the museum. Trustee Marcia Simon Weisman—instrumental in MOCA's founding, and a preeminent collector of works on paper—bequeathed 83 drawings and prints by 51 artists, including Johns, Gorky, and de Kooning. Artist Sam Francis—a founding trustee, as well as a force behind Isozaki's architecture commission—bestowed MOCA with ten of his major works, while artist Ed Moses chipped in 11 paintings and drawings. Other noteworthy bequests are the treasures from the Lowen Collection (painting, sculpture, photography, and drawing from 1960 to 1980); the Panza Collection (post-1980s works by L.A.-born or -based artists); the

Schreiber Collection (paintings, sculptures, and drawings by Pollock, Giacometti, Gorky, and Mondrian); and the Lannan Foundation (112 works by 52 artists, in a wide range of art movements, with particular emphasis on Southern California artists). Premier MOCA purchases include a comprehensive photographic series tracing primarily American documentary photography from 1930 to 1990 through the lenses of Brassaï, Diane Arbus, Robert Frank, and Helen Levitt, among others; and 80 major works from the Panza Collection, by such well-knowns as Oldenburg, Rauschenberg, and Rothko.

The "Art Talks" series (hosted by artists, critics, and curators), docent tours, lectures, and a free summer jazz series add to the fun. ■

The museum's exterior meshes perfectly with the contemporary art on display.

Underground art tour

Since its establishment in 1989, Metro Art, a department of the Metropolitan Transit Authority (M.T.A.), has commissioned more than 175 artists—well-known names as well as emerging talents—to create both permanent and temporary public art projects at 50 stations. Three crisscrossing lines include the Red Line (all subway), the Blue Line (above ground), and the Green Line (both above and below ground), covering a total of 59.4 miles. The goal is to put some pizzazz into the daily commute, to toss some catchy scenes at bleary-eyed travelers, and to turn a mundane ride into an art tour. The project will also give Angelenos some impetus to get out of their cars, and an estimated 200,000 passengers are expected to take a daily ride on the three Metro lines in 2000. Forty-seven stations are already up and running, and the remaining three should be open at the time of publication. All of the artwork is site specific, and while some has been integrated into the station, others are artist/architecture collaborations. The final product at each station is a unique "gallery." Described as one of the most imaginative public art programs in the country, the three lines expose residents and visitors to the city's diverse culture and history through a variety of media. Follow the tours given below or join one of the frequent onboard docent-led options.

RED LINE—DOWNTOWN TO NORTH HOLLYWOOD

Hop on the Red Line subway at **Union Station,** where you'll encounter Terry Schoonhoven's mural of traveling Angelenos through the eras near the ticket-vending machines. Christopher Sproat's "Union Chairs," on the platform, uses granite to mimic the old seating in the depot above. At **Civic Center Station,** Jonathan Borofsky's fiberglass figures are suspended above the platform, casting shadows on the ceiling. The stainless-steel ceiling at **Pershing Square Station** reflects Stephen Antonakos' colorful neon sculptures.

You'll begin to feel that Hollywood buzz at the **Seventh Street/Metro Center Station,** where Joyce Kozloff's handpainted tiles along the walls unfold like a filmstrip with imagery from hundreds of scenes and sequences. More tiles on the end walls of **Westlake/MacArthur Park Station** depict artist Francisco Letelier's take on major construction projects, MacArthur Park above, and L.A.'s more ordinary extraordinary folk. At the same station, Therman Statom's suspended oversize objects cast patterns on the pavement below the skylight. Peter Shire's industrial-object and abstract sculptures float overhead at **Wilshire/Vermont Station,** and the artist also designed the colorful wall tiles, skylight shapes, and plaza benches. The popular Festival of Masks Parade is commemorated at **Wilshire/Normandie Station** in Frank Romero's large mural of the same name (the annual parade takes place on the boulevard above). Los Angeles in transition is the theme for Richard Wyatt's 50-foot murals covering the end walls of **Wilshire/Western Station.**

It was only after three years of construction and public-relations mayhem that the five long-awaited stations that bring the Red Line into Hollywood were opened in 1999. Dramatic rock formations by multimedia artist George Stone are the focal point at **Vermont/Beverly Station.** The **Vermont/Santa Monica Station** emphasizes natural and artificial light, appropriate for viewing Robert Millar's polycarbonate/

Far left: L.A. car culture even finds a place in the subway. Above & right: Eye-catching art whether you're headed up or down

aluminum paintings and thousands of stenciled questions on the entryway walls. Artist Michael Davis incorporates science, astronomy, and medical imagery (in deference to the medical facilities on the streets above) with contemporary postmodern architectural design at **Vermont/Sunset Station.**

May Sun collides past and future at **Hollywood/Western Station,** using depictions of excavated animal bones, photos of the tunnel's construction workers, and replicas of the has-been Pacific Red Car, among other symbols. The long-awaited **Hollywood/Vine Station** is pure Tinseltown, with Gilbert "Magu" Lujan's homage to Hollywood's culture and glamour. Here the culture landmarks double as bus shelters, car-culture benches, palm-tree columns, and vintage film projectors.

Commissioned for the next stations in line (all scheduled to open in mid-2000) are Sheila Klein's theatrical projected images and sculptured platform columns at Hollywood/Highland Station; Margaret Garcia's historic tribute at Universal City Station, site of the treaty-signing where California was granted freedom from Mexico; and James Doolin and

---

🅰 See area map pp. 46–47

☎ Metro information: 800/266-6883. Metro Art information: 213/922-2727

🕐 Red Line: 20 minutes; Blue Line: 1 hour; Green Line: 30 minutes

NOT TO BE MISSED

- Terry Schoonhoven's mural, Union Station
- May Sun's symbols, replicas, and depictions, Hollywood/Western Station
- Gilbert "Magu" Lujan's homage to Hollywood, Hollywood/Vine Station
- Patrick Mohr's metaphorical journey, Transit Mall Station

Local geology inspired George Stone's rock art at the Red Line's Vermont/Beverly Station.

Anne Marie Karlsen's San Fernando Valley-related designs and murals at **North Hollywood Station.**

BLUE LINE—DOWNTOWN TO LONG BEACH

The ride begins at the **Seventh Street/ Metro Center Station** (see Red Line above). Thomas Eatherton's fiber-optic light "paintings" dance along the tunnel walls to **Pico/Convention Center Station,** where passengers await trains beneath Robin Brailsford's steel canopies with cosmic cutouts that cast shadows on the platform. **Grand Station** poses Mark Lere's travel-as-metaphor questions through symbols and text sandblasted underfoot. At **San Pedro Station,** Sandra Rowe honors neighborhood residents in stainless steel, while Elliott Pinkney has livened up **Washington Station** in bright primary colors and figurative sculptures. Horace Washington pays tribute to the surrounding industry at **Vernon Station** in sewing-design seating areas and paving tiles. At **Slauson Station,** the South Central area is celebrated in colorful "people's art" panels through a collaborative effort by East Los Streetscapers. The historic Red Cars of the Pacific Electric Railway are honored in

Roberto Salas' bright totems at **103rd Street/Kenneth Hahn Station,** while local schoolkids worked with JoeSam to create the "Hide-n-Seek" figures at **Imperial/ Wilmington Station.**

Eva Cockcroft's large ceramic-tile murals scope the local history and ethnic character at **Compton Station.** Wishes and water are Lynn Aldrich's themes at **Artesia Station,** reflected in mosaic waves and a wishing well. Local history is again addressed in Colin Gray's puzzle-ridden, cast-stone cartwheel at **Del Amo Station.** Jacqueline Dreager's sundial, inscribed with a Wallace Stevens poem, and aircraft-nosecone seating liven up **Wardlow Station,** while Ann Preston's overhead, gigantic magnifying discs are hard to ignore at **Willow Station.** Look up at Joe Lewis's 12 overhead discs at **Pacific Coast Highway Station** for a representation of values cited by local community members. **Anaheim Station** features Terry Braunstein's photomontages in porcelain-enamel panels that honor local heroes. Stained glass from unique Long Beach buildings can be appreciated in Jim Isermann's overhead circular discs at **Fifth Street Station,** while the local culture of people living around **First Street Station** comes alive with rotating, kinetic sculptures by Paul Tzanetopoulos. Take a metaphorical journey with two children through a train, trumpets, and text, created by Patrick Mohr at **Transit Mall Station.** Finally, **Pacific Station,** at the end of the line, features June Edmonds' images of neighborhood residents and their cultural identities in a series of Venetian glass-mosaic panels.

GREEN LINE—NORWALK TO REDONDO BEACH

The Green Line can be accessed from the Blue Line at the Imperial/Wilmington transfer station. The 13 additional stations along this route exhibit works that include a giant bee, a tile-mural replica of a Chumash cave painting, wishing-well buckets pouring text that becomes poems on the platform, a large hand launching a giant "paper" airplane, and, near the beach end of the line, a "wave"

The station exteriors are as provocative as the eye-catching interiors.

canopy made of blue glass.

Trains come every 5–10 minutes during peak hours, 15–20 minutes non-peak. Some artworks can be viewed from the train windows, depending on the station. ∎

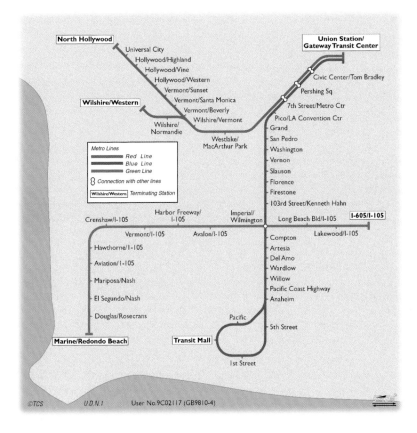

Central Library

NOT EVEN TWO CASES OF ARSON (IN THE 1980s) MANAGED to close the book on the much-loved Los Angeles Central Library. Though the doors were shut for a six-year remodeling stint, the 1920s landmark building has been elegantly restored.

Central Library

- Map pp. 46–47
- 630 W. 5th St.
- 213/228-7000 or 213/228-7040
- Guided tours of the library buildings are given daily

Architect Bertram Goodhue's extraordinarily creative combination of beaux arts design with bits of Roman, Byzantine, Egyptian, and art deco styling was far too spectacular to meet its doom even through the efforts of a fire-starter. The blazes razed a big chunk of the structure and destroyed or damaged more than a million books.

During the restoration period many Angeleno bibliophiles pined for their favorite library. When the building finally reopened in 1993, locals came barreling through the doors. The "new" library comprises a meticulous renovation of Goodhue's centerpiece masterwork, as well as the modernist Tom Bradley Wing. The combined structures, with over two million books and 500,000 historical photographs, make this one of the largest public libraries in the nation.

One of the Goodhue building's most prominent features is its signature pyramid tower with tiled-mosaic sunbursts and a handheld torch symbolizing the Light of Learning above the collective L.A. minds below. Other not-to-be-missed details include the rotunda with Dean Cornwall's elaborate murals depicting early California (painted in 1933); the one-ton chandelier; and the sculptured limestone figures of personages such as Goethe, Dante, and Shakespeare. The **Tom Bradley Wing** is an abrupt change in mood, with its soaring eight-story glass-roofed atrium and commissioned contemporary art. The 1.5-acre park-like garden within the complex holds yet another of chef Joachim Splichal's "casual" brasseries. ■

Biltmore Hotel

Positioned between the Central Library and Pershing Square, this Italianate beaux arts building was the creation of Schultze and Weaver, architects of New York's Waldorf-Astoria. When the hotel opened in 1923, it became the place to be seen. Its three brick towers, palatial lobby, and formal rooms were the site of many L.A. moments. The Academy Awards™ were held here during the 1930s and '40s and J.F.K. commanded his 1960 presidential campaign from the lobby.

Designated a Los Angeles historical cultural landmark in 1969, the hotel nonetheless began to languish. However, a makeover came to the Biltmore's rescue. By 1984, after the expenditure of some $40 million, the Biltmore had been impeccably restored to its grande-dame glory.

You needn't pay the price of a room to access many of the hotel's most beautiful areas. Go in through the old entrance on Olive Street, and if the soaring, ornate **Rendezvous Court** doesn't render you breathless then stay for the formal afternoon tea. The lobby is everything you would envision—a Spanish palace ambience. ■

Biltmore Hotel
- Map pp. 46–47
- 506 S. Grand Ave.
- 213/624-1011

White-glove service

Bradbury Building

The 1893 Bradbury Building, inspired by amateur architectural draftsman George Wyman's Ouija-board contact with a dead brother, landed him a mention in many history and architecture books (as well as travel guides), even though the building was named for the owner/financier Louis Bradbury. Famed as one of L.A.'s most astounding Victorian buildings and a superb example of Victorian-era commercial architecture, the Bradbury continues to wow visitors with its impeccable detailing and, for the era in which it was created, its futuristic styling. No wonder it was used as a setting in the film *Blade Runner.*

Although the public can access only the lobby level, that's usually enough of an eye-opener to keep most people happy. The comparatively plain brick facade belies what delights lay in store when you pass through the portal to enter an interior courtyard with five-story skylit atrium. Some of the classy, jaw-dropping details of this architectural treasure include highly ornate wrought-iron railings and bird-cage elevators, marble and tile floors, oak paneling, and glazed and unglazed brick walls. It all almost makes sense of the story that Wyman's Victorian-era design ideas came from some entity in tune with the future. ■

Bradbury Building
- Map pp. 46–47
- 304 S. Broadway
- 213/626-1893

Victorian attention to detail created a classic.

Grand Central Market

Map pp. 46–47

317 S. Broadway

213/624-2378

Grand Central Market

IN THIS CITY WHERE WHAT ONE EATS TENDS TO BE AS flashy as what one drives, the Grand Central Market is a refreshing throwback to the days of more simple fare. Though primarily a retail outlet for the city's diverse ethnic groups, the market has become a "flavor of the month" for yuppies, artists, and celebrity chefs.

Soak up the sights and smells of such incomparable delicacies as hand-rolled tortillas, sheep's brains, vine-ripened tomatoes, and bulls' testicles. This block-long bazaar, extending from Broadway to Hill Street between Third and Fourth streets, is one of the most colorful spots in the city, both because of its food and the people who buy and sell it.

The city's largest and most bustling food market is chock-full of common fruits, exotic herbs, and cast-off vital organs. A mainstay shopping mecca for the Latino community and other ethnic groups, the market also draws a clientele of senior citizens, low-budget families, and artistes and Westsiders who want to look trendy. Food stalls also sell to-go items for brown-baggers and hungry visitors. And don't pass up the tasty tacos, fresh juices, and ice-cream cones.

A word of caution: As with markets in other countries, it's forbidden to touch the merchandise. Ask or point and the vendor will wrap the goods for you; if you don't ask, that ripe banana or juicy lemon might turn out to be an impromptu facial. ■

Colorful goods are on display at the market's stalls.

Historic Theater District

L.A.'S VERSION OF BROADWAY MAY NOT QUITE MATCH THE
original, but in the prewar days it was the Big Orange's commercial
and entertainment thoroughfare. Portions of the street are still a
main shopping drag for the Latino community and other ethnic
groups, where local color and bargain stores intertwine with historic
architecture and provocative memories.

**Los Angeles
Conservancy**

Map pp. 46–47
523 W. 6th St.
213/622-4312
$$ (free tours
for Conservancy
members)

The historic theater district—the
first of its kind to rank a spot on
the National Register of Historic
Places—runs along Broadway
between Third Street and Ninth
Street. Though archival photos
chronicle the early movie palaces
(circa 1910–1931), with their fabu-
lous marquees and equally fabulous
moviegoers, many of the theaters
now show hard porn or Spanish-
language films and have a less fash-
ionably dressed clientele.

The most noteworthy theaters
include Million Dollar Theater
(307 S. Broadway), across from the
Bradbury Building, with an exquis-
ite baroque auditorium now used
by an evangelical church; Los
Angeles Theater *(615 S. Broadway)*,
another baroque theater with a
glorious lobby (built in the 1931 for
the premiere of Charlie Chaplin's
City Lights), still considered by
many to be the city's finest; Globe
Theater *(744 S. Broadway)*, a beaux
arts building-turned-flea market;
Orpheum Theater *(842 S.
Broadway)*, a 1926 monument
replete with Wurlitzer pipe organ;
and United Artists *(933 S.
Broadway)*, a 1927 Spanish-Gothic
affair with a cathedral-like lobby
(its original funding came from
Charlie Chaplin, Douglas
Fairbanks, Sr., and Mary Pickford,
but these days a ministry passes
the plate).

Some of the cinemas are still in
"normal" operation, while others
can be seen only on a tour or at
certain times. One of the best ways

to get a glimpse of the high points
and recapture the glory days of the
theater strip is to take a guided tour
with the **Los Angeles
Conservancy.** This will also
allow you to access buildings that
are otherwise closed to the public.

Theater and architecture buffs
might want to take a short detour
out of the designated historic dis-
trict at Hill Street, between
Olympic Boulevard and 11th
Street. Here, the ornamental pre-
Columbian-revival 1927 Mayan
Theater *(1040 S. Hill St.)* awaits,
complete with brightly painted
birds and dragons, sculptured
reliefs of Aztec gods, and all those
things that distinguish L.A. from
the rest of the planet—including its
various incarnations as a Gershwin-
revue house, porn theater, and (in
its current life) a hip disco. The
bright green, Spanish-baroque
Belasco Theater *(1050 S. Hill St.)* is
adjacent to the Mayan. ■

**Above & below:
Though present
marquees may
mislead, the early
movie palaces
still retain the
grand styling of
the early era.**

Museum of Neon Art

Museum of Neon Art

- Map pp. 46–47
- 501 W. Olympic Blvd.
- 213/489-9918
- Closed Sun.–Tues.
- $$. Free 2nd Thurs. of month 5–8 p.m.

YOU DON'T NEED TO WING IT TO VEGAS TO VIEW SOME flashy, eclectic, and amazing neon art—and, yes, it is classed as art, even though in past times it was seen merely as a form of advertising. Neon has been around since 1910, and it was in L.A., not Vegas, that America's first neon signs were installed.

The Museum of Neon Art (MONA), founded in 1981 as a nonprofit cultural and educational organization, may have moved around a bit in its time, but it still claims to be the only permanent institution of its kind in the world. Originally located in the loft district adjacent to Little Tokyo, MONA made a segue over to CityWalk in Universal City in 1993, where signage from its historic collection has jazzed up many of the building exteriors. In 1996, the museum moved again to its new exhibition space on the first floor of downtown's Renaissance Tower, adjacent to Grand Hope Park.

MONA founder, Lili Lakich, is an internationally recognized neon artist in her own right. The permanent collection contains superb examples of L.A. neon signs rescued and repaired by Lakich and her assistants, along with a fine art collection and displays that take you through the history and technology of this dazzling art form. Between five and eight temporary exhibitions are mounted annually, incorporating the works of more than 400 artists in both group and one-person shows. You'll see contemporary one-of-a-kinds and kinetic pieces, and hear a cacophony of flashers and hissers. The showcase piece, however, is Lakich's signature creation, her circa-1981 "MONA," the museum's logo, featuring none other than Leonardo da Vinci's "Mona Lisa" masterwork glowing in neon, enigmatic smile and all.

Call ahead for details of dates and reservations on MONA's bus tours of L.A.'s "neon jungle." These narrated tours, which depart at dusk, cruise by downtown's classic movie marquees and through the glitter of Hollywood, pointing out examples of unique signage and contemporary pieces. If you fall in love with the art form, you can always sign up for a variety of classes, where you'll be able to create your very own born-in-L.A. masterpiece. ∎

Neon lighting, another L.A. "first," is no longer used merely as advertising signage.

Blessed Oblivion

University of Southern California

USC turns out achievers in a wide range of pursuits, from filmmaking to football.

Straddling one of the city's most impoverished enclaves, the wealthy University of Southern California (USC) founded in 1880, with a student body of 53, claims to be the oldest major private coeducational university of significance on America's West Coast. Enrollment now hovers around 30,000, and some of the more formidable alumni include film director George Lucas, Neil Armstrong, and O.J. Simpson.

The 152-acre campus contains 191 buildings, and many of the earlier structures are built in lovely Romanesque style. Top professional schools abound, including dentistry (Angelenos in the know come here to have their teeth fixed by the best dental students in the city). Campus highlights include the Doheny Memorial Library, 1880 Widney Alumni House, Fisher Art Gallery, Helen Lindhurst Fine Arts Gallery and Helen Lindhurst Architecture Gallery and Library, Mudd Hall of Philosophy, and George Lucas Film School. Take a free hour-long walking tour or pick up a campus map at the Doheny Memorial Library and explore at your leisure. ∎

USC

- Map pp. 46–47
- S. Figueroa St., Vermont Ave., Exposition, & W. Jefferson Blvds.
- 213/740-2311 (general information) or 213/740-6605 (walking tour appointments)
- Walking tours Mon.–Fri. 10 a.m.–2 p.m.
- Free tours

Shrine Auditorium

Before the Music Center came along, the Shrine Auditorium was one of L.A.'s major venues for the mega-performances that traveled into town. This architectural oddity, across from the USC campus, was actually designed by the tassel-capped secret fraternal society of Shriners, who still use it for meetings and events.

Constructed in 1926, the cavernous fantasy mosque with its onion domes is perhaps most famous as the site of the annual Grammy Awards and, occasionally, the Academy Awards™—although both are to move elsewhere. At the time of publication the Grammys will have a new home at the Staples Center, and, come 2001, the Academy Awards™ will shift to the Hollywood-Highland Complex. ∎

Shrine Auditorium

- Map pp. 46–47
- 665 W. Jefferson Blvd.
- 213/749-5123
- $–$$$$

Exposition Park

Exposition Park
🅰 Map pp. 46–47
✉ Bounded by S. Figueroa St., Menlo Ave., & Exposition & Martin Luther King, Jr., Blvds.

EXPOSITION PARK'S ORIGINS DATE FROM 1872, WHEN IT was designated an agricultural park where farmers could showcase their produce. Other events organized by the Southern California Agricultural Society included fairs, carnivals, and, eventually, horse races. Unfortunately, around the turn of the 20th century the horsey crowd and its gambling vices led to the area's decline as assorted saloons and bawdy houses moved in. Judge William Miller Bowen, appalled by the park's downhill slide, banged his gavel and rose to action, reclaiming the land for more virtuous Angelenos.

California Science Center
www.casciencectr.org
🅰 Map pp. 46–47
✉ 700 State Dr.
☎ 213/744-7400
💲 Museum: free. IMAX: $$

By 1910, construction had begun on the park's first museum, the Natural History Museum of Los Angeles County. The park's entry back into "proper society" came when it hosted the 1932 Olympics at the Memorial Coliseum, built in 1923 and a national historic landmark. Since then, the Coliseum has hosted Super Bowls in 1967 and 1974, most of the games for the 1984 Olympics, Raiders football games (before the team moved back to Oakland), and USC football games. It was also the spot where J.F.K. accepted the 1960 Democratic nomination for president, and where Pope John Paul II celebrated public mass in 1987. Although the Coliseum suffered damage in the 1994 Northridge earthquake, it was repaired. The nearby Sports Arena, built in 1958, was the major venue for many other sporting events and concerts. At the time of writing, the future of both the Coliseum and the Sports Arena is up in the air. The new Staples Center has lured the Clippers and Kings away from the Sports Arena. If another N.F.L. team is acquired by L.A., it will take up residence at the Coliseum, and the Sports Arena will quite possibly become a parking lot.

The 1994 earthquake inspired a renewal plan to beautify and better utilize the park's 114 acres. The famous 7-acre sunken Rose Garden (16,000 specimens of 190 varieties) will stay intact, but expect to come across new playground and picnic areas. Also on the grounds are the California Science Center, an IMAX Theater, the Aerospace Hall, and the California African-American Museum.

CALIFORNIA SCIENCE CENTER

Formerly known as the California Museum of Science and Industry, the facility underwent major redevelopment and reopened in 1998 as the California Science Center. The "new and improved" Science Center has been expanded to 245,000 square feet to house the myriad interactive exhibits relating to space, physics, the environment, and health. Even non-science buffs can't help enjoying the fun. At **BodyWorks** learn how human organs function, via animatronics, from 50-foot-tall Tess. Or experience a zero-gravity environment through the **Space Docking Simulator** virtual-reality ride. Other exhibits within four unique theme areas allow you to build your own structure and then test it for earthquake preparedness (stand back!), to create and alter musical compositions at a digital jam session, and to ride a high-wire bicycle across a 1-inch cable more than 40 feet above the ground. For more sedentary entertainment (although no less thrilling), catch a science-

Opposite: The lobby of the California Science Center is an exhibit in its own right.

archival collection of books, vintage films, and audio- and videotapes related to African Americans. CAAM's Living Theatre offers performances, readings, films, and other presentations that bring impact to African-American stories.

NATURAL HISTORY MUSEUM OF LOS ANGELES COUNTY

The Natural History Museum was opened in 1913 in order to prove that Exposition Park was being returned to the people of culture. And big proof it was, for not only is the museum L.A.'s principal venue for exhibitions relating to science, art, and history, but it is also one of the largest, most-visited museums in California. The Petersen Automotive Museum and the Page Museum at the La Brea Tar Pits (see pp. 92–93 and p. 83 respectively) are satellite facilities.

The museum's original 1913 Spanish-Renaissance structure was awarded a place on the National Register of Historic Places in 1975. Domed rotundas (including one in stained glass by the local Judson Studios), travertine columns, marble walls and floors, and the east side porch all reflect Bowen's serious intentions for an elegant edifice. A restored 1926 mural by artist Charles R. Knight depicts the city's famous dinosaur life at the Rancho La Brea Tar Pits, and it is made even more evocative by the surrounding fossils of animals that lived during the prehistoric era. More than 30 galleries and halls hold the extensive exhibits, and the museum is the third-largest natural history exhibition arena in the country. The permanent collection consists of more than 35 million specimens and artifacts, all players in planet Earth's 4.5-billion-year history. The majority of collections fall within four primary depart-

African-American history and achievements receive homage in these spacious galleries.

Unusual collection
Hidden among the dinosaur bones and preserved insects at the Natural History Museum is a collection of quite another genre: Movie memorabilia. Although some might argue that Mary Pickford's hair, King Kong's miniature mechanical hand, Lon Chaney's wax head, and Fred Astaire's tap shoes are not exactly "natural" history, this is L.A. after all.

California African-American Museum
- 🗺 Map pp. 46–47
- ✉ 600 State Dr.
- ☎ 213/744-7432
- 🕐 Closed Mon.

related show in the seven-story, 90-foot-wide **IMAX Theater,** where you can get personal with everything from canyons and reefs to sealife and surfers.

CALIFORNIA AFRICAN-AMERICAN MUSEUM

Originally opened in 1981 in temporary quarters at the California Museum of Science and Industry, the California African-American Museum (CAAM) was moved to its permanent home just in time for the 1984 Olympic Arts Festival. Designed by African-American architects Jack Haywood and Vincent Proby, the building's breezy galleries are entered through a 13,000-square-foot sculpture court with tinted-glass roof. CAAM's permanent collection focuses on paintings, sculpture, photography, and works in other media by African-American artists from the 19th century to contemporary periods. The historical collection runs from the emancipation and reconstruction periods through the 20th century, with emphasis on the African-American experience in the West—particularly California. Other historical exhibitions have presented African Americans in their roles as golfers, inventors, and players in the California gold rush. The museum also houses an

ments: life sciences, earth sciences, anthropology, and history.

"Dueling Dinosaurs," portraying a duel between the late-Cretaceous *Tyrannosaurus rex* and *Triceratops* (unearthed from Hells Creek, Montana), will practically hit you in the face as you enter the main foyer. The perennially popular **Dinosaur Hall** also boasts the complete skeleton of a *Mamenchisaurus,* the longest-necked dino ever discovered.

On either side of the foyer are the African Mammal and North American Mammal habitat halls, with world-renowned displays of these animals in re-created natural environments.

More than 800 pieces in 16 interpretive areas can be viewed in the **Times Mirror Hall of Native American Culture.** Highlights include the William Randolph Hearst Collection, with about 200 Navajo textiles, thousands of baskets from California and the Great Basin, Plains beadwork, Southwestern pottery and jewelry, and replicas of both a California Craftsman house and a two-story Pueblo cliff dwelling. The **Gem and Mineral Hall** features more than 2,000 specimens, including rare meteorites, one of the world's largest gold exhibits, mining artifacts, and a walk-through vault filled with sapphires, emeralds, and star rubies.

Kids love the 6,000-square-foot **Ralph M. Parsons Discovery Center,** off the Rotunda, with its myriad interactive displays and science exhibits geared especially to smaller hands and inquiring minds. The **Insect Zoo,** on the mezzanine level above the Discovery Center, is another hit with youngsters, who delight over the selection of tarantulas, scorpions, and giant beetles. Other main floor areas include comprehensive exhibits of

fossils, pre-Columbian cultures, and the West Coast's premier American and regional history collections (1492–1914). The lower level houses a hall devoted solely to California history (1540–1940).

Schreiber Hall of Birds, on the upper level, is popular for its walk-through habitats, animated birds, and 27 learning stations. The ornithological collection numbers more than 100,000, including the world's largest holding of California condors. The **Marine Hall** features detailed sealife dioramas, many thousands of fish species, and the 14.5 foot-long megamouth (*Megachasma plagios*), the world's rarest shark and one of only five ever collected. The **Chaparral Exhibit,** anchoring the birds and the fish, demonstrates the importance of fire in the chaparral's life cycle.

In addition to the overwhelming permanent collection, the museum hosts marvelous traveling exhibitions on subjects as diverse as nomads and butterflies. A library, gift shop, and cafeteria sit on the lower level. ∎

In the main foyer two dinosaurs re-create an ancient duel.

Natural History Museum of Los Angeles County

✉ 900 Exposition Blvd.

☎ 213/763-3466

🕐 Daily. Free guided tours daily

💲 $$. Free 1st Tues. of each month

More places to visit in downtown & vicinity

GARMENT DISTRICT

Savvy Angelenos have been traipsing to the Garment District since the 1930s to pick through top-quality clothing at bargain-basement prices. Also referred to as the Fashion District, the area is crammed with jobbers and discount retailers just drooling to make you a deal on everything from swimsuits and kids' togs to leather coats and formal wear for men. The **Cooper Building** (860 S. Los Angeles St., tel 213/622-1139) has one of the best selections of women's clothing and shoes, while **Academy Award Clothes** (821 S. Los Angeles St., tel 213/622-9125) caters to the gents. South Los Angeles Street, between 7th and 9th Streets, is the prime discounter's strip. Map pp. 46–47 Bounded by Main, S. San Pedro, 7th, and 11th sts.

LOS ANGELES CHILDREN'S MUSEUM

A hands-on environment is designed especially for children under ten, with emphasis on arts, science, and environmental studies. Kids make recycled creations at Club ECO, learn the fine art of television production in the Video Zone, and become recording personalities in the Recording Studio. Play equipment and arts and crafts areas offer additional energy-burners. Map pp. 46–47 310 N. Main St. 213/687-8801 Closed Mon.–Fri. mid-Sept.–late June $$

SPRING STREET

The street formerly known as the "Wall Street of the West" may have lost most of its financial enterprises to Bunker Hill, but nonetheless it harbors some architectural treasures. Though the area became somewhat run down over time, this designated national historical district is now on the rebound. Buildings to watch for are **Banco Popular** (354 S. Spring St.), a 1903 beaux arts beauty; the **Continental Building** (408 S. Spring St.), built in 1904 and L.A.'s first skyscraper at 175 feet; and the 400-room **Alexandria Hotel** (501 S. Spring St.), built in 1906, and bed of choice for by-gone celebs. The L.A. Conservancy (tel 213/623-2489) provides walking maps. Map pp. 46–47

STAPLES CENTER

Adjacent to the Los Angeles Convention Center is L.A.'s newest showpiece. The $375 million Staples Center is a state-of-the-art sports and entertainment complex, proud new home to the L.A. Lakers, L.A. Kings, and L.A. Clippers sports teams, as well as a venue for major rock concerts. It includes five concourse levels, two restaurants, private clubs, business centers, and retail outlets. Map pp. 46–47 111 S. Figueroa St. 213/742-7340

WATTS TOWERS OF SIMON RODIA STATE HISTORIC PARK

Tile-setter Simon Rodia spent 33 years (1921–1954) creating these eight towers. Working alone, he haphazardly formed this monumental piece of folk art from salvaged steel rods, pipes, cement, and bed frames, and then adorned them with bits of tile, pottery, bottle fragments, and thousands and thousands of seashells. Rodia died in 1965, and the towers eventually were designated a national historical landmark. Extensive renovation following vandalism has kept the towers closed, but weekend tours should resume by the time of publication, and in any case you can see the towers from the outside whenever you like. The adjacent Watts Tower Art Center occasionally sponsors cultural events (note that this is not a good neighborhood, although a daytime visit should be safe). Map pp. 46–47 1765 E. 107th St. 213/847-4646

WELLS FARGO HISTORY MUSEUM

Housed inside the Wells Fargo Center, the museum presents displays and exhibits relating to the history of both the Wells Fargo Bank (founded in 1852) and the "Go West, young man" phenomenon. Highlights include original prospecting equipment, a 19th-century stagecoach, archival photos and lithographs, and a whopping two-pound gold nugget. Visitors get to sit aboard a stagecoach and relive a three-week journey (in just a few minutes) from St. Louis to San Francisco. Map pp. 46–47 333 S. Grand Ave. 213/253-7166 Closed Sat.–Sun. ∎

The midtown section of L.A. (a.k.a. mid-Wilshire) offers an extravaganza of diversity in terms of both history and culture. From Koreatown, through the La Brea Tar Pits and Museum Row, it ends in the ultra-modern Melrose Avenue.

Midtown

Introduction & map 76–77
Wilshire Boulevard 78–79
Koreatown 80
Hancock Park 81
Miracle Mile 82
Museum Row 82
La Brea Tar Pits 83
Los Angeles County Museum of Art 84–89
Petersen Automotive Museum 92–93
Carole & Barry Kaye Museum of Miniatures 94
Fairfax Avenue 94
City of Los Angeles Craft & Folk Art Museum 95
Farmers Market 95
Melrose Avenue shopping walk 96–97
More places to visit in midtown 98
Hotels & restaurants 246–47

Art deco detail, former Bullocks Wilshire department store

Midtown

An exploration of midtown leaves you reeling in a whirlwind of history, culture, ethnic diversity, and modern fashion. The area loosely encompasses Wilshire Boulevard, from the eastern edge of downtown to Beverly Hills and the Westside, as well as the territory from Olympic Boulevard to Melrose Avenue—the Hollywood border zone.

Wilshire Boulevard, from MacArthur Park to Hancock Park, traverses some of planet L.A.'s—and planet Earth's—most intriguing sights as it inches its way from bleak ethnic neighborhoods into the city's original old-money suburbs, then makes an abrupt shift back to the Pleistocene epoch at the La Brea Tar Pits. In between are such illustrious icons as the Ambassador Hotel (where Robert Kennedy was assassinated), some superb 1920s architecture and notable film sets, and the formerly fabulous Miracle Mile. This once glamorous shopping district, later reincarnated as Museum Row, is home to the Los Angeles County Museum of Art, the George C. Page

Museum of La Brea Discoveries, and the Petersen Automotive Museum, amongst other showcases. The La Brea Tar Pits (part of the Page Museum and within the renovated Hancock Park) are actually closer to Fairfax Avenue than to La Brea Avenue. You can't miss them—a replica mammoth juts from the Lake Pit, symbolizing one species of the many Ice Age animals that met their death here.

Midtown's ethnic enclaves include an interesting conglomeration of Hispanics, African Americans, Asians, Anglos, and Jewish people, in economic brackets ranging from welfare and trust-fund recipients to yuppies and old-money diehards who refuse to move to the

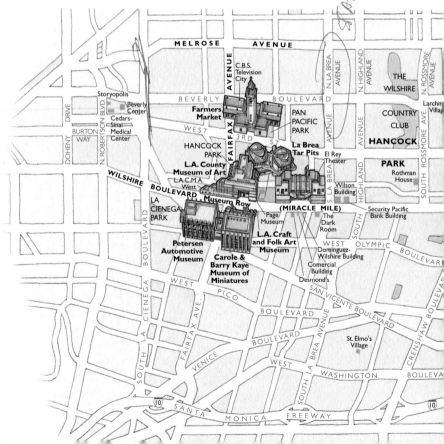

Westside. Koreatown, at the eastern end of midtown, is the cultural and social hub of the city's sizable Korean population. Since the 1992 riots, when Korean stores and businesses were torched, the district has managed to rebound and settle down; many of the new settlers are Hispanics.

At midtown's western flank is Fairfax Avenue, the heart and soul of the Jewish community since World War II. Stalwart Eastern European traditions have continued since that time, although some spots—such as Canter's deli—have been commandeered by kitsch-seeking trendsetters. The Farmers Market, at Fairfax Avenue and 3rd Street (established in the 1930s) is a longtime favorite on the tourist circuit. Nonetheless, the stalls, shops, restaurants, and ambience have changed little over the years. The adjacent CBS Television City has been a venue for TV shows since the 1950s. At the north end of Fairfax Avenue, just beyond the Jewish enclave, is Melrose Avenue, a shopping experience extraordinaire. ■

MacArthur Park, transition point from downtown to more "neighborhood-like" midtown

Wilshire Boulevard

RANKED AS ONE OF THE COUNTRY'S LONGEST AND WIDEST thoroughfares—and one of L.A.'s most historic—Wilshire Boulevard runs 16 miles from downtown, through Beverly Hills and Westwood, to Santa Monica and the Pacific Ocean. Although it has only become jammed with cars and buses since the mid-20th century, Wilshire has always been a busy stretch: Native American tribes trekked the route from the Elysian Hills to reach the sea, and the Spanish colonists used it to cart oily asphalt from the La Brea Tar Pits to waterproof their homes. Even back in the Ice Age, good old Wilshire was the habitat of more than 600 species of plants and animals, bizarre life-forms in what would become a bizarre city. Today, the boulevard passes through nearly a dozen diverse communities and is intersected by a couple of hundred streets.

Henry Gaylord Wilshire (1852–1927) was the befitting namesake for this historic boulevard. He was eccentric, entre-preneurial, a millionaire, and an out-of-the-closet socialist. Wilshire had an eclectic variety of interests and investments, including orange and walnut farming, gold mining, real-estate development, politics, and the then very New Age magnet-ic therapy. Some he won at, some he lost. Originally from Ohio, Wilshire headed out to California in the 1880s. There he founded the town of Fullerton in Orange County, became an avid socialist, and, as such, ran for Congress—and lost—in California as well as in New York. While he was taking a breather in London, Wilshire hung out with the likes of George Bernard Shaw, Upton Sinclair, and the Fabian Society. Then, on his return to L.A. at the turn of the century, he lost no time in becom-ing a property mogul, buying up huge parcels of land around the city, including the "Old Road" (Camino Viejo, a.k.a. Wilshire Boulevard), which he developed into a mighty thoroughfare linking downtown with the ocean. But it was after Edward Doheny struck oil on his land (while using an ordinary shovel) that wells began springing up in the neighborhood, fortunes were acquired, and Wilshire Boulevard became perma-nently etched in L.A.'s cartography.

FROM DOWNTOWN TO THE MIRACLE MILE

Viewing the four-level Harbor Freeway overpass from Wilshire, between Figueroa Street and Beaudry Avenue, will give you an amazingly concrete (pardon the pun) view of life in the fast lane (or very slow lane, depending on the time of day). Between South Alvarado and South Park View streets is MacArthur Park, originally Westlake Park and renamed for General Douglas MacArthur. It was, of course, also immortalized in song by Richard Harris and disco queen Donna Summer. Formerly a swampland, the 32-acre park is today filled with rare plants and trees, and it has a lake with rental paddleboats, recreation areas, a variety of public art, and, on the down side, a nasty sleaze and drug element after dark. The 1927 **Granada Building** *(672 S. Lafayette Park Pl., off Wilshire)* is a residential-commercial complex, combining Spanish Colonial architecture with Mission-style archways. **Otis School of Art and Design** *(2401 Wilshire Blvd.)*, established in 1918, is the city's oldest college of art and design. Though the building remains, Otis has moved to Santa Monica.

Five-story **Bullocks Wilshire** *(3050 Wilshire Blvd.)*, possibly L.A.'s most masterful art deco structure, was the city's premier shopping venue when it opened in 1929. Angelenos, by then already attached to their vehicles, could not resist the thoughtful porte cochere car entryway. Closed in 1993, the building now houses the Southwestern University law library. The exterior is still dazzling, with its terra-cotta base, oxidized copper tower, and Golden Age elegance.

The landmark **Ambassador Hotel** *(3400 Wilshire Blvd.)* was where many celebrities "wintered" during the area's Golden Age (1920s–40s). The hotel's Coconut Grove was one of the city's most glamorous nightclubs, drawing the preeminent social dance set. Early Academy Award™ ceremonies were held in the ballroom, and the hotel was also a setting for the film *A Star is Born*. The 1968 assassination of Robert F. Kennedy, near the restaurant's kitchen, propelled the hotel into notoriety and also drew all the joy out of the place. Closed since 1987, it is still used as a film location while the powers that be— Donald Trump, pitted against the L.A. City Board of Education—battle over the site's future.

Wilshire Boulevard's religious architecture includes **St. Basil's Roman Catholic Church** *(3611 Wilshire Blvd.)*, a massive, modern 1970s edifice, and the Byzantine **Wilshire Boulevard Temple** *(3663 Wilshire Blvd.)*, a synagogue rife with gold, marble, and exquisite murals by Hugo

Ballin, depicting Hebrew biblical scenes. The **Wiltern Theater** *(3790 Wilshire Blvd.)*, another of the city's favorite art deco movie palaces (built in 1931), is housed within the Wiltern Center. Saved from the wrecking ball, the restored building features a bluish-green terra-cotta Zigzag Moderne facade with copper embellishments, and a 12-story tower housing offices and stores. The 2,300-seat theater is now used as a concert hall for everything from opera and dance to rock and pop. ■

A favorite 1920s shopping spot, wonderful art deco Bullocks Wilshire now houses a law library.

Koreatown

KOREATOWN FUNCTIONS AS THE CULTURAL, BUSINESS, and social hub for L.A.'s 110,000-plus Koreans, the largest Korean population outside of Korea itself.

Korean-American Museum

⯐ Map pp. 76–77

✉ At time of going to press, the museum was searching for a new location

☎ 213/388-4229

$ Free; donations accepted

Korean Cultural Center

⯐ Map pp. 46–47

✉ 5505 Wilshire Blvd.

☎ 323/936-7141

🕐 Closed Sun.

Enjoy Korean culture and history in Koreatown— an area shared with Hispanics.

Bounded roughly by Wilshire and Pico Boulevards, and by Vermont and Western Avenues, the area took some heavy hitting during both the invasive Metrorail construction and the violent 1992 riots. The latter followed the Rodney King verdict, when police officers accused of assaulting the African-American motorist were acquitted. African Americans pitted themselves against their Korean neighbors, resulting in locals taking to roofs— guns in hand—to protect their homes and businesses from looters and arsonists. Although much of the area has since been rebuilt and tensions have somewhat eased, scars from the melee are still visible.

Nonetheless, Koreatown is a vibrant place to soak up the culture and to indulge in some top-notch authentic dining. Here, you're just as apt to find yourself feasting on stuffed plantain and Jerez chicken as you are on kimchi and table-top barbecue, for Koreatown is home to more Latino immigrants than Korean residents. Explore this area during the daytime.

KOREAN MUSEUMS

Two cultural venues along Wilshire Boulevard offer more in-depth coverage of Korean life. Located west of Vermont Avenue is the **Korean-American Museum,** which explores the culture and history of Korean immigrants and citizens, dating from their 1903 arrival in L.A. up to the present time. Exhibits include archival photos, arts and crafts, antiques, and period furnishings. Various educational programs supplement the visual displays. Farther west along Wilshire is the **Korean Cultural Center,** with a well-rounded Korean experience in the unlikely (though not by L.A. standards) arena of an Egyptian Revival-style bank building on the Miracle Mile. The center presents a variety of public programs on Korean history, art, and culture, with extensive focus on the Korean immigrant experience. Some of the offerings include subtitled Korean-language films, language classes, lectures, photo displays, juried art exhibits, and a 15,000-volume library. Local museums and universities often use the center as a resource facility. ■

Hancock Park

DURING THE 1920s, HANCOCK PARK (NOT TO BE CONFUSED with the Hancock Park near the La Brea Tar Pits) was the most elite residential neighborhood for rich Angelenos. Throughout the tumultuous and changing decades, the area has still managed to retain a sizable share of prominent names and old money. And all this is practically within the shadow of gritty Koreatown.

Bounded by Wilshire Boulevard, and by Van Ness, Highland, and Melrose Avenues, the district was named for G. Allan Hancock (another of the city's oil and real-estate tycoons), who subdivided his premium land parcel around the Wilshire Country Club. An exclusive residential district soon sprang up, filled with the opulent mansions of some of the most esteemed names in town, including Doheny, Huntington, and Crocker. Architectural styles spanned the whole range, from Historic Revival to Medieval Norman and mock-Tudor. Although the strictly Anglo neighborhood welcomed neither Jewish people nor African Americans, residents in 1948 "finally allowed" Nat King Cole to break the color barrier. Other wealthy, tradition-loving, African Americans eventually followed, including Muhammad Ali.

Prominent African-American architect Paul Revere Williams designed the grand, half-timbered **Rothman House** (*541 Rossmore Ave.*). The half-timbered, mock-Tudor **Getty House** (*605 S. Irving Blvd.*), built in 1921, is the L.A. mayor's official home. Although the current mayor lives elsewhere, the home is used for official city functions and is open for tours, call 323/930-6430 for information.

Tour this area by car—not because it's dangerous, but because patroling private security personnel may think you look suspicious.

SHOPPING AREAS

Larchmont Village, which stretches along Larchmont Boulevard, primarily between W. First Street and Beverly Boulevard, is a treasured shopping area with a hometown feel: The "village" features neighborhood shops, businesses, cafés, and trattorias. The surrounding residences provide good examples of early California bungalow architecture.

The once underloved **La Brea Avenue,** a few blocks west of the Hancock Park boundary, is now one of the city's hottest districts. The thoroughfare's 1930s art deco and Spanish buildings have been revived and are filled with contemporary art galleries, antiques dealers, chic boutiques, and hip restaurants. The road intersects Melrose Avenue, one of the city's (and the world's) most famous shopping strips (see pp. 96–97). ■

The mayor's official home, set in beautiful grounds, is now only used for official functions.

Miracle Mile

Once a strip of glorious department and retail shops, the current miracles on this mile are its museums and architectural district.

Miracle Mile
🔺 Map pp. 76–77

The length of Wilshire Boulevard, between La Brea and Fairfax Avenues, was particularly well suited to drivers and also to a bus line. Dubbed the "Miracle Mile" due to its commercial growth, this was L.A.'s preeminent shopping area before it was usurped by malls, Melrose, and museums. The section between La Brea and Burnside Avenues is a designated historic district, listed on the national register. Some of the exquisite structures to keep an eye out for on Wilshire Boulevard are the **Security Pacific Bank Building** *(No. 5209)*; **Wilson Building** *(No. 5217)*; **The Darkroom** *(No. 5370)*, particularly outstanding for its period camera facade; **Dominguez-Wilshire Building** *(No. 5410)*; the twin-turreted **commercial building** *(No. 5466)*; **Desmond's** *(No. 5514)*; and the **El Rey Theater** *(No. 5519)*. ■

Museum Row

Museum Row
🔺 Map pp. 76–77

Between Miracle Mile's art deco icons and Fairfax Avenue is stately Museum Row. In the 1970s the once busy shopping precinct lost a lot of business to the mega-malls, Melrose Avenue, and designer boutiques. Thanks to local politicians and patrons, the strip is now a dignified compound for some of L.A.'s finest museums: the Los Angeles County Museum of Art (see pp. 84–89); the George C. Page Museum of La Brea Discoveries (see p. 83); the Carole Barry Kaye Museum of Miniatures (see p. 94); and the Petersen Automotive Museum (see pp. 92–93). The old May Company department store presently houses the Southwest Museum's new satellite facility as well as additional space for the Los Angeles County Museum of Art (see p. 89). ■

La Brea Tar Pits

THE SITE'S NAME IS NOT ONLY DOUBLY REDUNDANT (*LA* means "the" in Spanish, while *brea* translates as "tar") but also erroneous—the tar pits aren't tar at all; they are asphalt deposits.

Located in what is now Hancock Park (not the neighborhood covered on p. 81, but an actual park with the same name), this 23-acre parcel was first mentioned in the diary of a Franciscan friar in 1769. It eventually fell into the hands of Major Henry Hancock. The major then bequeathed it to his son, G. Allan Hancock, who donated the historic land to Los Angeles County. Some of the fossils excavated from the 100 pits include saber-toothed cats—California's official state fossil. An observation pit enables visitors to see some specimens.

In a joint project between the Page Museum and the Los Angeles County Museum of Art, a 10-million-dollar redevelopment project was completed at Hancock Park in mid-1999. A replica mammoth now appears "trapped" in the Lake Pit adjacent to Wilshire Boulevard.

PAGE MUSEUM

The Page Museum at the La Brea Tar Pits, part of the Natural History Museum of Los Angeles County, opened in 1977 at the tar pits. The 57,000-square-foot building houses reconstructed skeletons, educational exhibits, and an introductory film. A glass-enclosed laboratory allows you to watch paleontologists clean and identify fossil bones from the pits. The 9,000-year-old La Brea Woman has flesh given to her bones with the aid of holography.

Pit 91, still rich with buried fossils, continues to be excavated for two months each summer by Page Museum paleontologists. More than 1,000 new fossils have been recovered in recent digs. The pit measures 28 feet square by 14 feet deep, and is divided into 3-foot-square grids. Visitors can watch from an observation area. ∎

La Brea Tar Pits
- Map pp. 76–77
- Observation pit is open Wed.–Sun. Guided tours available 1 p.m.

Page Museum
- Map pp. 76–77
- 5801 Wilshire Blvd.
- 323/934-7243
- $$ (free 1st Tues. of the month)

A Columbian mammoth poses at the Page. Below: The fossil vault

Within and upon LACMA's many walls, visitors can view one of the country's largest collections of art and artifacts.

Los Angeles
County Museum of Art

ALTHOUGH DEVELOPER A.W. ROSS NEVER ENVISIONED IT AS such, perhaps the biggest miracle to occur on his mile has been the Los Angeles County Museum of Art (LACMA). The museum's collection includes a magnificent assemblage of more than 110,000 works from all over the world, time-framed from ancient eras to the present day.

Los Angeles County Museum of Art

Map pp. 76–77
5905 Wilshire Blvd.
323/857-6000
Closed Wed.
$$. Free 2nd Tues. of each month

LACMA was originally incorporated within the Museum of Science, History, and Art (established in Exposition Park), but by the early 1960s the trustees and staff decided that the visual arts should be presented in an exclusive venue. As a result, in 1965 LACMA's three original buildings (the Ahmanson Gallery, Hammer Wing, and Bing Center) opened to the art-loving public at its present 6-acre site. During the 1980s the fast-growing museum added the Anderson Building and the Pavilion for Japanese Art to its original compound, bringing the exhibition and work areas up to an impressive 415,000 square feet, all contained within a hodgepodge of architectural styles. In 1994, the adjacent May Company department store was acquired. Christened LACMA West, this cherished art deco building added three new gallery spaces to the institution's total property, along with a satellite facility for the undervisited Southwest Museum.

A handful of the museum's departments (American, European, Islamic, Indian and Southeast Asian, and Far Eastern galleries) have undergone major reinstallations, with rarely seen pieces now out of vaults or confined spaces and on display in sumptuous galleries. Easily accessible, LACMA welcomes more than 600,000 visitors each year. An informative CD-ROM audio tour complements the wall texts.

AMERICAN ART

LACMA boasts one of the country's most significant collections of American art. Housed on the plaza level of the Ahmanson Building are masterpieces by Mary Cassatt, Winslow Homer, Diego Rivera, George Bellows, Henry Ossawa Turner, Benjamin West, and John Singer Sargent. Proud new additions are Rolph Scarlett's large, objective painting, "Allegro"; "View of Mt. Rainier," a landscape by Grafton Tyler Brown, California's first important African-American painter; and Paul Manship's "Flight of Europa," LACMA's finest example of American art deco sculpture.

ANCIENT & ISLAMIC ART

More than 1,000 works make up one of the most acclaimed ancient and Islamic art collections in the U.S. Exhibits spanning the 7th through the 19th centuries, from Central Asia to southern Spain, are mounted in the Ahmanson Gallery. Among the treasures are an alabaster eagle-headed deity from the palace of Ashurnasirpal II; the Egyptian bronze "Sekhmet," a part-human, part-animal dating from the 26th Dynasty; the free-blown, painted, and gilded glass "Beaker with a Theatrical Scene," from late second- to third-century Syria or Egypt; and "Standing Warrior," a Mexican ceramic, dated circa 100 B.C. to A.D. 300.

INDIAN & SOUTHEAST ASIAN ART

One of the finest collections of Indian and Southeast Asian works outside Asia also fills the Ahmanson space. Comprehensive collections of South and Southeast Asian stone and bronze sculptures, Himalayan painting and bronzes, and decorative arts are among the riches, including Buddhas and deities galore. "Buddha Sakyamuni," "Two Addorsed Tree Dryads," "Siva as the Lord of Dance," and "The Goddess Sarasvati" are notable Indian works.

One of the museum's illustrious special exhibits absorbs visitors.

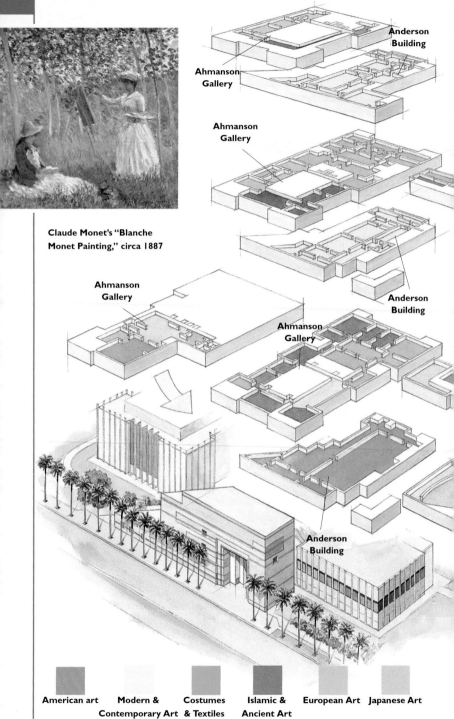

Claude Monet's "Blanche Monet Painting," circa 1887

Anderson Building

Ahmanson Gallery

Ahmanson Gallery

Ahmanson Gallery

Anderson Building

Ahmanson Gallery

Anderson Building

Anderson Building

American art   Modern & Contemporary Art   Costumes & Textiles   Islamic & Ancient Art   European Art   Japanese Art

"Beach at Honfleur," by French Impressionist artist Claude Monet

Hammer Wing

Pavilion for Japanese Art

Hammer Wing

Bing Center

Pavilion for Japanese Art

Eastern Art   Photography & Drawings   Special Exhibitions   Other Areas

FAR EASTERN ART

Most of the Far Eastern galleries on the Ahmanson's lower level have been redesigned, and many works never before seen are now on display. Early Chinese art and Southeast Asian ceramics are arranged in the first five galleries, with the art of later China displayed in the next six galleries in a mix that encompasses the neolithic, Bronze, early Imperial, and Song periods.

EUROPEAN PAINTING & SCULPTURE

More than 18,000 square feet of gallery space in both the Ahmanson and Hammer buildings is devoted to European painting and sculpture. Renowned artists include Rembrandt, Van Dyck, George de La Tour, and Degas. Works by Rubens, Monet, Gauguin, and Toulouse-Lautrec are also in the collection, along with a newer purchase, the masterpiece French painting, "A Musical Party," by Valentin de Boulogne. Rodin's bronze sculptures are ensconced in the **B. Gerald Cantor Sculpture Garden.**

COSTUMES & TEXTILES

Adorning the Ahmanson's third level is an exquisite array of costumes and textiles dating from the 16th century to the present day. Reigning supreme is the Ardabil Carpet, a 16th-century Iranian piece made of wool and silk, and one of only two such carpets in existence. A Peruvian burial mantle, the fragment of an Iranian dress or furnishing fabric, a Japanese priest's robe, a Chinese emperor's hunting cape, and an English gauntlet share the arena with varied special exhibits.

DECORATIVE ARTS

LACMA's decorative arts collection

"This is not a pipe," according to artist René Magritte.

The women of Paris' demimonde, as painted by Toulouse-Lautrec

is a trove of arts and crafts furnishings, silver serving pieces, superb Louis Comfort Tiffany and Venetian glass, Limoges enamels, and a vast assortment of art nouveau and art deco items. American pieces can be found on the Ahmanson's level one (including exquisite Craftsman furnishings by Greene and Greene, see pp. 212–14, and by Gustav Stickley), while the second level houses the reinstalled European Renaissance galleries.

HAMMER BUILDING

Although this building is named for industrialist Armand Hammer, you won't find any of his collection here. After a falling-out, Hammer left his building and took his art, installing it farther west along Wilshire Boulevard instead (see "UCLA at the Armand Hammer Museum of Art & Cultural Center" p. 172). Galleries linking this building with the adjacent Ahmanson allow visitors to meander among late 19th-century, Impressionist, and Postimpressionist paintings. The Hammer's second level houses excellent compilations of German Expressionist, European, and American prints and drawings. Among them are prominent works by Dürer, Rembrandt, Homer, and Whistler. Exciting new acquisitions include Jean Baptiste Greuze's "Christ Crucified," an old master drawing, and the very rare etching by Saint-Aubin, "View of the Salon at the Louvre." In addition, LACMA's photography stock consists of more than 6,000 picture-perfect works by famed shooters such as Stieglitz and Weston.

The museum shop is situated on the Hammer's plaza level, along with the visitor information center and a special exhibition area.

ANDERSON BUILDING

The immense Streamline Moderne Robert O. Anderson Building, completed in 1986, is devoted to LACMA's modern and contemporary art collection. Enshrined within the four-level, 115,000-square-foot structure are key works by Picasso, Matisse, Kandinsky, Hockney, Stella, and Rothko. "Portrait of Sebastian Juner" is representative of Picasso's Blue Period, while David Hockney's "Mulholland Drive: The Road to the Studio" is a monumental portrayal of L.A.'s ribbon-like road.

Creating excitement was the recent acquisition of more than 2,000 paintings and works on paper by esteemed Mexican artists, including Diego Rivera, David Alfaro Siqueiros, and Rufino Tamayo.

PAVILION FOR JAPANESE ART

The architecturally distinctive green stone and glass pavilion combines Japanese design with modern technology to create a dramatic and unusual 32,100-square-foot setting for the museum's collection of Japanese paintings, prints, sculptures, textiles, and decorative arts. Approximately 250 newly acquired Hirado porcelain pieces—an unusual catch for an American museum—join a compilation that includes fabulous Edo period screens and scroll paintings. An additional museum shop here specializes in Japanese items.

LACMA WEST

LACMA West was established in 1994 in the old May Company department store building, and comprises an experimental gallery used mostly by families and schoolkids and another gallery that hosts such major world-class traveling exhibitions as the 1999 "van Gogh's van Goghs: Masterpieces from the van Gogh Museum, Amsterdam." The Southwest Museum (see below) shares this level, while LACMA offices hold court on the upper floors.

The **Southwest Museum,** the oldest museum in L.A. (dating from 1907), opened a satellite facility within LACMA West. This affords a more convenient arena than its main Highland Park site (see p. 149) to showcase its premier collections of Native American textiles, decorative arts, and jewelry.

OTHER PROGRAMS

Other LACMA interests include an acclaimed music program (Friday evening jazz is hugely popular), a broad range of films, art workshops, specialized libraries, and research centers that include the Bing Center Art Research Library and the Doris Stein Research and Design Center for the Study of Costumes and Textiles. ■

A modern Japanese design, housing LACMA's Japanese collections

Southwest Museum at LACMA West
- ✉ Corner of Fairfax Ave. & Wilshire Blvd.
- ☎ 323/933-4510
- 🕐 Closed Wed.
- 💲 $$. Separate admission from LACMA

Car culture

There is perhaps no other city more geared to the automobile than Los Angeles; in fact, many Angelenos may be more concerned about their vehicles than they are about family members. Even in this style-conscious metropolis, it is far more permissible to send the spouse and kids off in slightly shoddy clothing than it is to drive to the office or mall in an unwashed vehicle.

How did it come to this? Once the automobile came to town, the Pacific Electric Cars didn't stand much of a chance. The city grew too far and too fast, and the discovery of oil ensured that fuel was cheap. Wilshire Boulevard's Bullocks department store took the lead in

establishing the city's first parking structure, and L.A.'s future thereafter was directed toward the motor car, and its passengers. Thus was shaped a car-oriented civilization that eventually boasted the world's first freeway, one of the first gas stations and parking meters. Next came drive-in motels, movies, and restaurants, then drive-through fast-food stops and services. And when the driver and passengers emerged, the beast could be left in a myriad of designated parking places, home driveways with carports and garages, and, in some cases, with valets and chauffeur stands.

Automobiles are the preeminent symbol of identity in the City of Angels' material world, somewhat akin to the caste system. After all,

the modern city was built for and around the car, and it is very difficult to get around without one. It is far more momentous for Angeleno youths to own their first car than to lose their virginity. In this town, you are what you drive. It doesn't have to be fabulous; it just has to be owned, although drivers are immediately placed in the same social strata as their vehicles. At the bottom of the caste system are the carless, scorned or considered as pitiable untouchables.

From low-riders to limo owners, car-crazy Angelenos depend on their vehicles for nearly all of their functions. They conceive children, give birth, and kill enemies in them. They eat, sleep, and watch soap operas in them, and they listen to music or traffic updates while strapped in bucket or back seats. Equipped with cell phones, notebook computers, paging systems, and portable faxes and printers, cars are used for an astounding array of wheeling, dealing, brainstorming, negotiating, and life-saving by plugged-in professionals, parents, rescue crews, security patrols, movie moguls, and drug dealers. Automobiles are also the setting for media events, as illustrated by O.J. Simpson's famous motor sprint, Hugh Grant's not-so-divine antics, and Eddie Murphy's early morning pickup. And while commuters complain endlessly about the traffic—as well as the smog—freeway car-pool lanes, which require just two passengers, are practically unused. After all, gridlock allows drivers more quality time to idle with their vehicles. ∎

Cars permeate L.A. life: Spectators flock to events such as car dance performances.

Petersen Automotive Museum

Petersen Automotive Museum

🅰 Map pp. 76–77

✉ 6060 Wilshire Blvd.

☎ 323/930-2277

🕐 Closed Mon.

💲 $$

IN A CITY WHERE AUTOMOBILES ARE WORSHIPED AS virtual spiritual deities, it is only fitting that the motorcar be honored with a museum. And this is not just any museum, but a 40-million-dollar, 300,000-square-foot-plus edifice/temple, run under the broad umbrella of the Natural History Museum of Los Angeles County.

Opened in 1994 in one of Miracle Mile's former department stores, the Petersen pays homage to the automobile and its influence on life and culture, particularly of Angeleno auto-maniacs, in one of the world's largest and most innovative automotive museums. Named for its principal donor, Robert E. Petersen (publisher of such magazines as *Road and Track*), the four-

story museum is, for some, a fundamental destination.

THE EXHIBITIONS

The first-floor **Streetscape** comprises interactive exhibits where visitors, rather than peering from the sidelines, actually walk through more than 30 detailed dioramas that simulate L.A.'s motoring history, from days past to thoughts

L.A.'s love affair with cars is a multigenerational thing.

of the future. Gas pumps, signage, and other paraphernalia change with the times. The opening diorama, "Stuck in the Mud," shows a 1911 American Underslung stuck in the mud with an overheated radiator, complete with live steam spewing forth. Against a background of Malibu and the Pacific Ocean, three life-size mannequin passengers find their own ways of dealing with the problem. The tour then winds through a variety of L.A.-as-car exhibits. Among them are the Louis Breer Blacksmith Shop in 1901, featuring a home-made steam-powered car; a 1915 racing scene with race-car driver Earl Cooper's Stutz Racer; Laurel and Hardy in a 1922 Model T; a 1928 middle-class home, with a 1922 Willys-Knight touring car in the driveway; a California Highway Patrolman hiding behind a billboard, atop his 1932 Harley-Davidson motorcycle; a full-scale replica of an actual 1929 Richfield gas station; a ritzy 1930s Lincoln dealership with three Zephyrs on display; a 1932 Twin Coach Helms Bakery truck awaiting delivery in one of the earliest alleys in the country; and a re-creation of the 1928 Dog Café, a landmark eatery that met its demise in the 1970s. A strip mall, a street scene, dry-lakes racing, a 1950s diner, a body customizing shop, 1960s and '70s youth lifestyles, a suburban garage, a wrecked car, and a semi-futuristic design studio are all part of the tantalizing look at L.A. history as it flew past the windshield.

The second-floor galleries present revolving exhibits that cover a broad variety of "car-isms" to lure repeat visitors. The **Hollywood Gallery** features changing collections of celebrity-owned vehicles as well as those appearing in films and on television. Golden Age cars include Howard Hughes's 1955

Packard, Greta Garbo's 1925 Lincoln limousine, and Mel Blanc's 1958 Edsel. **State of the Art Gallery** showcases fascinating specimens from the Natural History Museum's permanent collection. Classic hot rods liven up the **Bruce Meyer Gallery,** and the **Otis Chandler Motorcycle Gallery** revs enthusiasts through motorcycle history and also displays models such as a 1903 Orient and a 1969 Harley.

MAY FAMILY DISCOVERY CENTER

The third-floor May Family Discovery Center, opened in 1997, offers a hands-on learning environment for children, explaining basic scientific principles with the auto as the teaching vehicle (pardon the pun). Cartoon characters at the entrance point to the center's three different areas. The **Vroom Room** is a kid's dream and an adult's nightmare, where tots trigger an audio traffic jam via car horns, fire engine sirens, squealing tires, revving engines, and barking dogs. The **West Wing** provides a computerized driving simulator through a Virtual City, as well as an activity area, while the **East Wing** is rich with fun and interesting interactive demonstrations of gear ratios, rotational inertia, friction, hydroplaning, and the principles of force and motion. In one display kids can become human spark plugs in a giant combustion engine.

SPECIAL EXHIBITIONS

Along with its vast permanent collection, the Petersen regularly presents scintillating temporary displays. On the Millennium calendar alone there are tributes to woodies, the California surfer's dream vehicle; intricately engineered, mini-auto spindizzies; and customized low-riders. ■

Carole & Barry Kaye Museum of Miniatures

Carole & Barry
Kaye Museum of
Miniatures
⚠ Map pp. 76–77
✉ 5900 Wilshire Blvd.
☎ 323/937-6464
⏰ Closed Mon.
💲 $$

**Meticulously
crafted miniatures
invite detailed
pondering.**

What began as a hobby for founder Carole Kaye has evolved into one of the world's most comprehensive and extraordinary collections of miniatures. Situated across the street from the Los Angeles County Museum of Art, the Kaye Museum is a draw for old and young alike—admirers of hand-crafted miniatures, dollhouse connoisseurs, kitsch hounds, and those who prefer to view the world through the looking glass like Alice. More than 190 settings are meticulously decorated with beautifully crafted miniatures. Dioramas encompass a broad range of historical moments and varied locations, including a performance by Louis Armstrong and Ella Fitzgerald at the Hollywood Bowl, O.J. Simpson performing at his trial, and re-creations of France's Fontainebleau Palace, H.M.S. *Titanic,* the Vatican, and England's Hampton Court. "Mini-me" figurines run the gamut from Marie Antoinette to Michael Jackson and Nancy Reagan. The museum's **Eugene and Henry Kupjack Gallery** exhibits Eugene Kupjack's "Thorne Rooms," a circa-1930s project that is part of the Chicago Art Institute's holdings. Most of the miniatures are for sale, though browsers are welcome. ∎

Fairfax Avenue

Fairfax Avenue
⚠ Map pp. 76–77

**Jewish traditions
are still observed.**

Turn the corner from Museum Row onto Fairfax Avenue, and you'll find yourself taken back in time and space to post-World War II Eastern Europe. Fairfax Avenue (particularly the stretch between Beverly Boulevard and Melrose Avenue) has, since the 1940s, served the Jewish community and its strong religious, cultural, and retail traditions. To best soak up the vibrant culture, stroll the neighborhood on foot, toe-tapping as you go to Israeli songs and lilting Yiddish language. You'll pass refreshingly unyuppified delis (with the possible exception of touristy **Canter's** deli, at 419 North Fairfax Avenue), bakeries, kosher butcher shops and groceries, curio outlets, Judaica retailers, newsstands, yeshivas, and synagogues. Although the area is indeed rich, it is by no means wealthy, and has long been home to lower-income immigrants, elderly residents, and Orthodox Jewish people of all ages. The Westside and San Fernando Valley have lured the wealthier masses, though many still return "home" to shop. ∎

City of Los Angeles Craft & Folk Art Museum

Craft & Folk Art Museum

🅰 Map pp. 76–77
✉ 5814 Wilshire Blvd.
☎ 323/937-4230
🕐 Closed Mon.
💲 $ (free Thurs. evening & 1st Tues. of the month)

Known simply as the Craft & Folk Art Museum (CAFAM) when its doors opened in 1965, this former restaurant/gallery hit some hard times—including threat of closure—until "City of Los Angeles" was added to the front of its title. Now part of a joint venture with the city's Cultural Affairs Department, the nonprofit museum is assured a minimum ten-year life span. The restaurant is no longer part of the operation, but the museum has remained in its beautifully restored 1930s Georgian-style brick building with distinctive yellow awning. Changing displays consist of high-caliber contemporary, historic, and ethnic arts and crafts, from collectible teapots to wearable pieces. Recent exhibits include locally crafted surrealistic furniture, African and Cuban musical instruments, and girls' low-rider bicycles.

One of the museum's most popular events, the Festival of Masks, is scheduled to resume in 2000. Ordinarily held in October, the festival—which has been in existence for more than 20 years—hosts a huge neighborhood parade, where thousands of costumed and masked marchers show off ethnic garb. ∎

Ethnic treasures within invoke links with worlds away.

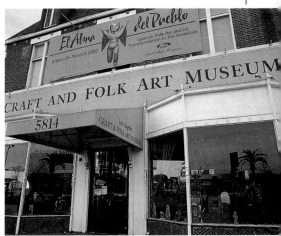

Farmers Market

Farmers Market

🅰 Map pp. 76–77
✉ 6333 W. 3rd St.
☎ 323/933-9211

At the corner of Fairfax Avenue and 3rd Street is the Farmers Market; established in 1934 it proved an immediate success. Farmers paid a 50 cent "parking fee," which entitled them to sell their farm-fresh goods from the beds and tailgates of their trucks. Far-thinking business-woman Blanche Magee soon opened **Magee's Kitchen and Deli,** still in operation and owned by the same family. Eventually the farmers moved their goods into stalls and produce stands, creating a colorful open-air market.

Today's Farmers Market is an icon for both residents and visitors, and it features more than 75 stands and food stalls where you can pick up everything from fruits and flowers to fine antiques and gaudy souvenirs. Alfresco dining comple-ments the pleasures of people-watching, and the market attracts everyone from wide-eyed tourists to celebrities and television execu-tives from the neighboring CBS Television City (**Kokomo Café,** also in the market, is a favorite breakfast and lunch spot.) ∎

Melrose Avenue shopping walk

It's hard to imagine that, until the 1980s, Melrose Avenue was just a common, ordinary L.A. thoroughfare. Today, it is world renowned as a trendy, "attitude"-driven mecca, where the coolest max out their credit cards on retro clothing, club wear, ethnic garb, shoes, jewelry, fine art, and kitsch decor. On this walk you'll find an eclectic mix of goods and people. You'll also bump into little theaters, star-studded eateries, and cafés. Allow one hour or all day, depending on your wallet, appetite, and shopping acumen.

Begin this unique shop-a-thon at **Necromance** *(No. 7220)*, where you can pick up your favorite skulls and bones, antique medical and funerary tools, and an assortment of real bone and tooth jewelry.

Meander west down the street to **Retail Slut** *(No. 7308)* for something a bit livelier—club wear with all the accoutrements, including leather and vinyl numbers, spiked dog collars and wristbands, and other L.A. must-haves. Cut over to **Vinyl Fetish ❶** *(No. 7305)* to check out the newest L.A. sounds and load up on punk merchandise and accessories.

Choose from Rolexes, antique pocket watches, clocks, and all manner of tick-tocks at **Wanna Buy a Watch** *(No. 7366)*. **Wound and Wound** *(No. 7374)* is a delight, with its huge assortment of windup toys, music boxes, and marching creatures. The collection includes everything from early tin toys to sci-fi and animation characters.

Across the street, at **Off the Wall** *(No. 7325)*, you can pick through a barrage of roadside antiquities, vintage Americana, old telephones, and other quirky items. Eyeglasses are art at **l.a. Eyeworks ❷** *(No. 7407)*, where the frame "gallery" comprises classic,

---

- 🗺 See area map pp. 76–77
- ▶ Necromance, No. 7220
- ↔ 2 miles (3.2 km)
- 🕐 Allow 1 hour minimum
- ▶ Bodhi Tree, No. 8385

NOT TO BE MISSED

- Necromance
- Vinyl Fetish
- Wound and Wound
- Wasteland
- Ron Herman/Fred Segal
- Bodhi Tree

MELROSE AVENUE SHOPPING WALK

Left & above: Try Melrose for dining, strolling, shopping, or people-watching.

contemporary, and extraordinary styles.

Wasteland *(No. 7428)*, at the southeast corner of Vista Street, stocks a vast assortment of retro clothing. The shop is popular with young and young-at-heart celebrities who crave bowling shirts, Hawaiian wear, faded denims, and vintage frocks and gowns.

Aardvark's Odd Ark ③ *(No. 7579)*, between Sierra Bonita and Curson Avenues, is also jam-packed with vintage wear. The store keeps an amazing inventory of 1950s through '70s garments, undergarments, and accessories.

Farther along, as you cross Fairfax Avenue, the shops become decidedly more upscale.

Ron Herman/Fred Segal ④ *(No. 8118)*,

at North Crescent Heights Boulevard, takes up an entire block with its boutique-like complex. In-the-trend Angelenos with their no-limit credit cards flock here for the latest collections of casual wear, designer gear, kids' apparel, lingerie, luggage, shoes, and gadgets. Continuing along Melrose toward Doheny Drive, the shops become increasingly elitist, focusing on home decor, rare books, and made-to-order cosmetics. An unmissable stop for bibliophiles and New Agers is the **Bodhi Tree** ⑤ *(No. 8385)*. This bookstore had titles on Eastern philosophy and *feng shui* even before Madonna's time. End with a coffee or herbal tea at **Sweet Lady Jane** *(No. 8360)*. ■

More places to visit in midtown

ALVARADO TERRACE

This is another of L.A.'s most fashionable early 20th-century residential districts, and it is a companion site to South Bonnie Brae Street (see below). Named for Juan Bautista Alvarado, Mexican California's governor from 1836 to 1842, the gently curving street features terraced lawns and stately mansions in a hodgepodge of architectural styles, including Mission Revival, Queen Anne, and English Tudor.

🅜 Map pp. 76–77 ✉ Runs from W. Pico Blvd. to S. Hoover St.

BEVERLY CENTER

This mega-mall will please those who prefer all their shops to be under one roof. Three levels, covering more than 7 acres, house over 160 stores, movie theaters, cafés, and restaurants. Among the residents are outlets of Macy's and Bloomingdale's department stores, and the Hard Rock Café. A five-level parking garage makes it even more convenient.

🅜 Map pp. 76–77 ✉ Bounded by La Cienega, San Vicente, and Beverly Blvds., & by W. 3rd St. ☎ 310/854-0070

CBS TELEVISION CITY

The Pereira and Luckman architectural team constructed this black-cube television studio in 1952, during the medium's heyday. Sitcoms and game shows are still taped here, and free tickets (first come, first served) are available at the information window. Age restrictions apply to some shows.

🅜 Map pp. 76–77 ✉ 7800 Beverly Blvd. (across the street from Farmers Market) ☎ 323/575-2458

CEDARS SINAI MEDICAL CENTER

Adjacent to the huge Beverly Center shopping mall is Cedars Sinai, which could almost be mistaken for part of the retail complex—until you get inside. This behemoth medical center is noteworthy not only because of its highly regarded staff and facilities but also because of the roster of celebrities who have been treated and/or died here. Muhammad Ali left by the front door; Lucille Ball was less fortunate.

🅜 Map pp. 76–77 ✉ 8700 Beverly Blvd. ☎ 310/855-5000

LOYOLA LAW SCHOOL

Frank Gehry's law-school-as-classical-temple was completed in 1987, and the noted architect even threw a Romanesque chapel and dramatic outside stairways into the works. The school maintains an impressive collection of fine art.

🅜 Map pp. 76–77 ✉ 1441 W. Olympic Blvd. ☎ 213/736-1000

SOUTH BONNIE BRAE STREET

Some of the city's most fashionable homes still stand in this residential neighborhood dating from the turn of the 20th century. Architectural styles include Queen Anne, Gothic, Moorish, and Colonial Revival.

🅜 Map pp. 76–77 ✉ Between W. 8th & W. 11th Sts.

ST. ELMO'S VILLAGE

Artist Roderick Sykes and his friends rallied to turn this once grubby group of bungalows into a delightful display of folk art. Brightly painted murals, found objects, sculptures, inspirational messages, and the representation of people of many colors and creeds on the walls offer a beacon of hope to all. Art and music festivals take place here throughout the year.

🅜 Map pp. 76–77 ✉ 4830 St. Elmo Dr. ☎ 323/931-3409

STORYOPOLIS

Storyopolis, situated close to the Beverly Center, presents a celebration of children's book illustrations in a 6,000-square-foot shop/gallery. Illustrations on display are the best of the genre and are also available for purchase. The spacious bookstore stocks thousands of children's titles and provides a comfortable reading area. Authors of children's books are often scheduled, and every Saturday features a craft and storytelling hour (*Tel 310/358-2512, $$*). This is an obvious hit with kids, especially if they've had to endure Melrose Avenue or the mall.

🅜 Map pp. 76–77 ✉ 116 N. Robertson Blvd. ☎ 310/358-2500 ⏲ Phone for opening times ∎

Mythical, magical Hollywood has for nearly a century been the epitome of glamour, the high life, and showbiz glitz. It's hard to believe that this town began as a puritanical, prohibitionist, agricultural community.

Hollywood & West Hollywood

Introduction & map 100–101
Hollywood 102–129
Hollywood Boulevard 102–109
A walk along Hollywood
  Boulevard 110–111
Hollywood & Highland 112–13
Hollywood & Vine 114–16
Hollyhock House & Barnsdall Park
  117
Hollywood Hills 120
Mulholland Drive 121
Paramount Pictures Studio 122
Gower Gulch 122
Hollywood Forever 123
Sunset Boulevard 126–28
Sunset & Crescent Heights 129
West Hollywood 130–37
Sunset Strip 131
Sunset Strip walking tour 132–35
Schindler House 136
Pacific Design Center 137
More places to visit in Hollywood
  & West Hollywood 138
Hotels & restaurants 247–51

Celebrity look-alikes turn heads on Hollywood Boulevard.

Hollywood & West Hollywood

DROVES OF VISITORS DESCEND UPON HOLLYWOOD EVERY DAY, EACH OF them with different dreams, expectations, fantasies, and demands. There are film buffs, Raymond Chandler fanatics, wanna-be stars, and star-crazed fans, all pilgrims mesmerized by the legacy of Tinseltown, the place where dreams not only come true but become larger than life (and can be rerun to earn residuals).

Many visitors envision Hollywood as a sophisticated environment filled with huge studios, celebrities at every street corner, popping-flashbulb premieres, and all things glamorous. The reality, however, is that most of the moviemaking and associated deals don't take place in Hollywood at all. With the exception of

Paramount Pictures—practically out in the boonies over on Melrose Avenue—the major studios have long since moved to Burbank, Culver City, and Century City. And, unless a film premiere is being held at Mann's Chinese or at one of the other movie palaces, the stars are difficult to spot.

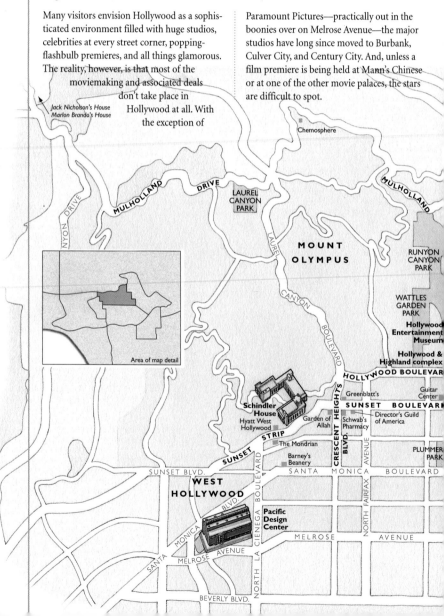

Jack Nicholson's House
Marlon Brando's House

Chemosphere

MULHOLLAND DRIVE

NYON DRIVE

MULHOLLAND

MULHOLLAND

LAUREL CANYON PARK

LAUREL CANYON BOULEVARD

MOUNT OLYMPUS

RUNYON CANYON PARK

WATTLES GARDEN PARK

Hollywood Entertainment Museum

Hollywood & Highland complex

Area of map detail

HOLLYWOOD BOULEVARD

Greenblatt's

Guitar Center

Schindler House

SUNSET BOULEVARD

Hyatt West Hollywood

Garden of Allah

Schwab's Pharmacy

Director's Guild of America

STRIP

The Mondrian

Barney's Beanery

CRESCENT HEIGHTS

BLVD.

AVENUE

PLUMMER PARK

SUNSET

SUNSET BLVD.

SANTA MONICA BOULEVARD

BOULEVARD

WEST HOLLYWOOD

BLVD.

MONICA

LA CIENEGA BOULEVARD

Pacific Design Center

NORTH FAIRFAX AVENUE

MELROSE

AVENUE

SANTA MONICA

MELROSE AVENUE

NORTH

BEVERLY BLVD.

Hollywood basked in glory during the 1920s and '30s, then was hit hard in the '40s by anti-Semitism and McCarthyism, and by competition in the '50s and '60s. By the 1980s, Hollywood's downtown was downtrodden, derelict, and anything but glamorous. In 1996, the local Business Improvement District launched an aggressive get-back-to-the-glitz revitalization campaign, tagging the area the "Hollywood Entertainment District." Already, new attractions have opened, the long-awaited Metro Red Line is in operation, and many icons have been restored. By the time this book is in print, a bevy of other clean-up projects will be in place, and the massive Hollywood & Highland complex should be near completion. In 2002, this new site will be the permanent home to the Academy Awards.

Hollywood "proper" runs from the Silver Lake neighborhood to Laurel Canyon Boulevard, and encompasses Hollywood and Sunset Boulevards, portions of Santa Monica Boulevard, and the Hollywood Hills. The territory is separated into the "flatlands" and the "hills." Businesses (many catering to the entertainment industry) are conglomerated in the flats, along with some major landmarks, older bungalows, and shabby apartments; here, there is a large population of recent immigrants from the former Soviet Union, Southeast Asia, and Latin America. Celebrities, artists, writers, and other creative (and wealthier) types still hide out in the cabins, castles, and cottages tucked away in the Hollywood Hills and along Mulholland Drive.

West Hollywood adjoins "old" Hollywood at a number of places east of La Brea Avenue (although that's about all they have in common), particularly as it nudges closer to Beverly Hills. This independent community is filled with hipsters who frequent the trendy shops, chic hotels, and famous nightclubs and restaurants on and around the infamous Sunset Strip. ■

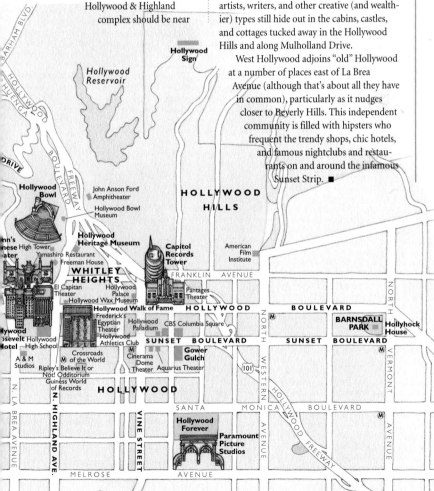

Hollywood Boulevard

THERE IS, PERHAPS, NO STREET IN THE WORLD THAT IS more famous—or infamous. Long associated with stardom and all that goes with it, Hollywood Boulevard remains a continual draw.

Hollywood Boulevard
- Map pp. 100–101
- Hollywood Blvd., between La Brea Ave. & Gower St.

Although the street had become downright sleazy over recent decades, practically no one seemed to notice (well, not the visitors anyway; residents took heed of the decay long ago and either headed for the hills, for West Hollywood, or for the Westside). Millions have gazed upon the street in utter fascination, blinded from the gritty reality by Tinseltown's mythical image of glamour, sophistication, and moviemaking magic. There have always been enough icons to satisfy: Mann's Chinese Theater, the Hollywood Roosevelt Hotel, movie palaces, the signpost at Hollywood and Vine, the Capitol Records Tower, and the thousands of Walk of Fame sidewalk stars. All of these are interspersed with rather dubious-looking groupings of honky-tonks, tourist traps, porn houses, and street people.

Believe it or not, Hollywood Boulevard was once lined with ornate mansions and prudish residents—that is, until the movie industry blasted into town and turned it into an unabashedly unprudish main drag. Indeed, during the 1920s and '30s, the stretch between La Brea Avenue and Vine Street very much exemplified the "Hollywood dream," with its fabulous movie palaces, fashionable shops, and ritzy hotels and restaurants. Stars, filmmakers, and entertainment-business types—dripping in diamonds, furs, and chic garb—could be seen carousing at snazzy nightclubs, sipping cocktails and smoking up a storm.

While the glory days are long over, Hollywood Boulevard is making a comeback, and doing it in no-holds-barred Tinseltown style. As at the time of writing, millions of dollars are being pumped into the Hollywood Entertainment District, an 18-block stretch between La Brea Avenue and Gower Street. The Hollywood Entertainment Museum and revamped Egyptian Theater are already up and running, as are the Metro Red Line's stations at Western Avenue, Vine Street, and Highland Avenue. The massive Hollywood & Highland project is bringing the revered Academy Awards ceremonies back home—to a site virtually opposite the Hollywood Roosevelt Hotel, where the first Oscars were presented in 1929. The fit-for-a-star face-lift also includes cleaning up building facades and the provision of new streetlamps, an on-foot security patrol, and signs that point to historic places. Even the sidewalk stars are gleaming again.

Hollywood Chamber of Commerce
- 7018 Hollywood Blvd.
- 323/469-8311

HOLLYWOOD WALK OF FAME

This is a town where people look down, instead of up, to see stars. The Walk of Fame "constellation" features more than 2,500 stars embedded along Hollywood Boulevard between La Brea Avenue and Gower Street, with some spilling on to Vine Street between Yucca Street and Sunset Boulevard. The honorees' engraved names twinkle from pink-coral stars, outlined in metal and ensconced in a gray terrazzo square. Beneath each name is an icon that designates the entertainer's field of fame: movie camera, television set, radio mike, theatrical mask, or record.

Although the Walk of Fame was the brainchild of the Hollywood Chamber of Commerce to pay tribute to entertainment industry artists, it's usually the celebrity's entertainment company who ends up paying some $15,000 a pop for the privilege of being enshrined in the street. A special committee selects prospective honorees, who must then cough up the money and await their slab and accompanying ceremony. Studios and public-relations firms have been more than eager to "fund" stars, having turned the process into a cool—and relatively cheap—promo tool for soon-to-be-launched movies or record albums. The selection process, as can be imagined, is somewhat haphazard. Some celebrities, just dying for a star, are turned down, while others—whose names are less familiar—seem to make it onto the street. There are also a number of well-known entertainers—including Meryl Streep and Dustin Hoffman—who seemingly could not care less about the whole matter.

The eight original stars, unveiled in 1960, can be seen at the northwest corner of Hollywood Boulevard and Highland Avenue. These are Olive Borden, Ronald Colman, Louise Fazenda, Preston Foster, Burt Lancaster, Edward Sedgwick, Ernest Torrence, and Joanne Woodward. From there, the trail leads to such legends as W.C. Fields *(7004 Hollywood Blvd.)*, Michael Jackson *(No. 6927)*, Elvis Presley *(No. 6777)*, Marilyn Monroe *(No. 6774)*, Charlie Chaplin *(No.*

Even glimpsing the stars in the street is a thrill for passersby along the Hollywood Walk of Fame.

Hollywood Entertainment Museum

- Map pp. 100–101
- 7021 Hollywood Blvd.
- 323/465-7900
- Closed Wed.
- $$

Opposite: Mann's Chinese Theater. Below: Bone up on the art of filmmaking and pore over important artifacts at the Hollywood Entertainment Museum.

6751), Ronald Reagan (No. 6374), and Rudolph Valentino (No. 6164). Even Rin Tin Tin has a star.

To take part in the fanfare of an induction ceremony (and get a peek at the inductee), call the Hollywood Chamber of Commerce for an upcoming schedule.

HOLLYWOOD ENTERTAINMENT MUSEUM

The Hollywood Entertainment Museum, occupying 33,000 square feet on the lower level of the Hollywood Galaxy Building, has considerably brightened a previously blighted plot just steps (or stars) away from Mann's Chinese Theater. Opened in 1996, the museum pays homage to Tinseltown, endeavoring to recapture the true spirit of its former self through treasured moviemaking artifacts, props, scripts, and exhibits.

The Exhibits

The 15-foot-tall Goddess of

Entertainment welcomes visitors into the main rotunda, where every 45 minutes Oscar-winner Chuck Workman's multimedia presentation whizzes through a retrospective of TV and filmdom's early days and legendary stars. The mini-model of Hollywood, also in the gallery, offers another fascinating glimpse at the district during its glory years. Constructed in 1936 by Joe Pellkofer, a cabinetmaker at Paramount Pictures, the 12-foot-square model details more than 400 buildings that once formed Tinseltown's core.

The "Dream Merchants" audio exhibit lets you have a one-sided conversation with an eclectic group of celebs, who offer words of wisdom—in their own voices—on various topics. Spouting off are Orson Welles on money, Tom Cruise on collaboration, Bill Cosby on comedy, and Tina Turner on sex appeal, among others. Other highlights include the bar from TV's Cheers, the bridge of the Starship Enterprise (you can sit in Captain Kirk's chair), and an interesting range of masks, costumes, and props. The education center is almost more interesting than the museum, with its electronic archive and library, recording studio, editing suite, and foley room, where visitors learn to create sound effects.

Max Factor Museum of Beauty

When the Max Factor Museum of Beauty closed its doors in 1996, the Hollywood Entertainment Museum inherited the treasured collection of early makeup and beauty paraphernalia. In 1914, Russian immigrant Max Factor created pancake makeup, flexible greasepaint that kept stars' faces from melting under the intense lights. The Factor display includes not only early makeup concoctions but

The old Max
Factor Building,
near the corner
of Hollywood and
Highland, once
housed the Max
Factor Museum
of Beauty.

**Mann's Chinese
Theater**

🅰 See map pp.
100–101

✉ 6925 Hollywood
Blvd.

☎ 323/464-8111

**Hollywood
Roosevelt Hotel**

🅰 See map pp.
100–101

✉ 7000 Hollywood
Blvd.

☎ 323/466-7000

intriguing implements such as the beauty calibrator, a horrific head cage-type device that seems made for beauties from another planet.

MANN'S CHINESE THEATER

The theater formerly known as Grauman's Chinese is, without doubt, the world's most famous cinema and remains a continual draw for throngs of film buffs. Owner-showman Sid Grauman, seeking an extravagant stage for his extravagant pre-film prologues, commissioned architects Meyer and Holler to come up with an elaborate design. And that they did. The duo put together a fanciful and elaborate pseudo-Chinese temple, complete with a pagoda-like entry guarded by a 30-foot-tall dragon. The well-preserved interior, with its red lobby, houses even more dragons, as well as other Chinese motifs and plenty of deep-red plush.

Completed in 1927, Grauman's opened in grand style, with Cecil B. DeMille's *King of Kings* bringing bright lights and long limos to the front door for the perfect gala

premiere. The theater continued to screen the biggest box-office hits, and the galas—complete with glittering celebrities and breathless fans—became a tradition. Although Grauman eventually sold up to the Mann chain (which couldn't resist the temptation to add more screens), the main theater behind the courtyard still retains much of its original ambience. And the flashbulb-popping premieres have continued through the decades.

Although the theater's building and premieres are fabulous indeed, the biggest attraction is the famous forecourt, where nearly 200 celebrities have left marks in the cement and where nearly two million visitors congregate each year. Legend has it that, on the 1927 opening day, visiting silent-film star Norma Talmadge accidentally stepped into the wet concrete. Grauman—always the showman—must have liked the concept, because he invited Mary Pickford and Douglas Fairbanks, Sr., to add their hand- and footprints as well. Under the Mann label, the inscriptions have gone on, with more recent honorees including Susan Sarandon, Harrison Ford, Mel Gibson, Meryl Streep, and Denzel Washington. Most of the prints are just the hands and feet of various Hollywood legends, but some have left the imprints of other parts of their bodies or accessories. Among the more unusual of these are Sonja Henje's ice skates, Betty Grable's legs, Jimmy Durante's schnoz, Donald Duck's webbed feet, Harpo Marx's harp, and Trigger's horseshoes.

HOLLYWOOD ROOSEVELT HOTEL

The Oscars' new home will be the Hollywood & Highland complex, just across the street from where the first presentation was held. Currently flying the Clarion banner, the Hollywood Roosevelt Hotel hosted the first Academy Awards ceremony in 1929. Douglas Fairbanks, Sr., presided over the event, which saw Janet Gaynor and Emil Jennings grabbing the acco-

lades for best actress and best actor.

Aside from the Oscars, the restored 1927 Spanish Colonial hotel has overseen plenty of other Tinseltown memories. During the glory years, the Roosevelt played host to numerous visiting

Above: Charlie Chaplin sits in the Hollywood Roosevelt Hotel. Below: Gwyneth Paltrow accepts her Oscar in 1999.

Catching the stars

One of the first things most visitors to Los Angeles want to know is where all the celebrities are. Truth be told, in Hollywood you are unlikely to see even one minor bit player, let alone a herd of top names. There are some notable exceptions along Hollywood Boulevard, including premieres at Mann's Chinese and the other big theaters. The Musso & Frank Grill, also on Hollywood Boulevard, has been a favorite celebrity hangout since the glory days, and it is still affordable for mere mortals (use the rear entrance and wait for a table on the "original" side). Otherwise, your best bet for celebrity gazing is over in West Hollywood and the Westside.

L.A.'s trendy restaurants and bars are the primary places where celebrities are apt to show up; here the major pastimes of eating and drinking often go hand and mouth with contract negotiations and agency sign-ups. Also keep in mind that celebrities bear little resemblance to their movie or television selves. Many are shorter, balder, and heavier or scrawnier than they appear on the screen. Porcelain complexions and sensuous features in that pulsing film romance can translate to a freckled face and chapped lips under the Tinseltown sun. And as for many of those dashing, heartthrob, action heros, keep your eyes trained on short guys with potbellies! ■

celebrities—and the legends that traveled with them. Tales include that of Errol Flynn concocting his gin recipe in the back of the barber shop, Bill "Bojangles" Robinson teaching Shirley Temple how to tap dance up the lobby staircase, and Montgomery Clift spontaneously blowing his bugle (Room 928 is said to be haunted by Clift's ghost). The Cinegrill bar was a favorite watering hole for serious drinkers such as Ernest Hemingway, F. Scott Fitzgerald, William Faulkner, and W.C. Fields, and portions of the film *The Fabulous Baker Boys* were filmed there. Artifacts, photos, props, and other memorabilia are displayed in the second floor's **History of Hollywood** exhibit. Finally, check out the hotel's Olympic-size swimming pool: Artist David Hockney painted the mural on the bottom.

MORE MOVIE PALACES
Although Mann's Chinese Theater has received the most fame—and notoriety—Hollywood Boulevard boasts an additional trio of Golden Age movie palaces.

Sid Grauman's first enterprise in Hollywood was not the famed hand- and footprint-laden Chinese temple, but the **Egyptian Theater** down the street. In 1922, Grauman—obviously into exotic themes—opened the Egyptian Theater, Hollywood's first movie palace, screening *Robin Hood* and launching Tinseltown's first gala premiere. Although a Spanish theme had initially been envisioned, Grauman decided to go Egyptian after King Tutankhamun's tomb was discovered. Designed by Meyer and Holler (architects of the Chinese Theater), the Egyptian Revival palace was a frenzy of hieroglyphic murals, sphinxes, mummy cases, banana palms, a bazaar (and bizarre) courtyard, and a grand sunburst- and scarab-adorned auditorium. Closed in 1992, the theater was given a major makeover and reopened in 1998. Blessedly, most of its original features were restored, from the marquee and period signs to the ornate ceiling and entrance portico. It is now the headquarters of the nonprofit American

This stained glass is part of the opulent decor of the Egyptian Theater.

Egyptian Theater
- Map pp. 100–101
- 6712 Hollywood Blvd.
- 323/466-3456

El Capitan Theater
- Map pp. 100–101
- 6838 Hollywood Blvd.
- 323/467-7674

Pantages Theater
- Map pp. 100–101
- 6233 Hollywood Blvd.
- 323/468-1700

Hollywood Wax Museum
- Map pp. 100–101
- 6767 Hollywood Blvd.
- 323/462-8860
- $$$

Ripley's Believe It or Not! Odditorium

⛰ Map pp. 100–101
✉ 6780 Hollywood Blvd.
☎ 323/466-6335
💲 $$

Guinness World of Records Museum

⛰ Map pp. 100–101
✉ 6764 Hollywood Blvd.
☎ 323/463-6433
💲 $$$

Frederick's of Hollywood Lingerie Museum

⛰ Map pp. 100–101
✉ 6608 Hollywood Blvd.
☎ 323/466-8506
🕐 Open until 9 p.m. Fri.

Cinematheque, whose weekly screenings range from classics and foreign films to indies and videos.

El Capitan Theater, a 1926 beauty, was used originally as a legitimate theater until it was bought by Paramount Pictures in 1941 and converted to a movie palace. Sensitively restored in 1991, this art deco gem is a blend of East Indian, baroque, and Moorish elements, with balcony boxes, stenciled ceiling coves, and other colorful ornamentation. Although the theater now shows Disney premieres and cartoons, it nonetheless has kept its single-screen status in a world of multiplexes.

The 1929 **Pantages Theater,** over near Hollywood and Vine, holds the distinction of being America's first art deco movie theater. It was the site of the Academy Awards presentations in the 1950s (under the ownership of Howard Hughes) and now operates as a venue for Broadway musicals. The facade is not particularly remarkable, but the zigzag Moderne interior—designed in 1929 by B. Marcus Priteca—is stunning, from the vaulted lobby to the ladies' rest room.

MORE HOLLYWOOD MUSEUMS

In addition to the Hollywood Entertainment Museum and Hollywood History Museum, the industry's most famous boulevard offers an eclectic quartet of Hollyweirdness.

If you are unable to get up close to stars in the flesh (or if they left their flesh long ago), you might want to opt for the wax version instead. The **Hollywood Wax Museum** is an opportunity to find the unlikely grouping of Elvis Presley, Humphrey Bogart, Mary Pickford, Brad Pitt, and the cast of *Star Trek* in one convenient

location. Contrary to popular belief, only the heads and hands are made of wax—the bodies are constructed of fiberglass. If a star falls from the galaxy, the body can be reused for the new kid on the block. This ever-popular visitor attraction continues to fascinate.

If you are visiting with kids, or if the L.A. street scene isn't odd enough for you, both the Ripley's and Guinness museums should satisfy any freak frenzies. It's difficult to miss **Ripley's Believe It or Not! Odditorium** as a *Tyrannosaurus rex* is poised on the museum's roof. Inside are hundreds of sideshow-type weirdnesses from around the world. The nearby **Guinness World of Records Museum** showcases all manner of strange world records, including videos of various peculiar achievements.

A purple-and-pink art deco tower heralds **Frederick's of Hollywood,** long-time bastion of interesting undergarments. Founded in 1946 by Frederick Mellinger, this establishment has catered to clientele from early pinup models to current drag queens and continues to epitomize flashy and trashy underwear, along with very high heels, skin-tight body stockings, and feather boas. The shop's upper-level **Lingerie Museum** is filled with titillating displays of celebrities' underthings, including items worn by Marilyn Monroe, Judy Garland, Zsa Zsa Gabor, Cher, Mae West, Tony Curtis and Milton Berle (in the film *Some Like it Hot*), and even Phyllis Diller. During the 1992 riots, Frederick's was looted and thieves made off with Ava Gardner's pantaloons and Madonna's bustier. Luckily for the viewing public, the guilt-ridden culprits eventually returned these too-hot-to-handle items, which are proudly on display once again. ■

El Capitan is one of L.A.'s few remaining single-screen movie theaters.

A walk along Hollywood Boulevard

A stroll along Hollywood Boulevard is de rigueur for a Tinseltown visit. Although the route doesn't have the glitz and glory of Hollywood's early days, major renovations to the designated 18-block Hollywood Entertainment District are brightening the neighborhood considerably. While it's unlikely you'll see any celebrities, you'll certainly come into contact with plenty of colorful characters.

Begin your walk west at the **Hollywood Entertainment Museum** (see p. 104) for a high-speed multimedia retrospective of Tinseltown. At **Mann's Chinese Theater ❶**, next door (see p. 106), the forecourt is fabled for its collection of celebrity hand- and footprints in cement blocks. Join the throngs trying to fit their favorites' shoes, or try to match up to Jimmy Durante's nose or Betty Grable's legs. When complete, the adjacent **Hollywood & Highland complex** (see p. 112) will keep visitors lingering around all day at its stylish shops, restaurants, and theaters, and in its Metro Station "gallery."

Across the street is the 1927 (Clarion) **Hollywood Roosevelt Hotel** (see p. 107), once the most happening place in town; stop here for a cool drink in the hotel's Cinegrill, a bar well used by Ernest Hemingway and F.

Scott Fitzgerald. Peek into the exquisite lobby of the 1926 **El Capitan Theater** (see p. 109), near the corner of Highland Avenue. Beyond Highland Avenue you'll pass **Ripley's Believe It or Not! Odditorium** and the **Guinness World of Records Museum;** the **Hollywood Wax Museum ❷** is across the street (see p. 109 for all three).

Step back to admire the magnificently restored **Egyptian Theater** (see p. 108), then take a close-up look at the courtyard and lobby. Can't you just imagine Hollywood's first premiere taking place here? Around the next corner, on Las Palmas Avenue, is the **Universal News Agency,** with its racks of newspapers and magazines.

Film and theater buffs will want to stop at **Larry Edmund's Cinema and Theater Bookshop ❸** (6644 Hollywood Blvd.), with one of the world's largest collections of new and out-of-print books related to the entertainment industry. And who could resist a browse through **Frederick's of Hollywood** (see p. 109). Pay tribute to celebrities' undergarments in the upstairs Lingerie Museum, or pick up some risqué unmentionables for take-home souvenirs. **Musso & Frank Grill,** across the street *(No. 6667),* has been in operation since 1919 and still retains its classic atmosphere, formal (and ancient) waiters, and comfort-food menu.

Continuing east, No. 6541 is Janes House, one of the boulevard's surviving Edwardian mansions (1903) and now the office of the Visitor Information Center. Cross the street again to view performance art, multimedia alternative art, and the video gallery at **LACE** ❹ *(No. 6522).* At Ivar Avenue, turn right to

Upstairs at Frederick's you can browse through celebrity underwear.

visit the Frank Gehry-designed **Frances Howard Goldwyn Hollywood Branch Library** *(1623 Ivar Ave.),* or left for a glimpse of the former **Knickerbocker Hotel** *(1714 Ivar Ave.).* Back on Hollywood, the next block you come to is Vine Street. The 1929 **Pantages Theater** ❺ (see p. 109) is on the opposite corner, while the Metro Red Line's Hollywood/Vine Station with its whimsical bus shelters, stands at this renowned intersection. Finally, face north to see the Hollywood sign in the distance. ∎

🅰 See area map pp. 100–101
▶ Hollywood Entertainment Museum, 7021 Hollywood Blvd.
↔ 1 mile (1.6 km)
🕐 Allow 20–30 minutes. Take this walk in daylight.
▶ Hollywood/Vine Metro Station

NOT TO BE MISSED
- Hollywood Entertainment Museum
- Mann's Chinese Theater
- Hollywood Roosevelt Hotel
- Egyptian Theater

Hollywood & Highland

TINSELTOWN'S UNSUNG HIGHLAND AVENUE DOESN'T enjoy even a twinge of the much-ballyhooed Vine Street, just a few stoplights away. Nonetheless it is closer to more Hollywood attractions, including the movie palaces, and Hollywood Bowl.

HOLLYWOOD & HIGHLAND COMPLEX

When complete in 2001, the four-hundred-and-thirty-million-dollar Hollywood & Highland project promises to inject some much-needed glitz not only into this corner of Hollywood, but through its entire artery. Positioned at one of Hollywood Boulevard's most strategic intersections and atop an MTA Red Line subway station, this development will have a profound effect on the future of Tinseltown.

The 640,000-square-foot, five-story, open-air complex will consist of a luxury hotel, theaters, restaurants, clubs, and retail outlets, along with Hollywoodisms such as movie studios, a live broadcast center, and a grand staircase leading to a panoramic view of the famous Hollywood sign. In addition, the site's Babylon Court will feature a re-creation of the extravagant set from D.W. Griffith's film *Intolerance* (1916). The project's centerpiece will be the 136,000-square-foot Academy Awards Theater, the only one of its kind designed especially for the Academy, and including a 3,300-seat auditorium, a 30,000-square-foot ballroom, a press area, a media cockpit, and an appropriately dramatic entryway for those idolized arrivals. The Oscars will officially return to Hollywood in March 2002.

HOLLYWOOD HERITAGE MUSEUM

In 1913, Cecil B. DeMille directed *The Squaw Man*—boasted to be Hollywood's first successful feature-length film—in this old $250-per-month horse barn, which served as set, offices, and dressing rooms. Originally located at Selma Avenue and Vine Street, the barn was instrumental in cementing the nearby Hollywood and Vine intersection as the heartbeat of the movie industry, and also in luring other filmmakers to the area. In 1926, DeMille, in partnership with Samuel Goldwyn and Jesse Lasky, had the barn moved to the backlot of Paramount Pictures, where it was used as an occasional set in the *Bonanza* television series. In 1956, the barn was designated the first California state landmark associated with moviemaking. Eventually, Paramount and the Hollywood Chamber of Commerce donated the historic structure to the Hollywood Heritage preservation group, and the old horse barn was relocated to its present site, near the Hollywood Bowl. A fire in 1996 caused serious damage to the building, but luckily most of the collections were saved. Scrupulously restored by Hollywood Heritage, it now houses a museum that focuses on Tinseltown's earliest—and greatest—years through various displays and presentations, including original silent-era Bell and Howell cameras, props, costumes, and other paraphernalia from the good old days. A re-creation of Cecil B. DeMille's old office allows a glimpse into the director's daily grind.

HOLLYWOOD BOWL

Since its inaugural season in 1922, the world-famous Hollywood Bowl

Hollywood & Highland complex
- Map pp. 100–101
- Corner of Hollywood Blvd. & Highland Ave.

Hollywood Heritage Museum
- Map pp. 100–101
- 2100 N. Highland Ave.
- 323/874-4005
- $$

Concert goers enjoy an evening event in the Bowl, a stage that has seen talents ranging from Rachmaninoff to the Beatles.

Hollywood Bowl

Map pp. 100–101 & inside back cover map C5

2301 N. Highland Ave.

323/850-2000

Hollywood Bowl Museum

323/850-2058

Closed Sun. & Mon. Open until 8:30 p.m. July–mid-Sept.

has been an ongoing source of pride for Angelenos. The natural amphitheater, situated north of Hollywood Boulevard and cradled below the Hollywood Hills, provides a lush and magical outdoor setting in which to enjoy the world's greatest talents performing under the summer skies.

Initially, the open-air stadium was a rough—and practically isolated—space, where audiences came for various concerts and religious plays. When the decision came to create a more permanent environment, some of the area's most talented architects were eager to help.

In 1927 and 1928, Lloyd Wright (son of Frank Lloyd Wright) designed and built the concert shells; Myron Hunt, designer of Pasadena's Rose Bowl, created the expansive seating in 1926; and in 1980, architect Frank Gehry added the floating fiberglass spheres inside the shell, which improved the acoustics considerably. The 15-foot statue, "The Muse of Music," designed by George Stanley (creator of the Oscar statuette), was

installed in 1940, as was the entrance fountain.

The bowl's season traditionally runs from July through mid-September, and it has been the summer home of the Los Angeles Philharmonic Orchestra since its inauguration. Evening concerts feature styles that range from classical and jazz to rock and pop. Easter sunrise services and Fourth of July spectacles are favorite ongoing events. Traditionally, Angelenos show up early to picnic on the grounds surrounding the bowl, then take their seats before the performance. More than 17,000 seats encompass everything from subscriber-only boxes (where gourmet meals can be provided), to high-in-the-sky wooden benches, all with excellent views.

The grounds are open all year, as is the **Edmund D. Edelman Hollywood Bowl Museum,** which houses a fascinating collection of bowl artifacts. Among them are photographs of Lloyd Wright's original drawings, early programs, and archival footage of Judy Garland's performance in the rain and the Beatles' 1964 concert. ■

Hollywood & Vine

EVER SINCE MOVIEDOM'S GLORY DAYS, THE INTERSECTION of Hollywood Boulevard and Vine Street has come to symbolize fame and stardom. It is difficult to fathom why, since, contrary to popular belief, the corner was never anything remarkable. Even though it really hit the skids during the area's sleazy years, no self-respecting visitor would leave without making a trip to this famous crossroads.

During the 1920s and '30s many of the big studios (Columbia, Paramount, Fox, and Warner Brothers) were all situated within a few blocks of Hollywood and Vine, so it's likely that the corner gained its mythical status simply because of its proximity to the action. Broadcasters grabbed the hook and would announce that they were reporting from "Hollywood and Vine." Movie-star wanna-bes then began descending on the intersection, waiting to be discovered by producers, directors, and talent scouts, all of whom were sure to be lingering on the streets or cruising by. And there really were passing stars and movie moguls, visiting their agents, on the way to the studios, headed for the nearby Brown Derby restaurant.

The real Hollywood and Vine houses nothing more than various

The famous Hollywood sign in the hills sometimes loses a letter, or is garbed for a special occasion.

Hollywood & Vine

🅰 Map pp. 100–101

office buildings, drugstores, souvenir shops, and fast-food outlets, as well as Walk of Fame stars honoring astronauts Neil Armstrong, Buzz Aldrin, Jr., and Michael Collins. There's still plenty of lingering and cruising, although certainly not of the stardom caliber. There are, however, some landmark sights that can be seen from the intersection, enough to keep it in the annals of Hollywood mythology.

The 1956 **Capitol Records Tower** (*1750 Vine St.*), a block north, was built as a distinctive stack of 45-rpm records topped with a stylus and was the world's first circular office building. Designed by Welton Becket, the idea allegedly came from the brains of Nat King Cole and Johnny Mercer. A rooftop beacon flashes "Hollywood" in Morse code, and the building still operates as Capitol's headquarters. The **Palace** (*1735 Vine St.*), across the street, once hosted TV's *This is Your Life;* it's now a state-of-the-art bi-level

dance club, where acts such as the Smashing Pumpkins and Nine Inch Nails perform. The art deco **Pantages Theater** (see p. 109) sits near the northeast corner of Hollywood and Vine, while the Metro Red Line station, across the street, provides some much-needed whimsy. This is also one of the best places to view the Hollywood sign.

HOLLYWOOD SIGN

Situated atop Mt. Lee, and heralding your arrival in Tinseltown, is the Hollywood sign, one of the world's most famous viewable pop icons. When it has been completed, the observation deck at the Hollywood & Highland complex will afford the best (and safest) view in town. The original purpose of the sign was not to advertise Hollywood at all, but to promote Hollywoodland, *Los Angeles Times* publisher Harry Chandler's real-estate development, now known as Beachwood. Erected in 1923, the gigantic 50-foot-tall letters—

Hollywood Sign

 Map pp. 100–101

✉ Via Beachwood Dr., off Franklin Ave., Hollywood Hills. However, the sign is now behind security gates, so your best view is from below.

Recording artists grin from a mural beneath the Capitol Records Tower.

Catch the action

Why settle for visiting the places where movies used to be made and the spots where stars used to stand? The L.A. Film Office *(7083 Hollywood Blvd., Fifth Floor, tel 323/957-1000)* will provide you with daily shoot sheets ($10) that tell you where and when movies, television shows, commercials, and videos are being shot on location around town. The sheets don't let you know if the action is going to take place inside or outdoors, but the list of locations is usually long and the odds of seeing some action are in your favor. ■

originally outlined in thousands of lights—were supposed to promote the various homes for sale in the gated 500-acre tract. Eventually, the sign fell into disrepair and, in 1949, it was deeded to the Hollywood Chamber of Commerce, which removed the "land" portion and kept the remaining letters as a Tinseltown landmark. By 1978, the sign had deteriorated into a mess, but not for long. Sentimental celebrities rallied to the cause, each taking on a particular letter: Hugh Hefner held a benefit for "Y," Alice Cooper purchased "O," Gene Autry donated funds for an "L."

Over the years, the sign has been associated with an interesting assortment of characteristically Hollywood urban legends. Vandals, pranksters, and acronym artists have had a field day altering the letters for athletic promotions, politics, or just because it's there. Some of the sign's temporary identity crises have included Hollyweed, in support of marijuana; Dollywood, to promote Dolly Parton; Ollywood, for Lieutenant Colonel Ollie North, during the Iran-Contra affair; Holywood, to welcome evangelist Aimee Semple McPherson; and Perotwood, during the 1992 presidential election. College students have been infamous for draping the sign before a big game, and on many an occasion visitors have looked up to see such slogans as "Go Navy," "USC," and "UCLA." During the Gulf War, the letters were wrapped with yellow ribbon in a show of support.

Surprisingly there has been only one recorded suicide at this icon. In 1932, 24-year-old starlet Lillian Entwistle (known as Peg), shattered after RKO studios refused to pick up her contract option, dragged herself through thick brush, climbed a ladder to the top of "H," and took a flying leap. In an attempt to ward off more tragedy or mischief, the sign has now been fenced and a high-tech security system has been installed. ■

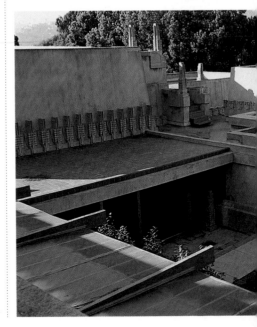

The Mayan-influenced design of the Hollyhock House incorporates a hollyhock motif throughout.

Hollyhock House & Barnsdall Park

IN 1915, HEIRESS ALINE BARNSDALL (1882–1946), FLUSH WITH money from her oil-tycoon grandfather, came West with the intention of setting up an artists' colony on a 36-acre site known as Olive Hill, at Hollywood's eastern edge. The development was to include her personal home, as well as a cinema, theater, and residences and studios for visiting artists and actors. Who better, then, to take on such a project than esteemed architect Frank Lloyd Wright?

Frank Lloyd Wright had met Aline Barnsdall previously in Chicago, and so he accepted his first L.A. commission. For Wright, it was also an opportunity to create one of his works of architectural art in a completely different location and climate. Completed in 1921, after a three-year construction period, Hollyhock House has since been officially acclaimed by the American Institute of Architects as one of the 20th century's most significant structures. Named for Barnsdall's favorite flower, the

Mayanesque concrete and stucco residence features hollyhock adornments both inside and out, and on Wright's original dining-room chairs. The home's dramatic layout incorporates theatrical spaces, proportional gardens, varying ceiling heights, and Craftsman-style furnishings. With the exception of the Wright chairs, detailed reproductions now furnish the home.

In 1923, after Wright had completed Hollyhock and two guest cottages (he received assistance from Rudolph Schindler and from his son, Lloyd Wright), Barnsdall abandoned the project and donated it to the city. The home was designated a historic cultural monument in 1963.

BARNSDALL PARK

Hollyhock House is not alone in Barnsdall Park, but shares the olive tree-ringed site with the Municipal Art Gallery, Junior Arts Center, and Barnsdall Art Center. The **Municipal Art Gallery** presents changing exhibits of cutting-edge works by regional artists, while the center's theater presents films, concerts, and exhibit-related readings by poets and writers. Budding young artists are offered classes at the **Junior Arts Center.** The **Barnsdall Art Center,** also known as Residence A, was one of Wright's original cottages and today promotes adult arts programs. ∎

Hollyhock House & Barnsdall Park

⬛ Map pp. 100–101

✉ 4800 Hollywood Blvd.

☎ 323/913-4157

🕐 Due to major restoration, Hollyhock House remains closed until spring 2003; the park grounds and Municipal Art Gallery until early 2001. The Barnsdall Art Center will temporarily re-locate across the street.

💲 $

Putting the tinsel into town

Early L.A. proved just too irresistible for the show-business crowd. The climate was divine year-round, the natural settings could handle anything from cowboys-and-Indians to sexy thrillers. Taxes were low, labor was cheap, and those navel oranges were just begging to be plucked.

D.W. Griffith, top dog at New York's Biograph film company, was the first director to make his mark on the town. In 1911, Griffith—with wife, Linda, teenaged Mary Pickford, and entourage—descended on the city for a winter film shoot. The season proved so productive, compared to weather-challenged and far-more-expensive New York City, that more directors headed West. A year later, Mack Sennett—following mentor Griffith's lead—formed the Keystone Company in East Hollywood, vehicle for vaudevillian Charlie Chaplin, slaphappy Laurel and Hardy, and the Keystone Kops.

It was Cecil B. DeMille who was the catalyst for the creation of L.A.'s major studios. In 1913, DeMille had merely come to town to rent a horse barn for the production of his successful film, *The Squaw Man*. His partners in the enterprise, Sam Goldwyn and Jesse Lasky, soon linked up with Adolph Zukor to form industry benchmark, Paramount Studios. By the 1930s, Hollywood was in full swing. Hollywood Boulevard—once a pathway for teetotaling churchgoers—was reeling with glitz, glamour, and hell-raising stars. Swanky nightclubs, chic restaurants, ritzy hotels, and movie palaces spread all the way to Sunset Strip. Highly paid stars were living in plush estates in Beverly Hills, the Hollywood Hills, and the beaches, while an ever increasing onslaught of wanna-be actors and starlets paraded into the city. By the 1940s, the heavyweight studios—M.G.M., R.K.O., Paramount, Warner Brothers, and Fox—were thriving.

Hollywood films had always been censored and regulated in some form: In the 1930s Will Hays, official censor, made sure sex and other "taboo" topics were never mentioned or alluded to in films; then the government began meddling, slapping Paramount with antitrust violations and breaking up the major studios' industry control. But nothing was as damaging as the House Un-American Activities Committee (H.U.A.C.), which between 1947 and 1954 spat its venom at the film industry. During the Cold War years, following World War II,

the U.S. was frenzied by the "Red Scare." The H.U.A.C. and its most famous member, Senator Joseph McCarthy, decided to hit on Hollywood, trying to eke out anyone who even made a left-leaning twitch. By the end of the ordeal, an ugly "blacklist" had been formed and many Hollywood talents went without work for a decade. Despite the carnage Otto Preminger—with his explicit-for-the-times film, *The Moon is Blue*—thumbed his nose at the Hays censorship code, and eventually the

hard-line attitude was replaced with the current ratings system. It took decades for the Hollywood studios to regain old ground, and, in fact, most moved to new turf in Culver City or the San Fernando Valley. Though the Golden Era is long gone, L.A. streets and attractions are often used for television and film shoots. ∎

Robin Hood **(1922) was one of the early films made in L.A.**

Pooches frolic on outings with their owners in a picturesque Laurel Canyon park.

Hollywood Hills

THE HOLLYWOOD HILLS RISE AND FALL LIKE STARS IN THE flatlands, forming the eastern edge of the Santa Monica Mountains and affording plenty of hidden crannies and canyons. Because of this privacy factor, the hills' proximity to Hollywood itself, and the great views from difficult-to-access streets, many celebrities continue to put down roots here, just as they did during Tinseltown's Golden Age.

The wooded hills shelter a dazzling mix of architectural house styles, most of them well hidden along a labyrinth of narrow, snaking roads. The residents include rock musicians, brat-pack stars, artists, writers, and creative-industry types.

The hills run almost parallel to Hollywood Boulevard, spilling from the western edge of Griffith Park across Laurel Canyon Boulevard and the area above West Hollywood. To the north, Mulholland Drive presents a physical and social borderline as the hills meet the San Fernando Valley. The main thoroughfares are Nichols Canyon Road and Laurel Canyon Boulevard, north of Hollywood Boulevard. The eastern Hollywood Hills consist predominantly of Harry Chandler's original **Hollywoodland** development, including its icon sign.

Hollywood Reservoir offers a respite from the hectic city and is reached via winding streets off Cahuenga Boulevard. **Whitley Heights,** west across Cahuenga Boulevard, is a pocket of 1920s and '30s Italian villa-esque residences.

South of the Hollywood Bowl, at 1962 Glencoe Way, is the **Freeman House,** Frank Lloyd Wright's 1922 concrete-block structure adorned with geometric decorations. **High Tower** (*High Tower Dr., south of Camrose Dr.*), a campanile built in 1920, conjures up images of a Tuscan hill town. ■

Mulholland Drive

Get your motor running: View-a-second Mulholland makes a thrilling road trip for gutsy drivers.

PRESIDING OVER BOTH LOS ANGELES AND THE SAN Fernando Valley is Mulholland Drive, which snakes a 25-mile path between Cahuenga Boulevard (just west of the Hollywood Freeway) and the Pacific Ocean. Also known as the Stars-to-Sea Highway, the gnarly mountain road has long reigned over the city lending ever more myth and intrigue to L.A.'s modern folklore.

The namesake of this particular byway was water pioneer William Mulholland, an Irish immigrant responsible for siphoning water from the Owens Valley into L.A.

The roadway's precarious cliffs, mesmerizing views, and seemingly endless twists and turns—with exclusive mansions either hidden or flaunted about them—have always been associated with celebrities, wealth, sex, car crashes, and various scandals, in television and film as well as in real life. Just as importantly, Mulholland Drive is L.A.'s designated lover's lane, the spot that every girl's mother warned her about. Aside from the regular lectures about parking, there have been plenty of events to inflame young minds. Roman Polanski was holed up at Jack Nicholson's home (No. 12850) when he had his infamous fling with a 13-year-old model, leading to his arrest, conviction, and eventual exile to Paris. Marlon Brando's compound (No. 12900), is where Brando's son shot and killed Brando's daughter's lover. Estate ruins just off Mulholland, at 2398 Laurel Canyon Boulevard, are alleged to have belonged to Harry Houdini and are now a hangout for his ghost and various psychics.

The lights of the city below are, indeed, magical. Parking is not allowed at night, but it's worth a stop at one of the designated viewpoints to ogle the City of Angels. ■

Paramount Pictures Studio

Paramount Pictures Studio
Map pp. 100–101
✉ 5555 Melrose Ave.
☎ 323/956-5575
🕐 Tours every half hour Mon.–Fri. 9 a.m.–2 p.m. (run on a first-come, first-served basis, so show up early). No children under ten.
💲 $$$

While other studios have moved out of Hollywood, Paramount has remained in this location since 1926. Originally erected in 1917 for Peralta Studios, thousands of famous films were turned out here. RKO Studios, part of the Paramount complex, produced Fred Astaire/Ginger Rogers musicals, as well as *King Kong* and *Citizen Kane*. Lucille Ball formed Desilu Studios here in 1957 churning out *I Love Lucy* episodes.

Perhaps the most famous part of Paramount is its side entrance at the corner of Bronson Avenue and Marathon Street. The wrought-iron gate here has appeared in many flicks, most notably in *Sunset Boulevard* (1950). There is a two-hour studio tour. Films and TV shows are still in production, but the tour focuses mainly on backlot sets and studio departments. ■

Gower Gulch

Gower Gulch
🗺 Map pp. 100–101

During the second two decades of the 20th century, the area around Gower Street and Sunset Boulevard came to be known as Gower Gulch, a sort of B-movie Poverty Row. Low-budget films, mainly of the Western variety, were being cranked out at dozens of small studios that lined the streets. CBS Columbia Square, on the intersection's northwest corner, was the site of radio broadcasts by Edgar Bergen and Charlie McCarthy and by George Burns and Gracie Allen. It was also the former home of the Nestor Film Company, Tinseltown's first movie studio. Sunset-Gower Studios, at the southeast corner, used to be Columbia Pictures, which turned out such classics as *From Here to Eternity, The Caine Mutiny,* and *It's a Wonderful Life. America's Funniest Home Videos* television show is one of the current tapings. ■

Hollywood Forever

Many stars and moguls played out their final act on these monument-laden grounds.

MOST OF THE HOLLYWOOD MAPS THAT CLAIM TO PINPOINT stars' homes prove to be inaccurate. A far more reliable map, however, is the one you pick up at the Hollywood Forever flower shop (formerly Hollywood Memorial Cemetery), as all of the celebrities listed are still in residence. Hollywood loves its famous dead people, and most visitors seem as enthralled by the stars' headstones as they would by their autographs.

Hollywood Forever

🅰 Map pp. 100–101
✉ 6000 Santa Monica Blvd.
☎ 323/469-1181

The roll call here reads like the A-list at a post-Oscar party, with Rudolph Valentino probably leading in the popularity stakes. Valentino, dashing hero of *The Sheik* and heartthrob of millions, died of peritonitis in 1926 at the age of 31 and was laid out inside the Cathedral Mausoleum. Some 10,000 fans packed the grounds to pay their tributes. For years after, a mysterious lady in black would show up with flowers on the anniversary of Valentino's death (August 23). Although this allegedly began as a publicity stunt, successors have kept the tradition going.

Other familiar names pop up at every turn: Charlie Chaplin Jr., Tyrone Power, Peter Finch, John Huston, Nelson Eddy, Bugsy Siegel, and the puritanical Harvey and Daeida Wilcox, founders of Hollywood. The Abbey of Psalms Mausoleum boasts the bones of Norma Talmadge and Clifton Webb, while director Cecil B. DeMille's crypt resides in the lake area. Also in this area is the predictably ostentatious resting place of Douglas Fairbanks, Sr. The largest monument, however, belongs to railroad heir and Los Angeles Philharmonic founder William A. Clark Jr., who is encased in an island tomb along with his two wives. In Pineland is the grave of Mel Blanc, voice of Bugs Bunny, whose epitaph aptly reads "That's all folks!" ■

Altars & egos

Contrary to some opinions, Los Angeles is not a city of shallow minds and questionable morals. The City of Angels is, in fact, a world center of religions, even if you've never heard of most of them. Angelenos simply love to worship, be it God, Allah, Buddha, Krishna, or a current favorite hairstylist, cosmetic surgeon, or personal trainer. They worship on bended knees or crossed legs, and with heads bowed or by standing on their heads. They count their beads on rosaries and sandalwood, burn pungent incense and votive candles, pour over litanies and Bible verses, and immerse themselves in meditation and in becoming one with the universe. And, Angelenos to the core, they most particularly worship themselves and their own reflected images, be it in snazzy boutique dressing rooms, in their oversize car's oversize mirrors, or—for the lucky ones—on television or film screens.

Death is also celebrated and prepared for in a worshipful manner, although Angelenos tend not to concentrate so much on theories of the afterlife and reincarnation, as to how their body, face, and grave will appear to those who come to pay their respects (Evelyn Waugh's novel *The Loved One,* later a film, was a scathing portrayal of L.A.'s inimitable take on death). Even when they are 6 feet under, Angelenos want to be surrounded by an A-list of corpses, encased, of course, in the best Italian silk-lined coffin with hand-fabricated fittings, and marked with a Carrara-marble slab. Visitors who never manage to see a living star during their stay can gape at the tombs of the late greats, who are no doubt far more approachable in death than they were in their blink-and-gone lives.

The truth is that since the Franciscans came to town, myriad preachers—from Pentecostal zealots and Eastern yogis to ufologists and New Age nudists—have made their way to L.A., proselytizing from the gritty city streets and parks to slick donation-built headquarters. Since the city's inception, offbeat religions have become the norm, and the more mumbo jumbo and hocus-pocus the better.

It's easy to strike up a congregation in L.A., and hard to get bored at the beach.

Performance art and escapism rule this town, and every kook and crackpot eventually cashes in. But, by the same token Angelenos—forever embracing eccentricity in all forms—are so open-minded that many ancient doctrines as well as pioneering philosophies have been launched on their home turf. In the 1920s alone, showy Aimee Semple McPherson, preaching Foursquare Gospel, set the tone for future televangelists, while Indian guru Paramahansa Yogananda espoused Eastern religion and meditation techniques. Both philosophies ultimately had a profound effect, not just on the L.A. community, but on the entire country. Not surprisingly, celebrities are always getting into the act (Richard Gere and the Dalai Lama are notable examples), while many star-endorsed channelers,

healers, and psychics have reeled in fortunes and fame.

Readers of literature will remember the main character in Nathanael West's novel *The Day of the Locust* (1939) catapulting among the city's bizarre churches, dabbling in the spirit world, Aztec secrets, and anti-salt crusades. And that was in the 1930s. Present-day L.A. embraces all of the major religions in their infinite varieties, as well as cults, sects, and movements that encompass channeling, chanting, shamanism, reincarnation, electromagnetic balancing, Wicca, transvestism, and nudism, among a literally mindboggling number of others. Many Angelenos, like dual nationalists, follow two or more belief systems. For example, a senior citizen Reform Jew might also delve into past-life regression, while a middle-aged Methodist quite possibly may attempt to conjure an Inca boogie man. Anything and everything is believable in L.A. ∎

Evangelist Aimee Semple McPherson, a dynamic preacher in 1920s L.A.

**Glitzy Sunset
Boulevard throngs
with traffic and life.**

Glitzy Sunset Boulevard throngs with traffic and life.

Sunset Boulevard
Map pp. 100–101

Sunset Boulevard

BEGINNING IN L.A.'S ORIGINAL PUEBLO AREA AS AN extension of Cesar Chavez Avenue, Sunset Boulevard stretches some 20 miles, ending at the Pacific Ocean. It runs through diverse neighborhoods, from low-rent districts such as the historic Pueblo and Echo Park, and then through the more arty Silver Lake and Los Feliz, where the boulevard turns north, paralleling Hollywood Boulevard for its course through Tinseltown. Beyond, it merges into West Hollywood, then wends a route through Beverly Hills, Westwood, Bel Air, Brentwood, and the Pacific Palisades, to reach the Pacific Ocean.

GOWER GULCH TO HIGHLAND AVENUE

Like Hollywood Boulevard, Sunset has been undergoing major changes—new developments, redevelopment, and a general clean-up. It is also practically unrecognizable from its heyday as a sophisticated celebrity hangout and starlet discovery zone. In Hollywood, the section between Gower Gulch and the Sunset Strip offers new complexes mixed in with old lore.

Sharing the intersection with CBS Columbia Square and Gower-Sunset Studios is **Gower Gulch**

dancers, who were referred to as the "most beautiful girls in the world." After Carroll died it was converted into the exclusive Moulin Rouge nightclub, and became the broadcasting site for the 1950s television show *Queen for a Day*. In the 1960s the club became the Aquarius Theater and venue for the live production of *Hair*.

At the time of writing, a new development is in the works at Sunset and Vine. The tri-level **Hollywood Marketplace,** designed to reflect the splendor of 1930s and '40s Tinseltown, will comprise restaurants, retail shops, a multiscreen movie house, a health club, and plenty of parking for Angelenos' vehicles. The historic white-concrete **Cinerama Dome Theater** *(No. 6360)* will be the centerpiece of the 6-acre complex and will also be glitzed up. Originally built in the 1950s as a venue for the three-projector Cinerama-film craze, the theater has continued to operate despite the redundancy of its technology.

During the 1920s, the **Hollywood Athletic Club** *(No. 6525)* was a private "boys' club" for stars such as Clark Gable, Charlie Chaplin, John Barrymore, Rudolph Valentino, and John Wayne, who rendered it notorious not just for the "health benefits" but for the heavy drinking bouts and boys-will-be-boys shenanigans. After a long period of closure, the club has reopened to a new breed of brat-pack celebrities who aspire to their predecessors' reputations. The conglomeration of architectural styles known as **Crossroads of the World** *(No. 6671)* was designed by Robert Derrah in 1936. This early shopping mall is a fantasy hodgepodge, with an ocean liner as the main building, surrounded by exotic "shops," which are now offices.

The unsigned Mondrian, a favorite celebrity hotel

shopping center, which provides a bit of nostalgia through the use of old frontier-style decor in its facades and signage. Famed chef Joachim Splichal's Pinot Hollywood and the Martini Bar can be found around the corner *(1448 Gower St.)*. The **Hollywood Palladium** *(6215 Sunset Blvd.)* has been swinging since the 1940s, with the big-band sounds of Glenn Miller, Stan Kenton, the Dorsey Brothers, and crooners such as Frank Sinatra. In the 1950s, Lawrence Welk (Mr. Bubble) taped his popular television show from here. The club is still open, although these days the headliners are usually rockers. Across the street is the **Aquarius Theater** *(No. 6230)*, originally Earl Carroll's theater and famed for its enormous revolving stage and 60

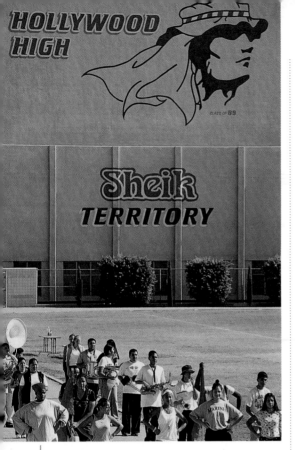

HOLLYWOOD HIGH

Sheik TERRITORY

The once glamorous Hollywood High School, now a fading star

into the area, Hollywood High graduates—though full of cultural color—are more blue collar than feather boa. Until that time, the school's drama department was top-notch, turning out professional productions that were well attended by the talent scouts. Hollywood High has not aged gracefully, and its previously open campus is now dank, tired, and guarded. The decorative reliefs and inspirational inscriptions on the buildings can, however, still be made out through the grime, and the football team is still known as the Sheiks in honor of Rudolph Valentino and his famous role.

At La Brea Avenue, just south of Sunset, is **A & M Recording Studios** *(1416 N. La Brea Ave.),* the 1919 studio of Charlie Chaplin and where he made such classics as *The Gold Rush, Modern Times, The Great Dictator,* and *City Lights.* Bought in the mid-1960s by Herb Alpert and Jerry Moss (A & M), and until recently home to Polygram Records, the studio has recorded numerous stars—including Sting, Bryan Adams, and Janet Jackson—and was the site where top vocalists got together to record the socially conscious hit "We Are the World." It is now owned by Henson Productions.

Guitar lovers should pay a visit to the **Guitar Center** *(No. 7425),* a huge musical instrument store where guitar wizards such as Eddie Van Halen have left embedded prints of their fast-flying hands. The circa-1980s **Director's Guild of America** *(No. 7920)* looms across Fairfax Avenue, just before Sunset Boulevard becomes the Sunset Strip. Here, public programs are occasionally presented at the three auditoriums. Sunset Strip is an ultra-trendy 1.75-mile stretch of the boulevard running through West Hollywood (see p. 130). ∎

HIGHLAND AVENUE TO SUNSET STRIP

At the corner of Sunset Boulevard and Highland Avenue is **Hollywood High School,** resting like a jaded star that can't afford a face-lift, Prozac, or a stint at the Betty Ford Center. Built in 1935 in Streamline Moderne style, America's most famous public high school used to turn out stars by the dozens. Alumni include Judy Garland, Sally Kellerman, Carol Burnett, James Garner, Fay Wray, Mickey Rooney, Jason Robards, and Lana Turner (Lana was reputedly discovered when she ditched class and went to the long-gone Top Hat malt shop across the street). Since the late 1960s, when school boundaries were changed and lower-income immigrants moved

Sunset & Crescent Heights

THE INTERSECTION OF SUNSET AND CRESCENT HEIGHTS boulevards is, for many residents, not merely the end of Hollywood in a geographical sense (West Hollywood's boundary begins about one block west of here), it is also the end, in a metaphorical sense, because it was the corner that both epitomized the glory years and also signaled their demise.

Sunset & Crescent Heights
Map pp. 100–101

Throughout the 1930s and '40s, Alla Nazimova's **Garden of Allah** hotel on the southwest corner of the Sunset and Crescent intersection was Hollywood's unofficial hub of literary and social activity, as well as the scene of some heavy partying and scandalous affairs. On any given day, the Garden's bar or poolside bungalows would shelter celebrities such as Ernest Hemingway, F. Scott Fitzgerald, Dorothy Parker, Tallulah Bankhead, Clara Bow, Errol Flynn, Clark Gable, Frank Sinatra, and Ava Gardner. In the early 1950s, when the hotel began to slide downhill, along with its fast-living clientele, it was sold to Lytton Savings and Loan, which demolished the Moorish paradise and constructed a depressing office block in its place. Singer/songwriter Joni Mitchell alluded to this desecration in her song, "Big Yellow Taxi:" "They paved paradise and put up a parking lot." For years afterward, aging stars as well as sentimental locals used to haunt that ugly parking lot, agonizing over paradise lost. Eventually, Lytton sold out, and the site is now a mini-mall.

Across the street, on the southeast corner of the intersection, was **Schwab's Pharmacy,** which achieved its claim to fame as Hollywood's prime spot for actors just dying to be discovered (the soda fountain was supposedly the best seat in the house). Allegedly, a Hollywood gossip columnist let it leak that Lana Turner was discov-

Like everywhere else in L.A., Sunset Boulevard is often blocked by cars.

ered while sipping atop one of his stools—a misnomer as Lana actually began her climb-to-fame over at the Top Hat opposite Hollywood High. A number of struggling writers and actors did indeed hang out at Schwab's, including William Holden in the movie *Sunset Boulevard,* and F. Scott Fitzgerald, who in real life suffered a heart attack in the store. Schwab's was bulldozed in the late 1980s and lingers today only as a memory within a block-long shopping complex that contains a Virgin Megastore and Wolfgang Puck Café. **Greenblatt's Delicatessen,** across the street *(No. 8017),* still stands as a monument to the residents of the Garden of Allah, who used to cross over for pastrami sandwiches and cheesecake. ■

Stars flock to celebrity chef **Wolfgang Puck's** eatery to be seen munching on designer pizzas.

West Hollywood

The independent kingdom of West Hollywood wants to remain associated with Tinseltown—it may have gotten a divorce, but it kept the family name. The two communities can be difficult to distinguish (some West Hollywood streets actually parallel and bisect those of Hollywood). Residents, however, will emphatically set you straight.

Even before the city's incorporation in 1984, West Hollywood was a neighborhood with a rebellious spirit. During the early 1900s, when it was the site of the Los Angeles Pacific Railway Terminal, West Hollywood (then known as Sherman) refused to be included within the City of Los Angeles. That hardly stopped the action though, for Sherman not only continued to be a hub for the rail lines but also became a haven for booze during the Prohibition era. Craftsman bungalows went up, stars moved in, and the 1920s nightclub scene—and the neighborhood's subsequent name change to West Hollywood—assured it an esteemed spot on the cool-L.A. map.

Demands for rent control and gay rights resulted in the incorporation of West Hollywood in 1984. The large gay population had complained of harassment, seniors were concerned over the lack of rent control, and Sunset Strip had become a hotbed of criminal activity. The media heralded West Hollywood's promotion to cityhood, with the associated appointment of gay- and senior-friendly police officers and city officials, as a big leap for civil rights and lauded its activism.

Ranking as the 84th city in Los Angeles County, West Hollywood today supports over 36,000 residents in just under 2 square miles. Its denizens are a mix of gays, lesbians, seniors, and immigrants from the former Soviet Union. The community policing system, working in partnership with residents, has been emulated throughout the country, while at the local level gays and seniors have fared well and crime has been cleaned up considerably. The Pacific Design Center, classy galleries, Craftsman architecture, chic shops, hip bookstores, and trendy clubs are all within West Hollywood's boundaries—particularly the side that abuts Beverly Hills. The main drag continues to be Sunset Strip. ■

Sunset Strip

IF YOU'RE WONDERING WHERE THE STARS MIGRATED after they disappeared from Hollywood, it was westward, taking with them all the glitz, glamour, and scandals that seem to be the natural companions to that fast-living, high-rolling, turned-on lifestyle.

Sunset Strip

Map pp. 100–101

Sunset Strip had been a thriving and sophisticated nightclub scene since the 1930s and '40s. Nightspots such as Ciro's, the Trocadero, and the Mocambo are legends. The 1950s television era kept people in front of the tube, but by the 1960s the Strip was packed with flower children, and the clubs became launching pads for some of rock 'n' roll's most famous bands. Best known of the clubs was the Whisky A Go Go, still in operation today.

Although peace and love eventually downslided into drugs, prostitution, and other sordid vices, West Hollywood's 1984 incorporation status turned the streets into bastions of trendiness. The Strip itself had never actually fallen into real decay and always had a smattering of prestigious hotels and restaurants, as well as the Sunset Plaza's chic boutiques. (It no doubt helped that chef Wolfgang Puck had opened the world-famous Spago a couple of years earlier.)

The majority of Sunset Strip tenants are entertainment industry professionals, and clubs are now owned by celebrity financiers such as Johnny Depp and *Hustler Magazine's* Larry Flynt. Celebrities covet the privacy of independent hotels such as the age-old Chateau Marmont, the art deco Argyle, and the super-classy Mondrian. And looming above the thriving scene are the Strip's famous billboards. While it is true that celebrities are always hovering about West Hollywood, some sighting spots are nearly impossible to get into unless you are someone already. ∎

The Strip's famous billboards light the way to exclusive hotels and celebrity-owned nightclubs.

Sunset Strip walking tour

Taking a walk on the Sunset Strip is exciting, day or night. You can't help but get caught up in the history and street energy, as Jaguars, BMWs, and Land Rovers zip past. At night, wild clubs and quiet bars set the scene for celebrities, models, and L.A. hipsters. If you're planning to try for a seat at Spago or a stool at the Sky Bar, book ahead, dress in your most expensive all-black outfit, and take plenty of money.

Billboards, luxury vehicles, and celebrity hideouts line either side of the Sunset Strip.

WESTWARD BOUND

There is no better place on Earth to begin an otherworldly journey than at a bona fide Jewish deli. **Greenblatt's Delicatessen** *(No. 8017, between Laurel Ave. & Laurel Canyon Blvd.)*, the only surviving landmark at the crossroads where the Garden of Allah hotel and Schwab's Drugstore once resided. Head west on the north side of Sunset to reach **Chateau Marmont** ❶ *(No. 8221)*, long a hideout for movie and film stars who crave privacy. Greta Garbo, Marilyn Monroe, Warren Beatty, and Mick Jagger have all come and gone unnoticed from this elegant 1927 Norman castle, while John Belushi made a

sensational final exit when he died in one of the bungalows. Nearby **Cajun Bistro** *(No. 8301)*, formerly The Source, was used for a scene in Woody Allen's film *Annie Hall*.

During the 1960s and '70s, rock 'n' roll musicians and their groupies used to throw wild parties at the Continental Hyatt House (now **Hyatt West Hollywood** ❷, *No. 8401)*. Legend has it that the band Led Zeppelin was the naughtiest. **The Comedy Store** *(No. 8433)* is nearby, with three rooms that host established comics alongside rising talents; alumni include Roseanne, Jim Carrey, David Letterman, and Robin Williams.

Only in L.A. could a former 1930s

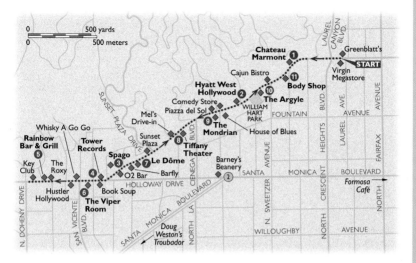

brothel—**Piazza del Sol** *(No. 8439)*—be given historic landmark status because of its Spanish Revival architecture. Another L.A. oddity is the retro **Mel's Drive-In** *(No. 8585)*, which does not provide any car service! Patrons feast on burgers and shakes in booths or at the counter, and they feed coins into the jukebox. **Sunset Plaza,** spilling across both sides of the street at the corner of Sunset Boulevard and Sunset Plaza Drive, dates from the 1930s and encompasses two blocks of exclusive boutiques, cafés, salons, and galleries. Renowned designer shops within the complex include such illustrious names as Nicole Miller, Laura Urbanati, Kenzo, Hervé Légèr Paris, BCBG, Vivienne Tam, Anna Sui, Dolce & Gabbana, and Armani Exchange.

Wolfgang Puck's **Spago** ❸ *(1114 N. Horn Ave., just off Sunset Blvd.)* sits at the top of most visitors' must-see lists and is still a celebrity favorite. Puck's designer pizzas live up to their reputation, and the smoked salmon "pie" remains the best seller. Back on Sunset is **Tower Records** ❹ *(No. 8801)*, which bills itself as the world's largest music store.

The 1960s were very good to **Whisky A Go Go** *(No. 8901, at Clark St.)*, the West Coast's first disco; it was renowned not only for launching the careers of groups such as The Doors, but also for the pretty young things in fringes and boots who danced inside

	See area map pp. 100–101
►	Greenblatt's Delicatessen, No. 8017
↔	3 miles (5 km)
⏱	Allow 20–30 minutes
►	Virgin Megastore, No. 8000

NOT TO BE MISSED
- Spago
- Whisky A Go Go
- The Roxy
- Book Soup

cages. Still going strong, the Whisky today hosts rock 'n' rollers, as well as uncaged dancing near the stage. Dating from 1972 is **The Roxy** *(No. 9009)*, another world-famous rock-your-socks-off club. Rockers, hipsters, and industry types pack in here every night to see headliners such as Rod Stewart and Jane's Addiction, as well as up-and-coming talents. The **Rainbow Bar and Grill** ❺ *(No. 9015)* draws the music execs these days, but as the Villa Nova Restaurant it was the place where Marilyn Monroe and Joe DiMaggio first met on a blind date. The **Key Club** *(No. 9039)* offers more musical entertainment in a slick, high-tech environment and has been ranked as one of the country's premier live-performance venues.

Count on crowds outside Sunset's
many nightclubs.

EASTWARD RETURN

Cross the street and head back east, pausing at
Larry Flynt's **Hustler Hollywood** *(No.
8920)*, a bit of porn kitsch as only L.A. can pull
off. Adult videos and an erotic novelty shop
coexist with an international newsstand, a café
and juice bar, and the Hustler Porn Walk of
Fame, popular with a hip, mixed clientele. The
hip and mixed also blaze a trail into **The
Viper Room** 6 *(No. 8852)*, co-owned by
actor Johnny Depp. Formerly the Melody
Room, a mobster hangout, the club now
presents a very cool atmosphere and music,
and it reels in bands such as Pearl Jam for
impromptu gigs. In 1993 actor River Phoenix
died on the pavement outside after overdoing
things inside.

The locally owned **Book Soup** *(No. 8818)*
offers a superb range of classic and current
literature, entertainment-industry tomes, and
an enormous assortment of international
newspapers and magazines. Woody
Harrelson's **O2 Bar** *(No. 8788)* will further
enhance your brain power with hits of oxygen
and mood-altering drinks, as well as organic
food. The European-style **Barfly** *(No. 8730)*
has no relation to Charles Bukowski except
through name. Also très chic is **Le Dôme** 7

The world's largest music store boasts
a lengthy roster of musicians among
its hip clientele.

(No. 8720), an elegant, celebrity-pulling dining
room with a great view and fine menu.
Tiffany Theater 8 *(No. 8532)* once
enshrined the facade used for the 1950s hit-
TV series 77 *Sunset Strip*. Dino's Lodge, once
next door, is long gone.

The **Mondrian** 9 *(No. 8440)* boasts no
sign, yet nonetheless is one of the most
sought-after addresses in town, an all-white,
contemporary oasis for both visiting and local
celebrities. The hotel's Sky Bar is perpetually
jammed with moguls, models, musicians, and
movie stars.

Blues Brother Dan Aykroyd is part-owner
in **House of Blues** *(No. 8430)*, which dishes
out Southern cuisine and doses of blues in a
large, colorful room. The 1929 art deco Sunset
Tower is now **The Argyle** 10 *(No. 8358)*,

another celebrity stay and play place, and on the National Register of Historic Places. John Wayne allegedly kept a cow on his penthouse balcony; hopefully, these days he'd find it more entertaining to hang out with Sharon Stone, who has sunbathed by the hotel's pool.

Exotic dancers have been bumping and grinding at the **Body Shop** ⑪ *(No. 8250),* at the Harper Avenue intersection, since 1938. The pseudo art deco **Virgin Megastore** complex *(No. 8000)* houses the chain's first U.S. store as well as shops, cafés, a health club, and a day spa. Renowned Schwab's Drugstore once stood on this spot. You are now back at the start point of your walk, the famous Sunset and Crescent Heights intersection. ■

Venerable venues

Three of West Hollywood's oldest celebrity hangouts are not even on renowned Sunset Strip. **Barney's Beanery** *(8447 Santa Monica Blvd.)* has been in operation since the 1920s, serving beer and roadhouse food to stars and musicians, many of whom created a ruckus (Janis Joplin and Jim Morrison had at least one nasty scene). Once a shrine to folk singers and rockers, **Troubador** *(9081 Santa Monica Blvd.)* presents acts such as Mötley Crüe, the Barenaked Ladies, and heavy metal bands. Across the street from Warner Hollywood Studios and open since 1934 is the **Formosa Café** *(No. 7156),* which once served the likes of Marilyn Monroe, Clark Gable, Humphrey Bogart, and Bugsy Siegel. Hipsters and celebrities still frequent the café, with its Chinese-American menu and stars' headshots plastered on the walls. ■

Schindler House

Schindler House

🗺 Map pp. 100–101
✉ 835 N. Kings Rd.
☎ 323/651-1510
🕐 Closed Mon.–Tues.
💲 $$

VIENNA ARCHITECT RUDOLPH SCHINDLER (1887–1953) originally came to L.A. to work on the Hollyhock House commission with his mentor, Frank Lloyd Wright (see p. 117). In 1921, Schindler constructed his own studio-residence—and future Modernist masterpiece—where he lived until his death. Enthralled by the airy, communal living arrangements of North African desert camps, Schindler embarked on a blueprint that would bring such a living style to his West Hollywood lot.

The house was designed as a two-family home (which proved very convenient when Schindler and his wife divorced) with a central communal kitchen, and it used materials and spatial elements that, for the time, were unconventional, even revolutionary. Concrete, redwood, exposed rafters, floor-to-ceiling glass, and removable canvas walls were incorporated into a highly textural, breezy open floor plan, where individual indoor studios blend into outdoor living areas, complete with outdoor fireplaces. Concrete walls on three sides, with the front an enormous glass window to the great outdoors, indeed gave the house a "desert living" feel. The kitchen also played out this concept; Schindler wanted cooking to be a sociable, campfire-type affair. And the sleeping arrangements? The architect installed rooftop "sleeping baskets" in which to enjoy those starry nights under the L.A. sky (unfortunately he obviously hadn't done his homework when he assumed that L.A. and North Africa have similar climates). Clyde and Marian Chace, the friends who had originally been scheduled to share the camping adventure with Schindler and his wife, eventually moved elsewhere. For a time, Schindler's friend and partner Richard Neutra moved in with his family, but then moved about five years later or so after falling out with Schindler. The architect's own wife, Pauline, like-wise left for a time, although she returned to live in the Chace's studio on the other side of the house.

For all its innovation, this house was not particularly well suited to its role as a residence. Not many people—especially in the pre-hippie days—wanted to share a kitchen, sleep on the roof, or live in a house that made them feel like they were in a desert camp. As a work of Modernist architecture, however, the building is brilliant, and is on the "must see" list of every architecture student and many artists. Preserved by Vienna's MAK (Museum of Applied Arts), to honor the city's esteemed offspring, Schindler House is now a center for experimental architecture, exhibitions, and symposia. Other Schindler buildings can be seen in the Silver Lake area (see p. 148). ∎

Desert styling, outdoor spaces, and communal living are hallmarks of Schindler's famous dwelling.

Pacific Design Center

IT'S IMPOSSIBLE TO IGNORE THE ENORMOUS, GLASS-sheathed, geometrically shaped Pacific Design Center (PDC), prominently positioned at Melrose Avenue and San Vicente Boulevard, and just a short hop from stylish Santa Monica, La Cienega, and Beverly Boulevards. Designed by Cesar Pelli, the two-building complex (affectionately known as the Blue Whale and the Green Whale) is the West Coast's largest interior-design marketplace.

Angelenos and their interior designers love to browse this striking center to keep up with the latest decorating trends.

The PDC's Center Blue dates from the mid-1970s, while the Center Green was added in 1998, together comprising a total of 1.2 million square feet, with more than 200 interior-design showrooms. Although the PDC used to be open only to decorators and others in the trade, mere mortals with designs of their own are now welcome to browse (though not purchase).

A hodgepodge of huge rooms and intimate boutiques showcases exclusive collections of furnishings, fabrics, lighting, floor and wall coverings, decorative accessories, kitchen and bath accoutrements, and European and Asian antiques. For more inspiration, visit the PDC's gigantic **IdeaHouse,** with its changing displays of fully furnished pseudo-interiors. The **Feldman Gallery,** located on the PDC Plaza, is dedicated exclusively to high-quality architectural design and the decorative arts. Public exhibitions and daily tours are held at the PDC throughout the year.

AVENUES OF ART & DESIGN
Near the PDC are the surrounding Avenues of Art and Design—Melrose Avenue and Robertson and Beverly Boulevards—which offer stylish art galleries, antiques stores, and plenty of outlets for home furnishings and accessories. ■

Pacific Design Center
- Map pp. 100–101
- 8687 Melrose Ave.
- 310/657-0800
- Closed Sat.–Sun.

More places to visit in Hollywood & West Hollywood

AMERICAN FILM INSTITUTE

Occupying the former site of the Immaculate Heart College campus, the nonprofit American Film Institute (AFI) was founded in 1967, although it didn't move to its present location until 1980. AFI is another player created under the National Endowment for the Arts, and its mission is to preserve American film heritage, as well as advance cinema, television, and other forms of the moving image. Classes and seminars include various workshops and labs, and the **Louis B. Mayer Library** houses the country's most extensive collection of movie scripts. The public is allowed access to the noncirculating library and is also invited to attend regular film and video screenings. The AFI's Lifetime Achievement Award, presented annually, is an esteemed honor within the film business. Past recipients include Elizabeth Taylor (1993), Jack Nicholson (1994), Steven Spielberg (1995), and Dustin Hoffman (1999). The Los Angeles International Film Festival, one of the country's most prestigious, is held during the last two weeks of October. The 1999 festival screened some 100 films at the historic Hollywood Boulevard movie palaces.

🅜 Map pp. 100–101 ✉ 2021 N. Western Ave. ☎ 323/856-7600

JOHN ANSON FORD AMPHITHEATER

Across the Hollywood Freeway from the Hollywood Bowl is this outdoor amphitheater, which hosts free jazz, multiethnic performances, thematic series, and a Shakespeare Festival. This is not, however, merely another venue for the performing arts: The site was also deeply embroiled in a local church-versus-state battle. It was originally constructed in 1920 by paint heiress Christine Wetherell Stevenson as the Pilgrimage Theater for staging her pilgrimage play, and friends raised an enormous illuminated cross there after her death. In 1964 the land was donated to L.A. County, and it was then that the cross began bothering plenty of citizens, who didn't think government money should have a hand in a religious symbol. And so the cross came and went, fell and was relit. In 1994,

Hollywood Heritage and local ministries decided to make it their cause.

🅜 Map pp. 100–101 ✉ 2580 Cahuenga Blvd. ☎ 323/461-3673

THE MAX FACTOR BUILDING

Makeup czar Max Factor once created faces fit for the silver screen in this spectacular art deco building. Plans are to turn this site into a Hollywood history museum.

🅜 Map pp. 100–101 ✉ 1660 N. Highland Ave.

WATTLES HOUSE & PARK

During Tinseltown's glory days, Wattles House and the adjoining formal gardens were a top visitor attraction. Nowadays, however, you're more apt to have the place all to yourself. The peaceful grounds are situated several blocks off La Brea Avenue and form a welcome respite from the Hollywood scene, while the 1907 Mission Revival manor, with Craftsman styling, can be toured by appointment. The grounds connect to Runyon Canyon Park, formerly a private estate (the house is now in ruins) and currently a city park; note that it's a steep climb from Wattles Gardens.

🅜 Map pp. 100–101 ✉ 1824 N. Curson Ave. ☎ 323/874-4005 🕓 Open by appointment only.

YAMASHIRO RESTAURANT

Where else in America would a city's oldest structure be a Japanese pagoda? Yes, LaLaland's most ancient edifice is an original 600-year-old turret that adorns the re-creation of a Japanese palace (the original stands in the Yamashiro Mountains near Kyoto, Japan). Built in 1913 by craftsmen imported from Japan, this architectural oddity sits atop a hillside about 250 feet above Hollywood Boulevard. The teak-and-cedar mansion was originally the private home for two brothers who dealt in oriental antiques. Then it became private apartments, until ending up as a restaurant in 1968. The site has been used in a number of films, including *Sayonara* with Marlon Brando (it starred as the officers' club). The view is exquisite, the food so-so.

🅜 Map pp. 100–101 ✉ 1999 N. Sycamore Ave. ☎ 323/466-5125 ■

L.A. is modest about Griffith Park, the largest city park in the U.S.A. Los Feliz and Silver Lake districts are home to some fine architecture, while on Mount Washington are the Southwest Museum's displays of Native American culture.

Griffith Park & vicinity

Introduction & map 140–41
Griffith Park 142–44
Autry Museum of Western Heritage 145
Los Angeles Zoo 146
Los Feliz 147
Silver Lake 148
Southwest Museum 149
More places to visit in Griffith Park & vicinity 150

Bronzed James Dean, Rebel Without a Cause

Griffith Park & vicinity

ONLY A TOP-OF-THE-LINE ASPHALT JUNGLE SUCH AS L.A. COULD HORDE A gem like Griffith Park, a 4,100-acre parcel filled with rolling parklands, urban wilderness, remote trails, scenic views, and a dizzying assortment of diverse amusements. From the bottom of its fern glades to the peak of Mount Hollywood (1,625 feet), the park offers something for everyone, even if just a few stolen moments (with a gourmet picnic) away from the madding crowds.

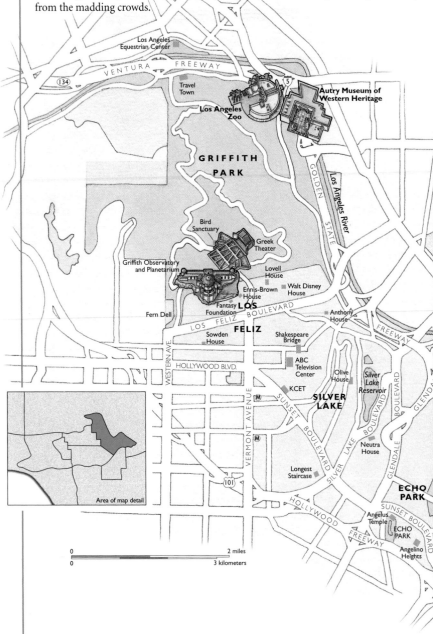

Los Angeles Equestrian Center

VENTURA FREEWAY

134

Travel Town

Autry Museum of Western Heritage

Los Angeles Zoo

GRIFFITH PARK

GOLDEN STATE

Los Angeles River

Bird Sanctuary

Greek Theater

Griffith Observatory and Planetarium

Lovell House

Walt Disney House

Ennis-Brown House

Fantasy Foundation

Fern Dell

LOS FELIZ BOULEVARD

LOS FELIZ

Anthony House

FREEWAY

Sowden House

Shakespeare Bridge

WESTERN AVE.

HOLLYWOOD BLVD.

ABC Television Center

Olive House

Silver Lake Reservoir

KCET

SILVER LAKE

GLENDALE

VERMONT AVENUE

M

M

SUNSET BOULEVARD

SILVER LAKE BOULEVARD

BOULEVARD

GLENDALE

Neutra House

GLENDALE BOULEVARD

101

Longest Staircase

ECHO PARK

Area of map detail

HOLLYWOOD

SUNSET BOULEVARD

Angelus Temple

ECHO PARK

FREEWAY

Angelino Heights

0   2 miles
0   3 kilometers

Sting on stage
at the Greek
Theater in 1993

Situated at the eastern end of the Santa Monica Mountains, Griffith Park was originally part of the Rancho Los Feliz Spanish Land Grant. When Welsh immigrant and mining millionaire Griffith J. Griffith donated the land to the city in 1896, there wasn't even access to the area. These days, with the Golden State Freeway to the east, the Ventura Freeway to the north, and Los Feliz Boulevard at the south, it is easily reached by an estimated 10 million annual visitors. Though many out-of-towners are included in this tally, most are Greater L.A. residents who use the park as their own giant backyard. Low-key baseball diamonds, horse stables, miniature steam

940ft
Mt. Washington

Southwest
Museum

110

Lummis
House

Heritage
Square
Museum

locomotives, and a vintage merry-go-round entwine around well-known attractions such as the Greek Theater, Observatory and Planetarium, L.A. Zoo, and Gene Autry Museum of Western Heritage. Donor Griffith would be ecstatic, for this is how he'd envisioned the land's usage: a gigantic resort for the masses.

The Los Feliz and Silver Lake communities, south of Griffith Park, were both early players in the city's film industry as well as designing grounds for top Modernist architects of the era such as Frank Lloyd Wright, Richard Neutra, and Rudolph Schindler. In a prime area just below Griffith Park is Los Feliz, which still maintains the glitzy 1920s mansions that belonged to such notables as W.C. Fields, Cecil B. DeMille and Walt Disney. Silver Lake, to the southeast, resembles a sloping Mediterranean-style hill town, with winding roads and tile-roofed homes, many looking down on the reservoir.

The North Central area, east of Silver Lake and wedging northward between Glendale and Pasadena, was once the stamping ground of the Yang-Na Native American tribe, who camped and hunted in Elysian Park. Later, a colorful and tightly knit Hispanic community took hold in practically hidden (and forgotten) Chavez Ravine. After Mack Sennett founded his Keystone Film Company here in the early days, the neighborhood became home turf for such slapstick comics as Laurel and Hardy and the Keystone Kops. Eventually residents were displaced by Dodger Stadium and the L.A. Police Academy. Southwest Museum, an almost-hidden treasure chest atop Mount Washington, shelters tribal art and artifacts lest anyone forget the original residents of this neighborhood. ■

Griffith Park

ENCOMPASSING AN AREA ROUGHLY FIVE TIMES THAT OF New York's Central Park, Griffith Park offers shelters and sights galore for out-of-towners and urban dwellers. Mountains meet the city in a 4,100-acre expanse that incorporates a multitude of recreation grounds and picnic opportunities, a premier amphitheater, a top-notch observatory and planetarium, the impressive Los Angeles Zoo, and the one-of-a-kind Gene Autry Museum of Western Heritage.

Most of the park's attractions are clumped in and around the bucolic flatlands, while the mountains in the central and western sections encompass hiking and horse trails within their undeveloped wilderness and untouched canyons. In all, the park contains 53 miles of hiking trails and 43 miles of horse trails, 24 tennis courts, four golf courses, numerous picnic areas, and uncountable numbers of plants, animals, and birds. And all this is within the city limits of a sprawling asphalt jungle. The park's main entry points are Fern Dell Drive, Vermont Avenue, and Crystal Springs/Griffith Park Drives, all of which run off Los Feliz

Boulevard. The visitor center provides road maps, trail maps, and information on all the attractions.

PARK SIGHTS

If you have kids in tow, they'll bellow for you to stop almost as soon as you enter the park from Crystal Springs Drive. On the east side of the road are miniature

Visitor Center & Park Ranger Headquarters

- Map pp. 140–41
- 4730 Crystal Springs Dr. (between Los Feliz Blvd. & Zoo Dr.)
- 323/913-4688
- Visitor center: open daily until 10 p.m. Bridle trails, hiking paths, & mountain roads close at sunset.

Main rotunda with Foucault pendulum

Planetarium

South gallery

12-inch Zeiss refracting telescope

East rotunda

East hall

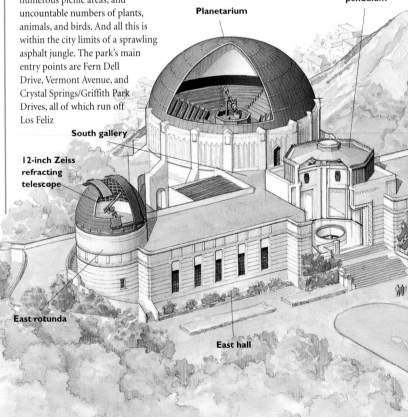

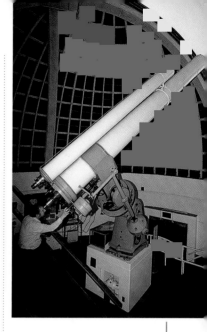

The public is invited to gaze at the evening skies through the powerful observatory telescope.

trains, covered wagons, and ponies reserved for youngsters only. Near the Visitor Center, off Griffith Park Drive, is the **merry-go-round,** another winner with kids and kids-at-heart. Constructed in 1926, the beautifully preserved carousel was one of the last built by Stillman Company craftsmen, and it features the original organ and wooden horses with authentic horsehair tails. At the top of Griffith Park Drive, south of the Ventura Freeway and in the northern portion of the park beyond the zoo, is **Travel Town,** which presents an open-air homage to the transportation industry. Displays include antique locomotives, railroad cars, and trolleys; vintage fire trucks are stored in the exhibition building. On Sunday mornings, the L.A. Live Steamers Club shows off its small but very detailed steam locomotives just east of Travel Town (kids get free rides on a miniature train).

Returning south down Griffith Park Drive, you can head out the way you came or opt for the Mount Hollywood fork, which twists and turns through peaceful, scenic hills and dales that are far removed from the chaotic city. The **Bird Sanctuary,** on Vermont Canyon Road, makes a terrific picnic or rest stop, where you are surrounded by canyons, ponds, and feathered friends. The observatory and planetarium are nearby (see p. 144), as is the **Greek Theater,** a seasonal (approximately June–October) outdoor venue for jazz, rock, classical, blues, and country and western concerts. In the southern corner of the park, and accessed from either Mount Hollywood Drive or Los Feliz Boulevard, is **Fern Dell,** a favorite oasis with locals. More than

Triple-beam solar telescope

West hall

Astronomer's monument

140 species of ferns share this shady glen with flowers, ponds, waterfalls, and humans tuning in with nature.

PARK SPORTS FACILITIES
Spread about the **Griffith Recreation Area** (*Los Feliz Blvd. at Riverside Dr.*) you'll find soccer fields, an Olympic-size pool (*closed winter*), and a well-equipped playground. Tennis is available at the Griffith-Vermont Canyon, Griffith-Riverside, and Griffith Park Drive courts which are lit up for night play. Golfers can pick and choose from two 18-hole and two 9-hole courses, accessible with a city golf registration card or on a space-available basis (18-hole Harding and Wilson courses are north of the Ranger Station). Rent saddle horses at the **L.A. Equestrian Center** (*480 Riverside Dr.*), a 75-acre complex across the L.A. River and Ventura Freeway at the northern edge of the park. The center will supply you with maps of the park's 43 miles of bridle trails, or you can sign up for a guided sunset ride. Friday evening moonlight rides are a popular event

Watching the sun set and the city light up is a magical experience.

at **Sunset Ranch** *(3400 N. Beachwood Dr.),* where excursions traverse wilderness areas and climb into the San Gabriel Mountains. The park's roads and pathways are havens for joggers, cyclists, and in-line skaters; wheels and blades can be rented in the parking lot near Los Feliz Boulevard and Riverside Drive.

Griffith Observatory and Planetarium
- Map pp. 140–41
- 2800 E. Observatory Rd.
- 323/664-1191 or 818/901-9405 (recorded information)
- Closed Mon. early Sept.–mid-June
- $$

GRIFFITH OBSERVATORY AND PLANETARIUM

One of L.A.'s most recognizable icons is this restored 1930s copper-domed Moderne building, regally positioned on the slopes of Mount Hollywood. A favorite L.A. pastime is to hang out on the observatory's terrace, gazing intently at the wide-open city panorama or the heavens twinkling above.

The observatory has been used as a set in numerous films, most notably the classic *Rebel Without a Cause* starring James Dean (a bronze bust of Dean is installed near the observatory entrance).

Griffith J. Griffith had, in fact, envisioned an observatory for "his" park much earlier and contributed

extra cash toward its construction. The city, however, wasn't terribly eager to accept anything else from the man quite yet, as the scandal surrounding the year he spent in San Quentin for the attempted murder of his wife hadn't quite simmered down. After Griffith's death in 1919, the money was gratefully accepted and the observatory duly built.

The 600-seat **planetarium,** beneath the 75-foot central dome, presents various planet and star shows throughout the year, as well as **laserium** light and sound shows (although these seem to be attended primarily by trippy teenagers). Two smaller domes, at either end of the building, house a triple-beam solar telescope and a 12-inch Zeiss refracting telescope (one of the world's largest public telescopes), and viewing is available most nights. The **Hall of Science,** in the corridors connecting the domes, presents related exhibits, including a cloud chamber, a Foucault pendulum, and a seismograph that monitors the region's shakes, rattles, and rolls. ∎

Autry Museum of Western Heritage

EVEN IF YOU HAVE NEVER WATCHED A WESTERN OR FELT nary a pang at the phrase "Go West, young man," the Autry Museum (across from the L.A. Zoo) might well fill you with the magic and romance of America's Wild West.

Although it is aptly named for America's favorite singing cowboy (and major museum benefactor), Gene Autry, don't be misled into thinking this is a showcase only for the actor. Rather, this museum focuses on the unique frontier culture that sprang up west of the Mississippi and defined America's "real" West. Add to that the special effects contributed by Disney Imagineers, and you have a history museum and Western gallery spiced up with high-tech features and Disneyland showmanship.

THE EXHIBITIONS

Seven diversely themed galleries detail and celebrate the history of the West through a plethora of art, artifacts, and films. The evolution of modern-day California is traced through a cast of characters, including native peoples, European explorers, early pioneers, shoot-'em-up gunslingers, Chinese laborers, and Catholic missionaries, ending—of course—in Hollywood.

The **Spirit of Romance** depicts both the genuine hardships of the West along with the delight at its natural beauty. Among the highlights are film footage of early Wild West shows (including a 1902 clip of Buffalo Bill Cody) and Annie Oakley's gold-plated pistols. Nearly 200 Colt revolvers are on display in the **Spirit of the Cowboy Gallery,** while the **Anheuser-Busch Gallery** sports an 1880 wooden saloon bar. If guns and gambling make you squirm, the

Spirit of Community will perk you up with its advertising signs, early machinery, 1873 fire engine, and Mormon history display. Kids can't resist The **Spirit of Imagination,** where they can watch themselves through video monitors on horseback and in cowboy scenarios. Little ones also gravi-

tate toward the **L.A. Times Children's Discovery Gallery,** where they can dress up in cowboy gear. Art lovers will appreciate a collection that includes works by Frederic Remington, Thomas Moran, Seth Eastman, and N.C. Wyeth. Classic Westerns and documentaries are screened regularly, and the **George Montgomery** and **Showcase** galleries present changing exhibitions. ∎

Western spirit and romance have been captured within the extensive galleries and displays.

Autry Museum of Western Heritage

⬛ Map pp. 140–41
✉ 4700 Western Heritage Way
☎ 323/667-2000
🕐 Closed Mon.
💲 $$ (free 2nd Tues. of month)

Los Angeles Zoo

Los Angeles Zoo
- Map pp. 140—41
- 5333 Zoo Dr.
- 323/644-6400
- $$

L.A.'s 75-ACRE ZOO, OPENED IN 1966 NEAR THE JUNCTION of the Golden State and Ventura freeways, is home to more than 1,300 mammals, birds, and reptiles representing 350 species, many of them on the rare and endangered list. An exquisite botanical garden is a bonus for flora- and fauna-loving visitors.

For orangutans and other primates watching visitors is a mutual pastime.

The zoo's inhabitants are separated into specialty areas, with many of the enclosures replicating natural habitats (North America and World Deserts, South America, Australia, etc.) and thereby doing away with insidious cages. It's fun to walk around the grounds, but those who prefer to ride can hop on a safari-type shuttle that runs between the various areas. Thanks to voter authorization and management restructuring, the zoo has been undergoing a much-needed clean-up and renovation; most notable is the new chimpanzee exhibit.

ZOO HIGHLIGHTS

Monkeys and flamingos positioned near the zoo entrance set the mood for visitors. Follow the chirps and trills to a tree-filled walk-through aviary. Alternatively, head straight for **Tiger Falls,** where you can admire the stripes, whiskers, and very big jaws of big cats from a safe distance. The **Koala House,** filled with cuddly looking marsupials, is always a big hit. Koalas tree-hug replica eucalyptuses in a simulated dusk-dawn environment that encourages activity amongst the natives. Sharing the limelight are echidnas (spiny anteaters), squirrel gliders, brush-tailed rat kangaroos, and high-flying possums.

The newest habitat is the **Chimpanzees of Mahale Mountains** exhibit, the first stage of the zoo's Great Ape Forest. The one-acre habitat includes a 9,100-square-foot forest, heated bedrooms, an indoor playroom, and an interactive play area for (human) children. Kids also have a ball at **Adventure Island,** a children's section with eye-level displays, an animal nursery, and a petting zoo. For reptilian delights check out the **Reptile Exhibit,** which features reptiles that were probably headed for the black market until the U.S. government confiscated them. ∎

Los Feliz

ALTHOUGH MORE SEDATE AND WEALTHIER THAN NEIGH-boring Silver Lake, Los Feliz is also moving steadily into the hip and arty mode. The former mansions of film stars still stand, and the neighborhood is a mix of ethnic groups, trend-setting denizens of the Cocktail Nation, and the gay contingency. Frank Lloyd Wright's Ennis-Brown House and Richard Neutra's Lovell House are just two of the standout architectural masterpieces above Los Feliz Boulevard.

Pre-Columbian art and architecture inspired the 1920s Ennis-Brown House.

Ennis-Brown House *(2655 Glendower Ave.)*, built by Frank Lloyd Wright in 1924, is an impressive concrete-block, pre-Columbianesque structure. Tours are offered by reservation. The contemporary styling of Richard Neutra's **Lovell House** *(4616 Dundee Dr.)* belies its 1929 construction. Neutra's international design launched the architect's career as one of L.A.'s most prominent Modernist architects.

Walt Disney House *(4053 Woking Way)* unsurprisingly poses like a cartoon-type cottage. The **Fantasy Foundation** *(2495 Glendower Ave.)* is the strange brainchild of Forrest J. Ackerman,

former editor of *Famous Monsters of Filmland,* containing 18 rooms packed with hundreds of thousands of sci-fi, horror, and fantasy-world memorabilia.

Below the hills is **Sowden House** *(5121 Franklin Ave.)*. The 1926 residence has an eclectic mix of styles and centers on a courtyard. **Shakespeare Bridge** *(Franklin Ave., between Myra Ave. & St. George St.)*, built in 1925, is distinctive with its Gothic turrets and arches. Also in this section of town are a couple of film industry pioneers, among them **KCET** *(4401 Sunset Blvd.)*, Hollywood's oldest film studio in continuous use. ∎

Ennis-Brown House

Map pp. 140–41

2655 Glendower Ave.

323/660-0607

Regular tours bimonthly every 2nd Sat., otherwise by reservation

**Architect
Richard Neutra's
reconstructed
"experimental"
house graces
Silver Lake
Boulevard.**

Silver Lake

THE 1907 SILVER LAKE RESERVOIR, NAMED FOR HERMAN Silver, the city water and power commissioner who okayed its construction, remains the focal point for the hill-town homes on the winding roads above. Thanks to the popularity of private housing in the 1950s, Silver Lake's "funky" neighborhood features L.A.'s highest number of signature homes by master architects.

Silver Lake

🅰 Map pp. 140–41

NEUTRA HOUSE & OTHER ARCHITECTURE

In 1933, after architect Richard Neutra left Rudolph Schindler's West Hollywood communal dwelling (see p. 136), he constructed his own family home in Silver Lake. The highly experimental **Neutra House** (*2300 E. Silver Lake Blvd.*) utilized light reflected from the water to bathe the upper-level living area, sleeping porches, and a roof deck, while a workshop and guest area were relegated to the lower level. After fire destroyed the home in 1963, it was reconstructed using new materials that would play off light, air, and water, including glass, stucco, mirrored walls, steel stairs, and shallow reflecting pools. The enclave adjacent to the

Silver Lake Boulevard home was also developed by Neutra. Other examples of the architect's work from 1948 to 1962 include Treweek House (*No. 2250*), Ivandomi House (*No. 2238*), and Yew House (*No. 2226*). Also nearby are Flavin House (*2218 Argent Pl.*), Akai House (*2200 Neutra Pl.*), and McIntosh House (*1317 Maltman Ave.*).

Olive House (*2236 Micheltorena St., between Rock & Angus Sts.*), was one of Rudolph Schindler's particularly intriguing works. In 1927, Bernard Maybeck (architect for San Francisco's Palace of Fine Arts) designed the eclectic **Anthony House** (*3412 Waverly Dr.*), which cost a whopping (for the time) $500,000 to build. ∎

Southwest Museum

THIS NEAR-HIDDEN TROVE OF NATIVE AMERICAN HISTORY and culture atop Mount Washington has the distinction of being L.A.'s oldest museum, a front-runner in the preservation and presentation of Native American peoples. A new satellite facility at LACMA West on Wilshire Boulevard's Museum Row (see pp. 82 and 89) makes the collections more accessible to a broader range of visi-

Native American art and crafts encompass the work of tribes from Alaska to South America.

Southwest Museum

- Map pp. 140–41
- 234 Museum Dr.
- 323/221-2164
- Closed Mon.
- $$

THE BUILDING

The museum complex consists of the original 1914 building, with its seven-story tower-with-a-view, the 1939 Poole wing, and the 1977 Braun Research Library. An interactive, simulated archaeology dig sits at the site's northwest corner, while the east side is planted with an Ethnobotanical Garden that features plants used by Native Americans. An access to the building is via a 250-foot-long tunnel burrowed into the hillside, followed by a 108-foot elevator ride up to the lower lobby entrance.

Of course, you can opt for the conventional entrance found just off the parking lot, but then you'd miss the historical dioramas along the tunnel walls.

THE COLLECTIONS

Art, crafts, and artifacts representing Native American cultures and history from Alaska to South America are displayed within exhibition halls totaling 16,000 square feet. Highlights include 11,000 pieces of basketry (one of the largest collections in the U.S.), more than 7,000 Southwestern pottery vessels, and thousands of colonial paintings, religious icons, textiles, and other folk and decorative arts from the Southwestern U.S. to South America.

The museum's **Braun Research Library,** with 10,260 square feet of archival books, manuscripts, photos, and rare correspondence and notes, is an important center for scholars. ■

More places to visit in Griffith Park & vicinity

ANGELINO HEIGHTS
L.A.'s first suburb flourished during the 1880s land boom, when lovely Victorian homes were created for commuters who rode the Pacific Electric trolley to their downtown offices. The views were superb, the city noise was a safe distance away, and all was well—that is until the boom went bust and the area downslid. A notable exception is the 1300 block of Carroll Avenue, where residents have painstakingly restored their homes to original splendor, with many now designated cultural historical landmarks by the City of L.A. The area is a popular location site for film and television crews, who are drawn to the juxtaposition of Victorian homes, Craftsman bungalows, and rooms-with-a-view.
⚑ Map pp. 140–41

ANGELUS TEMPLE
Modeled after Salt Lake City's Mormon Tabernacle, this large-domed circular structure (built in 1923) was the preaching ground for famed evangelist Aimee Semple McPherson.
⚑ Map pp. 140–41 ✉ 1100 Glendale Blvd.
☎ 213/484-1100

DODGER STADIUM
The 56,000-seat Dodger Stadium, designed by Emil Prager at the base of Chavez Ravine, is surrounded by a suitably gargantuan parking lot. It has been home to the L.A. Dodgers baseball team since its completion in 1962, even though the team had fled Brooklyn some years earlier. Cantilevered construction (there are no pillars), as well as a giant color screen in the outfield, ensures decent views for all. Its famous Dodger Dogs are ever popular.
⚑ Map pp. 140–41 ✉ 1000 Elysian Park Ave.
☎ 213/224-1400 🕐 Ticket office closed Sun.

EAGLE ROCK
One of L.A.'s true, natural landmarks, this 150-foot-high sandstone "eagle in flight" can be viewed without ever leaving the less-than-natural eastbound Ventura Freeway traveling from Glendale to Pasadena.
⚑ Map pp. 140–41 ✉ N. Figueroa St. & Scholl Canyon Rd.

ELYSIAN PARK
Designated for public use when L.A. was founded in 1781, the 600-acre Elysian is the city's second-largest park. The area has remained largely natural, occupying slopes and valleys that are covered in chaparral and crisscrossed with hiking trails. Off Stadium Way (between Scott Avenue and Academy Road) is **Chavez Ravine Arboretum,** which shelters acres of rare trees, many of them planted at the end of the 19th century. Picnic areas, a recreation center, and a small artificial lake are also part of the package. The public is invited to use the café at the Los Angeles Police Academy (as well as its shooting range). Note that it is not advisable to wander into isolated areas of the park or hang out there after dark.
⚑ Map pp. 140–41

HERITAGE SQUARE MUSEUM
Thanks to the Cultural Heritage Foundation of Southern California, eight historic buildings constructed between 1865 and 1914 were saved from the wrecking ball, authentically restored, and relocated in this outdoor museum. Rescued structures include the Hale House, Lincoln Avenue Methodist Church, and Palms Railroad Depot.
⚑ Map pp. 140–41 ✉ 3800 Homer St.
☎ 626/449-0193 🕐 Closed Mon.–Tues. 💲 $

LONGEST STAIRCASE
Laurel and Hardy fans won't want to miss a walk up (or down) the Longest Staircase, the steps where the comedy duo attempted to cart a grand piano in the 1932 film *The Music Box.*
⚑ Map pp. 140–41 ✉ 927 N. Vendome St.

LUMMIS HOUSE
Charles Fletcher Lummis, founder of the Southwest Museum (see p. 149), designed and built his unique private home between 1898 and 1910. Constructed around a sycamore tree, the L-shaped dwelling incorporates hand-hewn timbers, stones from an arroyo, telephone poles, an art nouveau fireplace, and a 2-acre garden.
⚑ Map pp. 140–41 ✉ 200 E. Ave. 43
☎ 323/222-0546 🕐 Open Fri.–Sun. p.m. ∎

Unlike Hollywood, which is steeped in myth and short on reality, Beverly Hills lives up to its image as a snooty city that caters to the elite, chic, celebrated, and super-wealthy.

Beverly Hills & vicinity

Introduction & map 152–53
The Golden Triangle 154–55
Shop till you drop along Rodeo
    Drive 156–57
Beverly Hills Hotel 160–61
Virginia Robinson Gardens 162
Greystone Mansion & Park 162
Museum of Television & Radio
    163
Century City 164–65
Museum of Tolerance 166–67
More places to visit in Beverly
    Hills & vicinity 168
Hotels & restaurants 251–53

Welcome to the Pink Palace

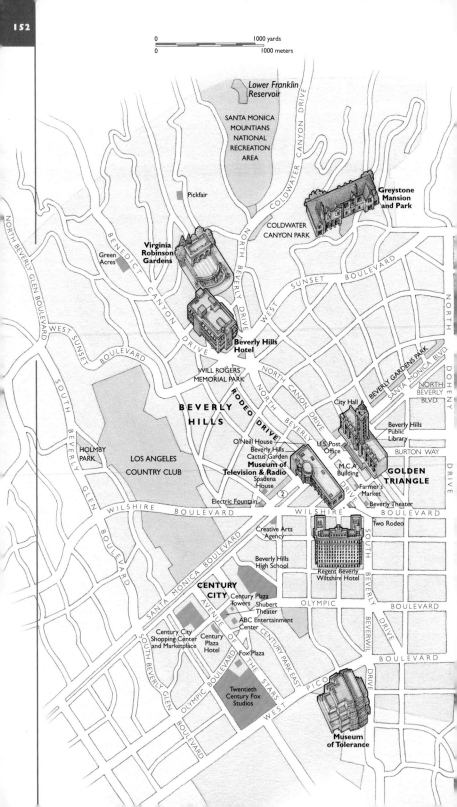

0   1000 yards

0   1000 meters

Lower Franklin Reservoir

SANTA MONICA MOUNTIANS NATIONAL RECREATION AREA

COLDWATER CANYON DRIVE

Pickfair

Greystone Mansion and Park

COLDWATER CANYON PARK

Green Acres

Virginia Robinson Gardens

BENEDICT CANYON DRIVE

NORTH BEVERLY DRIVE

WEST SUNSET

SUNSET BOULEVARD

Beverly Hills Hotel

WEST SUNSET BOULEVARD

NORTH BEVERLY GLEN BOULEVARD

SOUTH BEVERLY GLEN

WILL ROGERS MEMORIAL PARK

NORTH CANON DRIVE

City Hall

BEVERLY GARDENS PARK

SANTA MONICA BLVD.

NORTH BEVERLY BLVD.

DOHENY DRIVE

BEVERLY HILLS

RODEO DRIVE

NORTH BEVERLY DRIVE

O'Neill House

Beverly Hills Public Library

HOLMBY PARK

LOS ANGELES COUNTRY CLUB

Beverly Hills Cactus Garden
Museum of Television & Radio
Spadena House

U.S. Post Office

M.C.A Building

BURTON WAY

GOLDEN TRIANGLE

Farmer's Market

Electric Fountain

(2)

Beverly Theater

WILSHIRE BOULEVARD

WILSHIRE BOULEVARD

Two Rodeo

Creative Arts Agency

SOUTH BEVERLY DRIVE

Beverly Hills High School

SANTA MONICA BOULEVARD

Regent Beverly Wilshire Hotel

BEVERWIL DRIVE

CENTURY CITY

Century Plaza Towers

Shubert Theater

ABC Entertainment Center

OLYMPIC BOULEVARD

Century City Shopping Center and Marketplace

Century Plaza Hotel

AVENUE OF THE STARS

Fox Plaza

OLYMPIC BOULEVARD

CENTURY PARK EAST

WEST PICO

SOUTH BEVERLY GLEN

Twentieth Century Fox Studios

PICO DRIVE

BOULEVARD

Museum of Tolerance

Beverly Hills & vicinity

THE BOUNDARIES THAT SEPARATE THE CITY OF BEVERLY HILLS FROM THE rest of L.A. may barely be noticeable, but cross those lines laid in the asphalt and it will soon be obvious that you have entered another sphere, an honest-to-goodness fantasy world where the 32,000 or so residents' daily "grinds" play like scripts from *Lives of the Rich and Famous*. Even the air smells different.

The city's total area comprises just under 6 square miles, but within that enclave are superelegant shops, some of the finest restaurants in Southern California, splendid architectural sights and gardens, and a preponderance of opulent mansions. Sophisticated hotels add to the high-flying mix, including two historic beauties at either edge of town: the Beverly Hills Hotel and Regent Beverly Wilshire. Looking for celebrities? You won't have to search hard, just keep your eyes peeled in the Rodeo Drive shops, hotel lounges, and pricey restaurants. You can also pick up one of those maps to the stars' homes, hawked on street corners, though they often have inaccurate information.

Perhaps even more alluring than Hollywood, Beverly Hills had a similar start in life as an agricultural district. To put it simply, the place was a bunch of bean fields—lima beans, at that—known as Morocco Junction, and it was home to tumble-down shacks occupied by down-and-out farmworkers. It was originally part of the El Rancho Rodeo de las Aguas (Ranch of the Gathering of the Water) land grant, named for the streams cascading down from Benedict and Coldwater

Beverly Hills offers the ultimate "golden" shopping experience with its high-end jewelers and design shops.

canyons, purchased by Doña Maria Rita Valdez in 1810.

The oil boom around the turn of the 20th century changed things considerably. Little oil was found in B.H., but in 1906 three businessmen (Burton Green, Charles Canfield, and Max Whittier) formed the Rodeo Land and Water Company and developed the area into a combination of curving residential streets with a triangle-shaped business district, naming it Beverly Hills. Although settlement began slowly, the inclusion of canyons to the north raised the population figures to 500, the numbers required for incorporation.

In 1920 Douglas Fairbanks, Sr., and Mary Pickford moved into town, setting up house in Pickfair and bringing along all the accoutrements of wealth and status—as well as their celebrity pals. And so Beverly Hills came of age, famed home to stars, as well as to *The Beverly Hillbillies* and the "just regular kids" from *Beverly Hills 90210*. ■

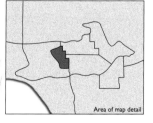

Area of map detail

The Golden Triangle

MANY OF BEVERLY HILLS' MOST SOUGHT-OUT ATTRACTIONS sit within a 20-block section tagged the Golden Triangle by the city's visitors bureau. This three-sided district—bounded by Wilshire Boulevard to the south, and by Santa Monica Boulevard and Rexford Drive to the west and east—harbors a conglomeration of exquisite historical architecture, numerous revered cosmetic surgeons and celebrity hairstylists, the ritziest retailers in the world, high-priced restaurants with attitude-espousing waitpersons, and office buildings occupied by such B.H. mainstays as agents and shrinks.

Each year some 12 million visitors square off in the Triangle, mesmerized by the trappings of wealth and power. The well-heeled leave with designer shopping bags and signature hairstyles, while those on a budget window-shop and wait for famous faces to pop by—which they most assuredly will. Whichever way you slice it, the Golden Triangle shapes up like a wedge of the richest-tasting pie on Earth.

GOLDEN TRIANGLE ARCHITECTURE

One of Beverly Hills' standout buildings is its **City Hall** (455 N. Rexford Dr.), a 1932 Spanish Renaissance design, with an ornate and colorful baroque dome. Architect Charles Moore's postmodern **Civic Center** (N. Rexford Dr., between Santa Monica & Little Santa Monica Blvds.) includes three landscaped courtyards that link City Hall with the public library, the fire and police departments, and a parking garage. The newer 92,000-square-foot **Beverly Hills Public Library** (444 N. Rexford Dr.), a mansion-like fortress fitted with mahogany, marble, and brass, has approximately 300,000 volumes, a children's reading section, computer stations, and a community auditorium. Nearby is the 1933 terracotta-and-brick **U.S. Post Office**

(9300 Santa Monica Blvd.), designed by Ralph Flewelling in Italian Renaissance style. Beaming like a beacon from the 1950s is the **Unocal Gas Station** (427 N. Crescent Dr.), with a cantilevered concrete canopy—proof that even B.H. is sentimental (or strange) at heart. A block away, the former **Music Corporation of America Building** (375 N. Crescent Dr.), designed in 1937 by architect Paul Williams, is a Georgian-style complex with a Florentine fountain and gardens that you can stroll around. The onion-domed, Moorish-style former **Beverly Theatre** (206 N. Beverly Dr.), built in 1925 by architect L.A. Smith, was a film-premiere venue during the 1920s to '40s, a branch of the hip Fiorucci retail house in the 1970s, and currently houses the Israel Discount Bank.

RODEO DRIVE

Famed Rodeo Drive cuts a neat slice through the Triangle's business district. And although the street extends both north and south of the area, fingering its way into the city's residential section, it's the portion between Wilshire and Santa Monica Boulevards that is revered by serious shoppers. There are surprises among the high-end shops, including a historic building, a

Elegant Rodeo Drive boutiques and salons epitomize the expression, "if you have to ask, you can't afford it."

Beverly Hills Visitors Bureau
✉ 239 S. Beverly Dr.
☎ 310/248-1015 or 800/345-2210
🕐 Closed Sat.–Sun.

Beverly Hills Public Library
✉ 444 N. Rexford Dr.
☎ 310/288-2221

Frank Lloyd Wright design, and Beverly Hills' first street, the cobblestone Via Rodeo walkway, dating from 1914 (see "Shop till you drop along Rodeo Drive" pp. 156–57).

BEYOND THE TRIANGLE

The **Electric Fountain** *(Wilshire & Santa Monica intersection)*, created in 1930 by the Beverly Hills Women's Club, continues to be a favorite attention-grabber for locals stuck at the traffic lights. The circular frieze tells the tale of early California history, while an Indian rain prayer is symbolized by the statue crowning the fountain's central column. Famed architect I.M. Pei designed the **Creative Artists Agency** *(9830 Wilshire Blvd.),* home to entertainment industry powermongers. The sleek

1989 building features an exquisite marble-and-glass facade.

Spadena House *(516 N. Walden Dr.),* in the residential district across Santa Monica Boulevard, is also referred to as the Witch's House, possibly because of its fairytale-style gnarled windows, steeply pitched roof, jagged fence, and "broomstick" entrance. The building originally stood in Culver City, where it was the headquarters for a movie studio. It was moved to its current location in 1931 and is now a private residence. About four blocks away is **O'Neill House** *(507 N. Rodeo Dr.),* another private abode, which is built in the style of Antonio Gaudí-meets-California. The undulating main home was constructed in 1986 by architect Don Ramos. ■

Trolley Tours

The Beverly Hills Trolley operates two tours. Both depart from the corner of Rodeo Drive and Dayton Way, Tues.– Fri. noon–5 p.m.; Sat. noon–4 p.m., May– June and Sept.–Nov. No reservations (first come, first served). For details, phone the Beverly Hills Visitors Bureau (see opposite).

Shop till you drop along Rodeo Drive

Every visitor to Beverly Hills—be they tycoon, royalty, Joe Blow from Middle America, or your average high-profile movie star—ends up on Rodeo Drive at some point. High-end designer shops and celebrity-watching are the draws of this walk. Along the way it's easy to tell the locals from the visitors, for the former emerge from luxury vehicles.

When undertaking serious shopping, it is important to have someone to carry the bags.

Above: Body beautiful—reflected images of fitness buffs working out at the downtown YMCA. Right: Appearance is everything, wrinkles are out.

count grams of fat, protein, or carbohydrate ratios, depending on which of the ubiquitous diets they're following. Complementing the diet is an exercise regime: jogging, in-line skating, pumping iron, and a health club membership. The wealthier residents swim in their backyard lap pools, work out with personal trainers, and tan in private booths. As for wrinkles and cellulite, if the day spa can't iron them out, then one of the many god-like cosmetic surgeons will. Only when you are thin, toned, tan, and trendy is it permissible to go out in public, and—more importantly—be allowed into one of the classier clubs and eateries. No matter what you've heard about the L.A.P.D., in this town the real power rests with the fashion police. ∎

Beverly Hills Hotel

Beverly Hills Hotel

⬛ Map pp. 152–53
✉ 9641 Sunset Blvd.
☎ 310/276-2251

IN 1912, IN A PUSH TO ATTRACT WEALTHY RESIDENTS AND visitors to the barely burgeoning Beverly Hills, developer Burton Green constructed the Beverly Hills Hotel. Situated at the base of the northern hills and canyons, the sprawling Mission Revival property soon became a symbol of both the city and the hedonistic lifestyle it aspired to, and attracted such fashionable clientele as Clark Gable, Charlie Chaplin, Marilyn Monroe, and Elizabeth Taylor.

Opposite: From the time the Rolls Royce pulls up, red carpet treatment is expected by the wealthy and famous guests. Below: Faye Dunaway studying her Oscar statuette while lounging by the pool

Dubbed the "Pink Palace," the Beverly Hills Hotel has enticed many of the world's wealthiest, best-known, and most powerful beings to its closely monitored doors. Twelve perfectly landscaped acres, with sheltering palms and lush gardens, keep Sunset Boulevard traffic noise where it belongs and offer peaceful respite to publicity-shy big shots. Most of the well-knowns favor one of the 21 luxurious bungalows, which afford more privacy from prying eyes and ears. Still, plenty of stories have leaked about the action on the other side of the pink walls.

Examples of reported bungalow goings-on include Marilyn Monroe trysting with her admirers, Liz Taylor doing the same with six of her husbands, and billionaire Howard Hughes asking hotel staff to hide his sandwiches in the trees (Hughes had a breakdown in Bungalow Four).

The hotel's **Polo Lounge,** a harbinger of dealmaking and power lunches, was added in the 1940s and has been a hot spot ever since. Though mere mortals are occasionally snubbed, it's worth enduring the humiliation to watch the action, gawk at the celebs, and dine on some very fine food. As an alternative, try the **Fountain Coffee Shop** (built in 1949), which has a curved soda fountain where you can sip malts, floats, and shakes along with many a slurping star.

The hotel was purchased in 1987 by the world's richest person, the Sultan of Brunei, who shelled out about $100,000,000 in pocket change to have it extensively renovated in 1995. Part of the extravaganza included a paint job and, though hotel officials swear the hotel was coated with its original distinctive pink, some say it now looks a tinge on the orange side. The hotel grounds and banquet facilities are heavily booked for pull-out-all-the-stops weddings and other celebrations—with bills that tally up to the combined annual incomes of entire small nations (though not Brunei!). ■

The main residence, palmed within a handful of fragrant Eden-esque gardens

Virginia Robinson Gardens

Virginia Robinson Gardens

- Map pp. 152–53
- 1008 Elden Way
- 310/276-5367
- Closed Sat.–Mon. Tours by appointment only
- $$

Sited on a 6.2-acre hillside, just north of the Beverly Hills Hotel, the former home of department-store heir Harry Robinson and his wife Virginia is ranked as the oldest estate in Beverly Hills. Virginia bequeathed the Mediterranean-style villa and its divine grounds (listed on the National Register of Historic Places) to Los Angeles County. Virginia's green thumb, with the assistance of 12 gardeners, created five distinctive garden areas, consisting of Italian Terrace, Formal Mall, Rose, and Kitchen gardens, as well as the main residence and Renaissance Revival **Pool Pavilion** (modeled after Italy's Villa Pisani). Fountains, ponds, brick pathways, and groves of camellias, gardenias, and king palms (supposedly the largest collection outside of the species' native Australia) are amongst the meanderings, along with specimen trees and rare plantings. ∎

Greystone Mansion & Park

Greystone Mansion & Park

- Map pp. 152–53
- 905 Loma Vista Dr.
- 310/550-4796

Oil tycoon Edward Doheny, Sr., originally purchased a 415-acre tract north of Sunset Boulevard for his private domain, making it the largest family estate in the city's history. The 46,000-square-foot, 55-room, English Tudor-style mansion, cost $3,000,000 to complete. In the mid-1950s, the brunt of the property was sold, leaving Greystone with about 18 acres of grounds. Visitors are allowed to peek through the windows, but otherwise the public is relegated to the lovely grounds, which also act as a center for local cultural events and activities. A self-guided walking tour will lead you through the Formal Gardens, Mansion Gardens, and Lower Grounds Estate. ∎

Museum of Television & Radio

OPENED IN 1996, THIS IS ONE OF GREATER L.A.'S NEWER museums. The New York branch, however, has been going strong since 1975, when it was founded by William S. Paley (also the father of CBS). Paley's aim was to collect, preserve, and interpret television and radio programming, and to keep as much of it as possible available to the media-loving public.

Museum of Television & Radio

🅼 Map pp. 152–53
🕐 465 N. Beverly Dr.
☎ 310/786-1000
🕐 Closed Mon.–Tues. Open until 9 p.m. Thurs.
$ $$

Originally established in Manhattan, the L.A. facility is extraordinary in that it has duplicated the entire New York collection, so that East and West coast visitors enjoy the exact same access.

THE BUILDING

The architects Meier & Partners created a vibrant showcase for Paley's dream. The 23,000-square-foot, two-level building features a natural-stone-and-glass exterior, skylit rotunda lobby, open gallery and promenade, a reflecting pool, and unique transparent facades on street-facing walls that permit two-way viewing. The museum also houses a 150-seat theater, an education room, and a retail shop.

COLLECTIONS & FACILITIES

You can choose from a collection of more than 100,000 programs—from documentaries and sitcoms to newscasts and commercials—covering more than 75 years of radio and television history, and you can enjoy them at private consoles or in listening booths. Special exhibits are also presented; recent calendars have included Barbara Streisand's television performances, *Monty Python's Flying Circus*, and a Hitchcock retrospective. ■

Visitors select their desired radio programs, then lean back and enjoy them in the listening room.

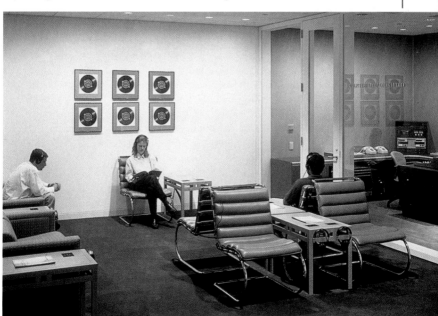

Century City

POSITIONED BETWEEN BEVERLY HILLS AND WESTWOOD, and stretching between Little Santa Monica and West Pico Boulevards, is Century City. This 176-acre development of sleek high-rise hotels and office buildings, condominiums, a shopping center, and an entertainment complex used to be the backlot of nearby Twentieth Century Fox. It was sold in the late 1950s and developed into what it is today: A looming glass-and-steel Modernist world of its own, where the plentiful parking is in hidden structures, and where streetlife is almost nonexistent.

Century City

Map pp. 152–53

Closer to the ground at the Little Santa Monica Boulevard end is the **Century City Shopping Center and Marketplace.** This low-lying, open-air complex seems more like a marketplace than a mall, with its bustling cafés, restaurants, 150-plus shops, department stores, and a multiplex cinema. Abercrombie

and Fitch, Godiva Chocolatier, and Steven Spielberg's Dive! restaurant are just a few of the tenants.

The twin triangular **Century Plaza Towers** *(Avenue of the Stars & Constellation Blvd.)* were designed in 1975 by Minoru Yamasaki, one of whose previous projects was the New York World

Trade Center. The **ABC Entertainment Center** (*2020 and 2040 Avenue of the Stars*) contains movie theaters, restaurants, offices, and the well-respected **Shubert Theater,** where extravagant musicals are often presented. An underpass links this section with the very exclusive 1,000-room **Century Plaza Hotel** (*2025 Avenue of the Stars*) across the way.

If the 34-story **Fox Plaza** (*2121 Avenue of the Stars*) looks familiar, it's probably because you have seen it featured in the action movie *Die Hard.* Although former President Ronald Reagan once had offices here, most of the viewing public will remember it as the place where Bruce Willis, playing a New York cop who just wanted to spend Christmas with his kids, went

through hell and back to save hostages, kill the bad guys, and win back his woman. No tours are offered at what's left of **Twentieth Century Fox** (*10201 W. Pico Blvd.*), and the sets are barely visible behind high walls. ■

Market day

Beverly Hills holds a farmers market at 300 Canon Drive each Sunday, 9 a.m.–1 p.m. But even in this town, a public market has a different twist. Unlike downtown's Grand Central Market (see p. 66), where you'll find dead ducks hanging by their feet and the brains of unrecognizable animals under glass, B.H.'s version offers only the most perfect-looking fruits, vegetables, and flowers, along with other edible delights. An added B.H. attraction is the Chef of the Month series, featuring cooking demos by Wolfgang Puck and other well-known celebrity chefs. ■

Museum of Tolerance

THE MUSEUM OF TOLERANCE, SITUATED JUST OUTSIDE THE
Beverly Hills perimeter within the Simon Wiesenthal Center, may be
one of the world's most important historical centers. Strong visual
and interactive exhibits challenge and enlighten viewers not only to
the Holocaust, but also about attitudes toward racism, and bigotry.

**Getting much
too close for
comfort to the
Holocaust and
Nazi atrocities**

**Museum of
Tolerance**

🅰 Map pp.152–53

🕐 9786 W. Pico Blvd.

☎ 310/553-8403

🕐 Closed Sat. & Jewish
hols.; early closing
Fri.

💲 $$

The museum emerged out of collec-
tive brainstorming from leaders of
the Simon Wiesenthal Center, an
organization dedicated to Jewish
human rights. The thought process
moved beyond the plights of Jewish
people and Holocaust atrocities to
include those of all races, colors,
creeds, and ages. In the museum,
all prejudices and belief systems
are brought to light, and not just
through the usual range of photos
and artifacts, but with the use of
state-of-the-art technology and
extraordinary consciousness-raising,
interactive exhibits. Since it was
established in 1993, the $55,000,000
museum has opened its doors to
more than 325,000 people per year,
including corporate, medical, and
law-enforcement groups in need of
some sensitivity training.

Within the 165,000-square-foot,
four-level complex is a 28,000-
square-foot permanent exhibition
level (where the important
Tolerancenter and Holocaust
Center are located), an 8,400-
square-foot Multimedia Learning
Center, an archival exhibit area,
gallery space for temporary
exhibits, a 32-seat screening room,
a 150-seat auditorium, and a 324-
seat theater where films and lec-
tures are presented. A large outdoor
Memorial Plaza and indoor cafete-
ria are part of the museum com-
plex, as are two gift shops that sell
fine, internationally created arts
and crafts items, as well as books,
videos, posters, and music.

The two central themes of the
museum are the Nazi Holocaust
and the history of racism and

prejudice in the U.S. The majority of displays have been designed to draw visitors into the various experiences, and they incorporate advanced technology, interactive exhibits, hands-on computer stations, films, graphics, and video monitors.

THE TOLERANCENTER

This area focuses on the many and varied intolerances regularly encountered in daily life. **The Point of View Diner,** a re-created 1950s American diner, complete with counter and red booths, allows "patrons" to sit before video jukeboxes and select a variety of controversial subjects. View various scenarios such as a hate speech or a drunk driver, then let the machine know your opinion on the matter. Using cutting-edge technology, the jukebox then spits out the results of your particular take on personal responsibility.

Also within the Tolerancenter is a huge computer-interactive map with information about more than 250 hate groups in the U.S.; a 16-screen civil-rights video wall; and a film that gives you the lowdown on current human-rights violations throughout the world.

THE HOLOCAUST CENTER

Through what has got to be the most dramatic and heart-wrenching historical and educational exhibits of all time, the Holocaust Center forces visitors to become witnesses to the events and atrocities that occurred during World War II. You will be handed a photo passport (each is different) of a child whose life was changed by the Nazi Holocaust. These passports are updated as the tour proceeds, through a 1930s prewar Berlin café where talk centers on the impending Nazi takeover, to the Wannsee

Conference where Nazi leaders decide on the "Final Solution," and into the Hall of Testimony, where survivors can be seen and heard. At the end of the tour, you find out the ultimate fate of the child whose photo you've been carrying around in your hands.

OTHER FACILITIES & EXHIBITS

The second-level Multimedia Learning Center enables visitors to access eight main subjects, including anti-Semitism, the Holocaust, and military strategies of World War II. More than 30 workstations with touch-screen technology allow fingertip research of more than 6,000 entries, 50,000 photographs, video testimonies, and documents and maps. This level also features Holocaust artifacts and documents, including original Anne Frank letters, Auschwitz artifacts, death-camp bunk beds, and highlights of crusader Simon Wiesenthal's work.

Theme-related temporary showings have recently focused on Polish Jews, the former Yugoslavia, and the children of Rwanda. ∎

No ordinary diner, the Point of View serves up some provocative food for thought.

More places to visit in Beverly Hills & vicinity

ACADEMY OF MOTION PICTURE ARTS AND SCIENCES

The rather lackluster exterior of this building belies its important role as headquarters of the Oscars, filmdom's most exciting awards. Visitors are welcome to scout the lobby exhibition areas, which are filled with changing displays of moviemaking memorabilia. Recent exhibitions have included costume collections spanning eight decades, including Jessica Lange's *King Kong* outfit and a 1930s Marie Antoinette number. The academy's main theater occasionally presents public screenings.

🅰 Map pp. 152–53   ✉ 8949 Wilshire Blvd.   ☎ 310/ 247-3000   🕐 Closed Wed.   💲 $$

BEVERLY HILLS CACTUS GARDEN

If you're into gardens, particularly the prickly type, the Beverly Hills Cactus Garden will appeal. Here you will find one of the largest collections of cactuses and succulents.

🅰 Map pp. 152–53   ✉ Santa Monica Blvd. between N. Camden and N. Bedford Drs.

BEVERLY HILLS HIGH SCHOOL

They may share a name, but this is not the setting for the television series *Beverly Hills 90210* (which gave its final farewell in spring 2000); shooting actually took place at Torrance High School, in a relatively ordinary part of L.A. Beverly Hills High was, however, the site for the classic Jimmy Stewart/Donna Reed film, *It's a Wonderful Life*. Hollywood High is by far a bigger (and longer) player in the city's high-school history books, but B.H. High has had its share of celebrity grads. Alumni include Albert Brooks, Nicolas Cage, Richard Chamberlain, Carrie Fisher, Rhonda Fleming, Rob Reiner, Marlo Thomas, Betty White, and, last but not least, White House intern Monica Lewinsky.

🅰 Map pp. 152–53   ✉ 241 S. Moreno Dr.

CENTER FOR MOTION PICTURE STUDY

Under the auspices of the Academy of Motion Picture Arts and Sciences, this former 1927 landmark Beverly Hills waterworks was creatively converted to house a film archive and the Margaret Herrick Library. The library preserves one of the country's most comprehensive collections of film-related books and materials, including 20,000 volumes, 60,000 scripts, 20,000 posters, and millions of still photos. The archive's 15,000 films—ranging from the silent era to the present day—are stored in the former water-filtration vaults. Access to special collections is by appointment. Researchers can peruse the collections as long as they have proper credentials.

🅰 Map pp. 152–53   ✉ 3359 S. La Cienega Blvd.   ☎ 310/247-3000   🕐 Closed Wed., Sat.–Sun.

GREEN ACRES

From the street, all you can see of silent-film star Harold Lloyd's estate is a single fountain. But inside those off-limits walls is a mega-mansion. The expansive grounds accommodate such parklike features as a nine-hole golf course, an Olympic-size pool, a 120-foot-high waterfall, an 800-foot-long canoe lake, and a further 11 fountains.

🅰 Map pp. 152–53   ✉ 1740 Green Acres Dr.

PICKFAIR

As soon as Mary Pickford and Douglas Fairbanks, Sr., moved to Beverly Hills, a large contingency of film stars and industry types followed, thereby granting the district its status as *the* place for the rich and famous to live. As America's most popular stars at the time, it was only natural that the couple's Pickfair estate became a focal point for the entire world. After they divorced in 1936, Mary Pickford stayed on in the residence and eventually was joined there by her next husband, Buddy Rogers. After Pickford's death in 1979, the house was eventually bought by L.A. Lakers' owner Jerry Buss, who later sold it to wanna-be star Pia Zadora and husband Meshulam Riklis. Sadly, Zadora immediately leveled Pickfair to build her own, much bigger, home on the site. Shortly thereafter she dumped her rich husband and let him keep the house.

🅰 Map pp. 152–53   ✉ 1143 Summit Dr. ∎

The Westside sits next door to Beverly Hills, is relatively close to the ocean, and is filled with hideaway hills and canyons, so it was only natural that the fabulously fashionable and famous would eventually spill over into its communities.

The Westside

Introduction & map 170–71
Westwood Village 172
UCLA 173
UCLA walking tour 174–75
Getty Center 176–82
Skirball Cultural Center & Museum 183
Other Westside communities 184–85
More places to visit in the Westside 186
Hotels & restaurants 253–54

Casting shadows on rich textures, the Getty Center

The Westside

IT'S UP FOR GRABS WHERE THE Westside actually begins. Some place the fine line at La Cienega Boulevard, which cuts through West Hollywood; others at Doheny Drive, where Beverly Hills begins; and still others lump Beverly Hills and Westwood into their own little worlds and decree that this section of L.A. begins west of I-405. No matter where the line is drawn, the Westside is home to many of L.A.'s wealthiest residents, whose mansions rival those in Beverly Hills over to the east.

Let's face it, Beverly Hills and the Hollywood Hills could hardly hold the city's entire flock of celebrities, industry moguls, and business tycoons; there are just too many of them. Neighborhoods such as Westwood, Brentwood, Bel Air, and Pacific Palisades, with their canyons, hills, lush greenery, open spaces, and ocean breezes (and lack of tourist sites)— were natural draws for privacy-seeking stars, as well as for doctors, lawyers, athletes, and other high-income Angelenos. And, in typical L.A. style, along with the bucks comes the pretentiousness. Although this is not quite as blatant as in B.H., Westsiders are typically hedonistic while at the same time trying to look cool, natural, and non-image-conscious. They jog with their babies and pets in the grassy median strips, sweat together in the health clubs, and dine on salads or other healthful foods in fashionable restaurants. They drop their own kids off at school in enormous gas-guzzling sport utility vehicles, and they nurse nonfat decaffeinated lattes at the local Starbucks coffeehouses. Many moments of every day are consumed

MULHOLLAND DRIVE

Skirball Cultural Center and Museum

MOUNTAINGATE

COUNTRY

CLUB

SAN DIEGO FREEWAY

405

NORTH SEPULVEDA BOULEVARD

The Getty Center

Sturges House

BRENTWOOD

Schnabel House

WEST SUNSET

BOULEVARD

Dutton's Bookstore

PACIFIC PALISADES

WILL ROGERS STATE HISTORIC PARK

RIVIERA COUNTRY CLUB

BRENTWOOD COUNTRY CLUB

WEST SUNSET

BOULEVARD

Rustic Canyon

Santa Monica Canyon

Self-Realization Fellowship Lake Shrine

Brentwood Country Mart

SAN VICENTE BOULEVARD

SANTA MONICA

26TH STREET

7TH STREET

MONTANA AVENUE

WILSHIRE BOULEVARD

SANTA MONICA BOULEVARD

COLORADO AVENUE

0   1 mile
0   1 kilometer

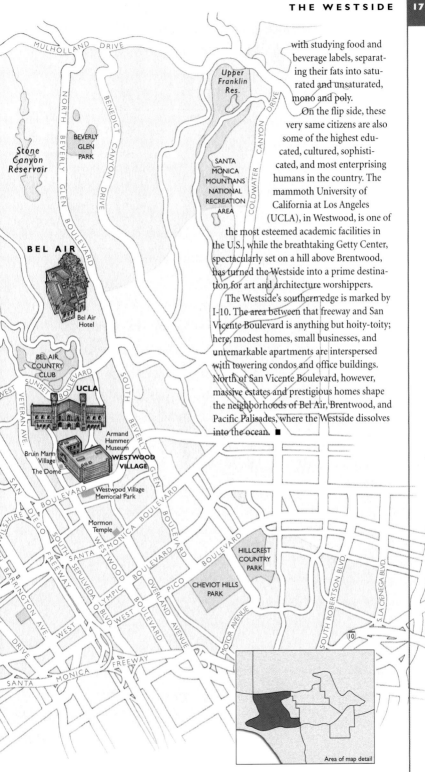

with studying food and beverage labels, separating their fats into saturated and unsaturated, mono and poly.

On the flip side, these very same citizens are also some of the highest educated, cultured, sophisticated, and most enterprising humans in the country. The mammoth University of California at Los Angeles (UCLA), in Westwood, is one of the most esteemed academic facilities in the U.S., while the breathtaking Getty Center, spectacularly set on a hill above Brentwood, has turned the Westside into a prime destination for art and architecture worshippers.

The Westside's southern edge is marked by I-10. The area between that freeway and San Vicente Boulevard is anything but hoity-toity; here, modest homes, small businesses, and unremarkable apartments are interspersed with towering condos and office buildings. North of San Vicente Boulevard, however, massive estates and prestigious homes shape the neighborhoods of Bel Air, Brentwood, and Pacific Palisades, where the Westside dissolves into the ocean. ■

Westwood Village

UCLA at the Armand Hammer Museum of Art

⚠ Map pp. 170–71

✉ 10899 Wilshire Blvd.

☎ 310/443-7000

🕐 Closed Mon.

💲 $$ (free Thurs.)

Historic movie palaces have managed to hang on, despite the blitz of local multiplexes.

POISED BETWEEN WILSHIRE BOULEVARD AND THE UCLA campus is Westwood Village, almost always abustle with college students, particularly on free-for-all weekend evenings.

Originally planned as a shopping district and dating from the late 1920s, Westwood's village atmosphere has endured throughout the years, despite the expansion of UCLA and the development of high-rise condos, office buildings, and movie multiplexes along Wilshire Boulevard. The core of the district is Broxton Avenue, which subsequently becomes Westwood Boulevard. The village pulses with a lively student-oriented street scene around its cluster of casual eateries, cafés, music stores, boutiques, and historic movie theaters.

For decades, weekend evenings have brought long lines of students and other moviegoers to two Broxton Avenue film houses: the 1931 Spanish Moderne **Mann Village** (*No. 961*) and the 1937 neon-spired **Bruin** (*No. 948*). The landmark 1929 **Dome** (*1099 Westwood Blvd.*), the former Islamic-style offices of Janss Investment Corporation, now houses a large music store.

UCLA AT THE ARMAND HAMMER MUSEUM OF ART & CULTURAL CENTER

After backing out of a deal with the Los Angeles County Museum of Art (see p. 88), industrialist Armand Hammer created a showcase for his considerable art holdings at this Westwood Village site, which now flies the UCLA banner. Regular selections from the Hammer collection include old masters and Impressionist and Postimpressionist paintings by such jaw-dropping artists as Rembrandt, van Gogh, Monet, Pissarro, and Cassatt. Works by 19th-century French satirist Honoré Daumier and his contemporaries are part of the ongoing rotating exhibits.

On the gallery level, the center also houses the distinguished **UCLA Grunwald Center for the Graphic Arts,** with 35,000-plus works of art on paper.

The museum presents traveling exhibits, a diverse range of cultural programs, and docent tours. ∎

UCLA

UCLA, FORMERLY LOCATED ON VERMONT AVENUE, WAS established in 1919 with an enrollment of 250 as a two-year college. The small facility—referred to as Berkeley's "southern branch"—grew quickly, and in 1929 the campus was shifted to purchased land in the up-and-coming Westwood community. Today, the world-renowned university boasts 419 lushly landscaped acres with more than 235 buildings and a student body numbering around 35,000.

As one of the country's most prominent universities, UCLA has a lengthy list of renowned departments and schools, including film, medicine, law, theater, earth and space sciences, chemistry, philosophy, history, and management. And, of course, athletes are highly revered, as confirmed by the myriad Bruins' sports team honors.

The real architectural standouts amid the diverse styles are the original four structures, glorious Italian Romanesque brick designs laid out around the grassy central quadrangle, itself always a hub of activity. **Royce Hall,** a campus architectural landmark, was constructed in 1929 and modeled by architect David Allison on a Milanese basilica. Named for philosopher Josiah Royce, the building hosts well-known performing artists in its 1,833-seat auditorium. **Powell Library,** another 1929 original and designed by architect George Kelham, features a 63-foot-high interior dome, a main entrance based on Verona's Church of San Zenove, and a reverent ambience. Haines and Kinsey Halls, also 1929 edifices, house classrooms. The 1931 Gothic **Kerckhoff Hall,** with student activity offices, was donated by the lumber and energy tycoon after whom it is named. The **Fowler Museum of Cultural History,** adjacent to Royce Hall, is considered one of the country's preeminent collections of African, Oceanic, and Native American art,

with four exhibition galleries and hundreds of thousands of artifacts. The **Wight Art Gallery** and **Franklin D. Murphy Sculpture Garden** should also be on the must-see list for artier visitors, while nature lovers will find fountains, gardens, and walkways galore.

Royce Hall and Powell Library, two of UCLA's earliest structures, dating from the 1920s and still a center for campus action

This is mainly a walking campus with limited vehicle traffic allowed in the central area. Parking is a real pain—don't leave your wheels in a restricted spot as the campus police are diligent at their jobs. Campus maps and self-guided walking brochures can be picked up at kiosks located at the major entrances. Alternatively, you can join a free 90- to 120-minute guided walking tour (weekdays and Saturday mornings, departing from the West Alumni Center next to the Pauley Pavilion—reservations are required) or follow the walk given on pp. 174–75. ■

UCLA

🅰 Map pp. 170–71 & inside back cover map C4

✉ 405 Hilgard Ave.

☎ 310/825-4321 or 310/825-8764 (walking tour reservations)

🕐 Tours weekdays from West Alumni Center

UCLA walking tour

This "city within a city" affords a delightful foray into one of America's most outstanding universities. Parklike landscaping, fountains, and gardens have been carefully interspersed with hundreds of hallowed halls abuzz with hungry minds.

Concerts and classes take place in Royce Hall, one of UCLA's original structures.

Visitors can walk to their feet's delight through the peaceful campus, and watch some of the country's finest as they flit in and out of class. Begin your walk in the center of action and where UCLA began, namely the **Quad** (sometimes called the Royce Quad), off Westwood Plaza Drive. Landmark **Royce Hall,** one of the original 1920s buildings, with grand archways and high bell towers, is an imitation basilica that houses classrooms as well as an auditorium. Renowned musicians and performing artists take to the stage here throughout the year. The three-story **Fowler Museum of Cultural History,** next door on Royce Hall's west side, is esteemed for its comprehensive exhibits and artifacts relating to African, Oceanic, and Native American cultures.

Moving in a counterclockwise fashion around the Quad, leave by its far corner to cross Westwood Plaza Drive and reach the **Morgan Intercollegiate Athletics Center.** To the west, **Pauley Pavilion ❶,** seats more than 12,500 spectators at UCLA Bruins basketball games, gym meets, and other events.

Turn eastward again, back across Westwood Plaza Drive, to reach the contemporary **Ackerman Student Union ❷,** a hive of student activity. Inside are a variety of restaurants and services, an arcade, and a skylit lounge, as well as a superb bookstore and all the insignia "bearwear" you could possibly hope for. **Kerckhoff Hall,** the 1931 Gothic edifice to the east, is where the student government functions and the *Daily Bruin* newspaper is turned out. The Romanesque **Moore Hall of Education** is next door, and beyond that is the **Schoenberg Hall,** location for the departments of music, musicology, and ethnomusicology, as well as the **Schoenberg Auditorium.**

Passing through the portals of **Powell Library** ❸ (across Bruin Walk and facing Royce Hall) is akin to entering a cathedral—not surprising, because the 1929 structure was modeled on a couple of churches. The many films and television tapings belonging to the Archive Research and Study Center

---

📷 See area map pp. 170–71

▶ The Quad

↔ 2.4 miles (3.8 km)

🕐 Allow 45 minutes–1 hour

▶ Mathias Botanical Garden

NOT TO BE MISSED

- Royce Hall
- Fowler Museum
- Ackerman Student Union
- Kerckhoff Hall
- Powell Library
- Murphy Sculpture Garden

(part of the Department of Film and Television) are stored within. North of the library and to the east of Royce Hall are Haines and Kinsey Halls, the final two remaining 1920s Romanesque structures, both of which house classrooms.

North of the Quad is the 5-acre **Franklin D. Murphy Sculpture Garden** ❹, boasting the West Coast's largest collection of outdoor sculpture; it's a favorite bucolic spot to linger and dream. Works by Rodin, Matisse, Henry Moore, Joan Miró, and Francisco Zuniga are among the 70-plus modern pieces on display. In the same North Campus section is the **Wight Art Gallery** ❺ (within the Dickson Art Center), with a good range of contemporary works and the famed UCLA film school, which often presents free film and television programs in Melnitz Hall.

End your tour in the wooded paradise of the **Mathias Botanical Garden** ❻, near Circle Drive at the southeast portion of the campus. The 7-acre grounds are planted with hundreds of tree and plant species. ∎

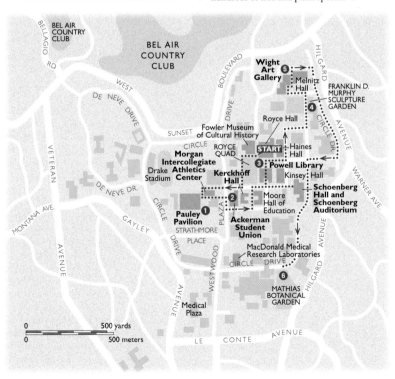

Sensuous curves, columns, and dramatic lighting effects comprise just some of the elements of the architecturally stunning Getty Center.

The Getty Center

COMMANDING A HILLTOP SITE ABOVE SUNSET BOULEVARD in the Santa Monica foothills, and beckoning like an ancient monument, is the Getty Center, L.A.'s largest and most expensive single-phase construction project. It is hard to describe without eliciting superlatives ad nauseum, so let's just say that it is simply "the most."

The Getty Center

- Map pp. 170–71
- 1200 Getty Center Dr.
- 310/440-7300
- Closed Mon. Open until 9 p.m. Thurs.–Fri.
- Free. $$ parking fee (reservations required)

The Getty Center, spread across 110 acres, is referred to neither as a museum nor as a facility, but as a campus, one that is devoted entirely to fine art. In addition to the J. Paul Getty Museum, this paean to the art world also consists of the Getty Research Institute for the History of Art and the Humanities, the Getty Conservation Institute, the Getty Leadership Institute for Museum Management, and the Getty Grant

Program. Since it opened in 1997, the Getty Center has welcomed more than a million visitors each year, greatly enhancing Brentwood's image as a destination for those in search of culture.

BEGINNINGS
Billionaire oil magnate J. Paul Getty purchased his first notable work of art in 1931: a Dutch landscape by Jan van Goyen, for which he paid

Risenburgh (somehow wrenched from the Dukes of Argyll, who had held onto it since the 18th century) and a life-size marble of Heracles (about A.D. 125), a piece that had lived in the London collection of the Marquess of Lansdowne since it was excavated from Hadrian's Villa in Tivoli in the late 18th century (obviously Getty had some persuasive ways). The "Heracles" acquisition, in particular, was a milestone for the oil tycoon, who had long been fascinated with Greek and Roman art. This got the ball rolling for what would eventually become one of the country's most comprehensive collections of antiquities.

When Getty opened his first museum in 1954 at his weekend ranch house in Malibu, it was "Heracles" that greeted visitors at the courtyard entrance. Opened to the public by appointment only, the museum had expanded by 1957 to include a second gallery. Come 1974, the ranch house had been replaced with a villa, modeled after the Roman country house Villa dei Papiri and housing antiquities, paintings, and decorative arts. During his lifetime, Getty was an irregular collector, adding pieces only every so often. However, after his death in 1976, and following the bequest of seven hundred million dollars in oil stock, the appointed Getty Trust embarked on a few-holds-barred buying spree.

Since the 1980s, thousands of new works have been purchased by the trust in the museum's three primary interests (antiquities, European paintings, and French furniture and decorative arts) as well as for four new collections. In addition, the Getty Trust has created four institutes to huddle together with the museum under the greatly expanding umbrella organization. But where would they

Visitors get their bearings in the grand entrance hall, with the information desk beneath the massive rotunda.

$1,100 at a Berlin auction. Although Getty didn't begin his serious collecting until 1938, exquisite art and antiquities were definitely coursing through his rich veins. A circa-1790 rolltop desk with gilt-bronze mounts by Bernard Molitor signaled the debut of what would become one of America's most important collections of 18th-century decorative arts. Soon after came Louis XIV's Savonnerie carpet and Rembrandt's portrait of Martin van Looten (later donated to the Los Angeles County Museum of Art).

GETTY VILLA

By the 1950s, Getty's collection contained a breathtaking assortment of works that included a double desk by Bernard van

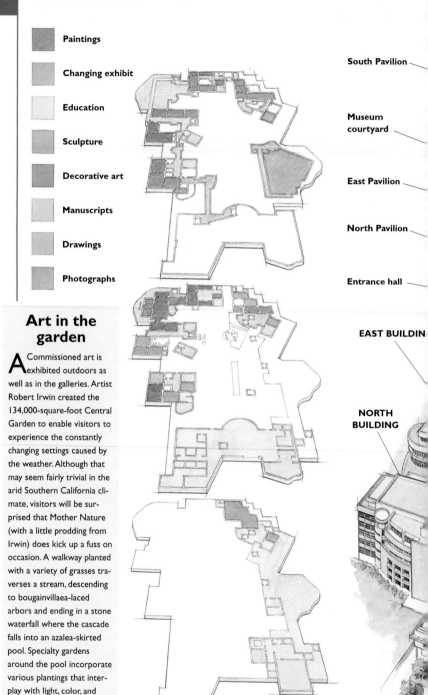

Paintings

Changing exhibit

Education

Sculpture

Decorative art

Manuscripts

Drawings

Photographs

South Pavilion

Museum courtyard

East Pavilion

North Pavilion

Entrance hall

EAST BUILDIN

NORTH BUILDING

Art in the garden

A Commissioned art is exhibited outdoors as well as in the galleries. Artist Robert Irwin created the 134,000-square-foot Central Garden to enable visitors to experience the constantly changing settings caused by the weather. Although that may seem fairly trivial in the arid Southern California climate, visitors will be surprised that Mother Nature (with a little prodding from Irwin) does kick up a fuss on occasion. A walkway planted with a variety of grasses traverses a stream, descending to bougainvillaea-laced arbors and ending in a stone waterfall where the cascade falls into an azalea-skirted pool. Specialty gardens around the pool incorporate various plantings that interplay with light, color, and reflection. ∎

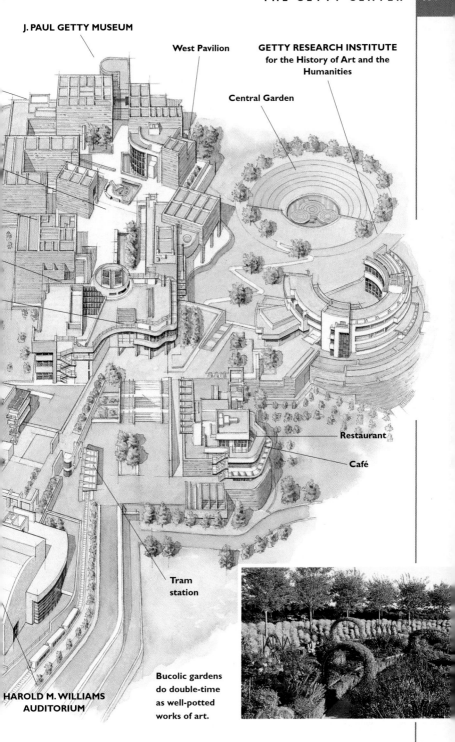

J. PAUL GETTY MUSEUM

West Pavilion

GETTY RESEARCH INSTITUTE
for the History of Art and the
Humanities

Central Garden

Restaurant

Café

Tram
station

HAROLD M. WILLIAMS
AUDITORIUM

Bucolic gardens
do double-time
as well-potted
works of art.

"The Entry of the Animals into Noah's Ark," by Flemish artist Jan Breughel, 1613

A colorful Ensor puppet poses in one of the welcoming outdoor spaces.

house all this great work? It would take an entire campus of exquisite edifices and pavilions, with landscaping to match, to do the job—hence the Getty Center.

THE ARCHITECTURE

Indeed, the Getty Center's architecture and landscaping are so phenomenal that many visitors come just to look at the exterior and don't even bother with what's hanging on the other side of the walls. In 1984 award-winning architect Richard Meier was chosen to bring the Getty Center to life—no small task for a project that would become one of the country's most significant works of architecture as well as a prominent cultural venue. But then it helps to have a billion-dollar budget. Along with a team of highly proficient project leaders, contractors, landscape and interior designers, and work crews, Meier & Partners were able to unveil the Getty in December 1997.

One of the first and most important elements for Meier to deal with was the hilltop site in the Santa Monica Mountains, just a

nod away from the San Diego Freeway. The campus had to maintain appearances from below, above, and all around. It was also necessary to maximize the view from above (of the Pacific Ocean, San Gabriel Mountains, and the city sprawl), to minimize the center's impact from the freeway and Sunset Boulevard below, and also to keep the high-rise-hating neighbors happy. Meier's solution? An organic environment that would highlight both nature and culture, following the topography and also encompassing the openness and light evoked by earlier Modernist architects.

The end result was six glorious, low-lying, geometric-shaped buildings clustered along the site's natural ridges, and affording panoramic views of the ocean, mountains, and cityscape from elevations rising to 900 feet. For those looking upward at it, the center's two ridges form a Y-shape, intersecting at the exact angle of the freeway below. And to appease the neighbors, Meier's plan dictated that only two stories be built above grade, with the remaining portions underground and connected to one another via subterranean corridors. Buildings were positioned on the site according to their relative public or private nature, and, though totaling 750,000 feet of space, they occupy a mere 110 acres of the enormous site. The remainder has been relegated to gardens and terraces or left in its natural state.

TRAVERTINE & LIGHT

The most stunning architectural elements of the Getty are Meier's use of stone and natural light. The travertine, a variety of limestone and a marble-look-alike, was quarried near Rome, and the rough-cut texture was achieved through a specially invented guillotine process. Just as unusual is the stone itself, which is 8,000–80,000 years old and contains the still-visible fossilized remains of leaves, branches, fish, and other matter. More than 290,000 blocks, cut into 30-inch squares, now cover the Getty's pavement as well as its buildings and retaining walls, interspersed with off-white, enamel-clad aluminum panels.

Putting Southern California's sunshine to good use, Meier's design features plenty of glass surfaces and two-story atria. All upper-level painting galleries are naturally lit, assisted by a sophisticated computerized system that adjusts louvers via sensors coordinated to the sun's movement. Visitors can therefore view paintings in conditions similar to those the artists experienced while creating them. Special filters keep any sun damage at bay.

THE MUSEUM BUILDING

The five interconnected two-story pavilions are designed around an exterior fountain-filled courtyard and are linked by crisscrossing

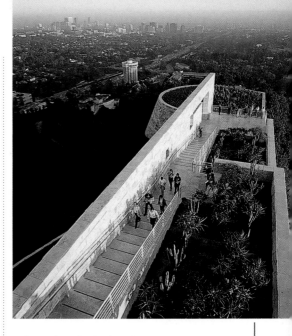

walkways, formal and informal gardens, and ever changing views. The layout allows freedom of movement throughout interior and exterior spaces, thereby encouraging independent exploration. A café adjacent to the courtyard enables visitors to ponder their surroundings over a cappuccino.

The Getty's permanent collection, presented in chronological order, is shown in four of the five pavilions. Pre-20th-century European paintings hang on the 22 skylit upper levels, while galleries on the courtyard level are filled with drawings, illuminated manuscripts, sculptures, decorative arts, and 19th- and 20th-century American and European photographs. The remaining pavilion is used for temporary exhibitions, including important international works on loan.

THE GRAND ENTRANCE

Whether you've arrived by car (a seven-floor parking structure is provided, though you must reserve a space), bus, or taxi, you enter the main gate and head to the tram

This walkway parallels lush plantings, leading to a panoramic viewpoint.

Portrait of Georgia O'Keeffe by American photographer Alfred Stieglitz

station, where a computer-operated, three-car tram takes you on a five-minute ride along a winding, wooded, view-filled route. Designed by Otis Transit especially for the Getty Center, each of two trams can accommodate 100 passengers and move 1,200 passengers per hour. Arriving at the plaza, visitors will immediately encounter the exotic travertine. Steps lead up to the museum

"Adoration of the Magi" by Italian Renaissance artist Andrea Mantegna

entrance, with its soaring rotunda, information desk, bookstore, and two small theaters (these screen orientation films).

HIGHLIGHTS

The galleries house such masterpieces as van Gogh's "Irises" and Mantegna's "Adoration of the Magi," as well as the country's best group of Rembrandt drawings, strong sculptures, exquisite decorative arts, and the world's finest photography collection. Paintings span the medieval to Postimpressionist eras and also include such eclectic offerings as Steen's "The Drawing Lesson," Jan Brueghel's "The Entry of the Animals into Noah's Ark," Cézanne's "Still Life with Apples," and works by Renoir, Monet, Goya,

and Turner. Along with the selection of Rembrandt drawings come others by da Vinci, Michelangelo, Raphael, Jean Antoine Watteau, Claude Lorrain, Manet, and Degas.

A purchase frenzy by the Getty Trust gleaned an additional 26,000 master photographs and related works from the medium's early 19th-century development to the present time. Represented are European pioneers such as Talbot and Nadar, daguerreotypes by Southworth and Hawes, and masterworks by Man Ray, Cunningham, Callahan, Kertész, Hockney, and Stieglitz.

Bernini's marble "Boy with a Dragon," carved by the artist at the age of 16, and Cellini's bronze "Satyr" are standouts in the sculpture department. Also included under the sculpture umbrella are ceramics, glass, and Italian furniture.

The important collection of illuminated manuscripts includes the Romanesque *Stammheim Missal* and the Franco-Flemish *The Visions of Tondal*. Getty's passion for 18th-century French furniture is well known, and it is so comprehensive that it completely spilled out of its Malibu space and into 14 galleries at the Getty Museum. This museum-within-a-museum shows off furnishings and decorative arts, including two paneled rooms that were never before seen by the public.

MUSEUM STORE

No mere run-of-the-mill museum shop, the Getty version rates as one of the West Coast's most comprehensive art bookstores. Along with books, visitors will find exhibition handbooks, CD-ROMs, videotapes, and computer software, as well as typical souvenir merchandise. ■

Skirball Cultural Center & Museum

CONCEPTUALIZED IN THE EARLY 1980s AS AN AFFILIATE OF L.A.'s Hebrew Union College, the Skirball Cultural Center & Museum finally came to fruition in 1996. Located on 15 acres at the top of Sepulveda Pass in the Santa Monica Mountains, the self-governing center interprets and celebrates the Jewish experience, past and present, through its museum and cultural and educational facilities.

Designed by architect Moshe Safdie, the 340,000-square-foot steel-and-concrete complex consists of the museum, a hands-on Discovery Center, an educational center, a study gallery, conference and banquet rooms, a full-service restaurant, and an outstanding gift and retail shop. The 350-seat auditorium holds regularly scheduled lectures, films, videos, concerts, and readings, while the Tapler Courtyard sets the scene for open-air concerts, performances, and special events. Many programs are timed to coincide with Jewish holidays.

THE MUSEUM

The heart and soul of the center is the museum and its core exhibition, "Visions and Values: Jewish Life from Antiquity to America." Twelve galleries enlighten visitors about the Jewish experience, focusing on life in the Old World, immigration, and successful assimilation into present-day American society. Although Jewish life is emphasized, the center's two-fold mission also seeks to encourage a cross-cultural exchange with other immigrants. While the center is undergoing expansion, its galleries also emphasize the connection between American-Jewish life and American democratic values.

Exhibits comprise multimedia installations, architectural reconstructions, and a vast collection of Judaica. The Torah, a scroll containing the Five Books of Moses, is the foundation of Judaism and the first item encountered. From here, visitors are pointed toward historic turning points, the weekly Sabbath and other traditional holidays, a reconstructed synagogue, and the passage of Jewish people to America both before and after World War II. "At Home in America," is a freestanding space in which eight elevated screens present a kaleidoscopic view of Jewish life in modern America.

DISCOVERY CENTER

Younger visitors enjoy the Discovery Center, with its exciting hands-on exhibits. Here, and in the outdoor archaeology classroom, students are encouraged to participate in a simulated dig. ■

Jewish journeys and traditions are highlighted at this mountain-top sight, also a venue for weddings.

Skirball Cultural Center & Museum
 Map pp. 170–71
✉ 2701 N. Sepulveda Blvd.
☎ 310/440-4500
🕐 Closed Mon.
💲 $$

You can see celebrities hidden by over-size hats and sunglasses lounging around the Bel Air Hotel pool.

Other Westside communities

BEL AIR, BRENTWOOD, AND PACIFIC PALISADES ARE THREE of the most sought-after neighborhoods in the city for wealthy professionals and celebrities. As you move northward and westward of UCLA, luxury and hedonism seep from the canyons, hills, and tree-shaded avenues in a sinuous curve all the way to the sea.

Other Westside Communities
 Map pp. 170–71

BEL AIR

There's not much going on—at least that you can see—in super-exclusive Bel Air, a hillside enclave northwest of UCLA and east of I-405. Nonetheless, once you drive through the gates fronting Sunset Boulevard, you'll know you've entered a separate money-drenched, privacy-obsessed world where someone famous dwells behind nearly every guarded wall.

Dating from the 1920s, Bel Air is hardly what you would call a community, although practically every mansion could be considered a community unto itself. Household staff usually outnumber residents, and most of the homes contain private tennis courts, putting greens, playgrounds, gyms, spas, swimming pools, ballrooms, enter-tainment centers, and pantries with enough food for entire nations. The ritzy residential neighborhood is devoid of shops and services, with the exception of the exquisite **Bel Air Hotel** (701 Stone Canyon Rd.), one of the loveliest hotels in Los Angeles and almost a sure bet for seeing some fabulously famous names. If you decide to drive along Bel Air's winding roads, do be discreet and don't loiter or trespass; security is very tight and patrols are vigilant. Unlikely residents include former President Ronald Reagan and wife Nancy (668 St. Cloud Rd.), and TV's Beverly Hillbillies (750 Bel Air Rd.).

BRENTWOOD

Until the 1995 O.J. Simpson debacle, this exclusive residential and retail

community was practically unknown to all except its denizens and other assorted Angelenos. But once the world was watching, Brentwood soon became besieged by fame—albeit unwanted—and an onslaught of media. After what seemed like an eternity, the excitement finally died down. These days, Brentwood has become world famous for yet another sensation: The magnificent billion-dollar Getty Center is an architectural and cultural gem (see pp. 176–182). The relatively new Skirball Cultural Center, north of the Getty, highlights the Jewish experience and provides yet another high-minded draw (see p. 183).

San Vicente Boulevard is Brentwood's main shopping and jogging street. The grassy, tree-shaded median strip stretches all the way to the ocean bluffs, and is a favorite path for runners. The boutiques, restaurants, antiques dealers, and beauty salons situated mainly between 26th Street and Wilshire Boulevard are suitably highbrow for the local trade. **Brentwood Country Mart** *(26th St., just south of San Vicente Blvd.)* is a delightful red-barn shopping center with more than two dozen shops, a post office, and espresso and juice bars. Many famed authors sign their tomes at **Dutton's Bookstore** *(11975 San Vicente Blvd.)*.

Celebrities and prominent Angelenos live along the leafy streets north of San Vicente Boulevard, although, unlike Bel Air, groupings of apartment buildings and condos also share the Brentwood zip code. Architecture buffs might want to check out Frank Lloyd Wright's **Sturges House** *(449 Skyeway Rd.)* and Frank Gehry's **Schnabel House** *(526 N. Carmelina Ave.)*. Marilyn Monroe allegedly overdosed at the very ordinary looking house at 12305 Fifth Helena Drive *(off Carmelina Ave.)*, where she lived alone with her dog.

PACIFIC PALISADES

Founded in 1922, this upper-crust residential community spills along the canyons and hills either side of Sunset Boulevard, calling it quits at the Pacific Ocean. Residences range from low-lying ranch houses, including the former home of President Ronald Reagan *(1669 San Onofre Dr.)*, to palatial mansions such as the one belonging to film director Steven Spielberg *(1515 Amalfi Dr.)*. The 1952 studio of architect Cliff May (credited with mastering the California ranch-style home) is located at 13151 Sunset Boulevard, and May residences can be seen along the 13000 blocks of adjacent Riviera Ranch and Old Oak roads. The **Will Rogers State Historic Park** and the **Self-Realization Fellowship Lake Shrine** (see p. 186), on either side of Sunset Boulevard, attract nature lovers and spirit seekers. ∎

It may look like a Dutch windmill, but this replica is actually a meditation chapel at Self-Realization Fellowship Lake Shrine.

More places to visit in the Westside

MORMON TEMPLE

Unless you're a card-carrying member of the Church of Jesus Christ of Latter-day Saints, you won't be able to enter the inner sanctum. Nevertheless, you can gawk at the enormous temple, tour the grounds, and access the visitor center. Designed by Edward Anderson in 1951, the temple features a 257-foot tower topped with a 15-foot gilded statue of the angel Moroni.
🅼 Map pp. 170–71 ✉ 10777 Santa Monica Blvd. ☎ 310/474-1549

SELF-REALIZATION FELLOWSHIP LAKE SHRINE

The Lake Shrine was founded in 1950 by Indian guru Paramahansa Yogananda and is situated beneath the dramatically poised homes in Pacific Palisades' Castellamare section, a couple of blocks east of the ocean.

Krishna is just one of the deities beckoning visitors to the Lake Shrine.

Although this place of worship is based on Eastern teachings, Yogananda tagged it a Church of All Religions. As such, everyone is welcome at the truly Edenesque grounds. Take a stroll around the swan-filled lake, where a pathway leads you through magnificent gardens with ponds, statuary, a bird refuge, plaques with inspirational quotes, and meditation nooks. Among the lakeside sights are the houseboat where Yogananda once lived, the Windmill Chapel, and the Mahatma Gandhi World Peace Memorial. A gift shop sells quality arts from India, crafts, jewelry, and artifacts, as well as spiritual books and tapes. At the rear of the shop is a small museum displaying historical photos and items that belonged to Yogananda. A recently built, gigantic, golden-domed temple sits on the hill above the lake.
🅼 Map pp. 170–71 ✉ 17190 Sunset Blvd. ☎ 310/454-4114 🕒 Closed Mon.

WESTWOOD VILLAGE MEMORIAL PARK & MORTUARY

Stashed behind an office building is the final resting place of, among others, Marilyn Monroe, Natalie Wood, Buddy Rich, Dean Martin, Donna Reed, Truman Capote, and ex-Playboy playmate Dorothy Stratten. Playboy magazine emperor Hugh Hefner has reportedly purchased the crypt adjacent to Marilyn's, so he can one day rest eternally next to the woman who launched his kingdom.
🅼 Map pp. 170–71 ✉ 1218 Glendon Ave. ☎ 310/474-1579

WILL ROGERS STATE HISTORIC PARK

Will Rogers, America's esteemed cowboy, humorist, performer, and writer, helped keep the country's spirits up during the dismal Depression era, hurling philosophical, common sense one-liners like life preservers. After he died in a plane crash in 1935, the entire nation was prompted to hold silence, in reverent tribute to the talkative Rogers, for 30 minutes. His former home, north of Sunset Boulevard in Pacific Palisades, is a popular nature getaway for Angelenos. Set on nearly 186 acres, the property encompasses miles of hiking and bridle trails, a huge polo field where weekend matches are often played, and Rogers's ranch home (now a casual museum filled with memorabilia and artifacts, including the mounted head of a Texas longhorn).
🅼 Map pp. 170–71 ✉ 1501 Will Rogers State Park Road ☎ 310/454-8212 🆂 Free, but $6 for parking ■

Holding steady at the edge of the continent, the beach communities contribute mightily to the quintessential L.A. experience. This is a post-card paradise of light blondes, deep tans, (mostly) great bodies, and carefree lifestyles.

Santa Monica, Venice, & Malibu

Introduction & map 188–89
Santa Monica 190–93
Venice Beach & Boardwalk 194–95
South of Venice 196
Malibu 197
Along beaches & through canyons 198–99
More places to visit in Santa Monica, Venice, & Malibu 202
Hotels & restaurants 254–56

It's a dog's life in Venice.

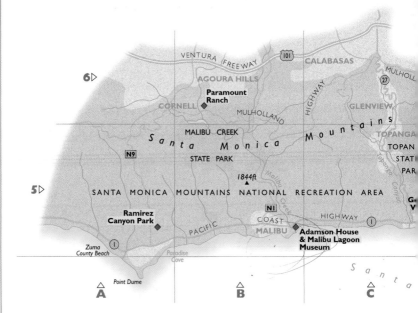

Santa Monica, Venice, & Malibu

ALONG WITH HOLLYWOOD AND BEVERLY HILLS, THE BEACH TOWNS (AND the lifestyles that go with them) complete most people's image of L.A., and almost every visitor eventually winds up (or down) on the sandy shore before leaving town. It's almost impossible to avoid the coast: Los Angeles International Airport faces the ocean south of Venice (Pacific Coast Highway actually cuts under the runway), and Wilshire, Santa Monica, and Sunset Boulevards all lead to the beaches or the bluffs above them. This is a far cry from the turn of the 20th century, when a visit to the seashore for most Angelenos meant a daylong trek by stagecoach to frolic in the waves and breathe the salt air.

Venice, Santa Monica, and Malibu—all facing onto Santa Monica Bay—are L.A. County's three most popular beach destinations. Which is best depends on taste and interests. Curvy in-line skaters and bodybuilders hang out in semiseedy Venice, while the super rich and famous are sequestered up the coast in Malibu. Santa Monica is the more mainstream choice.

Prominently positioned between Venice and Pacific Palisades, Santa Monica continues to be one of the most sought-after communities for "real" people who covet sea breezes, clean air, and the laid-back beach-resort lifestyle. In L.A.'s early days, the town (then citrus groves and farmlands) had been targeted by its Southern Pacific Railroad

owners as the city's port. Luckily for Santa Monica, San Pedro (down the coast) was chosen instead. Within its 8-square-mile boundaries, hitched to L.A. on three sides and to the ocean on the fourth, Santa Monica contains typical city services, prestigious art galleries, and several of the hottest retail meccas in L.A., namely bustling Third Street Promenade, hip Main Street, and snazzy Montana Avenue. Residential districts range from low-key bungalows and apartment buildings in middle-class neighborhoods, to stately homes and architectural wonders in the upper-class section between Wilshire and San Vicente Boulevards. Palisades Park, between Colorado Avenue and San Vicente Boulevard, is a bluffside haven for joggers, sunset-worshippers, and board-game-playing seniors.

Although today's Venice is a far cry from tycoon Abbot Kinney's early 20th-century dream of a re-created Venice, Italy (complete with canals and culture), at the Los Angeles seashore, it certainly isn't lacking in character (or characters). Even a few of the canals—long since paved over or turned to murky gunk—

have been rebuilt. The famous boardwalk, however, has endured, along with a peculiar population mix ranging from artists and bodies on wheels to charity cases and hipsters.

North of Santa Monica and Pacific Palisades, Malibu basks in its own bubble. The 27-mile-wide stretch between the Santa Monica Mountains and the Pacific Ocean has been an exclusive enclave for celebrities since the late 1920s. And neither fire, nor landslide, nor earthquake can make it burst. ■

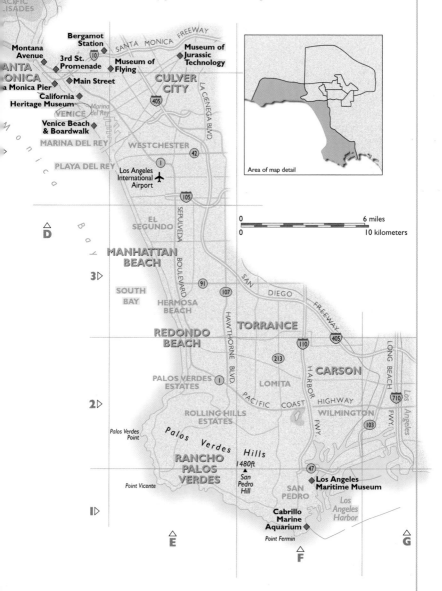

Santa Monica

Santa Monica
 189 D4/5

**Santa Monica
Pier**
 189 D4/5
✉ End of Colorado
Ave.
☎ 310/458-8900
$ Free (charge for
rides)

Main Street
 189 D4/5

IN RECENT YEARS, SANTA MONICA HAS BECOME ONE of L.A.'s coolest, hottest, and breeziest hangouts. Dumpy streets, dated shops, and roach-coach diners have metamorphosed into gracious thoroughfares, hip shops, and trendy cafés and bars. Added lures include the historic Santa Monica Pier.

SANTA MONICA PIER
Although it is but a shadow of its early self during the days when it was a prime tourist attraction, Santa Monica Pier still manages to provoke plenty of carnival- and boardwalk-type nostalgia.

Constructed in the early 1870s, Shoo-Fly Landing (as the original pier was known) was earmarked to be L.A.'s major port. Though San Pedro eventually won the honor, Santa Monica actually captured the grand prize—as a preeminent destination for Angelenos in search of beach getaways and boardwalk amusements. Shoo-Fly Landing was eventually replaced by two adjacent piers, the Santa Monica Municipal Pier and the Looff amusement pier. Diversions included La Monica Ballroom, a two-story hippodrome

with landmark carousel, a vibrant amusement park, the usual jangling arcades, lots of junk food, and offshore gambling (that is until the law shut it down). Raymond Chandler modeled his *Bay City* after the seedier section between the piers and Venice Beach, while wealthy stars laid out their mansions along Pacific Coast Highway to the north.

Threatened with demolition since the 1970s by developers, dilapidation, storms, and criminal activity, the piers became the focus of a zealous battle launched by citizens' groups. Against all the odds they won, and a full restoration program was completed in 1990. The neon sign spanning the entrance for more than 50 years once again welcomes visitors.

Attractions

The **UCLA Ocean Discovery Center,** near the entrance, features an aquarium, hands-on exhibits, and educational programs. The restored 1922 **Looff Carousel** (listed on the National Register of Historic Places) and its 44 handcrafted horses are irresistible to all ages. **Playland Arcade** offers all the favorite boardwalk-type coin-operated games, fortune-tellers in machines, and video games. The all-new 2-acre Pacific Park, located entirely on the pier, features all the good old family amusements.

MAIN STREET

Santa Monica's Main Street, running parallel to the ocean and best explored on foot, is one of L.A.'s most atmospheric retail and gustatory trails. Mingled among the older brick buildings is a grab-bag mix of celebrity restaurants, novelty shops, high-end boutiques, cafés, salons, and interesting architecture. The stretch between Ocean Park Boulevard and Rose Avenue (in Venice) is the prime area to target.

Hot restaurants along Main Street include Wolfgang Puck's **Chinois** *(No. 2709)* and Arnold Schwarzenegger and Maria Shriver's **Schatzi** *(No. 3110)*. **World Café** *(No. 2820)* provides a sophisticated setting for dining and cocktails, plus cyberspace communion at a six-station Internet-access kiosk.

Smokers should seek out the **Cigar Toscano** *(No. 2814)*, with a 200-square-foot humidor, 125 brands of cigars, and a blatant public smoking area. **Star Wares** *(No. 2817)* will garb you in celebrities' hand-me-downs and also stocks collectibles and props. **Homeworks** *(No. 2923)* sells an eclectic array of affordable novelty items that are perfectly geared for struggling souvenir hunters.

The Frank Gehry-designed **Edgemar Complex** *(No. 2427–2449)*, once an old egg company, houses more stores, salons, and eateries, including the Röckenwagner Restaurant, the Museum of Contemporary Art Store, and Form Zero Architectural Books and Gallery.

Sunset at Santa Monica Pier balances well with the lights of Pacific Park's rides and amusements.

Topiary dinosaurs line Third Street Promenade.

CALIFORNIA HERITAGE MUSEUM

An historic 1894 Queen Anne home is the setting for this museum, which depicts California's history and culture through reconstructed period rooms dating from the 1890s through the 1930s, among other displays. The building itself was originally designed by Sumner P. Hunt for Roy Jones (one of Santa Monica's founders). The dining room, living room, and kitchen have been fully restored to their original styles, while upper-level galleries display archival photos and other exhibits.

California Heritage Museum
🅰 189 D4
✉ 2612 Main St.
☎ 310/392-8537
🕐 Closed Mon. and Wed.
💲 $

THIRD STREET PROMENADE

This is where cool Santa Monicans come to strut and stroll, many of them escapees from the Melrose scene or nostalgic for the throngs that hung out around Westwood Village in times past.

A three-block, pedestrian-only thoroughfare between Broadway and Wilshire Boulevard, Third Street Promenade is all the rage with locals and visitors for people-watching, street performances, various entertainments, casual shopping, and outdoor dining. People mingle among the jacaranda trees and topiary dinosaur fountains, dodging in and out of clubs, coffeehouses, movie theaters, pool halls, specialty bookshops, restaurants and bars, and stores ranging from one-of-a-kinds to chain establishments. The atmosphere is especially lively on weekend nights, when street entertainers wow passersby with everything from acoustic guitar solos and psychic readings to tap dances.

Until the early 1990s, this was one of the last places anyone (aside from street people) would have hung out, and there probably wasn't a psychic around who foresaw the 360-degree turn the Promenade would take. Before it was given a major face-lift, this strip was one part mom-and-pop stores and one part down and dirty. Today, however, there's something for everyone of every age and every pocketbook. Some of the don't-miss spots are **Midnight Special Bookstore** (No. 1318), with a high-minded stock of books, literature, and journals; **Pyramid Music** (No. 1340A), for hard-to-find new and used CDs, LPs, and cassettes; **DOM** (No. 1245), highlighting mod home design; **Urban Outfitters** (No. 1440), for industrial styles with trendy labels for trendy people; and **Hennessey and Ingalls** (No. 1254), one of the West Coast's largest art and architecture bookstores. And if this isn't enough, **Santa Monica Place,** across Broadway, offers three levels of fine shopping in a Frank Gehry-designed enclosed mall.

BERGAMOT STATION

Far from the madding crowds, over by Santa Monica's beach, is

Third Street Promenade
🅰 189 D5

Bergamot Station, a former Red Car trolley station that has metamorphosed into one of Southern California's most happening art centers. Converted by architect Frederick Fisher, the old railroad sheds now house a premier collection of galleries. On display are the works of both emerging local and international artists, much of it with controversial or in-your-face (or, for some, nonsensical) political, cultural, and social messages.

When L.A.'s downtown area—once the core of the alternative art scene—took a seedy slide, galleries moved here en masse, all too happy to have a fresh, historical compound devoted to art (and out of the smog). The 5.5-acre complex is one of the largest art centers of its kind in the country and showcases more than 20 galleries, all open free of charge to the art-loving public who continue to keep the place afloat. Among the on-site galleries are the Peter Fetterman Photographic Works of Art, the Shoshana Wayne Gallery, the Craig Krull Gallery, the Rosamund Felsen Gallery, the Patricia Faure Gallery, the Rose Gallery, and Artworks-Book Arts. Many of the more overt cutting-edge works are exhibited in Track 16 Gallery and Mainspace, while the Gallery of Functional Art presents an ever amazing assemblage of home furnishings and accessories. The recent addition of the Santa Monica Museum of Art has further increased attendance.

Santa Monica Museum of Art

Established in 1985, the successful Santa Monica Museum of Art recently moved over to Bergamot Station from its previous location at Main Street's Edgemar complex. Positioned on the Michigan Avenue side of the art center, the museum continues to be a substantial force in the contemporary art scene, and is well established as a non-collecting, artist-driven organization. More than 1,000 local and international (lesser-known) artists have exhibited mostly edge art in a variety of media. Regularly scheduled Friday night salons are a big hit, and the museum shop and café also encourage lingering. ∎

Hip, colorful Third Street Promenade is shared by yuppies, tourists, shoppers, and buskers.

Bergamot Station
- 189 D5
- 2525 Michigan Ave.
- 310/829-5854
- Closed Mon.

Santa Monica Museum of Art
- 189 D5
- Bergamot Station, 2525 Michigan Ave.
- 310/586-6488
- Closed Sun. & Mon. Open until 10 p.m. Fri.
- $

Venice Beach & Boardwalk

Venice Beach & Boardwalk
⚠ 189 D4

LIKE COLLIS HUNTINGTON, THE SOUTHERN PACIFIC Railroad owner who tried to push Santa Monica as a port by building a massive pier, tobacco tycoon Abbot Kinney had a big plan for neighboring Venice. Kinney's dream, however, was a tad more fanciful than a harbor: He wanted to re-create the city of Venice, Italy, on the shores of the Pacific Ocean. And not just the canals either, for Kinney's vision also encompassed the exotic trappings of Venetian and Renaissance culture, including theaters, concert halls, architectural icons, restaurant sites, and, of course, a café society.

Kinney started off well enough, draining his 160-acre marshland property and developing more than 18 miles of wide, interconnected canals. Next, with the help of architect Norman F. Marsh, came the Italianate business district, with its St. Mark's Cathedral-style hotel, naturally christened the St. Mark Hotel. Savvy developer that he was, Kinney's next step was to bring in investors. On the Fourth of July, 1905, thousands of potential buyers were invited to Venice's grand opening. Suitably enthralled, many bought canal-front lots at exorbitant prices. Then, to Kinney's dismay, they built bungalows instead of grand Italianate mansions. It also became obvious that visitors were more interested in amusement and fun than they were in art and culture. Obligingly, Kinney shifted focus and built a casino, a dance pavilion, carnival amusements, a bowling alley, a pseudo-Arabian bathhouse, arcades and galleries, and various minaret-topped structures. *Voilà*, Venice Boardwalk! And so Venice, California, laid claim as another L.A. original.

Unfortunately, by the 1920s Venice had decayed. Kinney had died and the nearby oil fields had polluted the canals, so when voters agreed to be annexed to the City of L.A., most of the waterways were promptly filled in. However, the community was eventually revived by various groups—beatniks in the 1950s, hippies in the '60s, and artists in the '70s. So Kinney's dream had been realized after all, albeit with more opulence.

Today's Venice is a pulsing mix of *Architectural Digest* homes and businesses, plain bungalows, and positively condemnable shacks. The population is a vital, cross-cultural community. The Grand Canal, at Windward Avenue and Main Street, where all the canals originally met, has long since been a paved-over traffic circle. Several of the remaining canals and bridges have been refurbished, however, and can be seen from the southeast corner of Venice Boulevard and Pacific Avenue. The gang activity that sometimes plagues Venice is mostly confined to the Oakwood section, not far from the canals. Be sure to stay out of Oakwood at all times, and, although this district is removed from the tourist areas, explore Venice only during the day.

VENICE BOARDWALK
The famous Venice Boardwalk (also called Ocean Front Walk in some parts) is actually a paved walkway in the throes of renovation. By the time this book is published, the boardwalk will have been resurfaced, and more entertainment areas, new lighting, rest

The good life: a pair of in-line skates, favorite sounds through a headset, and the ocean alongside

rooms, and pagodas will have been added. What doesn't go on here? From its nucleus at historic Windward Avenue, Venice Boardwalk is nonstop performance art. Even during Kinney's day, the boardwalk was (pardon the political incorrectness) a freak show, and this holds true today. You'll encounter a year-round plethora of musicians, magicians, psychics, and artists, as well as almost-naked humans zipping by, not just on in-line skates, but on any object that can have wheels attached to it. But if you really want to bond, rent a pair of skates or a bicycle at one of the concessions at the boardwalk's southern end and join the parade. Just south of Windward Avenue is Muscle Beach, the infamous spot for fanatical iron-pumpers. ■

Palms sway above Venice's daily passing parade of in-line skaters, joggers, cyclists, and beachgoers.

South of Venice

South of Venice
⚠ 189

SOUTH OF VENICE, THE COAST BECOMES A REAL MISHMASH of nondescript developments, ghost towns, beach communities, gated estates, and the Los Angeles Harbor. Varied though they may be, all have the Pacific Ocean in common and so afford plenty of spots for swimming, surfing, boating, fishing, and other water-based pastimes.

The Pacific Coast Highway links L.A.'s surfing beaches, allowing easy access to the best waves.

MARINA DEL REY

Adjacent to Venice, south of Washington Boulevard, is Marina del Rey, an everyday coastal development crammed with condominiums and residential complexes. **Fisherman's Village** (*13855 Fiji Way*) is a Cape Cod-style retail and dining complex overlooking the harbor (nice ambience, but don't expect much from the food). **Burton Chace Park,** at the bottom of Mindanao Way, affords the best view of the thousands of colorful sailboats that are moored in the small-craft harbor.

PLAYA DEL REY

The peaceful little community of Playa del Rey offers beaches and fewer crowds, while Palisades del Rey (on the bluff) provides hiking options. In contrast to its populated neighbors to the north, the coastal area that runs the length of L.A. International Airport is a no-man's-land with an eerie ghost-town feel.

SOUTH BAY

Manhattan, Hermosa, and Redondo Beaches—collectively called the South Bay—are a hodgepodge of luxurious condos, beach cottages, and wealthy estates. Manhattan and Redondo Beaches cater to more upscale residents, while Hermosa Beach is a favorite with the sun-and-surf set. The Hermosa Beach Stand (between Hermosa Avenue and the pier) is a charming place to stroll or gaze out at the horizon. To the south are Palos Verdes Estates, Rolling Hills Estates, and Rancho Palos Verdes, well-established areas for the well-to-do. A drive along this stretch of coast is sublime, and on a clear day Catalina Island (22 miles away—see p. 232) appears almost close enough to touch.

LOS ANGELES HARBOR

L.A. Harbor, in San Pedro, ranks as the country's busiest import and export trade port, as well as Southern California's major stop for cruise ships. Nearby, the Frank Gehry-designed **Cabrillo Marine Aquarium** (*3720 Stephen White Dr.*) focuses on regional marine life, while the **Los Angeles Maritime Museum** (*Berth 84, foot of 6th St.*) displays nautical memorabilia and artifacts. ∎

Malibu

PERHAPS NO AREA OF THE CITY EPITOMIZES THE L.A. mystique more than Malibu, at the north end of Santa Monica Bay along the P.C.H. (Pacific Coast Highway). There are movie stars galore, extravagant mansions, film sites, exceptional wave breaks (and surfers who come to ride them), and seemingly one natural catastrophe after another—in fact, all the trappings of an action-packed film.

Malibu & the canyons
188 B5

Visitors are often surprised by Malibu's unremarkable retail center of surf shops, fast-food joints, and an ordinary supermarket. However, the fine grains of sand are trod upon daily by the biggest names in the movie business, and have also played key roles in the *Baywatch* television series, in Frankie Avalon and Annette Funicello beach flicks, and in the surf-breaking film *Gidget,* to name but a few.

Originally settled by the Chumash Indians (who were packed off to the missions), the cherished parcel, including its glorious 22 miles of Pacific frontage, was purchased in the late 1880s by wealthy Easterner Frederick Rindge. After Rindge's death in 1905, his widow, May (later known as Queen of Malibu),

spent years fighting to keep the railroad and the highway from getting near the land, but in the late 1920s, P.C.H. came barreling through. In an attempt to recoup some of the financial losses incurred by fighting City Hall, the Rindge family let loose of its beachfront property. The first resident was actress Anna Q. Nilsson, and within a couple of years Malibu Colony was home to Clara Bow, Ronald Colman, Gloria Swanson, and other big names of the era. Today, Malibu Colony is home to a camaraderie of fiercely private celebrities, as well as to artists, writers, and the routinely wealthy, all avidly guarding against trespassers as May Rindge once did. And neither fire, nor landslide, nor earthquake, nor flood can drive any one of them away. ■

Malibu's dreamlike setting has consistently lured the hottest stars, the coolest cars, and the surfer cult.

Along beaches & through canyons

Pacific Coast Highway (also known as P.C.H., or Highway 1), running from Santa Monica to Zuma Beach, is one of Southern California's most scenic drives. And, in addition, celebrities are most likely flying past, or stuck at a traffic light right alongside.

Begin your tour with a breathtaking hit of drama. Pointing north on Santa Monica's Ocean Avenue, cross Wilshire Boulevard, then veer off to the left onto the **California Incline** ramp for a grand Hollywood-style entrance onto the Pacific Coast Highway. An alternative start point is the Santa Monica Pier; the old beach clubs and movie tycoons' mansions still exist here, while the Gold Coast of early years lies just to the north. The wide, sunny sands of **Santa Monica State Beach** are favored by locals.

At Sunset Boulevard, you have the option of detouring to the **Self-Realization Fellowship Lake Shrine** and the **Will Rogers State Historic Park** ❶ (see p. 186). The **Getty Villa** (*17985 P.C.H.*), north of Sunset Boulevard on the right, is scheduled to reopen in 2002 as a showcase for Roman and Greek antiquities. North of Sunset Boulevard the seaside stretch becomes Will Rogers State Beach.

To zoom in on canyon culture and wilderness areas, take a right at Topanga Canyon. Unfortunately, this stunning natural area is often the victim of nature's evils, namely fires, mudslides, and quakes. Heavily forested **Topanga State Park** ❷ (*20825 Entrada Rd.*), east of the boulevard, provides a respite from the road and sensational views. At the community of Topanga—approximately midway between the coast and the San Fernando Valley—you'll feel as if you've tunneled back in time to the 1960s. Alternative lifestylers, artsy-craftsy shops, and a distinctive hippie ambience fill the woodsy air. Take the Old Topanga Canyon Road fork, and just to the west is the **Inn of the Seventh Ray** (*No. 128*), which serves moderately priced, healthful meals in a meditative outdoor atmosphere. Adventurous travelers can continue north on this road to Mulholland Highway; although it is a long, arduous trek through rugged wilderness, the scenery is eye-popping (inquire about road conditions

🅜	See area map pp. 188–89
▶	Santa Monica
↔	56 miles (89.6 km)
🕐	Allow about 30 minutes
▶	Zuma Beach

NOT TO BE MISSED
- Self-Realization Fellowship Lake Shrine
- Topanga State Park
- Malibu Pier
- Broad Beach

Santa Monica

before venturing along this route).

Return back the way you came, turning west at P.C.H. Dating back to the turn of the century, the landmark **Malibu Pier ❸,** between the Sweetwater Canyon and Serra roads, was closed at the time of writing, although plans for its reconstruction are on the books. Adjacent **Surfrider Beach,** the big surfing spot of the 1960s, is still a favorite with surfers today. Pull into one of the nearby lots to visit the **Adamson House and Malibu Lagoon Museum** (see p. 202), then stop at **Malibu Lagoon State Beach,** a bird refuge in surf city.

The road into famous Malibu Beach Colony (south of Malibu Road) is private and heavily guarded, but you stand a good chance of running into celebrities at Malibu Colony Plaza, near the entrance, or when dining on Wolfgang Puck classics at **Granita** (23725 Malibu Rd.). Continuing west from the town center, Pepperdine

University (a.k.a. Surfer's U) and its white cross hover over the highway at your right. The Malibu Gold Coast, with yet more powerhouse homes, runs from Escondido Beach Road to **Paradise Cove ❹.** The latter was the setting for several Frankie and Annette beach-party movies and numerous television shows, and it is home to The Sandcastle, a popular restaurant. **Broad Beach ❺,** about 6 miles west of Paradise Cove, is crammed with celebrity homes—and this time you're allowed to get out and sniff around. Take the path next to 31346 Broad Beach (note that the fence is unlocked from sunrise to sunset).

Backtrack to the expansive sands at **Zuma Beach** (30000 P.C.H.), to watch the sun set over L.A. County. ∎

Malibu Pier

Calamities & car crashes

A range of disasters, from brushfires to rockslides, collapsed bluffs, the occasional riots, and earthquakes have all affected L.A. at one time or another. What else could be expected of a place where many people are either living on the edge or have gone completely over it? But make no mistake, by and large Angelenos thrive on calamities; they're part of the seemingly endless grand movie. After all, there has to be the occasional action or disaster scene to keep things interesting.

A skateboarder nonchalantly wheels past some 1994 earthquake damage.

Unlike many events in this city, most of L.A.'s catastrophes are caused by Mother Nature, who crosses socioeconomic boundaries with no respect for celebrity status or money. In fact, far more natural disasters have occurred in the affluent neighborhoods than in the East and South Central sectors of the city. Ritzy, uppity (albeit heavily insured) Malibu always seems to take a beating when fires and landslides hit the region. The 1961 fire that began in Bel Air and then crossed over the San Diego Freeway into Brentwood was one of the most destructive blazes in the nation's history. Even though most of the world—and many L.A. residents—found it difficult to weep at mink coats reduced to ash, some illustrious artworks (including a van Gogh) were also destroyed.

Over the years, many more wildfires (fueled by Santa Ana winds and Southern California drought conditions) have whipped through the Westside canyons, the Santa Monica Mountains, and—especially—Malibu, which has been engulfed in dozens of deadly fires over the decades. Again, most of the victims have been superwealthy and overinsured, and they take it in their stride, simply rebuilding—an ideal opportunity to redecorate in the latest vogue style.

When rain does descend upon L.A., it's usually a doozy, causing massive flooding and leaving people stranded atop their vehicles or entombed in sinking homes. Landslides are commonplace, particularly along the Pacific Coast Highway between Santa Monica and (again) Malibu; many have been left homeless in the torrents, while other vicious death-and-destruction storms hit in 1978 and 1992. Later in 1992, just as the city was drying out from the winter floods, the Rodney King affair surfaced, triggering riots, looting, fires, mass destruction, and many hard feelings. It seemed L.A. had no sooner healed from that ordeal, than the O.J. Simpson antics hit the forefront. It was all too much to deal with, and the media promptly turned this local trauma into a miniseries and commercial enterprise. O.J.'s Bronco sprint also inspired an era of car chases. Locals revel in these high-speed pursuits, following the action beamed in from television helicopters, hoping for a demolition derby-type climax, but usually disappointed.

And then there are earthquakes. Those that caused major damage hit in 1933, 1971, and 1994, while hundreds—or even thousands—of smaller quakes have struck in between. The earthquakes hit home more than the fires and slides, as they have a pronounced affect on the lower- and middle-class communities. Still, the residents rebuild. Only recent arrivals go running back to wherever they came from; native Angelenos and long-timers don't budge—they just do lunch. ■

Top right: A tanker plane deployed to help quell the 1996 Malibu fire.
Right: For those who live on the edge of the ocean, storms can be terrifying.

More places to visit in Santa Monica, Venice, & Malibu

ADAMSON HOUSE & MALIBU LAGOON MUSEUM

Rhoda Rindge (the Queen of Malibu's daughter) and her husband, Merritt Adamson, were the original owners of this gorgeous Moorish and Mission Revival home. Designed by architect Stiles O. Clements, the 1929 romantic beachfront residence features intricate tilework (with tiles from the old Malibu Potteries), detailed ironwork, handcrafted woodwork, and other highly decorative touches. Furnishings are in keeping with the Spanish/Moorish theme, and the garden area blossoms around a central pool and fountain. Everything is pretty much the same as Rhoda left it when she died in 1962. Docent tours lead visitors through the home and grounds, offering an insight into the lavish lifestyle enjoyed by the Rindges before the celebrities took over. Self-guided tours are also available.

🅼 188 B5 ✉ 23200 Pacific Coast Highway ☎ 310/456-8432 🕒 Closed Sun.–Tues. 💲 $

MONTANA AVENUE

One of Santa Monica's ritziest shopping thoroughfares is Montana Avenue, bounded by Wilshire and San Vicente Boulevards, and by 7th and 17th Streets. Upscale boutiques, stylish cafés, hair salons, fine arts and hand-crafted goods, Italian footwear, yoga centers, garden shops, and high-end home furnishings occupy this strip, which lies off the beaten path and cuts through a residential area. The **Aero Theater,** a classic neighborhood movie house, has managed to remain independent and mono-screened.

🅼 189 D5

MUSEUM OF FLYING

More than 30 vintage aircraft are stored (and restored) in this three-level building at Santa Monica Airport, right on the site where Donald Douglas built the first DC3. Visitors can get up close to such flying machines as a 1924 Douglas World Cruiser biplane (the first airplane to circle the globe), World War II fighters, and modern jets, and most of the craft are flight-ready. Other diversions are an interactive flight area, Donald Douglas memorabilia displays, a library, a gift shop, and a

theater that screens aviation-themed films.

🅼 189 E5 ✉ 2772 Donald Douglas Loop North ☎ 310/392-8822 🕒 Closed Mon.–Tues. 💲 $$

MUSEUM OF JURASSIC TECHNOLOGY

Make no mistake, this Culver City museum is not a tribute to movieland's *Jurassic Park* and nor does it resemble a theme-park ride. Instead, it is more of a monument to strangeness (the museum decrees it "nature as metaphor"). Exhibits range from paranormal to fantasia to real life. Examples include the piercing devil bat, which uses radar to fly through solid mass and a bed-wetting cure that involves dead mice on toast. Kitschy temporary exhibits have involved minuscule figures mounted on sewing needles (viewable through microscopes).

🅼 189 E5 ✉ 9341 Venice Blvd. ☎ 310/836-6131 🕒 Closed Mon.–Wed. Open until 8 p.m. Thurs. 💲 $$

PARAMOUNT RANCH

If you take the Mulholland Highway route suggested in the drive tour on pp. 198–99, it's worthwhile stopping at this Agoura ranch, which has served as a backdrop for Westerns since the 1920s. The permanently set Western Town—with general store, wood shop, railway tracks, cemetery, and barn—has been used in dozens of films and television series, including *Dr. Quinn, Medicine Woman; Have Gun, Will Travel;* and *The Rifleman.* Hiking and picnicking are allowed on the 700-acre wooded property.

🅼 188 B6 ✉ 2813 Cornell Rd. ☎ 818/597-9192

RAMIREZ CANYON PARK

It costs a small fortune to tour Barbra's former four-home Malibu compound, which now houses an environmental think tank. One-hour walking tours take you through three of the homes and around the lush grounds and botanical gardens.

🅼 188 A5 ✉ 5750 Ramirez Canyon Rd. ☎ 310/589-2850 🕒 Open by appointment only 💲 $$$$$ ■

The San Fernando and San Gabriel Valleys, often thought of as dull, actually hold great treasures, including exquisite art and architecture, thrill-filled studios, celebrity-studded cemeteries, and the famous Valley Girl.

San Fernando & San Gabriel Valleys

Introduction & map **204–205**
Universal Studios Hollywood **206–207**
More studios **208**
Forest Lawn Memorial Park **209**
Pasadena 210–221
Rose Bowl **211**
Arroyo Seco **211**
The Gamble House **212–14**
Pasadena Historical Museum **215**
Other historic districts **215**
Norton Simon Museum **216–17**
Old Pasadena to the Playhouse District Walk **218–19**
Pacific Asia Museum **220**
California Institute of Technology **221**
The Huntington **222–23**
More places to visit in the San Fernando & San Gabriel Valleys **224**
Hotels & restaurants **256–57**

Not exactly your average Valley Girl

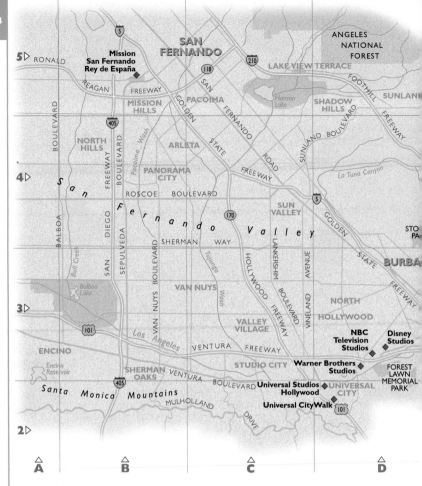

San Fernando & San Gabriel Valleys

THE SAN FERNANDO AND SAN GABRIEL VALLEYS, SKIRTING L.A.'S EASTERN and northern edges, often surprise visitors with their diversity. From the mundane (and somewhat bleak) suburbs and the contemporary estates, there is a socioeconomic leap to Craftsman architecture and old money, bridged by a smattering of amusement-parklike studios and star-filled graveyards. It's so L.A.!

SAN FERNANDO VALLEY

The sprawling, ever expanding San Fernando Valley does not have a particularly good reputation with locals, and most Angelenos tend to look down their noses at addresses in the "Valley." Although it's true that there is a lot of boring suburbia, celebrities and professionals long ago established roots in Encino,

Sherman Oaks, and other neighborhoods that edge up around Mulholland Drive, where the Santa Monica Mountains draw the line between the Valley and L.A. Annexed to the City of L.A. in 1915, today, the Valley is crammed with middle-class tract-type housing and endless strip malls, with some pretty hip restaurants and shops mixed in.

SAN GABRIEL VALLEY

The San Gabriel Valley, on the other hand, is well into old age—and quite happy about it. No Angeleno would dare refer to this section in the same derisive tone that San Fernando Valley incurs—this valley holds its

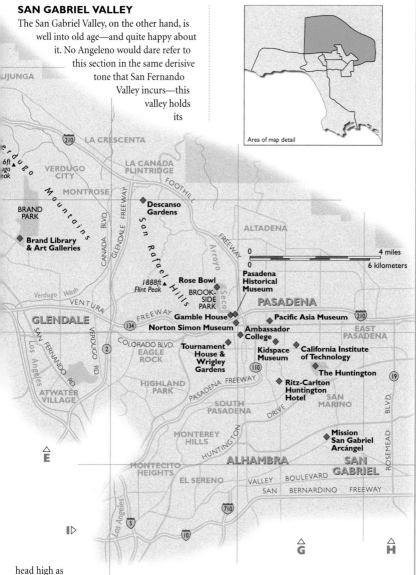

Area of map detail

head high as Greater L.A.'s first settlement. Mission San Gabriel Arcángel was established here in 1771, and Pasadena and San Marino, at the base of the San Gabriel Mountains, have been bastions of gentility, culture, and fortunes since the turn of the 20th century. The high concentration of Craftsman-style architecture and stately houses, along with the splendid Norton Simon

Museum and the Huntington cultural complex, are sure indicators that this area is one that prizes tradition. Even the Rose Bowl Parade dates back to the 1890s.

Filling the gap between the two valleys are the hectic film and television studios of Universal City and beautiful downtown Burbank, plus the far less lively Forest Lawn Cemetery in Glendale. ■

Universal Studios Hollywood

MILLIONS OF VISITORS FLOCK TO UNIVERSAL STUDIOS Hollywood annually, ranking it alongside the Disney kingdoms in the popularity stakes. Though you probably won't see any real moviemaking on the enormous 420-acre complex (the tourist portion is largely theme-park oriented), you'll certainly get up close and personal with sets, scenes, special effects, and television and film memorabilia (and, on occasion, some celebrities). And you'll also have the opportunity to experience some pretty amazing action-feature thrill rides.

Film pioneer Carl Laemmle moved his studio from Hollywood to this former 230-acre chicken ranch in 1915 in order to have a bigger backlot. In the early days 25-cent tours were offered—that is, until they became a distraction to the real business of moviemaking and were discontinued. In the ensuing years Universal merged with International Pictures, then with MCA, which reestablished the tours in 1964. By that time director Alfred Hitchcock was working out of the studio, later to be joined by George Lucas and Steven Spielberg, along with their collective stage sets and special effects. Today's VIP Experience trolley tour is the more expensive option open to visitors, but it allows access to behind-the-scenes areas as well as preferential entrance to rides.

TRAM TOUR
Ride down the long escalator near the entrance and hop on a tram for the narrated backlot tour. You'll cruise around sound stages and prop areas and be shown special-effects demos and movie sets. The sets alone provide a fascinating trek, affording Hollywood-style renditions of old Mexico, the Wild West, the homes of Beaver Cleaver and the Munsters, a New York street, and America's creepiest motel, The Bates, of *Psycho* fame. Tramsters will also experience the

parting of the Red Sea, a realistic-feeling 8.3 earthquake, a collapsing bridge, and a flash flood. They will also glimpse the waters where the killer-shark Jaws lived, and the Flintstones' town of Bedrock.

STUDIO CENTER
More long escalators lead down to the Studio Center, where you'll run into long lines for **Jurassic Park—The Ride.** Opened in 1996, this technological marvel cost $100,000,000 to create and bring to fruition. Along with the colossal five-story dinosaurs, visitors are treated to an 84-foot vertical plunge—the fastest water descent ever built. **Backdraft,** based on the movie of the same name, affords the terrifying sensation of life inside a fiery furnace. Happy, gentler entertainments are the **E.T. Adventure** and **Lucy: A Tribute,** a heart-shaped treasure chest of Lucille Ball memorabilia.

ENTERTAINMENT CENTER
This upper-level center houses some of the most sensational shows. The big buzz is **Terminator 2 3-D** (again, based on the film), opened in 1999, and combining live action with virtual effects—in short, you become part of the adventure. Billed as the world's most advanced film-based theme park attraction, it boasts the

Universal Studios Hollywood
- 204 D2
- Hollywood Freeway (US 101) at Lankershim Blvd.
- 818/622-3801
- $$$$$

These fearsome tentacles in the Terminator 2 3-D production seem a little too real to the screeching audience.

world's largest 3-D installation that not only was the first to use a triple-screen configuration but also incorporates original footage and specially created robots. **Back to the Future—The Ride** offers more techno-weirdness as participants journey through time in a DeLorean flight simulator.

Waterworld presents all the wateriness and spectacle of Kevin Costner's absurdly expensive flop and is far more entertaining than the screen version.

UNIVERSAL CITYWALK

Intended to give visitors a tour through urban life, CityWalk offers a sterile view of L.A. and its neighborhoods. There are no muggers, no gangs, no worries.

Opened in 1993, the two-block-long pedestrian strip links Universal Studios with the 6,000-seat Universal Amphitheater and the 18-screen Universal City multiplex cinemas. Along the route, visitors are treated to a whistle-stop tour through a variety of L.A. neighborhoods—including Venice Beach, Hollywood, Beverly Hills, and Melrose Avenue—via whimsical changing facades, landscapes, and decor. Props include towering palms, a genuine sand beach, vintage crackle-tube neon (from the Museum of Neon Art—see p. 68), and classic signage. More than 60 specialty restaurants, shops, and clubs line the walkway. Some of the best entertainment here is provided by top-caliber street-performing puppeteers, musicians, jugglers, and magicians. ∎

Universal CityWalk

🅼 204 D2 & inside front cover map C5

☎ 818/622-4455

✉ Universal Center Dr.

The seven dwarfs hold up the facade of Disney's Studio Office Building.

More studios

BURBANK AND THE SAN FERNANDO VALLEY ARE TWO OF the areas to which the Hollywood studios relocated. Universal Studios is certainly the biggest, busiest, and most commercial of the lots, but those who just want a no-frills peek behind the scenes might like to check out other studios nearby.

Warner Brothers Studios

🅰 204 B3 & inside back cover map C5

✉ 4000 Warner Blvd.

☎ 818/954-1669

🕐 Closed Sat.–Sun.

💲 $$$$$

NBC Television Studios

🅰 204 D3

✉ 3000 W. Alameda Ave.

☎ 818/840-3537

🕐 Closed Sat.–Sun.

💲 $$

Disney Studios

🅰 204 D3

✉ 500 S. Buena Vista St.

WARNER BROTHERS STUDIOS

The pricey VIP Tour through Warner Brothers Studios gives visitors a more serious look behind the scenes. Departing from Gate Four, the two-hour odyssey emphasizes the technical side of the business, moving through prop and costume shops, sound stages, backlot sets, and a museum with studio memorabilia. Whenever possible, live filming is included in the package. The studio houses 30 sound stages, including the *E.R.* set. Reserve in advance; children under ten years of age are not allowed.

NBC TELEVISION STUDIOS

Famed as the home of *The Tonight Show* (now starring funnyman Jay Leno), NBC offers a 70-minute tour through its wardrobe and makeup departments, prop shop, sound and special-effects rooms, and sound stages. You may get into Studio Three, where *The Tonight Show* is taped. If you want to be sure of a spot in the show's peanut gallery, write ahead for free tickets; otherwise, seats are handed out on a first-come, first-served basis, and the wait in line can be a long one.

DISNEY STUDIOS

Even though no tours (and no admittance) are on the books at Disney's animation studios, you can see bits and pieces from the outside world. Note Studio Office Building, designed by Michael Graves, in which the Seven Dwarfs hold up the roof. ∎

Forest Lawn Memorial Park

EVELYN WAUGH'S SCATHING SATIRE ON DEATH, *THE LOVED One,* was based on the denial and excesses at Forest Lawn. Set on 300 acres, the cemetery was founded in 1917 by Dr. Hubert Eaton, who envisioned a heavenly parklike setting for those who insisted on pretending to die. Forest Lawn soon became the best place in town to rest eternally. As such, the plots became coveted by celebrities and society's upper crust. Some of the well-known departed include George Burns, Gracie Allen, Walt Disney, W.C. Fields, Errol Flynn, Jean Harlow, Clark Gable, Carole Lombard, and Nat King Cole.

Forest Lawn Memorial Park

204 D3

1712 S. Glendale Ave.

818/241-4151

Prominently placed amid the extravagant landscaping is a plethora of Carrara-marble statuary and divine stained glass. One of the more awesome sights is the grand **Resurrection and Crucifixion Hall.** Housed within is artist Jan Styka's "The Crucifixion," one of the world's largest religious paintings, measuring 195 by 45 feet; it is unveiled with pomp every hour on the hour. A companion work, Robert Clark's "The Resurrection," commissioned by Eaton, is ceremonially unveiled at the same time. Eaton's stained-glass replica of Leonardo's "Last Supper" can be ogled in the Memorial Court of Honor in the Great Mausoleum (along with the tombs of Gable, Lombard, and Harlow). This is unveiled each half-hour. The Freedom Mausoleum also offers hospitality to deceased celebrity guests; Errol Flynn rests just outside the doors (reputedly with a few bottles of whiskey).

The cemetery's museum displays an eclectic range of artifacts such as medieval armor, ancient coins, a gem collection, photos, and illustrations. Also on the grounds are two replica English churches and one Scottish church (in 1940, former President Ronald Reagan married Jane Wyman at Wee Kirk o' the Heather, a replica 14th-century Scottish church), as well as the Court of David, with a reproduc-

tion of Michelangelo's famous statue. A map and self-guided tour can be picked up at the museum. Forest Lawn's Hollywood Hills branch *(6300 Forest Lawn Dr.)* is a last stop for other big names. ∎

Paying respects to the dead is not necessarily a solemn affair, especially at this celebrity-heavy parklike cemetery.

The San Gabriel Mountains rise behind Pasadena's baroque-domed city hall.

Pasadena

Notable for its annual Tournament of Roses Parade and Rose Bowl football game, as well as for its academically brilliant California Institute of Technology, Pasadena is also a community of stately homes, prized art and architecture, and a trendy retail district.

With a location at the base of the San Gabriel Mountains, and about 15 minutes north of downtown Los Angeles, Pasadena first came to light as a sought-after resort town in the 1880s. The area had briefly been settled earlier, in 1873, as a farming community by a group of expat Hoosiers, who initially sent teacher-turned-journalist Daniel M. Berry out West to find a climate less harsh than that of Indiana. Berry took one look at what was then Rancho San Pasqual and knew he'd found the perfect place. The Indiana Colony was renamed Pasadena after a Chippewa Indian term that roughly translates as crown of the valley.

Citrus groves, rose bushes, and vineyards soon gave way to the railroad, which brought a steady onslaught of wealthy Easterners who wanted to escape the cold winters back home. Elegant hotels sprang up, real estate boomed. New residents included top-level tycoons and industrialists such as William J. Wrigley, Henry E. Huntington, and Adolphus Busch. The big names and sunny, citrusy environment soon beckoned artists, musicians, writers, and other salon types. Today's Pasadena offers an intriguing mix of historic structures and old money, combined with lofty cultural and educational facilities. ■

Rose Bowl

To most people, the Rose Bowl is Pasadena's most famous icon. Although the Myron Hunt-designed stadium wasn't built until 1922, the fun actually began much earlier. In 1890, the Pasadena Valley Hunt Club (formed for ladies and gentlemen who wished to frolic outdoors) hosted the first Tournament of Roses Parade and games. An audience of about 2,000 locals came to watch a parade of flower-adorned horse-drawn buggies, followed by tugs of war, footraces, and a game known as the tourney of rings. Combining the tourney of rings with all the posies on display caused the parade's president to tag the event the Tournament of Roses. These days more than a million spectators attend the parade (held on New Year's Day), lining the 5.5-mile route along Colorado Avenue; another 450 million from more than 100 countries tune in on their TVs or modems. Each float is decorated with an average 100,000 blossoms.

The first Rose Bowl football game was played in 1902 in Tournament Park (University of

Michigan 49, Stanford 0), while the inaugural game in the completed Rose Bowl Stadium took place in 1923 (USC 14, Penn State 3). Apart from the New Year's Day hoopla, the 104,000-seat stadium hosts the UCLA Bruins home games and other special events (such as the 1994 Soccer World Cup Final and 1999 Women's Soccer World Cup Final). It is also the site of a terrific flea market on the second Sunday of each month. ■

Viewers around the world see the painstakingly crafted, flower-bedecked floats.

Rose Bowl
⬛ 205 F3 & inside back cover E5
✉ 1001 Rose Bowl Dr., Pasadena
☎ 626/577-3100

Arroyo Seco

Arroyo Seco
⬛ 205 F3

The Spanish name Arroyo Seco translates as "dry riverbed," and refers to a deep canyon expanse that stretches from the San Gabriel Mountains all the way to Los Angeles. At its northern edge is Caltech's Jet Propulsion Laboratory (JPL), home of NASA and the Sojourner robot that enabled earthlings to view the planet Mars from their own living rooms. The southern end of this area was changed forever when the Arroyo

Seco Parkway—L.A.'s first freeway, now called the Pasadena Freeway—blasted through in 1939. Arroyo landmarks include the **Rose Bowl** (see above), the nearby **Gamble House** and other extraordinary Craftsman bungalows (see pp. 212–214), and the Art Center College of Design. Spanning the ravine is the renovated 1913 **Colorado Street Bridge,** all curves and arches, and measuring 150 feet high and 1,468 feet long. ■

The Gamble House

THE ROSE BOWL MAY BE PASADENA'S BIG ICON TO SOME, but to architecture buffs the Gamble House (parallel to the 300 blocks of N. Orange Grove Boulevard, just north of Arroyo Terrace) is the city's claim to fame. Jointly managed by the city of Pasadena and the University of Southern California's School of Architecture, this 1908 residence is a renowned masterpiece of Craftsman-era styling and in 1971 was designated a national historic landmark.

The Gamble House

- 205 F3
- 4 Westmoreland Place, Pasadena
- 626/793-3334
- Closed Mon.–Wed.
- $$

David and Mary Gamble (members of the Proctor and Gamble family) of Cincinnati were part of the flock of Easterners who used Pasadena as a winter refuge. Choosing a lot near the Arroyo Seco, slightly removed from Millionaires' Row, the Gambles commissioned architect brothers Charles and Henry Greene to create the ultimate California bungalow. The Greene brothers ascribed heavily to the English-born Arts and Crafts movement of the time, and as they had already developed a chunk of nearby Arroyo Terrace, they threw their talents into the new project.

Incorporating function with aesthetics and precise detail, Gamble House epitomizes master-ful planning and craftsmanship, and all that a big budget can buy. Inspired by Swiss-chalet and Japanese influences, the three-story house features broad overhanging eaves, open sleeping porches, wide terraces, and airy rooms. Shingle siding, hand-rubbed woods (oak, teak, mahogany, maple, and Port Orford cedar), built-in cabinetry, carvings, leaded stained glass, and outdoor landscaping are all meticulously detailed, designed, and maintained. Almost every single element was painstakingly crafted in the Greenes' Pasadena studios. Much of the furniture (and research library) is housed at the Huntington Library in San Marino (see pp. 222–223), although the on-site

Gamble House architects: Henry (above) and Charles (facing right) Greene

This much-heralded Craftsman-era masterwork evokes the elegance and precise detailing of the Arts and Crafts movement.

Right: The Craftsman style of the Gamble House extends to the interior.

bookstore (in the former garage) stocks various books and brochures about the Greene brothers and the Arts and Crafts movement. ■

MORE CRAFTSMAN ARCHITECTURE

Greene and Greene didn't quit with the Gamble House, nor had they even begun there: The illustrious brothers had already bestowed their Craftsman-style artistry on a number of the area's homes. The so-called Greene and Greene Neighborhood is known primarily for its Arts and Crafts masterpieces, although a few other architects—including Frank Lloyd Wright, Lloyd Wright (his son), and Myron Hunt—also saw a piece of the action.

Westmoreland Place

The Greene brothers built the **Cole House** (2 Westmoreland Place) two years prior to the Gamble House next door. Currently used as a Unitarian Neighborhood

Church office, the building incorporated several Greene firsts, such as a porte cochere. Other Gamble neighbors are the 1913 **Ayers House** (No. 5), designed by Edwin Bergstrom, who also assisted with the Pasadena Civic Auditorium; and the 1911 **Jesse Hoyt Smith House** (No. 6), designed by Myron Hunt and Elmer Grey, whose simultaneous project was the San Marino Huntington Mansion (Hunt was also later architect of the Rose Bowl Stadium). The gate at the northern edge of this street was designed by the Greenes in 1917, alerting passersby (and, ultimately, tour buses) to this very special place.

Arroyo Terrace

South of the Gamble House is the Arroyo Terrace loop (also referred to as Little Switzerland), a treasured colony of Greene and Greene Arts and Crafts creations, including Charles Greene's own family home. As you round the loop, your first

encounter is with the 1907 **Ranney House** (*No. 440, corner of Orange Grove Blvd.*), the home of Mary Ranney, a draftsperson for the Greene firm who did much of her own design work. Next come the 1905 **Willett House** (*No. 424*), ultimately disguised as a Spanish Colonial remodel, and the chaletlike 1906 **Hawks House** (*No. 408*), which exhibits the Greenes's fieldstone touch. The meticulously restored 1903 **Van Rosem-Neill House** (*No. 400*), with a wall of arroyo boulders and burnt clinker brick, was featured in a 1915 edition of Gustav Stickley's *The Craftsman* magazine. The 1903 **White Sisters House** (*No. 370*) was built by Charles Greene for his three sisters-in-law (subsequent owners stuccoed the original exterior shingles). Right next door (*No. 440*) is Charles Greene's 1902 home, fitted with all of his favorite touches, including clinker brick, fieldstone, and a low-pitched roof; it was renovated several times by

On the small side for L.A., Frank Lloyd Wright's Millard House is also known as La Miniatura.

the architect. Greene's neighbor to the other side is the **Duncan-Irwin House** (*240 N. Grand Ave.*). Built as a single-level bungalow in 1901, it was expanded five years later to a whopping 6,000 square feet with mountain- and arroyo-view window banks, and is an exceptionally noteworthy Greene brothers design. The **Culbertson House,** across the street (*235 N. Grand Ave.*), underwent a 1950s remodel but still features the clinker-brick wall, a pergola, and a Tiffany-glassed front door. Also on Grand Avenue is a specification house commissioned by Josephine Van Rosem (*No. 210*), along with her own on Arroyo Terrace. **Hutchins House** (*No. 206*), an 1895 Queen Anne cottage tossed in with the bungalows, and architect Myron Hunt's 1905 home (*No. 200, near the intersection with Arroyo Terrace*) complete the lineup.

PROSPECT PARK

Prospect Park, north of the Gamble House, showcases assorted other treasures. The Greene and Greene circa-1910 stone entrance gates at the intersection of Orange Grove and Prospect Boulevards signal your arrival. The old camphor tree-lined neighborhood was developed by John C. Bentz, whose own well-preserved Greene brothers home (*No. 657*) was constructed in 1906. Mission-style **Hindry House** (*No. 781*), built by yet another duo of local brother architects, Alfred and Arthur Heineman, is big enough to be seen behind the shrubbery. An unexpected surprise is **Millard House,** along narrow Prospect Crescent (*No. 645*), a smallish concrete-block home designed in 1923 by Frank Lloyd Wright (son, Lloyd, added a studio later). Also known as La Miniatura, this ravine-set dwelling is best viewed from Rosemont Avenue. ■

Pasadena Historical Museum

205 F3

470 W. Walnut St., Pasadena

626/577-1660

Closed Mon.–Wed. Tours Thurs.–Sun. 1–4 p.m.

$$

Feynes House, the museum's neo-classic home, designed in 1905 by Robert Farquhar and known simply as "the mansion," is perhaps the grandest treasure in its collection. Situated just below the Greene and Greene Neighborhood, at the beginning of Millionaires' Row, the 18-room home (former residence of the Finnish consul) is furnished with many original 15th- and 16th-century antiques and works of art. Delve down into the basement to view photo exhibits, early newspapers, and other memorabilia that trace Pasadena's history. The **Finnish Folk Art Museum,** in a separate chaletlike building in the lovely gardens, features handmade furnishings, folk art, and decorative items that once belonged to Finnish Consul Paloheimo. ∎

Finnish folk art combined with local history

Other historic districts

Pasadena lays claim to more than 600 architectural landmarks, from grand mansions and smaller Craftsman bungalows to Spanish Revival and beaux arts buildings. Many are encompassed in various designated districts, in downtown as well as the surrounding areas. For self-guided tours, maps, and information, contact the Pasadena Convention and Visitors Bureau.

In the early 1900s, when wealthy Easterners arrived, they built palatial resort homes with showplace gardens along Orange Grove Boulevard, subsequently dubbed Millionaires' Row. The soaring property values of more recent decades have, unfortunately, seen most of the old mansions leveled to make way for more contemporary homes and condos. Survivors include chewing-gum magnate William J. Wrigley's **Tournament House and Wrigley Gardens** *(391 S. Orange Grove Blvd.),* now headquarters of the Tournament of Roses Association, and **Ambassador College** *(300 W. Green St.),* with four restored mansions open to the public.

The tree-shaded Oak Knoll area, southeast of Millionaires' Row, also attracted turn-of-the-century money. Splendid homes and estates were built here, as was the superbly restored **Ritz-Carlton Huntington Hotel** *(1401 S. Oak Knoll Ave.),* one of the grand old resorts. A variety of fine residences line Hillcrest Avenue, including two designed by Greene and Greene.

Bungalow Heaven (north of I-210) and the Historic Highlands district are filled with hundreds of renovated and restored middle-class Craftsman-era homes, and offer annual home tours. The downtown area straddles Colorado Boulevard, from Old Pasadena through the City Hall area to the Playhouse District (for more details of downtown sights, see the walking tour on pp. 218–19). ∎

Pasadena Convention & Visitors Bureau

205 F/G3

171 S. Los Robles Ave., Pasadena

626/795-9311

Closed Sun.

Norton Simon Museum

Simon Norton Museum
 205 F3
✉ 411 W. Colorado Blvd., Pasadena
☎ 626/449-6840
🕐 Closed Mon.–Tues.
💲 $$

WHILE EVERYONE ELSE IN THE 1950s WAS POURING THEIR money into backyard bomb shelters, industrialist Norton Simon (1907–1993) was investing in painting and sculpture by Degas, Gauguin, Cézanne, and Renoir. In the 1960s, Simon added old masters, more Impressionists, and modern artworks to his collection, and in the 1970s he focused on masterpieces from Southeast Asia and India. His holdings, collected over a 25-year period, evolved into what would become one of the world's last comprehensive private art collections.

A major renovation program shows the Norton Simon collection to its best advantage.

Simon not only had a fat wallet for serious shopping but also possessed formidable business acumen. By the time he was 24 years old, the college dropout decided to invest in a bankrupt orange juice-bottling plant in Fullerton, California. The juice plant was soon joined by other concerns, first under the umbrella of the Hunt Foods Company and eventually under Norton Simon Inc., a multi-industry empire that included McCall's Publishing, Max Factor, and Canada Dry Corporation. Still, art remained Simon's true love and was, in his opinion, a powerful tool of communication.

Simon loaned his collection to various other museums before taking over leadership of the Pasadena Art Museum in 1974 and reorga-

nizing it as the Norton Simon Museum. The 1969 museum has recently completed a major renovation by architect Frank Gehry. Interior improvements include heightened ceilings, more intimate gallery spaces, track lighting, oak hardwood flooring, and a much lighter look and feel. A major exterior change is the completely relandscaped 7-acre sculpture garden. Inspired by Monet's gardens at Giverny—a major focus of the Norton Simon collections—landscape architect Nancy Goslee Powers has traded the earlier tiled rectangular reflecting pool for a natural pond filled with water lilies and surrounded by plants indigenous to the environment. Sculptures will be reinstalled in the new outdoor area, including many works that didn't fit within the earlier design.

THE COLLECTIONS

The permanent collection consists of seven centuries of European art, spanning the Renaissance to the 20th century, with particular attention on Impressionist and Postimpressionist paintings. Remarkable South Asian sculptures complement the Western pieces, and much of the work will be reconfigured along with the renovations.

Most visitors head straight for the 19th- and 20th-century galleries

to the left of the main entrance. Here, there are more than 100 works by Edgar Degas, including paintings, drawings, pastels, mono-types, and a rare complete set of bronze sculptures cast from the artist's waxes. Other prominent works are Monet's "The Artist's Garden at Vétheuil," Renoir's "Pont des Arts, Paris" and "The Artist's Studio, Rue Saint-Georges," Pissarro's "The Boulevard des Fosses, Pontoise," Cézanne's "Tulips in a Vase," van Gogh's "Portrait of a Peasant," and Gauguin's "Tahitian Woman and Boy," as well as works by Corot, Rodin, Vuillard, and Seurat. The 20th-century gallery also has paintings by Picasso, Klee, Matisse, Modigliani, Braque, and Rousseau, and sculptures by Aristide Maillol and Henry Moore.

On the other side of the main entrance are the Renaissance galleries, which host gilded panels and Italian altarpieces, work by Botticelli and Raphael, Bellini and El Greco portraits, and other famous devotional images. The 17th and 18th centuries are well represented by masterworks such as Rubens' "David Slaying Goliath," Rembrandt's "Self Portrait" and "Portrait of a Bearded Man in a Wide-Brimmed Hat," and Jan Steen's "Wine is a Mocker," along with paintings by Nicolas de Largillière, Jean Honoré Fragonard, Jean Siméon Chardin, Francesco Guardi, and Francisco de Goya.

On the lower level, Indian and Southeast Asian pieces have been rearranged according to medium and geographical origin. ■

Paul Gauguin's "Self Portrait with a Palette" (1893), one of Norton Simon's many collected treasures on display

Old Pasadena to the Playhouse District walk

Pasadena's downtown area is broken up into various sections, all of them historical. Once left to languish, this neighborhood was revitalized in the 1990s into one of the trendiest in L.A. County; in particular, the stretch from Old Pasadena to the Playhouse District makes for a delightful stroll. From end to end, you'll come upon hundreds of elegant bistros, trendy sidewalk cafés, antiques outlets, fashionable boutiques, used-book and music shops, eclectic clothing and gift stores, and nightclubs, theaters, and museums. Maps are available from the Pasadena Convention and Visitors Bureau (see p. 215), or if you prefer to ride, Pasadena ARTS buses provide a free daily service along this route.

Start your stroll in Old Pasadena, a 20-block historic area bounded by Pasadena and Marengo Avenues, Walnut Street, and Del Mar Boulevard, and listed on the National Register of Historic Places. **One Colorado,** anchoring the west end, features dozens of shops, clubs, and eateries reeking with historic ambience. On either side of Colorado Boulevard

you'll see a trove of vintage brick buildings filled with boutiques and cafés.

At Raymond Avenue, turn right to view the domed and turreted **Castle Green ❶** (N. 99 S.), one of Pasadena's grand 1890s resort hotels, now private housing. The colorful 1935 Spanish Colonial **Santa Fe Railroad Station ❷** (N. 222 S.) up ahead, used to be

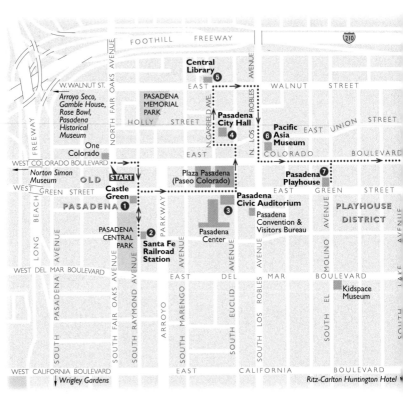

the main terminus for cross-country travelers before L.A.'s Union Station was built.

Head back to Green Street, then turn right again, leaving Old Pasadena as you cross Marengo Avenue. The 1932 **Pasadena Civic Auditorium** ❸ *(300 E. Green St.)* is home to the Pasadena Symphony Orchestra. Between Green Street and Colorado Boulevard, Paseo Colorado—an open-air "urban village"—is replacing the 1970s **Plaza Pasadena.** When complete in 2001, the new complex will feature retail shops, a multi-screen movie complex, alfresco eateries, and a residential community. Head north up Euclid and cross Colorado before turning left on Union Street then right up Garfield Avenue for a look at the 1925 **Pasadena City Hall** ❹ *(100 N. Garfield Ave.),* a domed building with a formal garden. The adjacent Robinson Memorial pays homage to athlete Jackie Robinson. Proceed three blocks up Garfield Avenue to the Renaissance-style **Central**

> ⓜ Also see area map pp. 204–205
> ➤ One Colorado, Old Pasadena
> ⬌ 4 miles (6.4 km)
> ⏱ Allow 30–45 minutes
> ➤ Caltech campus
>
> **NOT TO BE MISSED**
> * Castle Green
> * Pasadena City Hall
> * Robinson Memorial
> * Pacific Asia Museum
> * Pasadena Playhouse

Library ❺ *(285 E. Walnut St.).* Built in 1927, it is the northern anchor to the Civic Center area. Facing the library, walk right to Los Robles Avenue, then make another right to take you back to Colorado Boulevard. At the corner is the **Pacific Asia Museum** ❻ *(see p. 220),* that focuses on the arts and culture of East Asia and the Pacific Basin. Continuing left along Colorado Boulevard, you enter the Playhouse District, named for the **Pasadena Playhouse** ❼ *(39 S. El Molino Ave., between Colorado Blvd. & Green St., off to the right three blocks down Colorado).* Founded in 1917, the Playhouse is a registered historic landmark.

The tree-lined South Lake Avenue District, a right turn at Lake Avenue at the eastern end of the Playhouse District, features ten blocks of trendy shops and Continental restaurants reaching all the way to California Boulevard. Two blocks left along California Boulevard is the **Caltech campus** ❽ *(see p. 221).* ∎

Many prominent actors got their careers off to a start at the Pasadena Playhouse.

Pacific Asia Museum

AN UNLIKELY LOOKING ANCHOR TO THE PLAYHOUSE District, this Northern Chinese Imperial-style palace was designed in 1924 by architects Mayberry, Marston, and Van Pelt. The building, constructed for art-lover Grace Nicholson, is on the National Register of Historic Places, which cites its 1920s Period Revival design. Today, the palace houses the Pacific Asia Museum, which is devoted exclusively to the arts and cultures of the Far East and the Pacific Basin.

Pacific Asia Museum

- 205 G3
- ✉ 46 N. Los Robles Ave., Pasadena
- ☎ 626/449-2742
- 🕐 Closed Mon.–Tues.
- 💲 $$. Free 3rd Sat. of each month

THE BUILDING

The Chinese Treasure House features a green-tile roof (upturned to ward off evil), enemy-watching ceramic guard dogs, a meditative central courtyard with statuary, specimen rocks and plants, and a meditative koi pond.

Nicholson originally collected and sold Native American basketry and artifacts, and dealt well enough in it to indulge her appetite for Asian art, including a temple to house it all. The Treasure House served as Nicholson's remarkable home until her death in 1948, when she bequeathed it to the city of Pasadena. The pseudo-Chinese palace then housed the Pasadena Art Museum until it moved over to the present Norton Simon Museum (see pp. 216–217).

THE MUSEUM

The Pacific Asia Museum was established at the Treasure House in 1971 and has a permanent collection consisting of more than 17,000 pieces. Traveling exhibits are also on display. The research library (open on selected days or by appointment) has thousands of volumes on its shelves. A gift shop sells art books, children's literature, cards, jewelry, textiles, and other items. The Family Free Days (third Saturday of each month) also offer special events such as children's workshops, food-tasting, and music and dance performances. ■

California Institute of Technology

ALBERT EINSTEIN ONCE TAUGHT AT THIS WORLD-FAMOUS educational facility, where a student body of about 2,000 whiz kids immerse themselves in the school's renowned science, engineering, and astronomy programs. Faculty and alumni have laid collective claim to 27 Nobel prizes and copious National Medal of Science and Technology awards. Achievements hailing from within the Caltech walls include the development of aircraft design and the principles of flight, the creation of the Jet Propulsion Laboratory for NASA, and the invention of the Richter scale.

California Institute of Technology

🄰 205 G2

✉ 1200 E. California Blvd., Pasadena

☎ 626/395-6327 or 626/395-6977 (earthquake hotline)

$ Tours free

Founded in 1891 as the Throop University, the school originally focused on manual arts rather than scientific endeavors—that is until 1907, when astronomer George Ellery Hale joined the board of trustees and pushed for the transformation. Luckily for the world, Throop took his advice and in 1920 became the internationally acclaimed California Institute of Technology (Caltech).

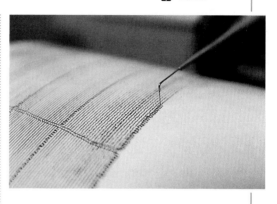

THE CAMPUS

Now occupying 124 acres southeast of downtown Pasadena and just north of San Marino, Caltech's Spanish- and Italian Renaissance-style buildings were laid out to harmonize with the surrounding landscape. The initial design came off the drawing boards of Myron Hunt and Elmer Grey, with later work taken over by Bertram Grosvenor Goodhue and his architectural firm. (Throop Hall, the original structure, was leveled after major earthquake damage in 1973, as were some other early buildings.)

Grouped according to the scientific disciplines studied within, the buildings were planned around an east–west axis (Olive Walk, the main thoroughfare), and a north–south axis that culminates at the 1964 Beckman Auditorium.

Positioned at the intersection of the axes is a central court patterned after Spain's city plazas (the Millikan Library pond resides at that site today). The campus is rich with arcades, vaulted ceilings, terra-cotta floor tiles, wrought-iron doors, and exterior decoration details (credited to Goodhue) such as sculptured shells, sea creatures, and floral and animal symbols.

Caltech's prized faculty club, the **Athenaeum,** was designed by British architect Gordon Kaufmann in 1930. He modeled it on the Oxford and Cambridge clubs, befitting the welcome dinner for Albert Einstein that signaled its opening. Architectural walking tours, as well as general tours, are offered when the university is in session. ∎

A seismograph keeps watch for the ever present threat of earthquake.

The Huntington

PIONEER RAILROAD MOGUL HENRY E. HUNTINGTON'S former 1910 home, set on 207 acres in superwealthy San Marino, houses one of the world's most impressive private cultural institutions and is an absolute must on any visitor's itinerary. The private, nonprofit educational and cultural complex, founded by Huntington in 1919, consists of a library, art collections, and botanical gardens, all packed with human- and nature-made superlatives.

The Huntington
www.huntington.org
- 205 G2 & inside back cover map E5
- 1151 Oxford Rd., San Marino
- 626/405-2100
- Closed Mon.
- $$ (free 1st Thurs. of month)

Among Huntington's illustrious feats was the development of L.A.'s Pacific Electric interurban rail system, which increased the population in the area threefold between 1902 and 1910. As he amassed his fortune in railroads, and later in water, power, and real estate, Huntington (along with his wife, Arabella) collected an amazing assortment of British art, rare books and manuscripts, and splendid plant species. Rumor has it that Arabella, much happier in New York and Paris, was loathe to move to Southern California and had to be wooed out West by Henry's ever expanding monument to culture (not to mention the hefty allowance that enabled her to continue art shopping in Europe). Henry's efforts worked on Arabella, as they continue to beckon more than half a million visitors and thousands of scholars each year.

THE LIBRARY

Don't forget your reading glasses, for the Huntington Library, one of the world's most esteemed research libraries, catalogues more than 3.5 million manuscripts, 357,000 volumes of rare books, some 31,000 reference works, and a plethora of prints and photographs. The five million items emphasize Anglo-American history, art, and literature from the 11th century through modern times. The **Library Exhibition Hall** (open to the public) displays such treasures as a Gutenberg Bible, the double-elephant folio edition of Audubon's *Birds of America,* an illuminated Ellesmere manuscript of Chaucer's *The Canterbury Tales,* and a prized collection of early Shakespeare editions. Other popular items include documents written by presidents Washington, Jefferson, and Lincoln, along with manuscripts and first editions penned by Blake, Wordsworth, Shelley, Twain, and Thoreau.

ART COLLECTIONS

Three separate buildings display the extensive Huntington Art Collections. The **Huntington Gallery,** in the hallowed halls of the Huntingtons' former Myron Hunt-designed mansion, contains all of the British collection and a portion of the European holdings. Here you'll find Gainsborough, Lawrence, Reynolds, and Turner. Eighteenth- and 19th-century British and French art are the hallmarks of the collection, and special changing exhibitions are presented throughout the year.

American paintings from the 1730s to the 1930s and Pasadena architects Charles and Henry Greene are showcased in the **Virginia Steele Scott Gallery of American Art,** a separate building in the Huntington complex that was opened in 1984. The four arms of the Greek cross-shaped, skylit gallery illuminate works such as Copley's "Sarah Jackson," Cassatt's "Breakfast in Bed," Hopper's "The Long Leg," Chase's "Tenth Street Studio," and Bingham's "In a Quandry." The **Dorothy Collins Brown Wing** is devoted to the Craftsman artistry of Greene and Greene. It showcases furniture, decorative items, and a

reassembled staircase. The new **Boone Gallery** is devoted primarily to changing exhibitions of American and English art. The **Arabella D. Huntington Memorial Collection** resides in the library's west wing and displays Renaissance paintings and 18th-century furnishings and art.

BOTANICAL GARDENS

The glorious gardens cover about 150 parklike acres of the grounds, enchanting visitors with 15 specialized sections containing 15,000 different plants. Major groupings are the 3-acre rose garden; the Shakespeare garden, honoring the English gardens of the bard's era; the herb garden, where the plants are arranged according to their uses, from medicines to potpourris; the 12-acre desert garden, a startling sight with more than 4,000 species of xerophytic plants; the traditional Japanese garden; and the Australian, subtropical, and palm gardens. The camellia collection is one of the largest in the country. Traditional high tea is served in the Rose Garden Room. ∎

Relax and take time to smell the roses!

More places to visit in the San Fernando & San Gabriel Valleys

BRAND LIBRARY & ART GALLERIES

Also known as El Miradero, this 1904 Moorish-style mansion was modeled on the East Indian Pavilion at the 1893 Chicago World Fair. Owner Leslie C. Brand subsequently donated his domed Islamic home to the city of Glendale on the condition that it be used as a public library. As the arts and music branch of the Glendale Public Library, the property also features beautiful grounds as well as studios and performance facilities.
🅰 205 E3 ✉ 1601 W. Mountain St., Glendale ☎ 818/548-2051 🕐 Closed Sun.–Mon.

DESCANSO GARDENS

This 160-acre woodland garden, in the foothills north of Pasadena, was developed in 1937 by *Los Angeles Daily News* owner, E. Manchester Boddy. Purchased by L.A. County in 1953, the refuge features about 25 acres of California live oaks and more than 100,000 camellia shrubs (representing 600 different varieties). The camellia blooming season (October–March) is a floral highlight. Those more inclined toward roses will prefer the 5-acre International Rosarium, where antique and modern roses are planted among annuals, perennials, and shrubs. Lilac shrubs, day-lily beds, iris gardens, Mantilja poppies, orchids, a Japanese-style garden, and a bird observation station also adorn the grounds.
🅰 205 F3/4 ✉ 1418 Descanso Dr., La Cañada-Flintridge ☎ 818/952-4400 🕐 Tram tours daily except Mon. 🅂 $$

KIDSPACE MUSEUM

This hands-on museum, designed for children ages two to ten, is housed in an elementary school gymnasium south of Pasadena's Playhouse District. Youngsters can take on various personae (complete with garb and gear), such as astronaut, football player, firefighter, or supermarket cashier. Kids can also try their hands as directors in the makeshift TV and radio stations. An indoor beach, tree house, and play equipment may be more enticing to some, while special programs and workshops are designed to interest all ages.
🅰 205 G2 ✉ 390 S. El Molino Ave., Pasadena ☎ 626/449-9143 🕐 Hours vary during school vacations 🅂 $$

MISSION SAN FERNANDO REY DE ESPAÑA

Named for Spain's King Ferdinand III, Mission San Fernando was founded in 1797 by Friar Fermin Lasuen and soon became an important element in L.A.'s economic structure. The food-sufficient community produced soap, candles, leather goods, and other necessities, and supplied not only the Native Americans who lived and worked there, but the burgeoning community as well. After Mexico began secularization in 1834, the once-thriving property soon became unproductive. The buildings were later sold off, fell into disrepair, sustained damage from various earthquakes, and were reconstructed. The simple adobe construction, arched corridors, and huge square pillars are inviting examples of the simple yet powerful design and craftsmanship of the early days. A small museum and gift shop are on the premises, and tours are offered.
🅰 204 B5 ✉ 15151 San Fernando Mission Blvd., San Fernando ☎ 818/361-0186 🅂 $$

MISSION SAN GABRIEL ARCÁNGEL

San Gabriel Valley's original settlement is located south of Sierra Madre. Dedicated in 1771, this site was named in honor of the archangel Gabriel, and for decades it was California's wealthiest mission. The earliest structure was erected by Native American workers, though subsequent earthquakes damaged the vaulted roof and the church tower. The mission was completely restored in 1828 (when the bell tower was moved to its present location), only to change hands several times and again be damaged by yet more earthquakes (including the 1994 Northridge shaker). Diligently restored once more, the adobe walls, cemetery, grape-vined gardens, and that same bell tower still stand.
🅰 205 G2 ✉ 537 W. Mission Dr., San Gabriel ☎ 626/457-3035 🅂 $$ ■

H ow many other cities can offer such a fantasy menu of nearby getaways? Within easy reach of L.A. are clear deserts, snowy mountains, beaches galore, a pristine island—dazzling country, and the happiest place on Earth!

Excursions

Introduction & map **226–27**
Disneyland Resort **228–29**
Coastal Orange County **230**
Long Beach **231**
Catalina Island **232**
Palm Springs & vicinity **233**
More places to visit around Los
    Angeles **234**

**Her time at sea over, the
Queen Mary is now moored
at Long Beach as a hotel
and visitor attraction.**

Excursions

LOS ANGELES IS INDEED BLESSED WITH AN ENVIABLE ASSORTMENT OF places to sneak off to for a day or longer. Although the big city and its communities can keep most visitors and residents occupied with their varied attractions, there is still often the desire to see and do more, more, more. Well, you've certainly come to the right place. Ever unique L.A. affords not merely a nearby beach or ski resort, but an entire mouth-dropping range of activities, climates, topography, and even an international border. Most can be reached via a freeway in less than an hour, and none takes longer than about two hours to access. Intrepid adventurers or even antsy travelers can actually hit the beach, the slopes, the desert, and an island in the course of one (very) full day.

For visitors with kids, or those who are kids at heart, Disneyland is a popular excursion, and one that usually takes up an entire day or weekend. Just 26 miles southeast of Los Angeles, the Magic Kingdom beckons millions of visitors to Orange County every year. Less glitzy and more Wild West is Knott's Berry Farm, with additional amusements in nearby Buena Park.

Over on the coastal section of Orange County, along Pacific Coast Highway, you'll find the usual watery pursuits and then some. Huntington Beach is a world-renowned surfer haven, while Newport Beach is favored by yachties. Laguna Beach, farther south still, has long been a popular artists' colony. Long Beach, between the Orange County line and Los Angeles Harbor, is California's fifth-largest city, with its own airport and harbor. The *Queen Mary* is anchored here, and the city also offers an art museum, an aquarium, and plenty of shopping.

From Los Angeles Harbor or Newport Beach, it's an easy cruise or catamaran ride over to Catalina Island. Most of the island is a nature reserve, cars are not allowed, and you'll feel eons away from city life (even though you can see the mainland on clear days).

Palm Springs—in the upper Colorado Desert, less than two hours from L.A.—is the place to go for middle-of-nowhere desert ambience. Although there's plenty to do in this fashionable resort (especially for golfers and tennis players), you can also easily venture out into nothingness. At the other end of the spectrum are the San Bernardino Mountains, with plenty of thrills for snow enthusiasts. ■

The harbor at Catalina Island, seen through Avalon Archway

⊲ **5**

⊲ **4**

⊲ **3**

⊲ **2**

⊲ **1**

Almdale

Victorville

Apple Valley

Mojave

Desert

138

California Aqueduct

Hesperia

Lucerne Valley

247

15

ANGELES

Wrightwood

SAN BERNARDINO

Flamingo Heights

San Gabriel Mountains

Crestline

Lake Arrowhead

Big Bear City

NATIONAL FOREST

Rancho Cucamonga

San Bernardino Mountains

Big Bear Lake

Yucca Valley

62

sadena Glendora

215

NATIONAL

38

11499ft

El Monte

210

San Bernardino

San Gorgonio Mt.

JOSHUA TREE NATIONAL PARK

Covina

10

Rialto

Ontario

Redlands

FOREST

Desert Hot Springs

Whittier Chino

60

Pomona

Santa Ana

Beaumont

Banning

Palm Springs

wney Fullerton Corona

Norco

Riverside

60

Moreno Valley

10

Aerial Tramway

111

Cathedral City

Thousand Palms

Knott's Berry Farm

215

SAN BERNARDINO

Mt. San Jacinto S.P.

Rancho Mirage

Indio

ewood Anaheim

CLEVELAND NATIONAL FOREST

San Jacinto

Palm Desert

Indian Wells

eyland Orange

Perris

NATIONAL

Coachella

den Grove Santa Ana

Hemet

Valle Vista

La Quinta

Seal Beach South Coast Plaza

Sun City

FOREST

ntington Irvine

Lake Elsinore

San Jacinto Mts.

74

ach 1

Costa Mesa

Rancho Santa Margarita

Wildomar

coastal Newport Beach

Mission Viejo

Cahuilla

Orange County

5 74

Murrieta

Laguna Beach

San Juan Capistrano

Temecula

79

Aguanga

ANZA - BORREGO

Dana Point

San Clemente

6140ft

Fallbrook

Pala

Bonsall

Borrego Springs

San Luis Rey

15

CLEVELAND NATIONAL FOREST

76

DESERT

Vista

78

Oceanside

78

San Marcos

Escondido

Santa Ysabel

Carlsbad

5

Julian

STATE PARK

Legoland

Ramona

79

Encinitas

78

Solana Beach

Rancho Santa Fe

Poway

6512ft

Del Mar

S2

La Jolla

Lakeside

San Diego

Santee

Pine Valley

Sea World

La Mesa

Alpine

8

Coronado

SAN DIEGO

El Cajon

CLEVELAND NATIONAL FOREST

Point Loma

Spring Valley

Cabrillo National Monument

Balboa Park

Dulzura

Campo

Boulevard

94

Imperial Beach

Chula Vista

Tijuana

MEXICO

Gulf of Santa Catalina

△ C

△ D

△ E

△ F

Disneyland Resort

IT'S A STRAIGHT RUN ALONG I-5 FROM THE CITY OF LOS Angeles to this other Magic Kingdom. When animator extraordinaire Walt Disney delivered Mickey Mouse to the world in an unconventional hand-birth back in 1928, he changed the amusement and entertainment world forever—along with the lives of kids whose deepest desire years later was to sport a pair of fake mouse ears. And Disney did not quit after he squeaked out Mickey; before he was finished, his biological clock had ticked out lady-mouse Minnie, the Duck couple, Snow White and her dwarfs, and assorted other extended-family members. In 1955—long before that Florida place existed —Disney created a home for his characters in Anaheim, a wonderful Magic Kingdom off the freeway in Orange County that has emptied countless wallets ever since.

With the exception of bringing the "technologically advanced" Tomorrowland out of the 1950s Dark Ages and making it more in tune with the next millennium, as well as updating the street parades, the basic structure of Disneyland hasn't varied much since it opened. It's a very hometownish affair, with plenty of fun (and food) for everyone, and is far more low key than Disney's Florida location—besides, this is the only park that was personally overseen by creator Walt Disney. Various shows and parades are scheduled in the park throughout the day, changing according to the current Disney Pictures blockbuster. Today's visitors no longer need fumble through ticket books, calculating coupons for various rides; instead, an unlimited passport allows access to all attractions for the price at the gate, though be prepared for some very long lines at the popular rides.

THE ATTRACTIONS

Eight "themed" lands encompass more than 60 major rides and attractions, and almost as many shops and eating places. You can walk (a lot) or board the Disneyland Railroad steam locomotives that circle the park. Visitors may encounter a human-size Mickey and many other cartoon characters, as well as stuff to buy, from the get-go as they enter **Main Street, U.S.A.,** a celebration of America's small towns circa 1890. This is a big thrill for little ones, but perhaps less so for parents who are keen to head toward the already-paid-for rides.

The big news is the long-awaited update of **Tomorrowland.** No longer merely retroland, this relandscaped and redecorated area now combines retro quirkiness with futurism. Along with big favorites such as Space Mountain and Star Tours, visitors can marvel at the 3-D Honey, I Shrunk the Audience attraction, pilot a spaceship at Astro Orbitor, or take a fast ride on Rocket Rods (which replaced the PeopleMover). The two-level Innoventions technology pavilion (in the former Carousel Theater) showcases the world of high tech and its applications to five major areas of life.

Especially appealing to young children are the gentle, happy rides of **Fantasyland,** including the Mad Tea Party, Peter Pan's Flight, It's a Small World, and Sleeping

Disneyland Resort

🅰 227 C4 & inside back cover map F2

✉ 1313 Harbor Blvd., Anaheim

☎ 714/781-4565

🕐 Extended opening hours in summer, check times prior to visit

💲 $$$$$

Beauty Castle. The snowcapped Matterhorn, a bobsled roller-coaster ride, is also in this section. **Mickey's Toontown** is another big hit with very little ones, who gape at all types of cartoon-land happenings and have a chance to meet (and have a photo taken with) Mickey in his very own house.

Frontierland offers the big-thrill Big Thunder Mountain Railroad, the explorable Tom Sawyer Island, the Mark Twain Riverboat, and the high-tech, pyrotech Fantasmic! show. Wild, wet, and scary Splash Mountain is located in the unlikely setting of **Critter Country,** along with Davy Crockett's Explorer Canoes and Country Bear Playhouse. **Adventureland**—filled with the exotic sounds and sights of the Far East, Middle East, and South Pacific—still operates its trusty Jungle Cruise, although the big draw now is the Indiana Jones Adventure through the Temple of the Forbidden Eye. The winding streets of **New Orleans Square** tempt with the ever popular Haunted Mansion, Pirates of the Caribbean, and hum-along Dixieland tunes.

WHAT'S NEXT?
Disney's **California Adventure**—set to open in mid-2001—is expected to celebrate the Golden State's charms in all the glory that about $1.5 billion can buy, including a deluxe 750-room hotel and a California Mission-inspired retail and dining complex. ■

Fireworks over Sleeping Beauty castle add to the Disneyland fun.

Coastal Orange County

PACIFIC COAST HIGHWAY (P.C.H.) DOES A SLOW, SINUOUS shimmy along California's seaside. As it moves through the coastal section of Orange County, the highway is almost always within eyeshot of the big blue sea, turning inland occasionally to meander through laid-back neighborhoods and chic villages.

**Coastal Orange
County**
227 C3

**Bolsa Chica
Interpretive
Center**
Inside back cover
map F1
✉ 3842 Warner Ave.,
Huntington Beach
☎ 714/846-1114
🕐 Closed Mon. Trail
open daily

Seal Beach is the first town across the L.A.–Orange County line. Here, the P.C.H. crosses the Seal Beach National Wildlife Refuge. More nature awaits you beyond at **Bolsa Chica Ecological Reserve,** a vast 1,000-acre wildlife sanctuary that nurtures over 300 species of birds and other wildlife.

Huntington Beach may be smitten with its snazzy Waterfront Hilton Beach Resort, but to surfers it's still the original Surf City famed in song and lore. The 1,800-foot **Huntington Pier** *(P.C.H. & Main St.)* is home to the U.S. Open professional surf competition each August. No surfing enthusiast or Beach Boys fan should miss a visit to the **International Surfing Museum** *(411 Olive St.; tel 714/960-3483; closed Mon. and Tues.*

in winter), with vintage boards, memorabilia, and a Surfing Hall of Fame.

Six miles south of Huntington Beach is **Newport Beach,** a well-heeled community famous for its marina and the accompanying yachtie life. Newport Harbor enchants with its thousands of colorful boats, and small islands dot the area. On weekends, Newport Pier turns into a kind of wholesome version of Venice. Inland from Newport Beach is **South Coast Plaza** *(3333 Bristol St., off I-405),* which features hundreds of shops.

Laguna Beach, about 12 miles down P.C.H., has long been a sought-after artists' colony for its Mediterranean feel, and its streets are packed with galleries, fine shops, restaurants, and cafés. ■

Long Beach

Regal *Queen Mary,* now a hotel, remains permanently berthed in Long Beach.

ALTHOUGH LONG BEACH IS JUST ACROSS THE BRIDGE from San Pedro, and Long Beach Harbor is practically a Siamese twin to the adjacent Los Angeles Harbor, this thriving city is a distinctly separate entity, with its 5.5 miles of sandy seashore beckoning thousands of Angelenos every year.

During the early 20th century, Long Beach became a favorite relocation spot for Midwesterners, and home-state get-togethers were common-place events. Far from common was aviator and eccentric billionaire Howard Hughes's 1947 takeoff in his *Spruce Goose,* the world's largest airplane. Leveled by a 1933 earthquake, the city was rebuilt with diversity and character. Since the late 1990s, a major redevelopment program has pumped millions of dollars into a gleaming new waterfront, convention center, the World Trade Center, and key attractions such as the Aquarium of the Pacific.

ON THE WATERFRONT
Shoreline Village (*between E. Ocean Blvd. & Queens Way*) draws visitors with its ambience and dozens of shops, while the 1906 Charles Looff carousel is a magnet for kids and woodcarvers. Built at a cost of more than $117 million dollars, **Long Beach Aquarium of the Pacific** (*100 Aquarium Way, tel 562/590-3100*) combines high-tech and splashy decor with the undersea world. An underwater tunnel allows visitors to walk right through a habitat for seals and sea lions. Across Queensway Bridge is the 81,237-ton **Queen Mary** (*1126 Queens Hwy., tel 562/435-3511*). This part hotel/part tourist attraction can be boarded by visitors. **Long Beach Museum of Art** (*2300 E. Ocean Blvd., tel 562/439-2119*), down the waterfront, displays contemporary regional works. ∎

Long Beach
🅜 226 B3 & inside back cover map D/E2

Long Beach Area Convention & Visitors Bureau
✉ One World Trade Center, Suite 300, Long Beach
☎ 562/436-3645
🕐 Closed Sat.–Sun.

Catalina Island

Catalina Island, a
pristine paradise,
is located just a
short boat ride
from Greater L.A.

Catalina Island
226 B3

Catalina Island
Visitors Bureau
226 B3
1 Green Pier, Avalon
310/510-1520

Santa Catalina
Island
Conservancy
310/510-2595

AMAZING AS IT MAY SEEM, AN ISLAND AWAITS VISITORS just 22 miles across the sea from L.A. County's sandy shores. Catalina offers a delightful and unexpected alternative, from the small community of Avalon to the untouched interior area—exquisite with rugged mountains and canyons—and to remote beaches and coves. The wilderness area is rich with countless species of native plants and over a hundred species of birds, plus boars, goats, and bison (left over from the 1920s filming of *The Vanishing American*).

Discovered in a 1542 voyage, it had already been home to the Gabrieliño Native Americans from as early as 500 B.C. Through its history the island has been used by pirates, smugglers, Russian fur trappers, bootleggers, and developers. In 1919 the Santa Catalina Island Company was purchased by William Wrigley, Jr. The millionaire built his mansion here, developed Avalon as a resort, and promoted the island as a sportfishing paradise. In the 1970s, the nonprofit Santa Catalina Island Conservancy acquired 86 percent of the island and is devoted to preserving its fragile environment.

Catalina is the second largest of the Channel Islands (it measures 21 miles long by 8 miles wide) and is home to approximately 3,200 residents. Most visitors and boaties anchor themselves in Avalon. The action is centered along Crescent Avenue boardwalk, the Green Pleasure Pier, and the circular Spanish Moderne Casino. Nonresident vehicles are not allowed, but bicycles and small gasoline-powered carts can be rented for use around Avalon. Those who wish to hike or cycle outside of town require permits from the conservancy, and a number of companies offer bus tours. ∎

Palm Springs & vicinity

Golfers call the desert communities heaven on earth, and tournaments galore are played here annually.

LOW-LYING PALM SPRINGS SPREADS OUT LIKE A MIRAGE IN the Coachella Valley at the base of Mount San Jacinto, about 110 miles southeast of L.A. along I-10, and has been a fashionable resort since the Hollywood stars began flocking here during the 1920s.

The early stars were drawn to the local mineral springs, as were the Cahuilla Native American tribe, who now own and operate the **Spa Hotel** *(100 N. Indian Canyon Dr.)* on the site. Golfing and tennis are the primary activities. Palm Springs hosts more than 100 golf tournaments every year, including the Nabisco Dinah Shore. The nearby residential communities and resorts of Rancho Mirage, Palm Desert, Indian Wells, and La Quinta, all blend into one big playground. The main thoroughfares—Tahquitz Canyon Way, and Palm Canyon and Indian Canyon Drives—are lined with boutiques, cafés, and galleries.

LOCAL ATTRACTIONS
Palm Springs Desert
Museum *(101 Museum Dr., tel 760/325-0189)* showcases regional art and natural history, including contemporary and Native American works. One of the world's largest collections of World War II vintage fighters is on display at **Palm Springs Air Museum** *(745 N. Gene Autry Trail, tel 760/778-6262)*. **Moorten Botanical Garden** *(1701 S. Palm Canyon Dr., tel 760/327-6555)* features cactuses and other desert plants, along with a bird sanctuary. Desert plants and wildlife are also exhibited in Palm Desert's 1,200-acre natural setting at the **Living Desert Wildlife and Botanical Park** *(47–900 Portola Ave., tel 760/346-5694)*. The **Palm Springs Aerial Tramway** *(Tramway Rd., west of N. Palm Canyon Dr., tel 760/325-1391)* offers a spectacular ride to the 8,516-foot summit of Mount San Jacinto. ■

Palm Springs
⚑ 227 B4

Palm Springs Desert Resorts Convention & Visitors Bureau
✉ 69-930 Hwy. 111, Suite 201, Rancho Mirage
☎ 760/770-9000
🕐 Closed Sat.–Sun.

Visitor Center
✉ 2781 N. Palm Canyon Dr.
☎ 760/778-8418

More places to visit around Los Angeles

KNOTT'S BERRY FARM

Situated in Buena Park, Orange County (not far from Disneyland), Knott's Berry Farm hails from the 1920s, when the Knott family did indeed sell their berries and jam, as well as Mrs. Knott's famous chicken and biscuit dinner (more than 1.5 million meals are still sold each year). In 1940, the Knotts decided to go Old West and built a replica ghost town, a cyclorama, and other homey rides. More amusements followed, and in the 1990s new ownership instigated new rides, many of them ranking with the nation's bigger parks. Ghost Rider is the region's most enormous wooden roller coaster, while Supreme Scream has a death-defying vertical descent.

🅰 227 C4 & inside back cover map D2
✉ 8039 Beach Blvd., Buena Park ☎ 714/220-5200 🕐 Extended hours during school vacations 💲 $$$$$

LEGOLAND CALIFORNIA

Legoland California opened in 1999 in San Diego's North County (off I-5) as a family-fun destination that pays tribute to the Danish-made interconnecting plastic bricks. Among the offerings are miniature cars and boats, a small roller coaster, a nature maze, and an ocean-view tower, all constructed from those colorful kiddies' construction blocks. Entertainment and eateries are geared to children.

🅰 227 D2 ✉ 1 Lego Dr., Carlsbad
☎ 760/918-5346 💲 $$$$$

SAN BERNARDINO MOUNTAINS

The 660,000-acre San Bernardino National Forest is just an hour or so from the desert and a couple of hours from L.A., depending where you go and how high you climb (elevations hit 11,502 feet). During winter, the ski resorts are usually snowy and bustling, while summer affords great hiking and picnicking opportunities. The most popular areas are upscale Lake Arrowhead (two hours from L.A.), with a small alpine village and shimmering lake (cruises available); and 6,750-foot-high Big Bear Lake, a more touristy town with lake sports and nearby ski resorts.

🅰 227 D/E4

Lake Arrowhead Communities Chamber of Commerce ✉ 28200 Hwy. 189, Bldg. F, Suite 290, Lake Arrowhead Village ☎ 909/337-3715. **Big Bear Chamber of Commerce** ✉ 630 Bartlett Rd., Big Bear Lake Village ☎ 909/866-4607

SAN DIEGO & TIJUANA

Two hours down the coast from L.A. via I-5 is San Diego, California's second-largest city, considered the birthplace of the state. The plethora of don't-miss sights here includes **Balboa Park** and the famous **San Diego Zoo,** most of the major museums, Old Town San Diego, Mission Bay Park and **SeaWorld, Cabrillo National Monument,** and the historic Gaslamp District.

Hop on a red trolley from the Santa Fe Depot for a quick ride and short walk across the border into frenzied, colorful Tijuana, Mexico.

🅰 227 D1

San Diego International Visitors Information Center ✉ 11 Horton Plaza, San Diego ☎ 619/236-1212. **Tijuana Convention & Tourism Bureau** ✉ Ave. Revolución, between calles 3 and 4, Tijuana ☎ 66/83-05-30

SIX FLAGS MAGIC MOUNTAIN

About an hour's drive northwest of L.A. into the Santa Clarita Valley is Six Flags Magic Mountain, yet another theme park offering a thrill a second for visitors who have strong hearts and are more than 48 inches tall (the cutoff for most of the sensational rides, rising to 54 inches for the penultimate thrills). Among the stomach-churners are Flashback, the world's only hairpin roller coaster; Batman the Ride, the ultimate floorless coaster; and the Riddler's Revenge, the world's fastest and tallest stand up coaster. There are milder, gentler amusements, too, while the adjacent Six Flags Hurricane Harbor offers the wet 'n' wild side of thrilldom.

🅰 226 B5 ✉ 26101 Magic Mountain Pkwy., Valencia ☎ 818/367-5965 🕐 Extended hours during school vacations 💲 $$$$$. Separate admissions or one combination ticket to both parks ∎

Travelwise

**Travelwise information
236–43**
Planning your trip **236**
How to get to Los Angeles
236–37
Getting around **237–39**
Practical advice **239–42**
Emergencies **242–43**
Activities **243**
Hotels & restaurants 244–57
**Shopping in Los Angeles
258–61**
Entertainment 262–64

**Art on the underground at
Hollywood and Vine Station**

TRAVELWISE INFORMATION

PLANNING YOUR TRIP

WHEN TO GO

The best thing about planning a trip to Los Angeles is that you can go virtually anytime and be assured of mild—and usually dry—travel-friendly weather. And, for better or worse, the city is practically seasonless. Nonetheless, in the course of one day it is possible to swim in the ocean, play in the snow, go off-road in the desert, and cha-cha into Mexico across one of the world's busiest international borders.

When it does rain, the drizzles and occasional downpours most often occur from November through March. Although summers are almost always dry, Los Angeles (and much of Southern California) experiences a phenomenon known as "June gloom," when the weather in coastal areas can be dreary, overcast, and glum—a delightful break for Angelenos, who tire of the eternal sun. Summer months also tend to be the smoggiest, and visitors with asthma or respiratory problems might want to avoid the city at this time. Infamous Santa Ana winds, which are hot, fiery, and wild, often appear in late summer or early fall, and again in early winter.

The city is so huge that it's easy to avoid the tourist crush in areas such as Hollywood, West Hollywood, downtown, the Westside, Santa Monica, and Pasadena. Major attractions are packed during summer months and holidays, making off-season weekdays the best times to visit hot spots such as Disneyland. Though the most popular beaches can be packed with bodies for much of the year, there's plenty of sand and surf for everyone to enjoy.

CLIMATE

Los Angeles has a fairly consistent, mild climate year-round. The Pacific Ocean keeps coastal communities such as Santa Monica, Venice, Pacific Palisades, and Malibu gentle and breezy, as well as foggy. Temperatures in inland areas can be 10–15 degrees warmer, but even the hottest days are usually followed by cool and comfortable evenings. Deserts sizzle in summer and freeze in winter evenings, and nearby mountain resorts almost always draw skiers and snowbirds with seasonal flurries and snowstorms.

WHAT TO TAKE

Bring casual clothing (cottons and linens are ideal) and dress in layers. Always have a sweater or light coat on hand for cool evenings. Good walking shoes are a must (make sure they're broken in), and sandals or thongs for the beach are a good idea. Bring bathing garb for water sports and sunbathing, a wide-brimmed hat, and plenty of sunscreen. Though you could live in walking shorts, T-shirts, and blue jeans, many restaurants and nightclubs require jackets and ties for men and something equally dressy for women. If you're going to snowy areas, bring a heavy coat, gloves, and boots.

INSURANCE

If you get sick or have an accident in Los Angeles, and you don't have medical insurance, you'll probably end up in the grim Los Angeles County General Hospital (used as the opening shot for the soap opera *General Hospital*). And that's if you're lucky. Most hospitals and private doctors won't even touch you in this city unless you have insurance or plenty of cash.

Check to make sure your policy or H.M.O. covers out-of-town incidents. If not, it is highly advisable to take out supplemental or travel insurance.

HOW TO GET TO LOS ANGELES

BY AIR

AIRLINES
All major domestic, and many international and regional carriers, fly into Los Angeles on either nonstop or connecting flights, including the following:
Alaska Airlines, tel 800/426-0333
America West Airlines, tel 800/235-9292
American Airlines, tel 800/433-7300
Continental Airlines, tel 800/525-0280
Delta Airlines, tel 800/221-1212
Hawaiian Airlines, tel 800/367-5320
Northwest Airlines, tel 800/225-2525
Southwest Airlines, tel 800/435-9792
TWA, tel 800/221-2000
United Airlines, tel 800/241-6522
USAirways, tel 800/428-4322

AIRPORTS
Los Angeles International Airport (LAX), tel 310/646-5252
Burbank/Glendale/Pasadena Airport (BUR), tel 818/840-8847
John Wayne Airport (SNA) (Orange County), tel 949/252-5252
Ontario International Airport (ONT) (in San Gabriel Valley), tel 909/987-2700

Los Angeles International Airport (more commonly known as LAX) serves more than 100 airlines in ten terminals, and is one of the country's busiest airports and the major gateway to Los Angeles. The other airports offer alternatives, especially for anyone staying in or near Anaheim, Palm Springs, the Burbank area, or the San Fernando Valley.

Once outside the baggage-claim areas, visitors will find an astonishing assortment of shuttles, vans, buses, taxis, and limousines to whisk them almost anywhere within the city as well as to surrounding areas (including Disneyland). The ticket/information booths, located outside each baggage-claim area, will direct you to the right ride. All big-name car-rental companies have shuttles to their nearby lots, where you can pick up your vehicle, and many hotels and motels provide free transportation as well (inquire when booking your room). Free buses run between the terminals, about every 10–20 minutes, 24 hours a day.

BY TRAIN

Union Station, 800 N. Alameda St., tel 800/872-7245

Long-distance runs into historic Union Station include the Southwest Chief, via Chicago; the Sunset Limited from Florida, via New Orleans and Texas; and the Coast Starlight, a super-scenic journey from Seattle, via Portland. All offer coach seating as well as sleeping compart-ments, with snack service, lounges, and dining cars.

GETTING AROUND

BY CAR

CAR RENTALS IN LOS ANGELES

Alamo, tel 800/327-9633
Avis, tel 800/331-1212
Budget, tel 800/527-0700
Budget's Exotic Car Rental, tel 310/274-9173
Dollar, tel 800/421-6878
Hertz, tel 800/654-3131
Luxury Line, tel 310/659-5555
National, tel 800/328-4567
Thrifty, tel 800/367-2277

Due to the size of L.A. and its lack of an efficient public transportation system, cars are a necessary evil in the city. Although L.A.'s reputation for horrendous traffic and manic drivers is occasionally right on target, navigating here is really not much different from any other large city. The sprawl also means there are gigantic pockets that have very little congestion and there is plentiful parking, unlike more concentrated metropolises such as New York or San Francisco. The freeways can be a pain and are quite daunting for novices, especially during rush hours (most of the time), and where one or more freeways merge. Tune in to the radio for traffic updates (KKTR, 1650 AM, provides continuous traffic reports 24 hours a day). Have good maps and plan your route beforehand. The down-town area is a bear, not only because of the traffic but also due to the confusing one-way streets.

Both parking lots and metered street parking are available in most parts of town, and most attractions, hotels, restaurants, and shopping malls offer facilities—often gratis—for visitors and guests. If you don't mind a walk, you'll be able to find free street parking in many residential areas. Unless you or your passengers are disabled, and have the appropriate license plates or placard, do not even think about parking in one of the blue zones reserved for people with disabilities. Police are fierce about slapping very costly parking tickets on violators, and locals also keep vigil. If you escape a ticket, you will most likely be greeted by several hecklers and at least one nasty note on your windshield.

DRIVING REGULATIONS

Speed limits vary, depending on where you are. Signs are posted at regular intervals, and in many places you can expect the limits to change abruptly—fun for the cops, and a challenge for sweating

motorists. As a general rule, the speed limit on most streets is 35 mph; in residential areas and in school zones it is 25 mph. Most of the freeways have a maximum speed of 65 mph. In California it is legal to turn right on a red light, but only after coming to a complete stop and if no vehicle is approaching from the left. Likewise, U-turns are permitted at intersections unless otherwise indicated. Pedestrians always have the right of way, whether crossing at a crosswalk or at an intersection. Always pull to the right and stop for emergency vehicles, whether they are passing from behind or approaching from ahead. Try to steer clear of car chases. Do not park in red zones or near fire hydrants, and never drive over the legal alcohol limit (0.5 percent).

Seat belts are mandatory for all passengers, and regulation car seats for infants and children are also musts. Advise car-rental agencies in advance if you require this equipment.

CAR BREAKDOWN

If you are driving a rental car, check your papers for the company's emergency number; it is advisable to ask for this beforehand, just in case. Emergency phones are located at regular intervals along most major freeways. If you belong to an automobile club, it will probably have reciprocal arrangements with a club in L.A. Inquire before your departure and keep the relevant numbers handy. It is best not to depend upon the kindness of strangers.

PUBLIC TRANSPORTATION

Metropolitan Transit Authority (M.T.A.)
Tel 800/266-6883 or 213/626-4455. Operates daily; some routes provide 24-hour service.
Downtown Area Short Hop (DASH)
Tel 213/808-2273. Operates 6 a.m.–6:30 p.m. weekdays and 10 a.m.–5 p.m. weekends.

Metro Rail

Tel 213/626-4455. Operates daily 4:45 a.m.–11:30 p.m.

Buses Although this is probably news to many Angelenos, public buses cover more than 200 routes throughout the entire metropolitan region. Maps and schedules are available at M.T.A. Customer Centers in downtown, Hollywood, East Los Angeles, Baldwin Hills/Crenshaw Plaza, the San Fernando Valley, Van Nuys, and in the Wilshire District.

Fares are $1.35 per trip (exact change only), and children under five travel free. Transfers cost an additional 25¢ (request these from the driver when you board). Tokens cost $9 per bag of ten, and are available at supermarkets and other shops. If you're in town for an extended stay, you might consider purchasing a monthly pass for $42, a semimonthly for $21, or a weekly for $11.

DASH These snappy silver and magenta minibus shuttles are a quick, convenient, stress-free, and cheap way to travel around the downtown area. Routes include most downtown attractions, business districts, shopping centers, hotels, and Metro Rail stations. Fares are 25¢ per trip, and the exact change is required.

Metro Rail The city's Metro stations also double as galleries, with public art on exhibit at almost every stop. Three lines operate daily. The Red Line (a bona fide subway) runs from downtown's Union Station to Wilshire Boulevard and to Hollywood and Vine in the Wilshire District. By the time this book is published Hollywood/Highland, Universal City and North Hollywood, should be open. The Blue Line connects to the Red Line at 7th and Figueroa streets in downtown, and travels above ground all the way to Long Beach. The Green Line is a little-

used run from Norwalk to Redondo Beach, ending up near (but not at) LAX. Fares are the same as for M.T.A. buses, and tokens and transfers between the Metro and buses are interchangeable.

TAXIS

Although it is not completely unheard of, don't expect to hail taxis off the street. Cabs can usually be found at the airport, train depot, bus terminals, and at major hotels. Otherwise, order ahead, allowing plenty of time—especially if you need to catch a flight or have dinner reservations.

The basic taxi fare is $1.90 plus $1.80 for each additional mile, and in L.A. those miles add up pretty fast. The flat-fare zone, however, is a good deal: Up to four passengers pay a flat fare of $4 for a ride in the downtown area, bounded by Main Street to the east, Pico Boulevard to the south, the Hollywood Freeway to the north, and the Harbor Freeway to the west.

Radio-dispatched taxis

Checker Cab Company, tel 800/300-5007 or 213/482-3456
Independent Cab Company, tel 800/521-8294 or 213/385-8294
L.A. Taxi Company, tel 310/859-0111
United Independent Taxi Drivers, tel 323/653-5050

Limousine services

A-1 West Coast Limousine Service, tel 310/671-8720
Carey Limousines, tel 800/336-4646 or 310/670-1166
Diva Limousines, tel 800/427-3482 or 310/278-3482
First Class, tel 800/400-9771 or 310/676-9771
Fox Limousines, tel 800/274-4369 or 310/641-9626
The Ultimate Limousine, tel 800/710-1498

In this town limos are as common and plentiful as celebrities. Amenities include such L.A.-isms as full bars, cell phones, televisions, VCRs, hot

tubs, aromatherapy and herbal essences, and vibrating double beds. Most companies charge an hourly rate (upwards of $40), with a three-hour minimum.

TRAINS

Metrolink The regional rail system serves mainly commuters on lines connecting downtown with 44 stations, including Orange, Riverside, and San Bernardino counties. Fares vary according to zones traveled and can be purchased at vending machines or stations. The service operates Mon.–Fri., although the San Bernardino and Santa Clarita lines also run on Sat. For information, phone 800/371-5465.

Amtrak Offers frequent and scenic (though not always reliable) rail services between Union Station and San Diego to the south, stopping at Fullerton, Anaheim, Santa Ana, Irvine, San Juan Capistrano, San Clemente, Oceanside, and Solana Beach. There are also services north to Santa Barbara, stopping at Glendale, Burbank Airport, Van Nuys, Chatsworth, Simi Valley, Oxnard, and Ventura. Amtrak buses continue on to Solvang, Lompoc, Santa Maria, and San Luis Obispo. Portions of both the southbound and northbound routes shimmy alongside the Pacific Ocean's sand and surf. Seating is unreserved, except for Custom Class cars (which have roomier seats, fewer kids, complimentary newspapers, and snacks and beverages). For information, tel 800/872-7245.

TOURS & ORGANIZED SIGHTSEEING

Bus Tours
These include general sightseeing tours of downtown, Hollywood, Farmers Market, and Beverly Hills, and some also take in stars' homes, beaches, Disneyland, Knott's Berry Farm, Universal Studios, and Magic Mountain. Casablanca Tours, tel 323/461-0156

GrayLine Tours, tel 213/689-8822 or 800/228-2452
Hollywood Fantasy Tours, tel 323/469-8184
L.A. Tours and Sightseeing, tel 800/286-8752 or 323/937-3361
Starline Tours, tel 800/959-3131 or 323/463-3333

Walking tours
Guided walking tours of downtown's historic and architectural icons:
El Pueblo de Los Angeles Historic Monument, tel 213/485-6885
Los Angeles Conservancy, tel 213/623-2489

Nature hikes
Santa Monica Mountains National Recreation Area, tel 805/370-2301
Sierra Club, tel 213/387-4287
State Parks Department, tel 916/653-6995

Personal tours
Personalized nightlife tour, complete with limo, guide, and club passes that whiz you right by the dreaded fashion police:
L.A. NightHawks, Box 7642, Santa Monica, 90406, tel 310/392-1500

Air & sea tours
See the city and coast from an open-cockpit biplane:
Bird's Nest, tel 818/753-0070

Or from a whirly bird
Helinet Tours, tel 818/902-0229

Cruises of the Los Angeles Harbor depart San Pedro. Tours of the inner and outer harbors, whale-watching, and coastal excursions are available:
Los Angeles Sightseeing Cruises, tel 310/831-0996

OFF BEAT "WHEN IN L.A." TOURS
Studio tours
NBC Studio Tour, tel 818/840-3537
Universal Studios Tour, tel 818/622-3801
Warner Brothers VIP Studio Tour, tel 818/954-1744

PRACTICAL ADVICE

COMMUNICATIONS

POST OFFICES
Main branch: 7101 S. Central Ave. tel 323/586-4414
General postal information: tel 800/725-2161
LAX branch: 9029 Airport Blvd., Inglewood, tel 310/337-8840

Both post offices and street mailboxes are plentiful. Regular post office hours are Mon.–Fri. 9 a.m.–5 p.m., and many branches open Sat. 9 a.m.–1 p.m. The LAX branch is open 24 hours. Mail deliveries are Mon.–Sat.

TELEPHONES
Local information, tel 411
Long-distance information, tel 1/area code of city/555-1212
Toll-free directory information, tel 1-800/555-1212

Public telephones are located in all hotels, at tourist attractions and other public places, at most restaurants, and along many city streets. Local calls cost 35¢ (payable in quarters, dimes, or nickels) and some privately owned phones set a time limit. Long-distance calls are easier and cheaper if you use your home carrier's telephone calling card or purchase a prepaid calling card (available at post offices and larger drugstores). Follow instructions on the telephone for collect calls. Hotels usually levy heavy surcharges for direct- or operator-dialed calls from your room—read the posted information or call the hotel operator before you dial.

Area codes The many area codes for Los Angeles and the surrounding districts can be confusing. The growing population (and its accompanying fax machines, cell phones, and computer modems) has turned almost every local call into a ten-digit finger dance. Dial

1 for all calls in different area codes, then the area code, and then the number you are trying to reach. If you are calling a number in the same area code, just dial the seven-digit number. For now, the city's area codes are broken up as follows:
Downtown Los Angeles, 213
Hollywood, 323
Beverly Hills, the Westside, and Santa Monica, 310
Northern Orange County, 714
Southern Orange County, 949
Portions of the San Gabriel Valley, 909
Portions of Long Beach, 562
Portions of Desert areas, 760
Portions of the San Fernando Valley, 818
Portions of Pasadena, 626

FAXES, COMPUTERS, & INTERNET ACCESS
Kinko's, tel 800/254-6507, www.kinkos.com

Kinko's offers comprehensive business services, including photocopying, fax services, computer rental, and Internet access, and has good lighting, efficient staff, and up-to-date equipment. Branches are located throughout L.A. and the surrounding areas, and all are open 24 hours.

NEWSPAPERS
The *Los Angeles Times,* published daily, is the major metropolitan newspaper and contains international, national, and local news (with local editions for suburban areas). The fat Sunday edition includes the "Calendar" section, with listings of movies, concerts, literary readings, and almost every other event in town. *U.S.A. Today,* the *New York Times,* the *Wall Street Journal,* and a bevy of local publications are also readily available. The free *L.A. Weekly,* distributed at restaurants and shops each Thursday, is another comprehensive arts and entertainment resource. The daily *La Opinión* is one of the country's largest Spanish-language newspapers. *Los Angeles Magazine* is a slick

monthly, filled with L.A.-oriented politics, profiles, events, restaurant reviews, and buzz on the local scene.

TELEVISION

L.A. boasts more than 30 cable and noncable stations, most of which feature 24-hour programming. Major noncable television stations are channels 2 (CBS), 4 (NBC), 7 (ABC), 11 (FOX), and 28 (PBS). Some of the more popular cable stations include American Movie Classics (AMC), Turner Classic Movies (TCM), Arts and Entertainment (A&E), as well as NICK's sitcom reruns, MTV's music videos, BRAVO's foreign films, and ESPN's sports coverage. HBO and Showtime are the premium channels, showing big-budget movies. Almost every hotel offers cable stations, and many toss in free or pay-per-view movie channels.

RADIO

More than 60 AM and FM stations keep listeners tuned in and stop commuters from tearing their hair out. AM stations offer talk shows, psychological advice, news, and traffic updates, while FM stations offer everything from classical and jazz to underground rock and heavy metal. Good choices are: KABC (790 AM), talk radio; KFWB (980 AM), news and weather; KKTR (1650 AM), 24-hour traffic reports; KPCC (89.3 FM), jazz and blues, talk radio; KCRW (89.9 FM), national public radio; KUSC (91.5 FM), jazz, classical, world music; KCBS (93.1 FM), classic rock; KRTH (101.1 FM), oldies; and KKGO (105.1 FM), classical.

LOS ANGELES SETTINGS

The whole city is like one big entertainment complex, a natural backdrop for everything from film noir and romantic comedies to shoot-'em-up Westerns and whodunits. The sun-kissed beaches, curvy

mountains, fringed palms, bad boys, bottle blondes, and decadent streets are all irresistible. Plenty of movies and television shows have been filmed here purporting to be far-away places such as the Sahara, deepest Africa, or Anytown U.S.A. In contrast, many celluloid creations—along with a fair number of notable novels, kitschy television programs, and catchy lyrics—have also inked L.A. into the script.

Movies

Films with blatant L.A. settings include *Sunset Boulevard, A Star is Born, L.A. Story, The Bad and The Beautiful, Barton Fink, Singin' in the Rain, Rebel Without a Cause, Gidget, Beach Blanket Bingo, Chinatown, Down and Out in Beverly Hills, Beverly Hills Cop, Ed Wood, Hollywood Canteen, Pretty Woman, Grand Canyon, Mulholland Falls, Ruthless People, Funny Girl, The Last Action Hero, Pulp Fiction, Get Shorty, Die Hard, The Player, Postcards from the Edge, Who Framed Roger Rabbit?, Whatever Happened to Baby Jane?, Falling Down, Speed, Lost Highway, The Terminator, Dead Again, Murder My Sweet, Clueless, Mi Familia, Shampoo, Barfly, Swingers, Colors, Boogie Nights, Lethal Weapon, L.A. Confidential,* and *Boyz 'n The Hood.*

Television series

The Brady Bunch, Beverly Hillbillies, Beverly Hills 90210, Rockford Files, Dragnet, 77 Sunset Strip, Fresh Prince of Bel Air, Marcus Welby M.D., Family, Melrose Place, L.A. Law, Baywatch, and the *Mickey Mouse Club* form an eclectic mix of L.A.-based T.V. shows.

Books

Novels, biographies, memoirs, poetry, exposés, and other literary works featuring L.A.-as-location are numerous. Some titles on the broad spectrum are *Hollywood Babylon,* by Kenneth Anger; *Hollywood,* by Charles Bukowski; *Double Indemnity, Mildred Pierce,* and *The Postman Always Rings Twice,* by James Cain; *The Big Sleep* and *The Long*

Goodbye, by Raymond Chandler; *The Black Dahlia* and *L.A. Confidential,* by James Ellroy; *The Last Tycoon,* by F. Scott Fitzgerald; *As Good as Their Words: Writers in Hollywood,* by Ian Hamilton; *In the Heart of the Valley of Love,* by Cynthia Kadohata; *Devil in a Blue Dress,* by Walter Mosley; *What Makes Sammy Run?,* by Budd Schulberg; *You'll Never Eat Lunch in This Town Again,* by Julia Phillips; *Translating L.A.: A Tour of the Rainbow City,* by Peter Theroux; *The New Centurions,* by Joseph Wambaugh; *The Loved One,* by Evelyn Waugh; and *The Day of the Locust,* by Nathanael West.

Song lyrics

Sing-and-dance-along L.A. culture has been immortalized in: "L.A. Woman," by The Doors; "Blue Jay Lane," by The Beatles; "MacArthur Park," by Richard Harris (and Donna Summer); "I Love L.A.," by Randy Newman; "Ladies of the Canyon," by Joni Mitchell; "It Never Rains in Southern California," by Albert Hammond; "Dead Man's Curve," by Jan and Dean; "California Dreamin'," by the Mamas and the Papas; "Hollywood Nights," by Bob Seger; "Hooray for Hollywood," by Doris Day; "L.A. Freeway," by Jerry Jeff Walker; and "L.A.'s My Lady," by Frank Sinatra.

Watching the action

Los Angeles Film and Video Office, 7083 Hollywood Blvd., Fifth Floor, Hollywood, tel 323/957-1000
Open: Mon.–Fri. 8:30 a.m.–6 p.m.

Daily "shoot sheets," listing movie and television productions being shot that day, are provided for $10. Look for street shots, as you won't be able to ogle the action on private property. Also, keep in mind that this business can be fickle and that some shoots are rescheduled or relocated.

Audiences Unlimited, 100 Universal City Plaza, Bldg. 3153, Universal City, tel 818/753-3470

Free tickets to television shows are distributed on a first-come, first-served basis. Check ahead for age requirements. Schedules can be obtained up to several weeks in advance by sending a self-addressed, stamped envelope to the Universal City address.

LIQUOR LAWS

The legal drinking age is 21. Bars, restaurants, clubs, liquor stores, supermarkets, and convenience stores are permitted to serve or sell alcohol daily 6 a.m.–2 a.m. Alcohol is not served at most strip clubs. The production of a photo I.D. (driver's license, passport, or state I.D.) is mandatory at most places before you can buy alcohol. Open containers holding alcohol are not allowed anywhere in a car while it is being driven, drinking on the streets is forbidden, and alcohol in any form is banished from beaches.

LOCAL CUSTOMS & QUIRKS

Expect to be hugged by complete strangers of both sexes at all times and in all places (this includes restaurant waitpersons, your concierge, tour guides, bodybuilders, the guy you buy a souvenir T-shirt from, and any celebrities you might encounter). You will be expected to return the cuddle—keep your body loose. If you're in town on business, that all-important deal you've been haggling over will most assuredly be sealed with a handshake as well as a hug. Angelenos also smile a lot—don't fight it, smile back.

At the first drizzle or drop of rain, havoc ensues. In L.A. moisture emerging from the heavens is far more paralyzing than any earthquake: Angelenos are used to getting wet in the ocean or hot tub, but not in the city streets. It's almost as though a collective shockwave spreads throughout the city. Windshield

wipers are turned on full blast, headlights are lit, and traffic (especially that on the normally aggressive freeways) either comes to a grinding halt—with many motorists pulling over to the shoulder—or slows to speeds that a toddler on a tricycle could overtake. You can bet that the weather will be the featured story on the evening news, put before war, politics, or a SWAT-team stand-off. Angelenos cannot cope with rain and certainly don't know how to drive in it.

MONEY MATTERS

ATM LOCATIONS
Cirrus, tel 800/424-7787
Plus, tel 800/843-7587

Banks and Automatic Teller Machines (ATMs) are ubiquitous, and most major attractions and shopping centers also have them. Check with your home bank to find out which system accepts your card. Credit cards, debit cards, and traveler's checks are accepted almost everywhere; make sure you have an official photo I.D. on you as some places require it before you can make a transaction. Don't count on using personal checks from your home bank to pay for services or purchases.

NATIONAL HOLIDAYS

New Year's Day; Martin Luther King, Jr., Day (3rd Mon. in Jan.); President's Day (3rd Mon. in Feb.); Easter Sunday; Memorial Day (last Mon. in May); Fourth of July; Labor Day (first Mon. in Sept.); Thanksgiving Day (4th Thurs. in Nov.); Christmas Day.

OPENING TIMES

Most banks open Mon.–Thurs. 9 a.m.–3 p.m., Fri. 9 a.m.–6 p.m. Many now stay open until 5 or 6 p.m. on weekdays, and some also open Sat. 9 a.m.–noon or 1 p.m. Shops and attractions have variable hours. Department

stores are normally open daily 9 a.m.–9 p.m., although some smaller shops and boutiques close at 5 p.m. Hours often depend upon location; shops in a major mall will uniformly stay open until 9 p.m., while those in suburban districts may close earlier. Almost every shop is open on Sun. and most holidays. Most museums and art galleries are closed on Mon., as are theaters. Convenience stores and many supermarkets do business 24 hours a day.

PLACES OF WORSHIP

L.A. holds top honors in the country (if not the world) for the number and variety of its religious services. You will find everything from charismatic churches to Orthodox synagogues, with a liberal spattering of eastern religions, Pentecostal sects, and out-and-out cults. Check the *Yellow Pages* or the Saturday edition of the *Los Angeles Times* for service listings.

SALES TAX

Price tags are misleading. Expect the cash registers to add an 8.25 percent state tax to purchases, while the hotel room tax will increase your bill by 14 percent.

SMOKING

Californians are militant when it comes to smoke in public places. A statewide law bans smoking in all public places, including restaurants and bars. Some smokers do rebel, but they usually give in to threats of lawsuits. Almost every hotel and motel offers separate smoking and nonsmoking rooms and floors.

TIME DIFFERENCES

L.A. is in the Pacific time zone, which is three hours earlier than New York City, two hours earlier than Chicago, and one hour earlier than Albuquerque. Daylight saving time is observed.

TIPPING

Leave at least 15 percent of the bill at restaurants (20 percent at upscale spots). It is not unheard of for miffed waitstaff to chase after bad tippers. Taxi-drivers expect 10–15 percent, bartenders should pocket 10 percent, hairdressers claim 15 percent, porters get at least a buck a bag, valet parking attendants should be palmed $2 or more, and doormen get a couple of bucks every time they whistle for a cab or blink in your direction. Tip the hotel concierge or restaurant maitre d' at your discretion, depending upon services performed and whether you plan to show your face again.

TOILETS

Weak bladders have few worries in L.A. Public restrooms are abundant at attractions, restaurants, shops, malls, department stores, service stations, and beaches (though it's best to exercise caution at beach restrooms as they attract unsavory characters). Unless you look particularly scruffy, it is doubtful whether you will be turned away or have to make a purchase in order to use the facilities.

TOURIST OFFICES

Los Angeles Convention and Visitors Bureau, 685 S. Figueroa St., Los Angeles, 90017, tel 213/689-8822
Open: Mon.–Fri. 8 a.m.–5 p.m., Sat. 8:30 a.m.–5 p.m.
Also at 6541 Hollywood Blvd., Hollywood, 90028, tel 213/689-8822
Open: Mon.–Sat. 9 a.m.–5 p.m.

Load up on visitor information, maps, current events, and tips on places to go, stay, and eat. Discounts to many attractions are also available, as is a 24-hour multilingual events hotline.

OTHER VISITOR INFORMATION CENTERS

West Hollywood, tel 310/289-2525
Beverly Hills, tel 310/248-1015
Santa Monica, tel 310/393-7593
Pasadena, tel 626/795-9311

TRAVELERS WITH DISABILITIES

INFORMATION
Mobility International U.S.A., P.O. Box 10767, Eugene, OR 97440, tel 541/343-1284
Society for the Advancement of Travel for the Handicapped (S.A.T.H.), 347 Fifth Ave., Suite 610, New York, NY 10016, tel 212/447-7284
Los Angeles County Commission on Disabilities, tel 213/974-1053 or 213/974-1053 (T.D.D. users)
Disabled Riders Hotline, tel 800/626-4455

Los Angeles is one of the world's leaders in terms of making facilities and attractions accessible to physically disabled travelers. The 1990 Americans with Disabilities Act decrees that all public buildings (and their toilets) must be wheelchair accessible. Almost every major hotel and motel chain offers accessible accommodations, as do most restaurants, attractions, and shops.
  Virtually every Amtrak train has seating and sleeping areas for disabled passengers, as well as for guide dogs. City buses offer automatic wheelchair lifts, designated seating space, and hand grips. Big-name car-rental companies provide vehicles with hand controls. Almost every street corner has sloped curbs.
  Disabled motorists enjoy special parking privileges in specially marked parking places near front entrances of buildings and attractions, unlimited parking in otherwise limited spaces, and free parking in metered zones. Placards with the international access symbol

(whether for permanent or temporary disability) must be hung from the car's rearview mirror, and I.D. from other states is acceptable.

WEATHER

Weather and Surf Report, tel 213/554-1212

EMERGENCIES

EMBASSIES & CONSULATES

British Consulate General, 11766 Wilshire Blvd., Suite 400, Los Angeles, 90025, tel 310/477-3322
Canadian Consulate General, 550 S. Hope St., 9th Floor, Los Angeles, 90071, tel 213/346-2700

EMERGENCY PHONE NUMBERS/ ADDRESSES

Police, fire, or emergency medical assistance, tel 911
Poison Control Center, tel 800/777-6476
American Red Cross, tel 213/739-5200
Missing Children Hotline, tel 800/222-3463
Department of Consumer Affairs, tel 800/344-9940
Dental Referrals Service, tel 800/422-8338

Hospitals with 24-hour emergency rooms are Cedars-Sinai Medical Center, 8700 Beverly Blvd., West Hollywood, tel 310/855-2000; UCLA Medical Center, 10833 Le Conte Ave., Westwood, tel 310/825-8611; Good Samaritan Hospital, 616 Witmer St., downtown, tel 213/977-2121; Century City Hospital, 2080 Century Park E., Century City, tel 310/553-6211; Children's Hospital, 4650 W. Sunset Blvd., Los Angeles, tel 213/660-2450

24-hour pharmacies: Sav-on Drugs, tel 800/627-2866 for

nearest location; Longs Drugs, 8490 Beverly Blvd., West Hollywood, tel 323/653-0880

LOST PROPERTY

LAX lost property, tel 310/417-0440

Report lost or rifled luggage immediately to your airline's or train depot's customer service desk, and also contact the lost-and-found department. If something is missing from your hotel room, contact the manager. Otherwise, file a report with the local police department; people have been known to turn in found items, including valuables and cash.

LOST CREDIT CARDS

American Express, tel 800/327-2177
Diners Club, tel 800/234-6377
Discover Card, tel 800/347-2683
MasterCard, tel 800/307-7309
Visa, tel 800/847-2911

ACTIVITIES

L.A.'s mild climate, seaside setting, and health-conscious lifestyle provide the ideal combination for outdoor activities. Visitors can indulge virtually year-round in a cornucopia of action—and much of it at little or no cost. Equipment rentals for all types of sports are available throughout the city.

The city's claim-to-fame surf culture thrives at many coastal beaches, particularly world-famed Malibu. Like gang members, some surfers closely guard their surf turf and can make outings less than pleasant for newcomers. Ask at lifeguard stations before hitting the waves. Other beaches cater to swimmers, body surfers, windsurfers, and kayakers. But, again, inquire with lifeguards before jumping in—Southern California waters can surprise with dangerous undertows. The undersea world around Catalina

Island is the preferred locale for snorkeling and scuba diving.

Wide, sandy beaches attract athletes as well as sunbathers, and volleyball at one of the many courts is a favorite out-of-water sport. Venice Beach boardwalk ranks as one of the country's most popular thoroughfares for scantily clad in-line skaters. Hang gliding can be arranged for those who would rather soar above the sands, and fishers can choose from pier fishing, shore fishing, surf casting, or various charters and expeditions.

Joggers and cyclists not only rank beachside paths, but have been bequeathed specially designated lanes along many city streets. Hikers favor trails in the Santa Monica Mountains, San Bernardino National Forest, and at Will Rogers Historic State Park and Griffith Park. Griffith Park, with more than 50 miles of public bridle trails, is also a popular area for horseback riding.

The city is packed with public golf courses and tennis courts, along with exclusive country clubs and private facilities. Numerous public high schools and colleges allow free use of handball and racquetball courts.

In winter months, the San Bernardino and San Gabriel mountains offer snow skiing and snowboarding, and Lake Arrowhead and Big Bear Lake become jet-ski havens during summer months.

Swimmers just looking for a sand-free dip will find pools at almost every hotel and motel, or at public parks and private health clubs.

SPECTATOR SPORTS

Baseball
The Anaheim Angels play their American League rivals, April through September.
Edison Field, 2000 E. Gene Autry Way, Anaheim, tel 714/663-9000
Dodger Stadium sets the scene for the National League's Dodgers home games, April through October.

Dodger Stadium, 1000 Elysian Park Ave., L.A., 323/224-1448

Basketball
The renowned L.A. Lakers take on other NBA teams during their regular season, October through May.
Staples Center, 1111 S. Figueroa St., Downtown, tel 213/742-7333
Not nearly as popular as the Lakers, the Clippers enjoy a loyal following—and tickets are cheaper and easier to come by during the October through May season.
Staples Center, 1111 S. Figueroa St., Downtown, tel 213/745-0500

Boxing
Fight fans can view championship matches, including world title fights, at the Great Western Forum.
Great Western Forum, 3900 W. Manchester Blvd., Inglewood, tel 310/419-3182

Hockey
The L.A. Kings, members of the National Hockey League, push their pucks at the Staples Center, October through April.
Staples Center, 1111 S. Figueroa St., Downtown, tel 310/673-6003

Horse racing
Referred to as the "track of lakes and flowers," Inglewood's Hollywood Park hosts thoroughbred racing, late April through mid-July and early November through late December.
Hollywood Park, 1050 S. Prairie Ave., Inglewood, tel 310/419-1500
Gloriously situated in the foothills of the San Gabriel Mountains, Santa Anita racetrack rates as one of the country's preeminent thoroughbred race tracks with top-stakes racing October through mid-November and late December through late April.
Santa Anita Raceway Park, 285 W. Huntington Dr., Arcadia, tel 626/574-7223

HOTELS & RESTAURANTS

One of the bonuses of L.A.'s vastness is the number of choices visitors have when it comes to both bedding down and chowing down. Stay put in one section of town, or move around to experience some of the many different neighborhoods and their essential flavors.

HOTELS

Los Angeles has an enormous array of accommodation choices, ranging from full-service high rises and discreet celebrity hideaways to comfortable hotels and pension-type establishments. The downtown area is primarily the domain of conventioneers and business travelers; Beverly Hills and the Westside draw a more upscale and sophisticated clientele; Sunset Strip and West Hollywood are where many rock stars and visiting celebrities hang out; Hollywood, though not the best neighborhood to hang your hat, still has its cult following; and Santa Monica and Malibu cater to a combination of all the above who can't resist the sniff of salt air.

Almost all accommodations have their own parking lots (though they are not always free), and the top establishments provide valet parking. Disabled guests will have no problem finding accessible rooms, and nonsmokers will be thrilled to know that larger hotels segregate the puffers on smoking-designated floors.

The room price categories given are rack rates and don't reflect seasonal or weekend rates, which may be considerably lower; it pays to ask. Package deals are often terrific bargains and might include a bottle of champagne, breakfast in bed, massage, or tickets to attractions. Whatever price you negotiate, expect an extra 14 percent hotel tax to be added to the tab. It's advisable to make reservations well in advance, especially during peak seasons and holidays. Hotels are listed here by price, and then in alphabetical order.

RESTAURANTS

Eating well, at any price, is one of L.A.'s greatest assets, and the natives take advantage of their famous restaurant scene as often as possible. Celebrity chefs such as Wolfgang Puck and Joachim Splichal, amongst others, continually draw foodies to their chic restaurants and innovative cuisine. The city's huge immigrant population ensures that Angelenos can also access the ethnic specialties of Central and South America, Asia, Europe, and Africa, all at moderate cost. Reservations for the top spots are mandatory, and though L.A. is a casual city, it's best to ask if a dress code is enforced. Restaurants are listed here by price, and then in alphabetical order.

Credit & debit cards

Most hotels and restaurants accept all major credit cards as well as traveler's checks. Smaller establishments and cafés may accept cash only.
AE = American Express
DIS = Discover
DC = Diners Club
MC = MasterCard
V = Visa

Dining hours

Lunch usually runs from noon until 2 p.m. Dinner is often served as early as 5 p.m., with 7 p.m.–8 p.m. the more sought-after time in better restaurants. Most places serve until 10 p.m.
L = lunch
D = dinner

Finding your hotel or restaurant

To help you pinpoint hotels and restaurants on the ground, we include the nearest cross street to each establishment as well as its address. This detail follows the letters NCS with the symbolized information toward the end of each entry.

DOWNTOWN & VICINITY

Due to downtown's proximity to the convention center and business district, most of the area's hotels tend to be imposing high rises with big names and plenty of services. Restaurants range from long-established ethnic eateries to foodies' musts.

HOTELS

SOMETHING SPECIAL

🏨 REGAL BILTMORE 🍴 HOTEL

The city's elegant grande dame, a social center when it was constructed in the 1920s, was gloriously and expensively restored in the 1980s. This palatial Italian Renaissance hotel features exquisite furnishings, deco murals, and loads of antiques, marble, and gold. Bernard's, one of the city's swankiest restaurants (see p. 245), is cloistered within. Site of early Academy Awards™ presentations, JFK's campaign headquarters, and spiritual leader Paramahansa Yogananda's final heaven-bound journey.
$$$$$
506 S. GRAND AVE., 90071
TEL 213/624-1011
FAX 213/612-1628
NCS: 5th St. 🛈 683 🅿
🔃 🐕 📧 🛗 🌀 All major cards

🏨 HYATT REGENCY 🍴 LOS ANGELES
$$$$
711 S. HOPE ST., 90017
TEL 213/683-1234
FAX 213/629-3230
Near the financial and legal center. Comfortable, with the gamut of business services and a shopping plaza accessed via the lobby.
NCS: Broadway Plaza
🛈 485 🅿 🔃 🐕 🛗
🌀 All major cards

INTER-CONTINENTAL LOS ANGELES
$$$$

231 S. OLIVE ST., 90012
TEL 213/617-3300
FAX 213/617-3399
Residential-style full-service hotel, somewhat more understated than others in this chain. Just a palette's throw from the Museum of Contemporary Art, and former home-from-home for the sequestered O.J. Simpson jury.
NCS: 4th St. ① 439 🅿
⇄ 🅢 ⬜ 🏋 🄰All major cards

LOS ANGELES DOWNTOWN MARRIOTT
$$$

333 S. FIGUEROA ST., 90071
TEL 213/617-1133
FAX 213/613-0291
Business-oriented hotel, close to the Pacific Stock Exchange and World Trade Center. Spacious guest rooms feature marble baths and plenty of glass for city (and smog) views. Abundant business services, including a free limo for nearby sprints or to the fitness center down the street.
NCS: adjacent to I-110
① 469 🅿 ⇄ 🅢 ⬜
🏋 🄰All major cards

WESTIN BONAVENTURE
$$$

404 S. FIGUEROA ST., 90071
TEL 213/624-1000
FAX 213/612-4800
Five cylindrical mirrored towers (rising 33 stories into the downtown sky), where a bustle of conventioneers, business types, and tourists wander eight levels of shops and restaurants or ride a glass elevator to the revolving rooftop restaurant. Extensive services and decent, though smallish, rooms.
NCS: W. 4th St. ① 1354 🅿
⇄ 🅢 ⬜ 🏋 🄰All major cards

WILSHIRE GRAND HOTEL & CENTER
$$$

930 WILSHIRE BLVD., 90017
TEL 213/688-7777
FAX 213/612-3989
High rise, convenient to downtown attractions and the convention center. Unexceptional rooms, but the many available services and amenities—including four imaginative restaurants—keep the house filled.
NCS: Figueroa St. ① 900
🅿 ⇄ 🅢 ⬜ 🏋
🄰All major cards

WYNDHAM CHECKERS
$$$

535 S. GRAND AVE., 90071
TEL 213/624-0000
FAX 213/626-9906
Refined, luxury establishment (originally the 1920s Mayflower Hotel), rife with antiques, oversize beds, marble baths, and an exquisite wood-paneled library where afternoon tea is served. (For the hotel's restaurant, Checkers, see p. 246.)
NCS: W. 5th St. ① 188 🅿
⇄ 🅢 ⬜ 🏋 🄰All major cards

FIGUEROA
$$

939 S. FIGUEROA ST., 90015
TEL 213/627-8971
FAX 213/689-0305
Spanish-style hotel near the convention center, with wrought-iron decor, terra-cotta color schemes, hand-painted furniture, and a decidedly early California ambience.
NCS: W. Olympic Blvd.
① 280 🅿 ⇄ 🅢 ⬜
🄰All major cards

THE INN AT 657
$$

657 W. 23RD ST., 90007
TEL 213/741-2200
B&B in an older residential neighborhood, and a friendly alternative to the big hotels. Apartment-size suites in a renovated 1940s building, full

PRICES

HOTELS
An indication of the cost of a double room without breakfast is given by $ signs.
$$$$$ Over $280
$$$$ $200– $280
$$$ $120–$200
$$ $80–$120
$ Under $80

RESTAURANTS
An indication of the cost of a three-course dinner without drinks is given by $ signs.
$$$$$ Over $80
$$$$ $50–$80
$$$ $35–$50
$$ $20–$35
$ Under $20

kitchens, private baths and entrances, and a homey decor. Full breakfast included.
NCS: Figueroa St. ① 5 🅿

RESTAURANTS

BERNARD'S
$$$$$

REGAL BILTMORE, 506 S. GRAND AVE.
TEL 213/612-1580
One of L.A.'s most elegant and romantic dining rooms, a throwback to an era when dining was a special event replete with silver service and harpsichord music. House specialties are rack of lamb, potato-crusted orange roughy, and a Caesar salad that is prepared at your table.
NCS: W. 5th St. 🅿
🕒 Closed Sun., Mon., & L
🅢 🄰All major cards

CAFÉ PINOT
$$$$

700 W. 5TH ST.
TEL 213/239-6500
Joachim and Christine Splichal have brought their gourmet magic—and their groupies— to the gardens of the Los Angeles Central Library. The brasserie-type fare includes French onion soup, steak

HOTELS & RESTAURANTS

frites, lighter California-French spa cuisine, and homemade ice cream. An olive tree-shaded terrace affords a divine setting.
NCS: Flower St. 🅿️
🕐 Closed Sat. & Sun. L 💲
👜 DC, MC, V

🍴 CHECKERS
$$$$
WYNDHAM CHECKERS,
535 S. OLIVE AVE.
TEL 213/891-0519
Local movers and shakers descend for Asian-influenced, contemporary American cuisine created by 1998 James Beard Award-nominated chef Tony Hodges. Feast in the intimate dining room or on the outside patio.
NCS: W. 5th St. 🅿️ ↕️
💲 👜 All major cards

🍴 CICADA
$$$$
617 S. OLIVE ST.
TEL 213/488-9488
Gorgeous art deco palace on the ground floor of the 1928 Oviatt Building. Chef Christian Shaffer's Italian specialties are outstanding—especially the pasta and seafood dishes.
NCS: W. 7th St. 🅿️
🕐 Closed Sun. & Mon. D
↕️ 💲 👜 All major cards

🍴 THE TOWER
$$$$
1150 S. OLIVE ST.
TEL 213/746-1554
On the Transamerica Center's 32nd floor, hence it offers one of the best views in town. Feast on French-Continental dishes in a romantic setting, while helicopters fly past the windows.
NCS: 11th St. 🅿️ ↕️ 💲
👜 All major cards

🍴 ENGINE COMPANY NO. 28
$$$
644 S. FIGUEROA ST.
TEL 213/624-6996
American comfort food and an excellent wine list at a

1912 fire station reincarnated as a trendy bar and grill. A complimentary shuttle whisks patrons to the nearby Music Center in time for the curtain.
NCS: W. 7th St. 🅿️
🕐 Closed Sat. & Sun. L 💲
👜 All major cards

🍴 TRAXX
$$$
800 N. ALAMEDA ST.
TEL 213/625-1999
Narrow art deco room inside L.A.'s historic Union Station, overseen by chef Tara Thomas, who produces a changing fusion menu incorporating Asian, California, and Italian dishes. The separate bar, in the station's former telephone room, specializes in single-malt Scotches.
NCS: Cesar Chavez Blvd.
🅿️ 🕐 Closed Sat. L & Sun. 💲 👜 All major cards

🍴 WATER GRILL
A runaway favorite fish house with local powerbrokers, business types, and theatergoers. Fresh seafood—such as black sea bass with eel potstickers, and a fabulous oyster bar—are the hallmarks of former Spago chef Michael Cimarusti.
$$$
544 S. GRAND AVE.
TEL 213/891-0900
NCS: W. 5th St. 🅿️
🕐 Closed Sat. & Sun. L 💲
👜 All major cards

🍴 YANG CHOW
$$
819 N. BROADWAY
TEL 213/625-0811
Famous for fiery Szechuan dishes, especially the slippery shrimp and panfried dumplings. The decor and ambience are everything you'd hope for in a Chinatown restaurant.
NCS: W. College St. 🅿️ 💲
👜 AE, MC, V

🍴 THE ORIGINAL PANTRY
$
877 S. FIGUEROA ST.
TEL 213/972-9279
Hearty, cholesterol-laden real American meals at a 1924 L.A. institution open 24 hours a day. Currently owned by city mayor Richard Riordan, who also eats here.
NCS: W. 9th St. 💲

🍴 PHILIPPE THE ORIGINAL
$
1001 N. ALAMEDA ST.
TEL 213/628-3781
Legendary birthplace (1908) of the French dip sandwich, made all the better with "double dipping." Sawdust covers the floor, customers sit at long wooden tables, and the coffee only costs a dime.
NCS: Ord St. 💲

MIDTOWN

Midtown encompasses the Miracle Mile, Museum Row, Fairfax Avenue, and the Farmers Market, ending at Melrose Avenue, where it practically merges with Hollywood, West Hollywood, and Beverly Hills. Hotels and motels in this area tend to be older and on the basic side, though some of the restaurants are noteworthy.

HOTEL

🏨 RADISSON WILSHIRE 🍴 PLAZA
$$$
3515 WILSHIRE BLVD., 90010
TEL 213/381-7411
FAX 213/386-7379
Nothing special, but comfortable, centrally located, and the nicest place to stay in the mid-Wilshire area. Its restau-rants include a sushi bar and a café serving Starbucks' coffee and Ben & Jerry's ice cream.
NCS: S. Normandie Ave.
🛏️ 383 🅿️ ↕️ 💲 🏊
🍴 👜 All major cards

RESTAURANTS

🍴 ATLAS BAR & GRILL
$$$$
3760 WILSHIRE BLVD.
TEL 213/380-8400
Glamorous and cavernous
1930s-style supper club, next
to the Wiltern Theater. Well-
dressed clientele come here
for the exotic Caribbean-style
dishes, flattering lighting, and
sometimes slow service.
NCS: Wiltern Ave. 🅿
🚪 Closed Sat. L & Sun. 🆑
🆂 All major cards

SOMETHING SPECIAL

🍴 CAMPANILE
South of France meets
midtown L.A. in the rustic
cuisine of chefs Mark Peel and
Nancy Silverton (both formerly
at Spago), dished up in a 1920s
building with sunny atrium.
Daily changing menu includes
such standouts as cedar-smoked
trout with fennel salad, and
weekend breakfasts are superb.
Silverton's La Brea Bakery
adjoins.
$$$$
624 S. LA BREA AVE.
TEL 323/938-1447
NCS: Wilshire Blvd. 🅿
🚪 Closed Sun. D 🆑
🆂 All major cards

🍴 GADSBY'S
$$$$
672 S. LA BREA AVE.
TEL 323/936-8471
New American/eclectic
cuisine created by chef/owner
Robert Gadsby, who can't
resist wowing fans with his
remarkable creations where
other chefs dare not go. Duck,
quail, and seafood are usually
on the menu.
NCS: Wilshire Blvd. 🅿
🚪 Closed Sat. L & Sun. 🆑
🆂 All major cards

🍴 PACIFIC DINING CAR
$$$$
1310 W. 6TH ST.
TEL 213/483-6000
The city's oldest steakhouse
(built around an old railroad
car) has served patrons since
1921. Top-quality steaks (the
prime beef is aged on the
premises), great side dishes,
breakfasts, and an extensive
wine list. Open 24 hours.
NCS: Witmer St. 🅿 🆑
🆂 All major cards

🍴 CA'BREA
$$$
346 S. LA BREA AVE.
TEL 323/938-2863
Large portions of excellent
pastas, whole roasted
chickens, osso buco, and daily
specials in a very happening
trattoria.
NCS: 4th St. 🅿 🚪 Closed
Sat. & Sun. L 🆑 🆂 All
major cards

🍴 SONORA CAFÉ
$$$
180 S. LA BREA AVE.
TEL 323/857-1800
Southwestern and
sophisticated south-of-the-
border fare can be enjoyed in
an attractive dining room or
on the outdoor patio. Same
owners as the beloved El
Cholo (see below).
NCS: W. 2nd St. 🅿
🚪 Closed Sat. L & Sun. 🆑
🆂 All major cards

🍴 CANTER'S FAIRFAX
$
419 N. FAIRFAX AVE.
TEL 323/651-2030
Favorite 24-hour "real" deli
with original 1928 decor and
grumpy waitresses. Noshers,
rock stars, and refugees all
gather round the pastrami,
chopped liver, and corned
beef sandwiches. Bakery on
premises; the Kibitz Room
features live music (see
p. 263).
NCS: Beverly Blvd. 🅿 🆑
🆂 MC, V

🍴 EL CHOLO
$
1121 S. WESTERN AVE.
TEL 323/734-2773
L.A.'s oldest Mexican
restaurant (1927), still family
owned and operated. Perfect
preparations of true-blue
Mexican dishes as well as
early California recipes.
Expect long waits, but great
margaritas.
NCS: Olympic Blvd. 🅿 🆑
🆂 AE, MC, V

HOLLYWOOD & WEST HOLLYWOOD

While Hollywood may still
conjure up images of glitz, most
of the accommodations and
much of the neighborhood are
in fact decidedly faded and best
seen by day. Many Hollywood
restaurants, particularly those
on the Melrose Avenue borderline, are some of the trendiest
spots in town. Meanwhile, rock
stars, younger celebs who want
to be near the club scene, super-
models, and their respective
groupies and entourages tend
to nestle happily into West
Hollywood's chic—and
expensive—hotels and hip
dining establishments.

HOTELS

🏨 SUNSET MARQUIS
🍴 HOTEL & VILLAS
$$$$$
1200 N. ALTA LOMA RD., 90069
TEL 310/657-1333
FAX 310/652-5300
The on-premises recording
studio (not to mention the
legendary Whiskey Bar) make
this the top address in town
for musicians and studio
execs. The slightly hidden
location, tight security, private
restaurant, and on-call
massage are added draws.
NCS: Sunset Blvd. 🛏 114
🅿 🔌 🆑 🏊 🏋
🆂 All major cards

🏨 THE ARGYLE
🍴 $$$$
8358 SUNSET BLVD., 90069
TEL 323/654-7100
FAX 323/654-9287
Beautifully restored 1929 art
deco delight befitting its star-
studded clientele. Deco

HOTELS & RESTAURANTS

theme permeates the deluxe guest rooms and suites, all of which have marble baths. Stars hang out at the rooftop pool or in the Fenix restaurant (see below). NCS: La Cienega Blvd. **ⓘ** 64 **P** **⊖** **⬚** **⬚** **⬚** 🃏 All major cards

🏨 CHATEAU 🍴 MARMONT

Pseudo French castle, just off Sunset Boulevard, that has closely guarded the privacy of film stars since it opened in the 1920s. Penthouses, cottages, bungalows, and suites are gently faded, just like some of the actors. Greta Garbo lived here, and John Belushi bid adieu.

$$$$
8221 SUNSET BLVD., 90046
TEL 323/656-1010
FAX 323/655-5311
NCS: Marmont Lane **ⓘ** 63 **P** **⊖** **⬚** **⬚** 🃏 All major cards

🏨 HYATT WEST 🍴 HOLLYWOOD

$$$$
8401 SUNSET BLVD., 90069
TEL 323/656-1234
FAX 323/650-7024
Across from the House of Blues, and with a spectacular view from its rooftop pool. Deco-ish rooms and predictable Hyatt service. Get a streetside room with balcony to keep tabs on the Sunset Strip action, otherwise you'll be facing the hills.
NCS: La Cienega Blvd.
ⓘ 262 **P** **⊖** **⬚** **⬚** 🃏 All major cards

🏨 MONDRIAN 🍴

$$$$
8440 SUNSET BLVD., 90069
TEL 323/650-8999
FAX 323/650-5215
Hipper than hip, contemporary California all-suite property. Spacious accommodations come with floor-to-ceiling windows, fresh flowers, and aromatherapy candles. Exclusive restaurant and bar, continually packed with industry honchos.
NCS: Olive Dr. **ⓘ** 263 **P** **⊖** **⬚** **⬚** **⬚** 🃏 All major cards

🏨 LE PARC 🍴

$$$$
733 N. WEST KNOLL DR., 90069
TEL 310/855-8888
FAX 310/659-7812
Glitzy all-suite hotel, just beyond the main hubbub, with sunken living rooms, fireplaces, stereos with CD players, private balconies, and microwave ovens.
NCS: Melrose Ave. **ⓘ** 154 **P** **⊖** **⬚** **⬚** **⬚** 🃏 All major cards

🏨 CLARION HOTEL 🍴 HOLLYWOOD ROOSEVELT

The historic 1927 Hollywood Roosevelt, site of the first Academy Awards™ presentation, and still a top stay for Tinseltown purists. Former social center for Errol Flynn, Ernest Hemingway, F. Scott Fitzgerald, and Shirley Temple, and the current hideaway for a ghost or two. Memorabilia from the good old days is on display throughout.

$$$
7000 HOLLYWOOD BLVD., 90028
TEL 323/466-7000
FAX 323/462-8056
NCS: N. Orange Dr. **ⓘ** 331 **P** **⊖** **⬚** **⬚** **⬚** 🃏 All major cards

🏨 WYNDHAM BEL AGE 🍴

$$$
1020 N. SAN VICENTE BLVD., 90069
TEL 310/854-1111
FAX 310/854-0926
All-suite property with an unremarkable facade, opulent interior, and residential ambience. South-facing

HOTELS
An indication of the cost of a double room without breakfast is given by $ signs.

$$$$$	Over $280
$$$$	$200– $280
$$$	$120–$200
$$	$80–$120
$	Under $80

RESTAURANTS
An indication of the cost of a three-course dinner without drinks is given by $ signs.

$$$$$	Over $80
$$$$	$50–$80
$$$	$35–$50
$$	$20–$35
$	Under $20

accommodations have private balconies and drop-dead views. Comprehensive rooftop fitness center. (For the hotel's Diaghilev restaurant, see p. 249.)
NCS: Sunset Blvd. **ⓘ** 200 **P** **⊖** **⬚** **⬚** **⬚** 🃏 All major cards

🍴 FENIX AT THE ARGYLE

$$$$$
THE ARGYLE, 8358 SUNSET BLVD.
TEL 323/848-6677
French-American-Cajun fare—including jambalaya and pecan-crusted chicken breast—in a stunning art deco room, which often takes second place to the celebs that show up.
NCS: La Cienega Blvd. **P** **⊕** Closed Sun. D **⊖** **⬚** 🃏 All major cards

🍴 L'ORANGERIE

$$$$$
903 N. LA CIENEGA BLVD.
TEL 310/652-9770
World-class French fare from chef Ludovic Lefèbvre: whole lamb loin, roast chicken, lobster pot pie. One of L.A.'s most palatial, rapturous, and expensive restaurants.

KEY 🏨 Hotel 🍴 Restaurant ⓘ No. of bedrooms **P** Parking ⊕ Closed ⊖ Elevator

NCS: Melrose Ave. 🅿
🕐 Closed L & Mon. 🕙
🚫 All major cards

SOMETHING SPECIAL

🍴 PATINA
Superstar chef Joachim Splichal's flagship restaurant remains an icon in this town of grandiose dining, and is a study in understated elegance. The contemporary French-California cuisine is not mere food, but a true culinary experience more akin to manna from heaven. Corn blinis with marinated salmon and crème fraîche are a favorite.
$$$$$
5955 MELROSE AVE.
TEL 323/467-1108
NCS: Cahuenga Blvd. 🅿
🕐 Closed Sat. & Sun. L, Mon.
🕙 🚫 All major cards

🍴 LE CHARDONNAY
$$$$
8284 MELROSE AVE.
TEL 323/655-8880
Pretend you're in Paris in this replica of Boulevard Saint-Germain's Vagenende. A *belle époque*, unrushed setting, for lovers and Francophiles.
NCS: Sweetzer St. 🅿
🕐 Closed L & Mon. 🕙
🚫 All major cards

🍴 CITRUS
$$$$
6703 MELROSE AVE.
TEL 323/857-0034
Originally opened by Michel Richard, who has since moved on, Citrus still woos industry types with its creative California-French glories. Guests watch from umbrella-shaded tables as their food is prepared in the glass-fronted kitchen.
NCS: Highland Ave. 🅿
🕐 Closed Sun. 🚫 AE, MC, V

🍴 LE COLONIAL
$$$$
8783 BEVERLY BLVD.
TEL 310/289-0660

Very cool spot where local hipsters and stars linger over small portions of nouveau Vietnamese dishes.
NCS: Robertson Blvd. 🅿
🕐 Closed Sat. & Sun. L 🕙
🚫 All major cards

🍴 LES DEUX CAFÉS
$$$$
1638 LAS PALMAS AVE.
TEL 323/465-0509
Join the ultra-cool (most of whom dress in black) at this bistro, hidden within a refurbished early 20th-century house. Chic diners with snazzy inventions such as lobster and tabbouleh salad.
NCS: Sunset Blvd. 🅿
🕐 Closed Sat. L & Sun. 🕙
🚫 All major cards

🍴 DIAGHILEV
$$$$
WYNDHAM BEL AGE, 1020 N. SAN VICENTE BLVD.
TEL 310/854-1111
French-Russian dinner-only place, where you'll be treated like a czar and will feel like one, too, after downing flavored vodkas with beluga caviar.
NCS: Sunset Blvd. 🅿
🕐 Closed L, Sun., & Mon.
🔄 🕙 🚫 All major cards

🍴 LE DÔME
$$$$
8720 SUNSET BLVD.
TEL 310/659-6919
Usually packed with industry power-lunchers, who chomp down the traditional French food, and stars, who lean toward slimming salads.
NCS: Robertson Blvd. 🅿
🕐 Closed Sat. L & Sun. 🕙
🚫 All major cards

🍴 THE IVY
$$$$
113 N. ROBERTSON BLVD.
TEL 310/274-8303
Star and industry heavyweights frequent the flatteringly lit dining room, or outdoor heated patio. American menu with wondrous fried chicken and

hot fudge sundaes, as well as some fancier fare.
NCS: Beverly Blvd. 🅿 🕙
🚫 All major cards

SOMETHING SPECIAL

🍴 JOZU
A Zen-inspired dining experience, where chef Hiasashi Yoshiara enlightens with her perfect preparations (try the Chilean sea bass). Owner Andy Nakano often greets and treats with a glass of sake.
$$$$
8360 MELROSE AVE.
TEL 323/655-5600
NCS: La Cienega Blvd. 🅿
🕙 🚫 All major cards

🍴 LOCANDA VENETA
$$$$
8638 W. 3RD ST.
TEL 310/274-1893
Tiny place with grand Venetian specialties from chef Massio Ornani and owner Antonio Tomassi. Don't pass up the gnocchi.
NCS: Robertson Blvd. 🅿
🕐 Closed Sat. L & Sun. 🕙
🚫 All major cards

🍴 MIMOSA
$$$$
8009 BEVERLY BLVD.
TEL 310/655-8895
Although the setting is low key, chef Jean-Pierre Bosc transports diners to Paris with authentic country French bistro fare, including steak frites and charcuterie plates.
NCS: Crescent Heights Blvd.
🅿 🕐 Closed Sat. L & Sun.
🕙 🚫 All major cards

🍴 MORTON'S
$$$$
8764 MELROSE AVE.
TEL 310/276-5205
Superhyped (it's all true) L.A. institution, dripping with movie stars and moviemakers. Mon. night is the time to go, though ordinary peons

HOTELS & RESTAURANTS

are often snubbed.
NCS: Robertson Blvd. **P**
⊕ Closed Sat. L & Sun. **S**
🅰 All major cards

🍴 THE PALM
$$$$
9901 SANTA MONICA BLVD.
TEL 310/550-8811
Favored spot for the really big
money crowd, who feast on
delectable lobster, mouth-
watering steaks, and finely
tuned martinis.
NCS: Robertson Blvd. **P**
⊕ Closed Sat. & Sun. L **S**
🅰 All major cards

🍴 PINOT HOLLYWOOD
$$$$
1448 N. GOWER ST.
TEL 323/461-8800
One of co-owner/chef
Splichal's burgeoning baby
Patinas serves French bistro
fare just a kiss away from
Paramount Studios. Daily
specials are always
remarkable, and the outdoor
patio is the place to sit.
Fabulous martini bar.
NCS: Sunset Blvd. **P**
⊕ Closed Sat. L & Sun. **S**
🅰 All major cards

SOMETHING SPECIAL

🍴 SPAGO HOLLYWOOD

The heart and soul of
Wolfgang Puck's restaurant
kingdom. Celebrities still make
this a regular haunt, and the
food hasn't slipped one iota.
Anyone who's anyone orders the
Jewish pizza, topped with
smoked salmon and cream
cheese.
$$$$
1114 HORN AVE.
TEL 310/652-4025
NCS: Sunset Blvd. **P**
⊕ Closed L & Mon. **S**
🅰 All major cards

🍴 TOMMY TANG'S
$$$
7313 MELROSE AVE.
TEL 323/937-5733
Modern Thai dishes (small

portions), an animated sushi
bar, and a hip Hollywood
attitude keep the people-
watching trendies coming
through the doorway.
NCS: Fairfax Ave. **P**
⊕ Closed Mon. **S** 🅰 All
major cards

🍴 GEORGIA
$$$
7250 MELROSE AVE.
TEL 323/933-8420
Upscale soul food without the
need to head South or into an
L.A. ghetto. Beautiful people
(including co-owner Denzel
Washington) slum it on
Melrose for okra stew, catfish,
gumbo, and peach cobbler.
NCS: La Brea Ave. **P**
⊕ Closed L **S** 🅰 All
major cards

SOMETHING SPECIAL

🍴 MUSSO & FRANK GRILL

One of Hollywood's most
venerable institutions
(opened in 1919) today retains
much the same ambience, menu,
and, possibly, gruff waiters as it
did when it hosted the likes of
Papa Hemingway, William
Faulkner, Aldous Huxley, and
gossip queens Hedda Hopper
and Louella Parsons. Chicken
potpie, prime rib, turkey with
the works, creamed spinach, and
possibly the most perfect
cocktails on Earth. If only the
walls could talk!
$$$
6667 HOLLYWOOD BLVD.
TEL 323/467-7788
NCS: Cahuenga Blvd. **P**
⊕ Closed Sun. & Mon. **S**
🅰 All major cards

🍴 GREENBLATT'S DELI & FINE WINES
$$
8017 SUNSET BLVD.
TEL 323/656-0606
This 1920s deli/fine wine
shop once served the likes
of Dorothy Parker, in
residence at the long-gone

Garden of Allah Hotel across
the street. Come for
matzo-ball soup, chopped
liver, great sandwiches, and
Sun. breakfast.
NCS: Fairfax Ave. **P** **S**
🅰 All major cards

🍴 HOLLYWOOD CANTEEN
$$
1006 N. SEWARD ST.
TEL 323/465-0961
Upscale "canteen," in the
heart of Hollywood, which
draws industry types from
nearby studios and sound
stages. Although not what it
was in its heyday, it is still a
cool place for an organic salad
or a hefty burger.
NCS: Santa Monica Blvd. **P**
⊕ Closed Sat. L & Sun. **S**
🅰 All major cards

🍴 HOLLYWOOD HILLS COFFEE SHOP
$$
6145 FRANKLIN AVE.
TEL 323/467-7678
The perfect, kitschy
Hollywood coffee shop. Blue-
plate specials, Denver
omelets, corned-beef hash,
and all the eccentricity you
could hope for.
NCS: Vine St. **P** **S**
🅰 MC, V

🍴 PINK'S FAMOUS CHILI DOGS
$
709 N. LA BREA AVE.
TEL 323/9391-4223
Funky hot dog stand, an L.A.
icon since the 1930s, and the
world's most famous place to
down a chili dog. Join hookers,
cops, yuppies, movie stars, and
other wienie fiends.
NCS: Melrose Ave. **P**

🍴 SWINGER'S
$
BEVERLY LAUREL MOTOR
HOTEL, 8020 BEVERLY BLVD.
TEL 323/653-5858
Hip diner, favored by an
alternative crowd in the
wee hours, and by
insignificant others during

---

the daytime. Breakfast includes tofu scramblers. NCS: Crescent Heights Blvd.

P ☀ ❄ Ⓒ All major cards

BEVERLY HILLS & VICINITY

Jet-setters, movie stars, foreign dignitaries, and the superwealthy feel quite at home here, in one of the world's most renowned cities. Beverly Hills hotels are used to pampering the rich and spoilt, and special requests are de rigueur. Restaurants, though remarkable, can be snooty. It's all part of the scene.

SOMETHING SPECIAL

🏨 BEVERLY HILLS 🍴 HOTEL

The legendary 1912 Mission Revival "Pink Palace" has always symbolized Beverly Hills and its glamour, wealth, and rarefied air. Gable, Garbo, Monroe, and Chaplin have all been guests here, most opting for one of the bungalows that nestle amid acres of lush tropical gardens. The hotel's famed Polo Lounge is still a hot spot for those make-or-break Hollywood meetings (see p. 252). Renovated rooms and bungalows feature lavish appointments, marble baths, original art, and butler service.

$$$$$
9641 RODEO DR., 90210
TEL 310/276-2251
FAX 310/281-2905
NCS: Sunset Blvd. 234
P ☀ ❄ 🏊 💪
Ⓒ All major cards

🏨 BEVERLY HILTON 🍴 $$$$$
9876 WILSHIRE BLVD., 90210
TEL 310/274-7777
FAX 310/285-1313
Many Beverly Hills regulars would not think of staying anywhere other than this imposing and somewhat flashy hotel, home to the annual Golden Globe Awards as well

as the marvelously kitschy Trader Vic's restaurant (see pp. 252–53). Tastefully decorated rooms, most with private balconies.
NCS: Santa Monica Blvd.
583 P ☀ ❄ 🏊 💪 Ⓒ All major cards

🏨 L'ERMITAGE BEVERLY 🍴 HILLS $$$$$
9291 BURTON WAY, 90210
TEL 310/278-3344
FAX 310/278-8247
A spectacularly renovated minimalist property, with Asian flair. Spacious rooms adorned with silk bed coverings, stocked bars, marble baths, and French doors opening to views of the Hollywood Hills.
NCS: Foothill Rd. 124
P ☀ ❄ 🏊 💪
Ⓒ All major cards

🏨 FOUR SEASONS 🍴 $$$$$
300 S. DOHENY DR., 90048
TEL 310/273-2222
FAX 310/859-3824
European styling, personal service, and gorgeous public areas with marble floors, original art, and knock-out floral arrangements. Rooms are elegant, and guests are treated to such L.A. essentials as complimentary cell phones and limo rides to Rodeo Drive. (For the hotel's Gardens restaurant, see p. 252.)
NCS: Burton Way 285
P ☀ ❄ 🏊 💪
Ⓒ All major cards

🏨 LE MÉRIDIEN AT 🍴 BEVERLY HILLS $$$$$
465 S. LA CIENEGA BLVD., 90048
TEL 310/247-0400
FAX 310/247-0315
Positioned smack in the middle of La Cienega's restaurant row. Oriental decor and traditional service blend flawlessly with guest rooms and public spaces that are stacked with high-tech gadgets.

NCS: Clifton Way 300
P ☀ ❄ 🏊 💪
Ⓒ All major cards

🏨 THE PENINSULA 🍴 BEVERLY HILLS $$$$$
9882 LITTLE SANTA MONICA BLVD., 90212
TEL 310/551-2888
FAX 310/788-2319
French Renaissance-style boutique property filled with exquisite antiques, tapestries, artwork, and an elite clientele. Guests have access to a chauffeured Rolls Royce. (For the hotel's Belvedere restaurant, see p. 252.)
NCS: Lasky Dr. 196 P
☀ ❄ 🏊 💪 Ⓒ All major cards

🏨 REGENT BEVERLY 🍴 WILSHIRE $$$$$
9500 WILSHIRE BLVD., 90212
TEL 310/275-5200
FAX 310/274-2851
A regal, classic, landmark property with service fit for traditionalist royals (many of whom stay here when in town) and spoilt stars. The magnificent marble lobby, spacious rooms, clubby lounge, and superb restaurant (see p. 252) are part of the glory.
NCS: Rodeo Dr. 394
P ☀ ❄ 🏊 💪
Ⓒ All major cards

🏨 SOFITEL 🍴 $$$$$
8555 BEVERLY BLVD., 90048
TEL 310/278-5444
FAX 310/657-2816
A hit with Francophiles, who feel à maison with cabaret music in the lobby, Provençal-style rooms, Pierre Deux fabrics, and Nina Ricci amenities. And, in case you left your personal trainer at home, the Sofitel will provide a temporary replacement.
NCS: N. La Cienega Blvd.
311 P ☀ ❄ 🏊
💪 Ⓒ All major cards

Air-conditioning ❄ Indoor/🏊 Outdoor swimming pool 💪 Health club Ⓒ Credit cards **KEY**

TRAVELWISE **251**

HOTELS & RESTAURANTS

🏨 BEVERLY PLAZA
🍴 HOTEL
$$$
8384 W. 3RD ST., 90048
TEL 323/658-6600
FAX 323/653-3464
Small hotel with tastefully decorated rooms, limited complimentary limo service, and in-house supper club with dancing.
NCS: N. La Cienega Blvd.
ℹ️ 98 🅿️ ⬆️ 🚭 🏊
🍷 🚫 All major cards

🏨 SUMMIT HOTEL
🍴 RODEO DRIVE
$$$
360 N. RODEO DR., 90210
TEL 310/273-0300
FAX 310/440-3890
An affordable stay in the high-rent district. Nicely renovated boutique-style inn with comfortable guest rooms, but without too much fuss and froufrou.
NCS: Wilshire Blvd. ℹ️ 86
🅿️ ⬆️ 🚭 🚫 All major cards

RESTAURANTS

🍴 THE BELVEDERE
$$$$$
THE PENINSULA BEVERLY HILLS, 9882 LITTLE SANTA MONICA BLVD.
TEL 310/788-2306
The ultimate name in power breakfasts and lunches for somebodies. Creative California menu includes chef Bill Bracken's signature potato-crusted Chilean sea bass with orange reduction sauce and fresh dill.
NCS: Wilshire Blvd. 🅿️
⬆️ 🚭 🚫 All major cards

🍴 THE DINING ROOM
$$$$$
REGENT BEVERLY WILSHIRE, 9500 WILSHIRE BLVD., 90212
TEL 310/275-5200
Formal dining on distinguished Continental cuisine in a European-style room with hand-painted ceilings and murals. Save room for the

Regent trio *brûlées* dessert.
NCS: Rodeo Dr. 🅿️
🔒 Closed Sun. ⬆️ 🚭
🚫 All major cards

🍴 MATSUHISA
$$$$$
129 N. LA CIENEGA BLVD.
TEL 310/659-9639
Prepare to pour over chef Nobu Matsuhisa's copious 30-plus-page menu, containing not only great sushi, but also exceptional seafood specialties such as sea urchin wrapped in shiso leaf.
NCS: Wilshire Blvd. 🅿️
🔒 Closed Sat. & Sun. L 🚭
🚫 All major cards

SOMETHING SPECIAL

🍴 SPAGO BEVERLY HILLS
Chef Lee Hefter turns out traditional meals at this branch of Wolfgang Puck's legendary Hollywood establishment. Much of the Hollywood restaurant's star-studded clientele has, in fact, migrated to this jewel to dine on such delights as French pigeon with foie gras and filet mignon tartare.
$$$$$
176 N. CANON DR.
TEL 310/385-0880
NCS: Wilshire Blvd. 🅿️
🔒 Closed Sun. L 🚭 🚫 All major cards

SOMETHING SPECIAL

🍴 CRUSTACEAN
Dramatic setting, complete with reeds and koi-filled stream, for nouvelle Vietnamese seafood specialties. The roasted whole Dungeness crab is the hands-down favorite.
$$$$
9646 LITTLE SANTA MONICA BLVD.
TEL 310/205-8990
NCS: Bedford Dr. 🅿️
🔒 Closed Sat. L & Sun. 🚭
🚫 All major cards

🍴 GARDENS
$$$$
FOUR SEASONS HOTEL, 300 S. DOHENY DR.
TEL 310/273-2222
Refined, peaceful atmosphere featuring gourmet California cuisine and an extravagant Sun. brunch, with celebrities usually out in force.
NCS: Burton Way 🅿️ ⬆️
🚭 🚫 All major cards

🍴 IL CIELO
$$$$
9018 BURTON WAY
TEL 310/276-9990
Very romantic garden cottage, equally popular for weddings and anniversaries, serving homemade pasta and northern Italian specialties.
NCS: Foothill Rd. 🅿️
🔒 Closed Sun. 🚭 🚫 All major cards

🍴 MAPLE DRIVE
$$$$
345 N. MAPLE DR.
TEL 310/274-9800
High-tech room, with private back entrance for the rich and famous, who come here for meatloaf and other "new" American meals.
NCS: Burton Way 🅿️
🔒 Closed Sun. 🚭 🚫 All major cards

🍴 POLO LOUNGE
$$$$
BEVERLY HILLS HOTEL, 9641 SUNSET BLVD.
TEL 310/276-2251
Sentimental favorite, and most well-known haunt for celebrities and those who seek them out. If you've come to eat, stick with the traditional dishes: You can't go wrong with the McCarthy salad or Polo club sandwich.
NCS: Sunset Blvd. 🅿️ ⬆️
🚭 🚫 All major cards

🍴 TRADER VIC'S
$$$$
BEVERLY HILTON, 9876 WILSHIRE BLVD.
TEL 310/276-6345
Polynesian decor that's so

tacky it's kitschy. Food and drink include *pupu* (appetizer) platters and froufrou rum and juice concoctions. Angelenos will always keep a place in their hearts and bellies for this old-timer.
NCS: Santa Monica Blvd. 🅿️
🕒 Closed L ⬌ 🅢 🅢All major cards

🍴 **FARM OF BEVERLY HILLS**
$$$
439 N. BEVERLY DR.
TEL 310/273-5578
So comfy and down to earth, it's hard to believe it's in Beverly Hills. Chicken and mashed potatoes, sandwiches made with fresh bread, and other happy meals.
NCS: Brighton Way 🅿️ 🅢
🅢 All major cards

🍴 **KATE MANTILINI**
$$$
9101 WILSHIRE BLVD.
TEL 310/278-3699
Warehouse ambience, popular with L.A. trendies for late-night dining on chicken, burgers, and meatloaf. Expect plenty of attitude from the waitpersons.
NCS: Doheny Dr. 🅿️ 🅢
🅢 All major cards

🍴 **PREGO**
$$$
362 N. CAMDEN DR.
TEL 310/277-7346
Long-time favorite trattoria, with excellent pastas, pizzas, grilled seafood, and other northern Italian specialties.
NCS: Rodeo Dr. 🅿️
🕒 Closed Sun. L 🅢
🅢 All major cards

THE WESTSIDE

The Westside—incorporating Westwood, Brentwood, Bel Air, and Pacific Palisades—comprises everything from the student enclave of UCLA to the ritzy neighborhood of Bel Air. Accommodations range from university-oriented motels and a few excellent hotels to the

esteemed Hotel Bel Air. Restaurants run the same course.

HOTELS

SOMETHING SPECIAL

🏨 **HOTEL BEL AIR**
🍴
This ultra-stylish retreat is as famous with upscale locals as it is with very well-heeled visitors. The Mission-style buildings are tucked around acres of magnificent gardens and a swan-filled lake, and the entire property is hidden in a wooded canyon. Rooms and suites are glorious, boasting fireplaces and fresh flowers. Superb restaurant (see below).
$$$$$
701 STONE CANYON RD., 90077
TEL 310/472-1211
FAX 310/476-5890
NCS: Sunset Blvd. 🛈 92
🅿️ ⬌ 🅢 ⛱ 🅥
🅢 All major cards

🏨 **WESTWOOD**
🍴 **MARQUIS HOTEL & GARDENS**
$$$$
930 HILGARD AVE., 90024
TEL 310/208-8765
FAX 310/824-0355
All-suite luxury property, a diploma's throw from the UCLA campus and Westwood village. Apartment-size accommodations and a full range of amenities, including formal teas and limousine service.
NCS: Wilshire Blvd. 🛈 257
🅿️ 🕒 Closed L 🅢 ⛱
🅥 🅢 All major cards

🏨 **LUXE SUMMIT HOTEL**
🍴 **BEL AIR**
$$$
11461 SUNSET BLVD., 90069
TEL 310/476-6571
FAX 310/471-6310
Attractive low-rise, convenient for the Getty Center but a little too close to I-405. Rooms are contemporary and spacious, and many of

PRICES

HOTELS
An indication of the cost of a double room without breakfast is given by $ signs.
$$$$$	Over $280
$$$$	$200– $280
$$$	$120–$200
$$	$80–$120
$	Under $80

RESTAURANTS
An indication of the cost of a three-course dinner without drinks is given by $ signs.
$$$$$	Over $80
$$$$	$50–$80
$$$	$35–$50
$$	$20–$35
$	Under $20

them have balconies.
NCS: I-405 🛈 161 🅿️ ⬌
🅢 ⛱ 🅥 🅢All major cards

RESTAURANTS

🍴 **THE DINING ROOM**
$$$$$
HOTEL BEL AIR, 701 STONE CANYON RD.
TEL 310/472-1211
Everything you'd expect of the posh Hotel Bel Air. A garden path leads past swan-filled streams to a much-romanticized dining room, aglow from both the perpetually lit fireplace and ubiquitous stars. California-French fare.
NCS: Sunset Blvd. 🅿️
🕒 Closed L 🅢 🅢All major cards

🍴 **LA CACHETTE**
$$$$
10506 LITTLE SANTA MONICA BLVD.
TEL 310/470-4992
Chef Jean François Meteigner understands Angelenos who adore French food but who can't handle all the heavy sauces and calories. A relaxing room to exult on bistro fare such as cassoulet and tuna

tartare, without having to rush off to the gym afterwards.
NCS: Beverly Glen Blvd. 🅿
🕐 Closed Sat. & Sun. L 🚭
♿ All major cards

🍴 FOUR OAKS
$$$$
2181 N. BEVERLY GLEN BLVD.
TEL 310/470-2265
Secluded, rustic-style garden spot, overseen by chef Peter Roelant, who turns out country French delights.
NCS: Sunset Blvd. 🅿
🕐 Closed Mon. L ♿ All major cards

🍴 TOSCANA
$$$$
11633 SAN VICENTE BLVD.
TEL 310/820-2448
Solid northern Italian pastas and pizzas in a permanently packed, very noisy trattoria. Service is often brusque but not so much as to deter Brentwoodites.
NCS: Darlington Ave.
🅿 🕐 Closed Sun. L
🚭 ♿ All major cards

🍴 LA BRUSCHETTA
$$$
1621 WESTWOOD BLVD.
TEL 310/477-1052
Publicity-shy celebrities love this down-to-earth trattoria, with its hearty Italian comfort food.
NCS: Santa Monica Blvd. 🅿
🕐 Closed Sat. L & Sun. 🚭
♿ All major cards

SANTA MONICA, VENICE, & MALIBU

Wonderful seaside hotels, historic inns, and trendy restaurants (particularly on the Third Street Promenade or Main Street) share the salt air with older motels and cheap eateries in Santa Monica and Venice. This is the perfect area for beach lovers and smog haters. Malibu, however, doesn't offer much in the way of accommodations despite the reputation it has for its beaches. Visitors who don't have an invitation to some cele-

brity's guest cabana usually opt to stay in Santa Monica instead. Restaurants in Malibu cater to discerning palates and bellies.

HOTELS

🏨🍴 LOEW'S SANTA MONICA BEACH HOTEL
$$$$$
1700 OCEAN AVE., SANTA MONICA, 90401
TEL 310/458-6700
FAX 310/458-0020
Sophisticated atmosphere, with the sand outside the door and Santa Monica Pier just a short stroll away. Most rooms have ocean views, and all come with entry to one of the best fitness centers in town.
NCS: Pico Blvd. 🛏 343 🅿
🛗 🚭 🏊 🏋 ♿ All major cards

🏨🍴 MIRAMAR SHERATON
$$$$$
101 WILSHIRE BLVD., SANTA MONICA, 90401
TEL 310/576-7777
FAX 310/458-7912
Ten-story tower and very private luxury bungalows, built around the original 1889 mansion. Most tower rooms have balconies and boggling ocean views, while those in the historic wing have a residential ambience.
NCS: Ocean Ave. 🛏 300
🅿 🛗 🚭 🏊 🏋
♿ All major cards

🏨🍴 THE RITZ-CARLTON, MARINA DEL REY
$$$$
4375 ADMIRALTY WAY, MARINA DEL REY, 90292
TEL 310/823-1700
FAX 310/823-2403
Another ritzy Ritz-Carlton, this one overlooking the colorful yachts on the marina as well as the Pacific Ocean. Rooms and services follow the signature Ritz tradition, though this one also includes boat charters.
🛏 306 🛗 🚭 🏊 🏋
♿ All major cards

🏨🍴 SHUTTERS ON THE BEACH
$$$$
ONE PICO BLVD., SANTA MONICA, 90405
TEL 310/458-0030
FAX 310/458-4589
Great plantation-like hideaway in the classic style of an early 1900s oceanfront resort. Spacious rooms with shutter doors, soaking tubs (some with surf views), and right-on-the-sand location.
NCS: Ocean Ave. 🛏 198
🅿 🛗 🚭 🏊 🏋
♿ All major cards

🏨 CHANNEL ROAD INN BED & BREAKFAST
$$$
219 W. CHANNEL RD., SANTA MONICA, 90402
TEL 310/459-1920
FAX 310/454-9920
Historic 1910 Colonial Revival inn, off the beaten path in Santa Monica Canyon. Some rooms have ocean views and fireplaces; all have private baths and period furnishings and decor.
NCS: Pacific Coast Hwy.
🛏 14 🅿 🚭 ♿ AE, MC, V

🏨🍴 THE GEORGIAN
$$$
1415 OCEAN AVE., SANTA MONICA, 90401
TEL 310/395-6333
FAX 310/656-0904
Historic hotel, with a loyal following of celebrities seeking anonymity, and visitors who don't swim or gym. Many rooms and suites have ocean views, and there is a restaurant with patio dining.
NCS: Wilshire Blvd. 🛏 84
🅿 🛗 🚭 ♿ All major cards

🏨 MALIBU BEACH INN
$$$
22878 PACIFIC COAST HWY., MALIBU, 90265
TEL 310/456-6444
FAX 310/456-1499
Surprisingly well-priced

Spanish-style beachfront motor inn in the heart of Malibu. The romantic rooms have private oceanfront balconies and fireplaces, and some have Jacuzzis.
NCS: Sweetwater Canyon Rd. ⓘ 47 🅿 🔄 ❄ 🏋
❄ All major cards

RESTAURANTS

SOMETHING SPECIAL

🍴 CHINOIS ON MAIN

Wolfgang Puck comes to Santa Monica (his wife, Barbara Lazaroff, designed the sharp setting). Palate-pleasing, rich French-Chinese-style Puckisms, including barbecued salmon with black and gold pasta, and tempura ahi sashimi in sea-urchin sauce.
$$$$$
2709 MAIN ST., SANTA MONICA
TEL 310/392-9025
NCS: Rose Ave. 🅿
🕐 Closed Sun.–Tues. L ❄
❄ All major cards

🍴 LAVANDE

$$$$$
LOEW'S SANTA MONICA BEACH HOTEL, 1700 OCEAN AVE., SANTA MONICA
TEL 310/576-3181
For lavender lovers—it's in the air, it's in the food, and it's in the sachet that you get to take home after paying the tab. Chef Scott Reed's Provençal oceanfront star.
NCS: Pico Blvd. 🅿 ❄
❄ All major cards

🍴 MICHAEL'S

$$$$$
1147 3RD ST., SANTA MONICA
TEL 310/451-0843
California cuisine got its start in chef Michael McCarty's upscale restaurant. Still special, with a lovely garden and heavenly squab with foie gras.
NCS: Wilshire Blvd. 🅿
🕐 Closed Sat. L, Sun., & Mon. ❄ ❄ All major cards

SOMETHING SPECIAL

🍴 VALENTINO

Piero Selvaggio's flagship restaurant set the standard for Italian cuisine, turning Tuscany into a household word. Chef Angelo Auriana uses top-quality ingredients, including white truffles and prosciutto from heaven; there are also more than 100,000 bottles in the wine cellar. Fri. lunch is quite special.
$$$$$
3115 PICO BLVD., SANTA MONICA
TEL 310/829-4313
NCS: 31st St. 🅿
🕐 Closed Sat. L & Sun.
❄ ❄ All major cards

🍴 GEOFFREY'S

$$$$
27400 PACIFIC COAST HWY., MALIBU
TEL 310/457-1519
Take your pick at this gorgeous clifftop location—the stars or the sunset? Terrific food and ultimate L.A.-style ambience. Enjoy!
NCS: Malibu Canyon Rd. 🅿
❄ ❄ All major cards

🍴 GRANITA

$$$$
23725 W. MALIBU RD., MALIBU
TEL 310/456-0488
Puck at the beach. The master presents sublime seafood, including the signature Mediterranean fish soup with half a lobster and couscous.
NCS: Pacific Coast Hwy. 🅿
❄ ❄ All major cards

🍴 JIRAFFE

$$$$
502 SANTA MONICA BLVD., SANTA MONICA
TEL 310/917-8871
Chef Josiah Citrin serves intensely flavored French-California dishes such as sautéed scallops sprinkled with rock salt and garlic, and fresh fig and arugula salad. Two-story dining room with arched windows.
NCS: 5th St. 🅿 🕐 Closed

Sat. & Sun. L, Mon. ❄
❄ All major cards

🍴 JOE'S RESTAURANT

$$$$
1023 ABBOT KINNEY BLVD., VENICE
TEL 310/399-5811
Casual storefront restaurant very popular with locals, who love chef Joe Miller's real home cookin' (the fish dishes, such as slow-roasted salmon with parsnip purée, are divine), and great weekend brunches.
NCS: Main St. 🅿
🕐 Closed Mon. ❄
❄ All major cards

🍴 ONE PICO

$$$$
SHUTTERS ON THE BEACH, 1 PICO BLVD., SANTA MONICA
TEL 310/587-1717
Modern American cuisine in a gorgeous and romantic oceanview setting. The room is elegant yet comforting, especially when you are eating roast salmon or grilled sword-fish. High prices, but worth it.
NCS: Ocean Ave. 🅿 ❄
❄ All major cards

🍴 RÖCKENWAGNER

$$$$
2435 MAIN ST., SANTA MONICA
TEL 310/399-6504
In the unlikely setting of a mini-mall, chef/owner Hans Röckenwagner turns out eclectic California-German sensations. The crab soufflé is a winner—that is if you get beyond the tantalizing appetizers. Also serves weekend brunch.
NCS: Pico Blvd. 🅿
🕐 Closed Mon. L ❄
❄ All major cards

🍴 SADDLE PEAK LODGE

$$$$
419 COLD CANYON RD., MALIBU
TEL 818/222-3888
It's a fair trek up the canyon to this 1918 stone-and-timber restaurant, but this is where you come for exotic meat

meals. Kangaroo with burgundy-poached pear, or buffalo carpaccio, anyone? NCS: Malibu Canyon Rd. ◨ ⊕ Closed Sat. L, Mon., & Tues. ⑤ ⊗ All major cards

🍴 72 MARKET STREET
$$$$
72 MARKET ST., VENICE
TEL 310/ 392-8720
Co-owners Dudley Moore and Tony Bill have brought American food back into the lives of Angeleno foodies. Meatloaf, chili, and all your favorites, done up with a hint of French.
NCS: Pacific Ave. ◨ ⊕ Closed Sat. & Sun. L ⑤ ⊗ All major cards

🍴 ALLEGRIA
$$$
22821 PACIFIC COAST HWY., MALIBU
TEL 310/456-3132
Casual spot for authentic rustic Italian fare. Go for the thin-crust pizzas.
NCS: Malibu Pier ◨ ⑤ ⊗ All major cards

🍴 INN OF THE SEVENTH RAY
$$$
128 OLD TOPANGA CANYON RD., MALIBU
TEL 310/455-1311
New Age, mostly vegetarian food, and a combination Zen/ Summer of Love ambience.
NCS: Pacific Coast Hwy. ◨ ⊗ All major cards

🍴 OCEAN AVENUE SEAFOOD
$$$
1401 OCEAN AVE., SANTA MONICA
TEL 310/394-5669
A cheery fish house with high-quality produce (including fresh oysters), excellent preparation, not-bad chowder, and ocean views.
NCS: Santa Monica Blvd. ⑤ ⊗ All major cards

🍴 LA SERENATA DE GARIBALDI
$$$
1416 4TH ST., SANTA MONICA
TEL 310/656-7017
Enjoy Mexican classics in a more upscale environment than your everyday taco stand.
NCS: Wilshire Blvd. ◨ ⑤ ⊗ All major cards

🍴 BABALU
$$
1002 MONTANA AVE., SANTA MONICA
TEL 310/395-2500
Eclectic, Caribbean-flavored menu and decor, and almost always crowded. Go for the jerk chicken and sublime desserts.
NCS: 10th St. ◨ ⑤ ⊗ All major cards

🍴 ROSE CAFÉ
$$
220 ROSE AVE., SANTA MONICA
TEL 310/399-0711
Cool and artsy hangout with California-American dishes, plus an attached market. Dine on the patio, but don't expect great service. A hot spot for Sun. breakfast.
NCS: Main St. ◨ ⊗ All major cards

🍴 PATRICK'S ROADHOUSE
$
106 ENTRADA DR., SANTA MONICA
TEL 310/459-4544
Funky spot for burgers and omelets. It looks dumpy, but celebrities love it.
NCS: Pacific Coast Hwy. ◨ ⑤

SAN FERNANDO & SAN GABRIEL VALLEYS

Craftsman-style architecture, old-money mansions, the refined Norton Simon Museum and Huntington Library, and the heavenly scented Tournament of Roses Parade draw discerning travelers to Pasadena and San Marino. Meanwhile, many movie and TV stars hang their hats in the Universal City/Burbank area, where they can be near the studio lots for early morning makeup calls.

HOTELS

SOMETHING SPECIAL

🏨 RITZ-CARLTON 🍴 HUNTINGTON
This splendid 1906 estate-like historic property is reason alone to visit Pasadena. Accommodations are in the tile-roofed main structure, bungalows, or in cottages, all surrounded by acres of impeccably landscaped grounds that also shelter the splendid mural-adorned Picture Bridge. Public rooms are grandiose and amenities profuse. (For the hotel's restaurant, The Grill, see p. 257.)
$$$$$
1401 S. OAK KNOLL AVE., 91106
TEL 626/568-3900
FAX 626/568-3700
NCS: Lake Ave. ⓘ 392 ◨ ⊖ ⑤ ▨ ▼ ⊗ All major cards

🏨 DOUBLETREE HOTEL 🍴 PASADENA
$$$$
191 N. LOS ROBLES AVE., 91101
TEL 626/792-2727
FAX 626/795-7669
Luxury hotel with a spacious lobby, well-appointed guest rooms, and a lovely plaza and restaurant area. Good weekend deals.
NCS: Walnut Ave. ⓘ 350 ◨ ⊖ ⑤ ▨ ▼ ⊗ All major cards

🏨 SHERATON 🍴 UNIVERSAL
$$$
333 UNIVERSAL TERRACE PKWY., 91608
TEL 818/980-1212
FAX 818/985-4980
Literally on the Universal Studios backlot, and a prime stamping ground for working celebs. Extensive amenities include complimentary

transportation to the studios. Package deals often toss in studio tour tickets.
NCS: Lankershim Blvd.
ⓘ 483 P 🔄 🛇 🏊
🏋 🆑 All major cards

🏨 SPORTSMEN'S LODGE
🍴 $$$
12825 VENTURA BLVD., 91604
TEL 818/769-4700
FAX 818/769-4798
Low-lying resort-type property offering a calm oasis from the city bustle, with tropical landscaping, a lagoon, and waterfalls. Transportation to Universal Studios is provided.
NCS: Coldwater Canyon Ave. ⓘ 191 P 🔄 🛇 🏊 🏋 🆑 All major cards

🏨 UNIVERSAL CITY
🍴 HILTON & TOWERS
$$$
555 UNIVERSAL TERRACE PKWY., 91608
TEL 818/506-2500
FAX 818/509-2058
Modern steel-and-glass high rise with spacious rooms, marble baths, big-hotel services and amenities, and a convenient location. Complimentary transportation to the studios.
NCS: Lankershim Blvd.
ⓘ 484 P 🔄 🛇 🏊
🏋 🆑 All major cards

RESTAURANTS

🍴 THE GRILL
$$$$$
RITZ-CARLTON HUNTINGTON, 1401 S. OAK KNOLL AVE.
TEL 626/568-3900
Continental cuisine, including rack of lamb, roasted venison, and chateaubriand, in a clubby semiformal dining room.
NCS: Lake Ave. P
🕐 Closed L 🛇 🆑 All major cards

🍴 ARROYO CHOP HOUSE
$$$$
536 S. ARROYO PKWY.
TEL 626/577-7463

Prime beef, martinis, and cigars are standard fare at this successful dinner-only house. The owners also boast the Parkway Grill, next door (see below).
NCS: E. California Blvd. P
🕐 Closed L 🛇 🆑 All major cards

🍴 PINOT BISTRO
$$$$
12969 VENTURA BLVD.
TEL 818/990-0500
Chef Joachim Splichal lets his hair down in a Dali-esque café that serves classic bistro dishes.
NCS: Coldwater Canyon Ave.
P 🕐 Closed Sat. & Sun. L
🛇 🆑 All major cards

🍴 THE RAYMOND
$$$$
1250 S. FAIROAKS AVE.
TEL 626/441-3136
Frequently changing California/Continental menu and weekend brunches, served in a splendidly restored classic Craftsman cottage. Cozy and romantic.
NCS: Columbia St. P
🕐 Closed Mon. 🛇 🆑 All major cards

SOMETHING SPECIAL

🍴 YUJEAN KANG'S
Nouvelle California/Chinese fusion creations by chef Kang continually fascinate and include lobster stir-fried with fava beans, sea bass with kumquats, and meringue-topped soup.
$$$$
67 N. RAYMOND AVE.
TEL 626/585-0855
NCS: Colorado Blvd. P
🛇 🆑 All major cards

🍴 BISTRO 45
$$$
45 S. MENTOR AVE.
TEL 626/795-2478
Romantic art deco bistro with California-French cuisine and an excellent wine list.

Artistically served bouillabaisse, hearty cassoulets, and seared ahi tuna.
NCS: Colorado Blvd. P
🕐 Closed Sat. & Sun. L, Mon.
🛇 🆑 All major cards

🍴 CA' DEL SOLE
$$$
4100 CAHUENGA BLVD.
TEL 818/985-4669
Italian trattoria with great pasta and seafood. Favorite haunt of Universal Studio execs.
NCS: Lankershim Blvd. P
🕐 Closed Sat. L 🛇 🆑 All major cards

🍴 PARKWAY GRILL
$$$
510 S. ARROYO PKWY.
TEL 626/795-1001
Contemporary California offerings in the Puck tradition, including wood-fired pizzas. Open kitchen, herbs and greens grown on premises, and always a festive atmosphere.
NCS: California Blvd. P
🕐 Closed Sat. & Sun. L 🛇
🆑 All major cards

🍴 ART'S DELI
$$
12224 VENTURA BLVD.
TEL 818/762-1221
Huge sandwiches and magnificent corned beef in a place where you're likely to hear the latest comedy spiel from local sitcom writers.
NCS: Laurel Canyon Blvd.
P 🛇 🆑 All major cards

🍴 JULIENNE
$$
2649 MISSION ST.
TEL 626/441-2299
Casual country-French café, popular with ladies who lunch on light entrées such as apricot chicken, quiches, brioches, soups, and sandwiches. Box lunches available for concerts and picnics.
NCS: El Molino Ave.
P 🕐 Closed Mon.–Sat. D, Sun. 🛇 🆑 All major cards

SHOPPING IN LOS ANGELES

L.A. is shop-till-you-drop territory. You'll find everything you desire and, no doubt, a few things you'd never before imagined. Spend a little or a lot, and shop every day if the urge takes you—most stores open Sundays and holidays. Unless you're dressed to the nines, you might get the cold shoulder by snobby sales clerks at high-class stores and boutiques. Don't be afraid to shop around for what you want; the city is so large, and there are so many choices, that you can almost always find a good deal. After all, this city runs on deals.

Department stores Greater L.A. has no shortage of department stores. Barney's of Beverly Hills (9570 Wilshire Blvd.), a branch of the New York company, is the most exclusive, with five floors of high-priced fashions and home accessories, and plenty of snooty attitude. Neiman-Marcus (9700 Wilshire Blvd.) and Saks Fifth Avenue (9600 Wilshire Blvd.), also in Beverly Hills, are appropriately stocked with opulent clothing, accessories, and jewelry. Nordstrom (Westside Pavilion, West L.A.) is renowned for its personal service, while Bloomingdale's (Century City Shopping Center and Beverly Center) is another New York transplant; both offer quality without bank-breaking prices. Mid-range mainstays include Macy's and Robinsons-May—you'll find one or both in most shopping malls.

Shopping malls Was there life in L.A. before the shopping mall? Most Angeleno consumers, young and old, spend plentiful hours thinking about, dreaming about, and going to the mall. After all, the Valley Girl phenomenon originated at the Sherman Oaks Galleria (Ventura & Sepulveda Blvds., San Fernando Valley). L.A.'s most popular malls are the Beverly Center (Beverly & La Cienega Blvds., West Hollywood); Century City Shopping Center & Marketplace (Santa Monica Blvd. at Avenue of the Stars, Century City); Santa Monica Place (Broadway at 2nd Street, Santa Monica); Westside Pavilion (Pico & Westwood Blvds., West L.A.), and Seventh Street Marketplace (7th & Figueroa Sts.,

downtown). Very serious shoppers will definitely want to trek to Orange County's South Coast Plaza, a mega-mall with nearly 300 shops.

Nearly every mall is anchored by at least one, if not several, large department stores, along with smaller retail chain stores, some one-of-a-kind shops, and a barrage of others that might include restaurants, food courts, movie theaters, cafés, bars, hair salons, and day spas. Parking is almost always free and most stores are open every day. Even nonshoppers find it difficult to resist the mall as cultural event.

Antiques shops Antiques hounds can scour everything from fine to funky in the shops around Melrose Avenue, La Brea Avenue, and Beverly Boulevard in the Melrose shopping district; along San Fernando Valley's Ventura Boulevard; and at antiques malls such as Cranberry House (12318 Ventura Blvd., Studio City), Santa Monica Antique Market (1607 Lincoln Blvd., Santa Monica), and the Pasadena Antique Center (480 S. Fair Oaks Ave., Pasadena). All are open daily.

Boutiques Rodeo Drive, the Melrose Avenue area, and Sunset Strip are the prime venues for designer salons and unique boutiques, although there is also a smattering along Brentwood's San Vicente Boulevard, and Santa Monica's Third Street Promenade, Montana Avenue, and Main Street.

Flea markets Flea markets are also called swap meets. The best is at the Rose Bowl (1001 Rose

Bowl Dr., Pasadena), held the second Sunday of each month. The array of merchandise is boggling, and even the heartiest and most efficient shoppers rarely make it through every aisle. Come early, wear good shoes, and keep taking deep breaths.

CLOTHING

You can find any style you could wish for, from preworn, hole-in-the-knees Levis to one-of-a-kind designer creations and celebrities' old movie costumes, and from skin-tight spandex to free-flowing chiffon. After all, this is the land of fashion statements.

Alfred Dunhill of London 201 N. Rodeo Dr., Beverly Hills. Tel 310/274-5351.
Very gentlemanly British-made suits, sweaters, shirts, and other garb, as well as Dunhill's signature pipes and tobacco.
American Rag 150 S. La Brea Ave. Tel 323/935-3154.
Chic denim jeans and jackets, as well as high-quality vintage wear for men and women. Coffee bar on the premises.
Ann Taylor 406 N. Beverly Dr. Tel 310/385-0051.
Classic, conservative, day and evening wear for women.
A/X Armani Exchange 2940 Main St., Santa Monica. Tel 310/396-8799.
Armani for regular folk. Casual wear, including T-shirts, at affordable prices and with the labels intact.
Battaglia 306 N. Rodeo Dr. Tel 310/276-7184.
For men who appreciate fine Italian silk suits, cashmere sweaters, and all the accoutrements.
Betsey Johnson 8050 Melrose Ave. Tel 323/852-1534.
Somewhat outlandish fine urban-hip polyester and spandex creations on Melrose Avenue.
Chanel 400 N. Rodeo Dr. Tel 310/278-5500.
Coco Chanel's signature suit is among the superior offerings on

two Chanel collection floors filled with fashion, perfume, and jewelry.

Christian Dior 230 N. Rodeo Dr. Tel 310/859-4700. Closed Sun.
The Dior line of clothing, perfume, and accessories.

Diavolina Shoes 7383 Beverly Blvd. Tel 323/936-3000.
One of the hippest shoe shops in town for everything from thongs and mules to pumps and stilettos. L.A.'s sculptural Sky Shoes are also stocked.

Emporio Armani 9533 Brighton Way. Tel 310/271-7790.
More affordable Armani sportswear and accessories for men and women, housed on three levels.

Georgio Armani 436 N. Rodeo Dr. Tel 310/271-5555. Closed Sun.
Armani elegance for both sexes, at high prices.

Govinda's 3764 Watseka Ave. Tel 301/204-3263.
Cool Indian hippie-wear, along with baby clothes, jewelry, bags, and other accessories.

Harari 110 N. Robertson. Tel 310/275-3211.
Stylish, yet hip, flowing fashions and accessories for women.

Jonathan A. Logan 8336 Melrose Ave. Tel 323/653-9155. Closed Sun.
Custom leather pants, jackets, and coats from the leather king used by the stars.

Laura Urbinati 8667 Sunset Blvd. Tel 310/652-3183.
Urbinati's prestigious knitwear and swimming suits, as well as clothing by an elite group of other designers, housed on two levels.

Madison 106 S. Robertson Ave. Tel 310/275-1930.
Interesting assortment of trendy ware for contemporary women.

Maxfield 8825 Melrose Ave. Tel 310/274-8800. Closed Sun.
Celebrities and costumers pay top dollar here for designer names such as Armani, Missoni, Sander, and Yamamoto.

Polo/Ralph Lauren 444 N. Rodeo Dr. Tel 310/281-7200.
Lauren's extensive collection of

sportswear, active wear, career gear, and accessories for men and women.

Ron Herman/Fred Segal 8100 Melrose Ave. Tel 323/651-4129.
Superhip shopping for both cutting-edge and designer duds.

Tommy Hilfiger 468 N. Rodeo Dr. Tel 310/888-0132.
An enormous store with sporty Hilfiger classics for everyone, including kids.

Tyler Trafficante 7290 Beverly Blvd. Tel 323/931-9678. Closed Sun.
Expensive, impeccably tailored women's wear in a ring-the-bell atelier. Julia Roberts might possibly be in the dressing room.

Urban Outfitters 1440 3rd St. Tel 310/394-1404.
Huge industrial space where hipsters and wanna-bes bag sportswear with trendy labels. Lots of accessories and toys.

ACCESSORIES

Hermès scarves, Gucci bags, feather boas, and other adornments are found throughout the shopping enclaves, some pricey and some downright cheap. Choose wisely, as accessories make the outfit!

Del Mano Gallery 11981 San Vicente Blvd., Brentwood. Tel 310/476-8508.
Artisan-crafted handbags, belts, jewelry, and other wearable art.

Frederick's of Hollywood 6608 Hollywood Blvd. Tel 323/466-8506.
No description is needed for Hollywood's icon of froufrou and kinky underthings (see p. 109).

Gucci 347 N. Rodeo Dr. Tel 310/278-3451.
Handbags and luggage, emblazoned with one of the most famous insignias in the fashion world.

Harry Winston 371 N. Rodeo Dr. Tel 310/271-8554.
In business for more than 100 years, often adorning Oscar nominees with the kind of dazzle that makes you adjust your TV

set. Not cheap.

Hermès 434 N. Rodeo Dr. Tel 310/278-6440. Closed Sun.
Famous for signature silk scarves (foulards).

l.a. Eyeworks 7407 Melrose Ave. Tel 323/653-8255.
Eyeglasses as art, from the ordinary to the outrageous. High quality, but prices to match.

La Perla 433 No. Rodeo Dr., Beverly Hills. Tel 310/860-0561.
Top-of-the-line (at Rodeo Drive prices) lingerie, nighties, and swimsuits, favored by celebrity clientele.

Louis Vuitton 295 N. Rodeo Dr. Tel 310/859-0457.
Another impressive and recognizable logo on luggage, wallets, and leather goods.

M.A.C. 8500 Beverly Blvd., Beverly Center. Tel 310/659-6201.
One of the in-crowd's favorite makeup stores, often frequented by makeup artists.

Moondance Jewelry Gallery 1530 Montana Ave. Tel 310/395-5516.
More than 50 jewelry artists exhibit an eclectic assortment of designs in a variety of price ranges.

Tiffany & Co. 210 N. Rodeo Dr. Tel 310/273-8880.
World famous for all those baubles and bangles that make life bearable.

Trashy Lingerie 402 N. La Cienega Blvd. Tel 310/652-4543.
Become a member for a few bucks, then enter this friendly world of corsets, lace, leather, and special orders. Celebrities often stock up here.

CHILDREN

Every self-respecting L.A. kid has a wardrobe that can accommodate restaurant dining, beach outings, casting calls, and the theater and concerts.

And Apple Pie 1211 Montana Ave. Tel 310/393-4588.
Infant and toddler specialty shop with a large selection of adorable styles and popular brands.

FAO Schwarz Glendale Galleria. Tel 818/547-5900.

L.A. branch of the famous New York toy shop, packed with dolls, stuffed animals, and creative, educational, and high-tech toys and games.

Harry Harris Shoes for Children 409 N. Canon Dr. Tel 310/274-8481.
Terrific selection of sport shoes and European leather for happy little feet.

Jacadi 10250 Santa Monica Blvd., Century City Shopping Center. Tel 310/203-0101.
High-quality play clothes, dress-up wear, shoes, and accessories for infants through elementary school age.

Mille Petites Fleurs 10250 Santa Monica Blvd., Century City Shopping Center. Tel 310/203-0424.
Exquisite, European-style clothing and accessories for dress-to-impress boys and girls.

Pixie Town 400 N. Beverly Dr. Tel 310/323-6415. Closed Sun.
Delightful—and delightfully expensive—designer duds for newborns and bigger kids.

Pom D'Api 9411 Brighton Way. Tel 310/278-7663.
French footwear for children, including sandals, loafers, dress shoes, and slippers.

BOOKS

Branches of the big chains, such as Barnes & Noble, Crown, Bookstar, and Borders, are prominent throughout L.A.'s neighborhoods and suburbs. Nonetheless, this city thrives on its unique independent and smaller enterprises.

Bodhi Tree 8585 Melrose Ave. Tel 310/659-1733.
Wonderful New Age/ metaphysical shop, once catering only to L.A.'s weird but now reeling in the Deepak Chopra celebrity crowd. Lots of workshops, readings, and the like.

Book Soup 8818 Sunset Blvd. Tel 310/659-3110.
Narrow aisles packed with books, many of them travel, photography, and Hollywood-type titles. In the middle of Sunset Strip and open every day until midnight.

Brentano's 10250 Santa Monica Blvd., Century City Shopping Center. Tel 310/785-0204.
Excellent selection, including art books and coffee-table show-offs. Frequent author readings.

The Cook's Library 8373 W. 3rd St. Tel 323/655-3141. Closed Sun.
Thousands of books on food and wine, including new, used, and rare titles.

A Different Light 8853 Santa Monica Blvd. Tel 310/854-6601.
L.A.'s premier gay and lesbian-oriented shop, with readings as well as art and music events.

Distant Lands 56 S. Raymond Ave., Pasadena. Tel 626/449-3220.
Thousands of travel guides and travel-related books and literature, videos, maps, and travel gear. Occasional guest speakers and slide presentations.

Dutton's 11975 San Vicente Blvd. Tel 310/476-6263.
An L.A. chain with rooms full of new and used books, plus music CDs and cassettes. Readings by many prominent authors. Other branches in Burbank and the San Fernando Valley.

Elliot Katt Bookseller 8568 Melrose Ave. Tel 310/652-5178. Closed Sun.
One of the city's best sources for books on theater and other performing arts. Producers, directors, and other movie types pay frequent visits.

Hennessey & Ingalls 1254 3rd St., Santa Monica. Tel 310/458-9074.
Comprehensive collection of art and architecture titles, on Santa Monica's promenade.

Larry Edmunds Book Shop 6644 Hollywood Blvd. Tel 323/463-3273. Closed Sun.
Stacks of tomes relating to film and theater. Also posters, movie stills, movie magazines, scripts, and rare titles.

Midnight Special 1318 3rd St., Santa Monica. Tel 310/393-2923.
Large shop on the promenade, with eclectic assortments of everything from fiction and poetry to political science and humanities. Good selection of magazines and literary journals.

The Mysterious Bookshop 8763 Beverly Blvd. Tel 310/659-2959.
Old and new mysteries and thrillers, plus browsers that include private eyes and spies.

Rand McNally 10250 Santa Monica Blvd., Century City Mall. Tel 310/556-2202.
Heaps of maps, travel books, and related accessories.

Samuel French 7623 Sunset Blvd. Tel 323/876-0570. Closed Sun.
Every film script and theater book you'd ever hope to find is housed in this Hollywood institution.

Traveler's Bookcase 8375 W. 3rd St. Tel 323/655-0575.
Good selection of travel guides, related literature, and maps.

Vroman's 695 E. Colorado Blvd., Pasadena. Tel 626/449-5320.
The region's largest independent bookstore, in operation for more than a century, is crammed with books, magazines, audio books, stationery, and gift items.

MUSIC

As with bookstores, there are numerous independent music outlets in addition to the well-known chains. The large establishments, such as Tower, do indeed tower. But this is L.A., a major pulse in the industry, and so there are alternatives galore for music lovers.

A-1 Record Finders 5639 Melrose Ave. Tel 323/732-6737.
Large stock of hard-to-find music, and if they don't have it, they'll get it. Vinyl only, please.

Penny Lane 12 W. Colorado Blvd., Pasadena. Tel 626/564-0161.
Reasonably priced new and used records and CDs, as well as listening stations so you can sample before you buy.

Pyramid Music 1340 Third

Street Promenade, Santa Monica. Tel 310/393-5877.
Eclectic mix of new and used CDs, cassettes, and vinyl. Hard-to-find titles, as well as those high on the charts.
Rhino Records 1720 Westwood Blvd. Tel 310/474-8685.
In addition to CDs put out on its own label, Rhino offers an excellent array of new and used CDs from other international independent artists and companies.
Vinyl Fetish 7305 Melrose Ave. Tel 323/935-1300.
The latest releases from the ever changing L.A. music scene.
Virgin Megastore 8000 Sunset Blvd. Tel 323/650-8666.
Richard Branson's musical megapolis in the center of Sunset Strip. Everything from classical to cutting edge, plus videos, computer games, listening stations, and free parking.

HOUSEWARES & INTERIOR DESIGN

Every type of home accessory can be found in L.A., from cheap plastic fruit to pure silk linens.

Details 8625 Melrose Ave. Tel 310/659-1550. Closed Sun.
European- and American-designed architectural elements.
Diva 8802 Beverly Blvd. Tel 310/278-3191.
Unique light fixtures, plus stylish accessories.
Freehand 8413 W. 3rd St. Tel 323/655-2607.
One-of-a-kind handmade pottery, ceramics, and other craftwork.
Geary's 351 N. Beverly Dr. Tel 310/273-4741.
Load up on Wedgewood and Baccarat at this très exclusive store.
Goat 306 S. Edinburgh Ave. Tel 323/651-3133.
Out-of-the-ordinary gifts and decor for those looking for less expensive and less showy items.
Highlights 2427 Main St., Santa Monica. Tel 310/450-5886. Closed Sun.

Top-of-the-line lamps and lighting, plus special orders.
Homeworks 2923 Main St., Santa Monica. Tel 310/396-0101.
Affordable and unusual housewares and decorative items.
Orange 2455 Robertson Blvd. Tel 310/652-5195.
Fabulous couches, chairs, filing cabinets, and garbage pails—done in hot colors, fake fur, and other in-tune finishes.
Pratesi 9024 Burton Way. Tel 310/274-7661. Closed Sun.
Why sleep on cotton when you can snuggle into pure silk sheets and cashmere coverlets?
Shabby Chic 1013 Montana Ave., Santa Monica. Tel 310/394-1975.
A frequent haunt of celebrities in search of eye-catching accessories and furnishings.
Urban Outfitters 1440 Third Street Promenade, Santa Monica. Tel 310/394-1404.
Change establishment offering hip sportswear, trendy labels, and funky accessories in converted-warehouse ambience.
Williams Sonoma 339 N. Beverly Dr. Tel 310/274-9127.
A full range of exquisite cookware, kitchen utensils, and culinary accessories.
Z Gallerie 42 W. Colorado Blvd., Pasadena. Tel 626/578-1538.
A chain store with unique and affordable designer pieces, including home accessories, furnishings, and gifts.

FOOD & WINE

Long a haven for foodies, L.A. offers a superb range of ambrosiac edibles and sips, for take-home souvenirs or to enjoy on the spot.

Bristol Farms 7880 Sunset Blvd. Tel 323/874-6301.
In business for decades, this terrific gourmet shop stocks gorgeous foodstuffs, as well as flowers, and fine wines. A deli counter is an added bonus.
The Candy Factory 12508 Magnolia Blvd., North Hollywood. Tel 818/766-8220.

Celebrities seeking one-of-a-kind novelty chocolates or sweet occasions beat a path to this San Fernando Valley shop.
Epicurus 625 Montana Ave., Santa Monica. Tel 310/395-1352.
This popular wine shop stocks California and imported wines, including hard-to-find vintages.
See's Candies
Established in 1921, See's was one of California's first chocolatiers and is still one of the best. Counters are laden with everything from lollipops to original-recipe creams and chews. Look for the black-and-white shops, in just about every shopping mall in the city.

ONLY IN L.A.

Paris has perfume, New York has bagels, Tahiti has black pearls, and L.A. has the strange and the theatrical.

Cinema Glamour Shop 343 La Brea Ave. Tel 323/933-5289.
This is no ordinary thrift shop—donations of clothing and accessories come from the estates of celebrities and showbiz personalities. Scheduled auctions are prime events for collectors.
It's A Wrap 3315 W. Magnolia Blvd., Burbank. Tel 818/567-7366.
Costumes are purchased straight from the films. Dress the part of action hero, nasty villain, or sultry temptress.
L.A. County Coroner Gift Shop 1104 N. Mission Rd. Tel 323/343-0760. Closed Sun.
Toe-tag key chains, replica skeletons, screen-printed T-shirts, and other kitschy death-related items.
Star Wares 2817 Main St., Santa Monica. Tel 310/399-0224.
Celebrities such as Cher and Mel Gibson clean out their very own closets for this store, so if you want to feel their vibes against your skin this is the place to come.

ENTERTAINMENT

The entertainment capital of the world wows visitors with every conceivable type of entertainment, much of it on the city streets. For listings, check Sunday's *Los Angeles Times* "Calendar" section, the free *L.A. Weekly* (distributed at restaurants and shops each Thursday), or the monthly *L.A. Magazine*. Book way ahead for top performances.

THEATER

L.A. offers everything from star-studded spectacles to local theater and avant-garde performance art.

Actors' Gang Theater 6209 Santa Monica Blvd. Tel 323/465-0566.
Actor Tim Robbins was one of the founders of this venue, which presents everything from Molière to musicals, as well as some alternative pieces.

Ahmanson Theater 135 N. Grand Ave., at the Performing Arts Center. Tel 213/972-7401.
Many Broadway mega-productions, such as *Miss Saigon* and *Phantom of the Opera*, in a 2,000-seat space. Bring your high-powered binoculars.

Coronet Theater 366 N. La Cienega Blvd. Tel 310/657-7377.
An intimate playhouse, home to the L.A. Public Theater and the Youth Academy of Dramatic Arts.

Geffen Playhouse 10886 Le Conte Ave. Tel 310/208-5454.
Lovely Spanish Revival theater with fine acoustics for one-person shows, pre- or post-Broadway works, celebrity-turned-playwright productions, and a plethora of prominent actors.

Henry Fonda Theater 6126 Hollywood Blvd. Tel 213/468-1700.
Impressive name (although not a great neighborhood) for musicals and touring shows.

James A. Doolittle Theater 1615 N. Vine St. Tel 323/462-6666.
Year-round roster of musicals, dramas, comedies, and new works presented at a 1,038-seat venue in the center of Hollywood.

Mark Taper Forum 135 N. Grand Ave., at the Performing Arts Center. Tel 213/628-2772.

Less daunting than the Ahmanson, with a mere 750 seats in a three-quarter round. Director Gordon Davidson has offered hundreds of classics as well as new works, including *Black Elk Speaks* and *Children of a Lesser God*.

Matrix Theater Company 7657 Melrose Ave. Tel 323/852-1445.
Award-winning L.A. equivalent of off-Broadway theater, with excellent productions of works by Harold Pinter, Samuel Beckett, Simon Gray, and other fine playwrights.

Odyssey Theater Ensemble 2055 S. Sepulveda Blvd. Tel 310/477-2055.
Noteworthy smaller theater company, offering avant-garde reproductions with mostly unknown (as yet) actors.

Pantages Theater 6233 Hollywood Blvd. Tel 323/468-1700.
Grand 2,600-seat art deco palace, former home of the Academy Awards™ presentations, and now site of lavish Broadway musicals and concerts.

Pasadena Playhouse 39 S. El Molino Ave., Pasadena. Tel 626/356-7529.
Landmark theater, opened at the turn of the 20th century, and at its present location since 1925. Many big-name actors have been given their start here. Mostly non-controversial old-money favorites such as *Steel Magnolias* and *Bus Stop*.

OPERA, DANCE, & CLASSICAL MUSIC

While the greatest international names are almost always playing in town, don't miss out on L.A.'s own prestigious local companies, many either already famous or well on their way. The Music Center is the foremost venue, and the Hollywood Bowl and Greek Theater are favorites for outdoor productions.

Dorothy Chandler Pavilion 135 N. Grand Ave., in the Performing Arts Center. Tel 213/972-8001.
An enormous 3,200-seat, acoustically fabulous auditorium, and grand dame of spaces. Home to the world-class Los Angeles Philharmonic Orchestra. The Los Angeles Opera performs classics, Sept.–June, bringing superstars such as Placido Domingo and Maria Ewing to the stage. Touring ballet companies—including the American Ballet Theater and the Joffrey Ballet—are also hosted here.

Greek Theater 2700 N. Vermont Ave. Tel 323/665-1927.
An outdoor Greek-style amphitheater at Griffith Park, presenting a summer schedule of renowned classical, pop, rock, and jazz stars.

Hollywood Bowl 2301 N. Highland Ave. Tel 323/850-2000.
This local landmark is a favorite with residents and tourists, who adore picnicking under the stars while enjoying a roster that has included such diverse performers as The Beatles, Elton John, and the Philharmonic Orchestra during its summer season, as well as prestigious jazz and classical music festivals.

Shrine Auditorium 665 W. Jefferson Blvd. Tel 213/749-5123.
This bizarre white mosque, built for the Shriners, was formerly the setting for the Grammy Awards and the Academy Awards, and hosts such esteemed touring dance companies as the Bolshoi, the Kirov, and the American Ballet Theater. Choral gospel groups practically raise the dome with their fervor.

UCLA Center for the Arts 405 N. Hilgard Ave. Tel 310/825-2101.
Royce Hall, designed in 1919, hosts year-round performances of elite musicians, and theater

and dance companies, including visiting troupes such as Paul Taylor and Martha Graham.

POP, ROCK, JAZZ, & BLUES

This is Musicville, U.S.A., where you can listen to anything your heart, ears, and feet desire. Lots of celebrities are regular club items, although you probably won't see them as most places provide private rooms for the big names. Some of the clubs require advance tickets, and most of the action doesn't get going until 9 or 10 p.m.

The Baked Potato 3787 Cahuenga Blvd. W. Tel 818/980-1615.
Venue for terrific jazz sessions since the mid-1970s.
Catalina Bar & Grill 1640 N. Cahuenga Blvd. Tel 323/466-2210.
An intimate club with great acoustics and best-in-the-business jazz performers.
Daddy's 1610 N. Vine St. Tel 323/463-7777.
Cool jazz, especially on Mon. nights, when owner/actor Jeff Goldblum and his five-piece combo take over the stage.
Doug Weston's Troubador 9081 Santa Monica Blvd. Tel 310/276-6168.
One of L.A.'s old-timers. It has metamorphosed from its original folk sounds to hot alternative music.
Genghis Cohen Cantina 740 N. Fairfax Ave. Tel 323/653-0640.
Popular with talent scouts in search of future Grammy winners. Mellow rock, unplugged performances.
Harvelle's 1432 4th St., Santa Monica. Tel 310/395-1676.
One of the oldest blues clubs on the Westside, but with a Southside Chicago groove.
Hollywood Athletic Club 6525 Sunset Blvd. Tel 323/962-6600.
Deejays from London and L.A. spin rock and techno.
House of Blues 8430 Sunset Blvd. Tel 323/848-5100.

Top blues talents, including such notables as Charlie Musselwhite and Etta James.
Jack's Sugar Shack 1707 N. Vine St. Tel 323/466-7005.
Friendly Polynesian-style venue for well-known rock and pop stars, as well as those who are up and coming. Paper umbrellas in the drinks.
Lunaria 10351 Santa Monica Blvd. Tel 310/282-8870.
Top-notch jazz and blues acts hit the stage most evenings.
McCabe's Guitar Shop 3101 Pico Blvd., Santa Monica. Tel 310/828-4403.
Long-time venue for unplugged punk and rock, country music and rockabilly.
The Mint 6010 W. Pico Blvd. Tel 323/954-9630.
Blues and jazz in an out-of-the-limelight setting. Don't be surprised to find big names either performing or toe-tapping in the audience.
The Palace 1735 N. Vine St. Tel 323/467-4571.
Art deco Hollywood icon, with a killer sound system and big-name rock acts.
The Roxy 9009 Sunset Blvd. Tel 310/276-2222.
Hot rock, pop, and jazz acts in a happening Sunset Strip nightspot.
The Viper Room 8852 Sunset Blvd. Tel 310/358-1880.
Co-owner Johnny Depp's infamous place, where many young celebrities are apt to be playing on stage. Mon. is jam night; other evenings have different themes.
Whisky A Go Go 8901 Sunset Blvd. Tel 310/625-4202.
The infamous club where it all happened. You won't see The Doors here these days, but plenty of alternative and hard-rock talent is still on the bill. Expect long lines to get in.

BARS & NIGHTCLUBS

L.A. has plenty of cool bars and hot dives, many with waits in line while "fashion police" check you out to see if you're cool enough

to gain entry. If you're even remotely dorky, at least try to pick up a fashionable companion. Your best chance is to wear all black and order martinis. Welcome to the Cocktail Nation.

Atlas Supper Club 3760 Wilshire Blvd. Tel 213/380-8400.
Superb deejays, popular with the après-performance spillover from the adjacent Wiltern Theater.
Chez Jay 1657 Ocean Ave., Santa Monica. Tel 310/395-1741.
Saloon-type bar near the Santa Monica Pier that has catered to a mixed clientele (including former governor Jerry Brown) for decades.
Conga Room 5364 Wilshire Blvd. Tel 323/938-1696.
Huge dance floor with some of the best names in salsa, samba, ska, and swing.
The Derby 4500 Los Feliz Blvd. Tel 323/663-8979.
Elegant 1940s-style supper club for '40s-style swingers in zoot suits and vintage wear.
Le Dôme 8720 W. Sunset Blvd. Tel 310/659-6969.
After the dinner crowd have folded their napkins, the bar action begins—often elbow-deep in celebrity imbibers.
Formosa 7156 Santa Monica Blvd. Tel 323/850-9050.
One of L.A.'s long-time favorite bars, with hideaway booths and celebrity photos on the walls. Used as a setting for the film L.A. Confidential.
Goldfinger's 6423 Yucca St. Tel 323/962-2913.
A martini and dancing spot for spies and Bond girls.
Gotham Hall 11431 Third Street Promenade, Santa Monica. Tel 310/394-8865.
Purple decor (including the pool tables) and Batman ambience.
Kibitz Room 419 N. Fairfax Ave. Tel 323/651-2030.
Popular spot with hipsters and oldsters, adjacent to Canter's deli. Live music almost every night.
Lava Lounge 1533 N. La Brea Ave. Tel 323/876-6612.

ENTERTAINMENT

Kitschy and cool. A very hip gathering spot for L.A.'s scene.
Liquid Kitty 11780 W. Pico Blvd. Tel 310/473-3707.
Hip Westsiders hit this place for cocktails and the latest sounds.
Molly Malone's 575 S. Fairfax Ave. Tel 323/935-1577.
Irish ales and traditional music for those who wish they were in the Emerald Isle rather than LaLaLand.
Q's 11835 Wilshire Blvd. Tel 310/477-7550.
Brentwood trendies drink brews and shoot pool, pretending to be just regular folk.
La Scala 410 N. Canon Dr. Tel 310/275-0579.
Celebrities frequent this intimate bar, which has a star-studded wine list.
Ye Olde King's Head 116 Santa Monica Blvd. Tel 310/451-1402.
For Brits and Anglophiles, who come to share ales and tales.

CABARET & COMEDY

These days the Cocktail Nation dons its best designer duds to sip martinis and listen to lounge acts that, until a few years ago, they wouldn't have been caught dead at. The Atlas Supper Club and Canter's Kibitz Room (see p. 263) both offer cabaret enter-tainment once or twice a week. Comedy clubs parade big-name performers as well as wanna-bes; many of the country's most famous comedians got their start on local stages.

Cinegrill 7000 Hollywood Blvd. Tel 323/466-7000.
L.A.'s most popular cabaret club, housed in the landmark Clarion Hollywood Roosevelt Hotel.
Comedy Store 8433 Sunset Blvd. Tel 323/656-6225.
Wonderful comedy acts at L.A.'s top laugh-a-second, three-room venue. Famous names, such as Jerry Seinfeld, often make impromptu appearances.
Gardenia Club 7066 Santa Monica Blvd. Tel 323/467-7444.
Upscale, New York-style cabaret acts with contemporary vocalists and variety performers.

Groundlings Theater 7307 Melrose Ave. Tel 323/934-9700.
Ground-breaking improvisation, where the crowd-pleasers move on to shows like *Saturday Night Live*. Pee Wee Herman started out here.
The Improvisation 8162 Melrose Ave. Tel 323/651-2583.
This East Coast transplant—live from New York—is one of L.A.'s premier comedy clubs, with plenty of hot new talent as well as already-made-it-big names.
Laugh Factory 8001 Sunset Blvd. Tel 323/656-1336.
Stand-up comics and improv acts nightly, some terrific, others mediocre. Take your chances.

CINEMA

Not surprisingly, the words "film" and "L.A." are synonymous. Film buffs can catch everything from new releases (often months before they screen in other cities) to art and classic films. Alas, L.A. has abandoned most of its treasured movie palaces and gone the megaplex route, though there are a few plush old glories left. Many cinemas offer bargain matinees. The daily *Los Angeles Times* features comprehensive listings.

Cinerama Dome Theater 6360 Sunset Blvd. Tel 323/466-3401.
Originally built for the Cinerama craze (*It's a Mad Mad Mad Mad World* played here for years), the spacious venue with its superscreen and multitrack sound system is now popular for mainstream films.
El Capitan Theater 6838 Hollywood Blvd. Tel 323/467-7674.
An exquisite art deco palace with mostly mainstream and Disney-oriented features.
Egyptian Theater 6712 Hollywood Blvd. Tel 323/466-3456.
The American Cinemateque Independent Film Series is held at this Egyptian Revival movie palace, one of Hollywood's favorites. Art films and experi-

mental works are also on the bill.
Fine Arts Theater 8556 Wilshire Blvd. Tel 310/652-1330.
The unassuming exterior shelters a decorative interior, where both art and mainstream offerings are shown.
Goldwyn Pavilion 10800 Pico Blvd. Tel 310/475-0202.
Multiplex in a mall, with both mainstream and art films.
Laemmle's Royal Theatre 11523 Santa Monica Blvd. Tel 310/477-5581.
Foreign and independent films are shown at this comfortable theater (unfortunately in a semi-ugly area).
Mann's Bruin 925 Broxton Ave. Tel 310/208-8998.
A 1930s Westwood landmark, with a wraparound marquee and first-run movies.
Mann's Chinese Theater 6925 Hollywood Blvd. Tel 323/464-8111.
The world's most famous movie house and Hollywood icon shows mainstream films to audiences who love the wide screen and top-notch sound system. Glitzy premieres are still held here, and the footprints are still out front.
Mann's Village 961 Broxton Ave. Tel 310/208-5576.
A 1920s exterior, yet modern screen and sound within. Comfortable seating, a real balcony (with good viewing), and mostly first-run features.
Melnitz Hall 405 Hilgard Ave. Tel 310/825-2345.
This theater on the UCLA campus (with its famed film school) offers film aficionados avant-garde, lesser-known, and classic movies.
New Beverly Cinema 7165 Beverly Blvd. Tel 323/938-4038.
Hollywood classics, documentaries, foreign films and—that endangered species—the double bill.
Nuart Theater 11272 Santa Monica Blvd. Tel 310/478-6379.
The city's best revival house has long lines for its classics, independent films, documentaries, double bills, and midnight specials.

INDEX

Bold page numbers
indicate illustrations

A

A & M Recording Studios 128
ABC Entertainment Center
165
Academy of Motion Picture
Arts and Sciences 168
Activities 243
Adamson House 199, 202
Ahmanson Theater 53
Airports and air services
236–37
Alcohol 241
Alexandria Hotel 74
Alvarado Terrace 98
Ambassador College 215
Ambassador Hotel 79
American Film Institute 138
Anaheim Station 62
Anderton Court 157
Angelino Heights 150
Angel's Flight Railway 57, **57**
Angelus Temple 150
Anthony House 148
Aquarius Theater 127
Architecture 39–41
The Argyle 135
Arroyo Seco 211
  Colorado Street Bridge
  211
  Jet Propulsion Laboratory
  211
Art 36–39
Art museums and galleries
36–37
Artesia Station 62
Artists and Writers
Building 157
ATMs 241
Autry Museum of Western
Heritage 145, **145**
Avila Adobe 49
Ayers House 213

B

Banco Popular 74
Banks 241
Banning, Phineas 25–26
Barfly 134
Barney's Beanery 135
Barnsdall Art Center 117
Barnsdall Park 117
  Barnsdall Art Center 117
  Junior Arts Center 117
  Municipal Art Gallery 117
Bars and nightclubs 263–64
Beat scene 35–36
Bel Air 184
Bel Air Hotel 184, **184**
Belasco Theater 67
Bergamot Station 192–93
Beverly Center 98
Beverly Hills Cactus
Garden 168
Beverly Hills High School 168
Beverly Hills Hotel 160, **161**

Beverly Hills Public Library
154
Beverly Hills Trolley 155
Beverly Hills and vicinity
151–68
  Academy of Motion
  Picture Arts and
  Sciences 168
  Beverly Hills Cactus
  Garden 168
  Beverly Hills High School
  168
  Beverly Hills Hotel 160
  Center for Motion
  Picture Study 168
  Century City 164–65
  Golden Triangle 154–55
  Green Acres 168
  Greystone Mansion and
  Park 162
  Holocaust Center 167
  hotels and restaurants
  251–53
  map 152–53
  Museum of Television and
  Radio 163
  Museum of Tolerance
  166–67
  Pickfair 168
  Virginia Robinson
  Gardens 162
Beverly Theatre 154
Big Bear Lake 234
Biltmore Hotel 65, **65**
Bird Sanctuary 143
Body Shop 135
Bolsa Chica Ecological
Reserve 230
Book Soup 134
Bradbury Building 65, **65**
Brand Library and Art
Galleries 224
Braun Research Library 149
Brentwood 184–85
  Brentwood Country Mart
  185
  Dutton's Bookstore 185
  Schnabel House 185
  Sturges House 185
Broad Beach 199
Bruin 172
Bullocks Wilshire 79, **79**
Bunker Hill 46, 57–59
  Angel's Flight Railway 57,
  57
  Bunker Hill Steps 57
  Museum of Contemporary
  Art (MOCA) 58–59, **58**
Bus tours 238–39
Buses 238
Business services 239

C

Cabaret and comedy 264
Cabrillo Marine Aquarium
196
Cajun Bistro 132
California African-American
Museum 72, **72**

California Heritage
Museum 192
California Incline 198
California Institute of
Technology (Caltech) 221
California Science Center
70, **71**, 72
Capitol Records Tower
115, **115**
Car breakdown 237
Car culture 90–91
Car rental 237
Carole & Barry Kaye
Museum of Miniatures 94,
94
Catalina Island 226, **227**,
232, **232**
CBS Television City 77, 98
Cedars Sinai Medical
Center 98
Celebrity gazing 107, 116
Center for Motion Picture
Study 168
Central Library 64, **64**
Century City 164–65
  ABC Entertainment
  Center 165
  Century City Shopping
  Center and Marketplace
  164, **164–65**
  Century Plaza Hotel 165
  Century Plaza Towers 164
  Farmers Market 165
  Fox Plaza 165
  Shubert Theater 165
  Twentieth Century Fox
  165
Century Plaza Hotel 165
Century Plaza Towers 164
Chandler, Raymond 35
Chateau Marmont 132
Chavez Ravine Arboretum
150
Chinatown 46, 51, **51**
Cinema 42, 264
Cinerama Dome Theater
127
City Hall 46, 52
City of Los Angeles Craft &
Folk Art Museum 95, **95**
Civic Center 52
Classical music 262–63
Climate and seasons 236
Clothing 236
Cole House 213
Colorado Street Bridge 211
The Comedy Store 132
Compton Station 62
Continental Building 74
Creative Artists Agency 155
Credit and debit cards 241,
243, 244
Crescent Heights
Boulevard 129
Crossroads of the World
127
Cruises 239
Culbertson House 214
Culture and the arts 34–44

D

Dance 44, 262–63
The Darkroom 82
DASH 238
Del Amo Station 62
Descanso Gardens 224
Desmond's 82
Director's Guild of America
128
Disabilities, travelers with 242
Disney Concert Hall 53
Disney Studios 208, **208**
Disneyland 226, 228–29,
228–29
Dodger Stadium 150
Dome 172
Dominguez-Wilshire
Building 82
Dorothy Chandler Pavilion 53
Downtown 45–74
  Biltmore Hotel 65, **65**
  Bradbury Building 65, **65**
  Bunker Hill 46, 57–59
  Central Library 64, **64**
  Chinatown 46, 51
  Civic Center and City
  Hall 46, 52
  El Pueblo de Los Angeles
  21–23, 48–49
  Exposition Park 46–47,
  70–73
  Garment District 74
  Grand Central Market 66,
  66
  Historic Theater District
  67, **67**
  hotels and restaurants
  244–46
  Little Tokyo 46, 55–56
  Los Angeles Children's
  Museum 74
  Los Angeles Times
  Building 54, **54**
  map 46–47
  Metro Art 37–38, 60–63,
  60, 61
  Museum of Neon Art
  (MONA) 68, **68**
  Performing Arts Center
  53, **53**
  Shrine Auditorium 69
  Spring Street 74
  Staples Center 74
  Union Station 50, **50**, 60
  University of Southern
  California 69, **69**
  Watts Towers **39**, 74
  Wells Fargo History
  Museum 74
Driving 237
Driving regulations 237
Duncan-Irwin House 214
Dutton's Bookstore 185

E

Earthquakes 200
Edmund D. Edelman
Hollywood Bowl Museum
113

Egyptian Theater 108, **108–109**, 110
El Capitan Theater 109, 110, **110**
El Pueblo de Los Angeles 21–23, 48–49, **49**
  Avila Adobe 49
  Italian Hall 48
  Old Plaza 48–49, **49**
  Olvera Street **48**, 49
  Pelanconi House 49
  Sepulveda House 49
  Zanja Madre 49
El Rey Theater 82
Electric Fountain 155
Elysian Park 150
Embassies and consulates 242
Emergencies 242–43
Emergency phone numbers/ addresses 242–43
Ennis-Brown House 147, **147**
Entertainment 262–64
Excursions 225–34
  Catalina Island 226, **227**, 232, **232**
  Disneyland 226, 228–29
  Knott's Berry Farm 226, 234
  Legoland 234
  Long Beach 231
  map 226–27
  Orange County 226, 230
  Palm Springs and vicinity 226, 233
  San Bernardino Mountains 226, 234
  San Diego 234
  Six Flags Magic Mountain 234
  Tijuana 234
Exposition Park 46, 70–73
  California African-American Museum 72, **72**
  California Science Center 70, 72
  Natural History Museum of Los Angeles County 72–73, **73**

F

Fairfax Avenue 77, 94
Fantasy Foundation 147
Farmers Markets **26–27**, 77, 95, 165
Faxes and Internet access 239
Fern Dell 143
Fifth Street Station 62
Film industry 29, 100, 114, 116, 118–19, 122, 206–208
Finnish Folk Art Museum 215
First Street Station 62–63
Fisher Art Gallery 69
Floods 200
Forest Lawn Memorial Park 209, **209**

Formosa Café 135
Fowler Museum of Cultural History 173, 174
Fox Plaza 165
Frances Howard Goldwyn Hollywood Branch Library 111
Franklin D. Murphy Sculpture Garden 173, 175
Frederick's of Hollywood 109, 111, **111**
Freeman House 120

G

Gamble House **40–41**, 211, 212–13, **212–13**
Garden of Allah 129
Garment District 74
Geffen Contemporary at MOCA 56, **59**
Gehry, Frank O. 41, 98, 196
George Lucas Film School 69
Getty Center **42–43**, 171, **176–77**, 176–82
Getty House 81, **81**
Getty Villa 198
Gin Ling Way 51
Globe Theater 67
Golden Triangle 154–55
  Beverly Hills Public Library 154
  Beverly Theatre 154
  City Hall 154
  Civic Center 154
  Creative Artists Agency 155
  Electric Fountain 155
  Music Corporation of America Building 154
  O'Neill House 155
  Rodeo Drive 154–55, 156–57
  Spadena House 155
  Unocal Gas Station 154
  U.S. Post Office 154
Golf Rush 24–25
Gower Gulch 122, 126–27
Granada Building 78–79
Grand Central Market 66, **66**
Grand Station 62
Greek Theater 143
Green Acres 168
Greenblatt's Delicatessen 129, 132
Greystone Mansion and Park 162
Griffith Observatory and Planetarium 144
Griffith Park 142–45
  Autry Museum of Western Heritage 145
  Bird Sanctuary 143
  Fern Dell 143
  Greek Theater 143
  Griffith Observatory and Planetarium 144
  Griffith Recreation Area 143

  L.A. Equestrian Center 143–44
  map 140–41
  merry-go-round 143
  Sunset Ranch 144
  Travel Town 143
Griffith Park and vicinity 139–50
  Angelino Heights 150
  Angelus Temple 150
  Braun Research Library 149
  Chavez Ravine Arboretum 150
  Dodger Stadium 150
  Elysian Park 150
  Heritage Square Museum 150
  Longest Staircase 150
  Los Angeles Zoo 146
  Los Feliz 141, 147
  Lummis House 150
  Silver Lake 141, 148
  Southwest Museum 141, 149
Griffith Recreation Area 143
Guinness World of Records Museum 109, 110
Guitar Centre 128

H

Hancock Park 81
  Getty House 81
  La Brea Avenue 81
  Larchmont Village 81
  Rothman House 81
Harry Winston 157
Hawks House 214
Helen Lindhurst Architecture Gallery and Library 69
Helen Lindhurst Fine Arts Gallery 69
Heritage Square Museum 150
Hermosa Beach 196
High Tower 120
Hiking 239
Hindry House 214
Historic Theater District 67, **67**
Hollyhock House **116–17**, 117
Hollywood & Highland complex 101, 110, 112
Hollywood Athletic Club 127
Hollywood Boulevard 102–11
  Egyptian Theater 108, 110
  El Capitan Theater 109, 110
  Frances Howard Goldwyn Hollywood Branch Library 111
  Frederick's of Hollywood 109, 111
  Guinness World of Records Museum 109, 110

Hollywood & Highland complex 101, 110, 112
Hollywood Entertainment Museum 104, 110
Hollywood Roosevelt Hotel 107–108, 110
Hollywood Wax Museum 109, 110
  Knickerbocker Hotel 111
  LACE 111
  Larry Edmund's Cinema and Theater Bookshop 110–11
  Lingerie Museum 109
  Mann's Chinese Theater 106–107, 110
  map 111
  Max Factor Museum of Beauty 104–105
  Musso & Frank Grill 107, 111
  Pantages Theater 109, 111
  Ripley's Believe It or Not! Odditorium 109, 110
  Universal News Agency 110
  Walk of Fame **2–3**, 102–104, **103**
  walking tour 110–11
Hollywood Bowl 112–13
Hollywood Entertainment Museum **104**, 104–106, 110
Hollywood Forever 123
Hollywood Heritage Museum 112
Hollywood High School 128, **128**
Hollywood Hills 120
  Freeman House 120
  High Tower 120
  Hollywood Reservoir 120
  Hollywoodland 120
  Whitley Heights 120
Hollywood Marketplace 127
Hollywood Palladium 127
Hollywood Reservoir 120
Hollywood Roosevelt Hotel 107–108, 110
Hollywood Sign **16–17**, **114–115**, 115–16
Hollywood and Vine 114–16
Hollywood Wax Museum 109, 110
Hollywood and West Hollywood 29, 99–138
  American Film Institute 138
  Barnsdall Park 117
  Edmund D. Edelman Hollywood Bowl Museum 113
  Gower Gulch 122, 126–27
  Hollyhock House **116–17**, 117
  Hollywood & Highland Complex 101, 110, 112
  Hollywood Boulevard 102–11

Hollywood Bowl 112–13, **112–13**
Hollywood Forever 123, **123**
Hollywood Heritage Museum 112
Hollywood Hills 120
Hollywood & Vine 114–16
hotels and restaurants 247–51
John Anson Ford Amphitheater 138
Louis B. Mayer Library 138
map 100–1
Max Factor Building 138
Mulholland Drive 121
Paramount Pictures Studio 122, **122**
Sunset Boulevard 126–28
Sunset and Crescent Heights 129
Wattles House and Park 138
West Hollywood 101, 130–37
Yamashiro Restaurant 138
Hollywood/Vine Station 61
Hollywood/Western Station 61
Hollywoodland 120
Holocaust Center 167
Hospitals 242
Hotels and restaurants 244–57
House of Blues 134
House Un-American Activities Committee (H.U.A.C.) 31, 118–19
Huntington, Henry 25–26, 222
The Huntington 222–23
Huntington Beach 230
Huntington Pier 230
Hustler Hollywood 134
Hutchins House 214
Hyatt West Hollywood 132

I

Imperial/Wilmington Station 62, 63
Inn of the Seventh Ray 198
Insurance 236
International Surfing Museum 230
Italian Hall 48

J

Japanese Cultural and Community Center 55–56
Japanese Village Plaza 56
Japanese-American National Museum 56
Jesse Hoyt Smith House 213
Jet Propulsion Laboratory 211
John Anson Ford Amphitheater 138
Junior Arts Center 117

K

KCET 147
Kenneth Hahn Station 62
Key Club 133
Kidspace Museum 224
Knickerbocker Hotel 111
Knott's Berry Farm 226, 234
Korean Cultural Center 80
Korean-American Museum 80
Koreatown 76–77, 80, **80**

L

La Brea Avenue 81
La Brea Tar Pits 76, 83
L.A. County Courthouse 52, **52**
L.A. Equestrian Center 143–44
L.A. Film Office 116
LACE 111
Laguna Beach 230
Lake Arrowhead 234
Landslides 200
Larchmont Village 81
Larry Edmund's Cinema and Theater Bookshop 110–11
Le Dôme 134
Legoland 234
Lingerie Museum 109
Liquor laws 241
Literature 34–36
Little Tokyo 46, 55–56
  Geffen Contemporary at MOCA 56, **59**
  Japanese Cultural and Community Center 55–56
  Japanese Village Plaza 56
  Japanese-American National Museum 56
Living Desert Wildlife and Botanical Park 233
Local customs 241
Locations, book, film and TV 240–41
Long Beach 231
  Long Beach Aquarium of the Pacific 231
  Long Beach Museum of Art 231
  Queen Mary 231
  Shoreline Village 231
Longest Staircase 150
Looff Carousel 191
Los Angeles
  appearance and image 158–59
  architecture 39–41
  car culture 90–91
  celebrity gazing 107, 116
  culture and the arts 34–44
  film industry 29, 100, 114, 116, 118–19, 122, 206–208
  history 18–33

natural disasters 200
population 11, 31
religions and cults 124–25
Los Angeles Children's Museum 74
Los Angeles County Museum of Art 84–89, **84, 85**
Los Angeles Harbor 196
  Cabrillo Marine Aquarium 196
  Los Angles Maritime Museum 196
Los Angeles Maritime Museum 196
Los Angeles Theater 67
Los Angeles Times Building 54, **54**
Los Angeles Zoo 146
Los Feliz 147. 141
  Ennis-Brown House 147
  Fantasy Foundation 147
  KCET 147
  Lovell House 147
  Shakespeare Bridge 147
  Sowden House 147
  Walt Disney House 147
Lost property 243
Louis B. Mayer Library 138
Lovell House 147
Loyola Law School 98
Lummis House 150

M

MacArthur Park **77**, 78
Malibu 188, 189, **197**, 197–99
  Adamson House 199, 202
  Malibu Lagoon Museum 199, 202
  Malibu Lagoon State Beach 199
  Malibu Pier 199
Manhattan Beach 196
Mann Village 172
Mann's Chinese Theater **105**, 106–107, 110
Marina del Rey 196
  Burton Chace Park 196
  Fisherman's Village 196
Mark Taper Forum 53
Mathias Botanical Garden 175
Max Factor Building 138
Max Factor Museum of Beauty 104–106
Mayan Theater 67
Medical insurance 236
Melrose Avenue 77, **96**, 96–97, **97**
Metro 238
Metro Art 37–38, 60–63, **60, 61, 62**
Metro Center Station 60, 62
Metro map 63
Midtown 75–98
  Alvarado Terrace 98
  Beverly Center 98

Carole & Barry Kaye Museum of Miniatures 94, **94**
CBS Television City 77, 98
Cedars Sinai Medical Center 98
City of Los Angeles Craft & Folk Art Museum 95, **95**
Fairfax Avenue 77, 94
Farmers Market 77, 95
Hancock Park 81
hotels and restaurants 246–47
Koreatown 77, 80, **80**
La Brea Tar Pits 76, 83
Los Angeles County Museum of Art 84–89, **84, 85**
Loyola Law School 98
map 76–77
Melrose Avenue 77, 96–97
Miracle Mile 76, 82, **82**
Museum Row 82
Petersen Automotive Museum 92–93, **92–93**
St. Elmo's Village 98
South Bonnie Brae Street 98
Storyopolis 98
Wilshire Boulevard 76, 78–79, 82
Millard House 214, **214**
Million Dollar Theater 67
Miracle Mile 76, 82, **82**
Mission San Fernando Rey de España 20, 224
Mission San Gabriel Arcángel 20, 224
Missions 20–21, 39
Mondrian **127**, 134
Money 241
Moorten Botanical Garden 233
Morgan Intercollegiate Athletics Center 174
Mormon Temple 186
Mulholland, William 28–29
Mulholland Drive 121
Municipal Art Gallery 117
Murals 38–39
Museum of Contemporary Art (MOCA) 58–59, **58, 59**
Museum of Flying 202
Museum of Jurassic Technology 202
Museum of Neon Art (MONA) 68, **68**
Museum Row 82
Museum of Television and Radio 163, **163**
Museum of Tolerance **166**, 166–67
Music Corporation of America Building 154
Music scene 44, 262–63
Musso & Frank Grill 107, 111

N

National holidays 241
Native Americans 18,
 20–21, 24, 39
Natural disasters 200
Natural History Museum of
 Los Angeles County
 72–73, **73**
NBC Television Studios 208
Neutra House 148, **148**
Newport Beach 230
Newspapers 239–40
Norton Simon Museum
 216, 216–17

O

O2 Bar 134
Oil 29, 78, 153
Old Plaza 48–49, **49**
Olive House 148
Olvera Street **48**, 49
Olympic Plant 54
One Rodeo Drive 157
O'Neill House 155
Opening times 241
Opera 44, 262–63
Orange County 226, 230
 Bolsa Chica Ecological
  Reserve 230
 Huntington Beach 230
 Huntington Pier 230
 International Surfing
  Museum 230
 Laguna Beach 230
 Newport Beach 230
 Seal Beach 230
Oranges 25
Orpheum Theater 67, **67**
Otis School of Art and
 Design 79

P

Pacific Asia Museum 219, 220
Pacific Coast Highway 198–99
Pacific Coast Highway
 Station 62
Pacific Design Center 137,
 137
Pacific Palisades 185
 Self-Realization Fellowship
  Lake Shrine 185, 186
 Will Rogers State
  Historic Park 185, 186
Pacific Station 63
Page Museum 83, **83**
The Palace 115
Palm Springs and vicinity
 226, 233
 Living Desert Wildlife and
  Botanical Park 233
 Moorten Botanical
  Garden 233
 Palm Springs Aerial
  Tramway 233
 Palm Springs Air Museum
  233
 Palm Springs Desert
  Museum 233
 Spa Hotel 233

Palos Verdes Estates 196
Pantages Theater 109, 111
Paradise Cove 199
Paramount Pictures Studio
 122, **122**
Paramount Ranch 202
Parking 237
Pasadena 210–21
 Ambassador College 215
 Arroyo Terrace 213–14
 Ayers House 213
 California Institute of
  Technology (Caltech)
  221
 Central Library 219
 Cole House 213
 Culbertson House 214
 Duncan-Irwin House
  214
 Finnish Folk Art Museum
  215
 Gamble House 211,
  212–13
 Hawks House 214
 Hindry House 214
 Hutchins House 214
 Jesse Hoyt Smith House
  213
 Kidspace Museum 224
 map 218–19
 Millard House 214
 Norton Simon Museum
  216–17, **216–17**
 Pacific Asia Museum 219,
  220
 Pasadena City Hall **210**,
  219
 Pasadena Civic
  Auditorium 219
 Pasadena Historical
  Museum 215, **215**
 Pasadena Playhouse 219,
  219
 Prospect Park 214
 Ranney House 214
 Ritz-Carlton Huntington
  Hotel 215
 Rose Bowl 211
 Santa Fe Railroad Station
  218
 Tournament House and
  Wrigley Gardens 215
 Van Rosem-Neill House
  214
 walking tour 218–19
 Westmoreland Place 213
 White Sisters House 214
 Willett House 214
Pelanconi House 49
Performing Arts 42–44
Performing Arts Center 53,
 53
 Ahmanson Theater 53
 Disney Concert Hall 53
 Dorothy Chandler
  Pavilion 53
 Mark Taper Forum 53
Petersen Automotive
 Museum 92–93, **92–93**

Pharmacies 242
Piazza del Sol 133
Pickfair 168
Pico/Convention Center
 Station 62
Places of worship 241
Planning a trip 236
Playa del Rey 196
Playland Arcade 191
Pop, rock, jazz, and blues
 venues 263
Post offices 239
Powell Library 173, 175
Public arts programs 37–38
Public transportation 237–38

Q

Queen Mary **225**, 231, **231**

R

Radio 240
Rainbow Bar and Grill 133
Ramirez Canyon Park 202
Rancho Palos Verdes 196
Ranney House 214
Redondo Beach 196
Regent Beverly Wilshire
 Hotel 157
Religions and cults 124–25
Restaurants 158
 see also Hotels and
  restaurants
Riots 31–32, 33
Ripley's Believe It or Not!
 Odditorium 109, 110
Ritz-Carlton Huntington
 Hotel 215
Rodeo Collection 157
Rodeo Drive 154–55,
 154–55, 156–57
 Anderton Court 157
 Artists and Writers
  Building 157
 Harry Winston 157
 One Rodeo Drive 157
 Regent Beverly Wilshire
  Hotel 157
 Rodeo Collection 157
 Two Rodeo 157
 Van Cleef & Arpels 157
Rolling Hills Estates 196
Rose Bowl 211, **211**
Rothman House 81
The Roxy 133
Runyon Canyon Park 138

S

St. Basil's Roman Catholic
 Cathedral 79
St. Elmo's Village 98
Sales tax 241
San Bernardino Mountains
 226, 234
San Diego 234
San Fernando and San
 Gabriel Valleys 203–24
 Arroyo Seco 211
 Brand Library and Art
  Galleries 224

 Descanso Gardens 224
 Disney Studios 208
 Forest Lawn Memorial
  Park 209
 hotels and restaurants
  256–57
 The Huntington 222–23
 map 204–205
 Mission San Fernando Rey
  de España 224
 Mission San Gabriel
  Arcángel 224
 NBC Television Studios
  208
 Pasadena 210–21
 San Fernando Valley 204
 San Gabriel Valley 205
 Universal Studios
  Hollywood 206–207
 Warner Brothers Studios
  208
San Fernando Valley 204
San Gabriel Valley 205
San Pedro Station 62
Santa Monica 188–89,
 190–93
 Bergamot Station 192–93
 California Heritage
  Museum 192
 Looff Carousel 191
 Main Street 191–92
 Montana Avenue 202
 Museum of Flying 202
 Playland Arcade 191
 Santa Monica Museum of
  Art 193
 Santa Monica Pier
  190–91, **190–91**
 Third Street Promenade
  192, **192**, 193
 UCLA Ocean Discovery
  Center 191
Santa Monica State Beach
 198
Santa Monica, Venice, and
 Malibu 187–202
 driving tour 198–99
 hotels and restaurants
  254–56
 Malibu 188, 189, 197–99
 map 188–89
 Museum of Jurassic
  Technology 202
 Paramount Ranch 202
 Ramirez Canyon Park
  202
 Santa Monica 188–89,
  190–93
 Venice 188, 189, 194–96
Schindler House 136, **136**
Schnabel House 185
Schwab's Pharmacy 129
Seal Beach 230
Security Pacific Bank
 Building 82
Self-Realization Fellowship
 Lake Shrine 185, **185**, 186,
 186
Sepulveda House 49

Serra, Father Junípero 20, 21
Shakespeare Bridge 147
Shopping 241, 258–61
Shoreline Village 231
Shrine Auditorium 69
Shubert Theater 165
Silver Lake 141, 148
    Anthony House 148
    Neutra House 148
    Olive House 148
Simon Rodia State Historic
    Park 74
Six Flags Magic Mountain
    234
Skirball Cultural Center &
    Museum 183
Slauson Station 62
Smoking 241
South Bay 196
South Bonnie Brae Street 98
Southwest Museum 141,
    149, **149**
Sowden House 147
Spadena House 155
Spago **130,** 133
Spring Street 74
Staples Center 74
Storyopolis 98
Sturges House 185
Sunset Boulevard **126–27,**
126–28, 129, **129**
    A & M Recording Studios
    128
    Aquarius Theater 127
    Cinerama Dome Theater
    127
    Crossroads of the World
    127
    Director's Guild of
    America 128
    Garden of Allah 129
    Guitar Centre 128
    Hollywood Athletic Club
    127
    Hollywood High School
    128
    Hollywood Marketplace
    127
    Hollywood Palladium 127
    Schwab's Pharmacy 129
Sunset Plaza 133
Sunset Ranch 144
Sunset Strip 131–35, **131,**
132
    The Argyle 134
    Barfly 134
    Body Shop 135
    Book Soup 134
    Cajun Bistro 132
    Chateau Marmont 132
    The Comedy Store 132
    Greenblatt's Delicatessen
    129, 132
    House of Blues 134
    Hustler Hollywood 134
    Hyatt West Hollywood
    132
    Key Club 133
    Le Dôme 134

map 133
Mondrian 134
O2 Bar 134
Piazza del Sol 133
Rainbow Bar and Grill
    133
The Roxy 133
Spago 133
Sunset Plaza 133
Tiffany Theater 134
Tower Records 133
The Viper Room 134
Virgin Megastore 135
Whisky A Go Go 133
Surfrider Beach 199

T

Taxis 238
Telephones 239
Television 240
Theater 42–44, 262
Tiffany Theater 134
Tijuana 234
Time differences 241
Tipping 242
Toilets 242
Topanga State Park 198
Tourist offices 242
Tournament House and
    Wrigley Gardens 215
Tours 238–39
Tower Records 133, **134–35**
Trains 237, 238
Transit Mall Station 63
Travel Town 143
Trolley tours 155
Troubadour 135
Twentieth Century Fox 165
Two Rodeo 157

U

UCLA 171, **173,** 173–75
    Ackerman Student Union
    174
    Fowler Museum of
    Cultural History 173,
    174
    Franklin D. Murphy
    Sculpture Garden 173,
    175
    Kerckhoff Hall 173, 174
    map 175
    Mathias Botanical Garden
    175
    Moore Hall of Education
    174
    Morgan Intercollegiate
    Athletics Center 174
    Pauley Pavilion 174
    Powell Library 173, **175**
    Royce Hall 173, 174, **174**
    Schoenberg Auditorium
    175
    Schoenberg Hall 174
    Wight Art Gallery 173,
    175
UCLA at the Armand
    Hammer Museum of Art
    & Cultural Center 172

UCLA Grunwald Center
    for the Graphic Arts 172
UCLA Ocean Discovery
    Center 191
Union Station 50, **50,** 60
United Artists 67
Universal News Agency
    110
Universal Studios Hollywood
    206–207, **206–207**
University of Southern
    California 69, **69**
Unocal Gas Station 154
U.S. Post Office 154

V

Valentino, Rudolph 123
Van Cleef & Arpels 157
Van Rosem-Neill House
    214
Venice and vicinity 188, 189,
    194–96
    Los Angeles Harbor 196
    Marina del Rey 196
    Playa del Rey 196
    South Bay 196
    Venice Boardwalk
    194–95, **195**
Vermont/Beverly Station
    60, **62**
Vermont/Santa Monica
    Station 60–61
Vermont/Sunset Station 61
Vernon Station 62
Vine Street 114, 115
The Viper Room 134
Virgin Megastore 135
Virginia Robinson Gardens
    162
Virginia Steele Scott Gallery
    of American Art 223

W

Walk of Fame 102–104
Walking tours 239
    Hollywood Boulevard
    110–11
    Melrose Avenue 96–97
    Pasadena 218–19
    Rodeo Drive 156–57
    Sunset Strip 132–35
    UCLA 174–75
Walt Disney House 147
Wardlow Station 62
Warner Brothers Studios
    208
Washington Station 62
Water supply 26–29
Wattles House and Park
    138
Watts Towers **39,** 74
Watts Towers Art Center
    74
Weather reports 242
Wells Fargo History
    Museum 74
West Hollywood 101,
    130–37

Pacific Design Center 137
Schindler House 136
Sunset Strip 131–35
Westlake/MacArthur Park
    Station 60
The Westside 169–86
    Bel Air 184
    Brentwood 184–85
    Getty Center 171, 176–82
    hotels and restaurants
    253–54
    map 170–71
    Mormon Temple 186
    Pacific Palisades 185
    Skirball Cultural Center &
    Museum 183
    UCLA 171, 173–75
    Westwood Village 172
        Bruin 172
        Dome 172
        Mann Village 172
    UCLA at the Armand
        Hammer Museum of Art
        & Cultural Center 172
    UCLA Grunwald Center
        for the Graphic Arts
        172
    Westwood Village
        Memorial Park &
        Mortuary 186
Whisky A Go Go 133
White Sisters House 214
Whitley Heights 120
Wight Art Gallery 173, 175
Will Rogers State Historic
    Park 185, 186
Willett House 214
Willow Station 62
Wilshire, Henry Gaylord 78
Wilshire Boulevard 76,
    78–79, 82
    Ambassador Hotel 79
    Bullocks Wilshire 79, **79**
    Granada Building 78–79
    MacArthur Park **77,** 78
    Otis School of Art and
    Design 79
    St. Basil's Roman Catholic
    Cathedral 79
    Wilshire Boulevard
    Temple 79
    Wiltern Theater 79
Wilshire Boulevard Temple
    79
Wilshire/Normandie
    Station 60
Wilshire/Vermont Station 60
Wilshire/Western Station 60
Wilson Building 82
Wiltern Theater 79
Wright, Frank Lloyd 40,
    117, 120, 157, 185, 214

Y

Yamashiro Restaurant 138

Z

Zanja Madre 49
Zuma Beach 199

ILLUSTRATIONS CREDITS

Abbreviations for terms appearing below: (t) top; (b) bottom;(c) center; (l) left; (r) right:

Cover (tl), Gettyone/Stone. (tr), Frank Spooner Pictures Ltd. (br), Craig Aurness/Corbis UK Ltd. (bl), AA Photo Library/Max Jordan (with permission from Mel's Drive-In). (spine), Frank Spooner Pictures Ltd

1, Superstock Inc. 2, Steve Weinberg/Gettyone/Stone. 4, Ken Biggs/Gettyone/Stone. 9, Catherine Karnow. 12/3, Robert Yager/Gettyone/Stone. 14/5, Steve McCurry/Magnum Photos. 16/7, Joe McNally/National Geographic Society. 19, Bettmann/Corbis UK Ltd. 20, Catherine Karnow. 21, Private Collection/Ken Welsh /Bridgeman Art Library. 22/3, Library of Congress, Washington D. C, USA/Bridgeman Art Library. 24, Bettmann/Corbis UK Ltd. 25, Trip & Art Directors Photo Library. 26/7, Bison Productions. 28/9, Bettmann/Corbis UK Ltd. 30, Bison Productions. 31, Paul Fusco/Magnum Photos. 32/3, Michael Ochs Arch/Redferns Music Picture Library. 34/5, David Hockney Studio. 36/7, Ronald Grant Archive. 38, Robert Yager/Gettyone/Stone. 39, Paul Fusco/Magnum Photos. 40/1, Robert Holmes. 42/3, Mark Harris/Gettyone/Stone. 44, Steve McCurry/Magnum Photos. 45, Sylvain Gandadam/Colorific! 48, AA Photo Library/Max Jourdan. 49, AA Photo Library/Max Jourdan. 50, AA Photo Library/Max Jourdan. 51, Deborah Davis/Gettyone/Stone. 52, AA Photo Library/Max Jourdan. 53, Ed Rooney/Gettyone/Stone. 54t, AA Photo Library/Max Jourdan. 54b, AA Photo Library/Max Jourdan. 55, AA Photo Library/Max Jourdan. 57, AA Photo Library/Max Jourdan. 58, AA Photo Library/Max Jourdan. 59, AA Photo Library/Max Jourdan. 60, Brian McGilloway/Robert Holmes. 61t, AA Photo Library/Max Jourdan. 61b, AA Photo Library/Max Jourdan. 62, AA Photo Library/Max Jourdan. 63, AA Photo Library/Max Jourdan. 64, AA Photo Library/Max Jourdan. 65t, AA Photo Library/Phil Wood. 65b, S. Grant/Trip & Art Directors Photo Library. 66, AA Photo Library/Max Jourdan. 67t, Catherine Karnow. 67b, Bernard Boutrit/Woodfin Camp & Associates Inc. 68, Catherine Karnow. 69, AA Photo Library/Max Jourdan. 71, Robert Holmes. 72, Robert Holmes. 73, AA Photo Library/Max Jourdan. 75, Catherine Karnow. 77, Topham Picturepoint. 79, Brian McGilloway/Robert Holmes. 80, J. Nordell/The Image Works/Topham Picturepoint. 81, Robert Holmes. 82, Brian McGilloway/Robert Holmes. 83t, Tony Wright/PowerStock/Zefa. 83b, Dick Meier/Natural History Museum of Los Angeles County. 84, Catherine Karnow/Colorific! 85, Los Angeles County Museum of Art. 86, Los Angeles County Museum of Art, CA, USA/Bridgeman Art Library. 87, Los Angeles County Museum of Art, CA, USA/Bridgeman Art Library. 88t, Los Angeles County Museum of Art, CA, USA/Bridgeman Art Library. 88b, Los Angeles County Museum of Art, CA, USA/Bridgeman Art Library. 89, Catherine Karnow/Woodfin Camp & Associates Inc. 90t, Robert Yager/Gettyone/Stone. 90c, Robert Yager/Gettyone/Stone. 90b, Catherine Karnow. 90/1, Robert Yager/Gettyone/Stone. 92/3, Barbara Filet/Gettyone/Stone. 94t, Brian McGilloway/Robert Holmes. 94b, Catherine Karnow. 95t, Brian McGilloway/Robert Holmes. 95b, Tony Wright/PowerStock/Zefa. 96, A. Ramey/Woodfin Camp & Associates Inc. 97t, A. Gin/PowerStock/Zefa. 99, Catherine Karnow. 103, Catherine Karnow. 104, AA Photo Library/Max Jourdan. 105, Reza Estakhrian/Gettyone/Stone. 106, Robert Holmes. 107t, AA Photo Library/Max Jourdan. 107b, Alpha. 108/9, S. Grant/Trip & Art Directors Photo Library. 110, Bernard Boutrit/Woodfin Camp & Associates Inc. 111, AA Photo Library/Max Jourdan. 112/3, Joseph Sohm; ChromoSohm Inc./Corbis UK Ltd. 114/5, Telegraph Colour Library. 115, Catherine Karnow. 116/7, AA Photo Library/Max Jourdan. 118/9, British Film Institute. 120, Catherine Karnow. 121, Catherine Karnow. 122, Alan Levenson/Gettyone/Stone. 123t, Brian McGilloway/Robert Holmes. 123b, AA Photo Library/Max Jourdan. 124/5, S. Grant/Trip & Art Directors Photo Library. 125, Popperfoto. 126/7, Mecky Fogeling. 127, AA Photo Library/Max Jourdan. 128, AA Photo Library/Max Jourdan. 129, Paul Fusco/Magnum Photos. 130, AA Photo Library/Max Jourdan. 131, Steve McCurry/Magnum Photos. 132, AA Photo Library/Max Jourdan. 134, Catherine Karnow. 134/5, Bernard Boutrit/Woodfin Camp & Associates Inc. 136, AA Photo Library/Max Jourdan. 137, Robert Landau/Corbis UK Ltd. 139, AA Photo Library/Max Jourdan. 141, Joseph Sohm; ChromoSohm Inc./Corbis UK Ltd. 143, Brian McGilloway/Robert Holmes. 144, Jim Corwin/Gettyone/Stone. 145, Autry Museum of Western Heritage. 146, Ralph A. Clevenger/Corbis UK Ltd. 147, Photovault. 148, Photovault. 149t, Assassi '98/Southwest Museum. 149b, Don Meyer/Southwest Museum. 151, Catherine Karnow. 153, Ian Cook/Colorific! 154/5, AA Photo Library/Max Jourdan. 156, Colorific. 158/9, Catherine Karnow. 159, Philip Jones-Griffiths/Magnum Photos. 160, Terry O'Neill. 161, Beverly Hills Hotel. 162, Virginia Robinson Gardens. 163, Grant Mudford/Museum of Television and Radio. 164/5, Catherine Karnow. 166, Robert Holmes. 167, Robert Holmes. 169, AA Photo Library/Max Jourdan. 172, Catherine Karnow. 173, Phil Schermeister/Corbis UK Ltd. 174, Phil Schermeister/Corbis UK Ltd. 176/7, B. Tanaka/Telegraph Colour Library. 177, AA Photo Library/Max Jourdan. 179, AA Photo Library/Max Jourdan. 180t, J. Paul Getty Trust. 180b, S. Grant/Trip & Art Directors Photo Library. 181t, AA Photo Library/Max Jourdan. 181b, J. Paul Getty Trust. 182, J. Paul Getty Trust. 183, Timothy Hursley/Skirball Cultural Center. 184, Victoria King Public Relations, Inc. 185, Catherine Karnow. 186, Catherine Karnow. 187, AA Photo Library/Max Jourdan. 190/1, Siegfried Layda/Gettyone/Stone. 192, AA Photo Library/Max Jourdan, 193, Deborah Davis/Gettyone/Stone. 194, AA Photo Library/Max Jourdan. 195, AA Photo Library/Max Jourdan. 196, AA Photo Library/Max Jourdan. 197, AA Photo Library/Max Jourdan. 198, AA Photo Library/Max Jourdan. 199t, AA Photo Library/Max Jourdan. 199b, AA Photo Library/Max Jourdan. 200, Catherine Karnow/Woodfin Camp & Associates Inc. 201t, Popperfoto. 201b, A. Ramey/Woodfin Camp & Associates Inc. 203, Catherine Karnow. 206/7, Universal Pictures. 208, Robert Holmes/Corbis UK Ltd. 209, Catherine Karnow. 210, Ken Biggs/Gettyone/Stone. 211, Frank Balthis. 212, Greene & Greene Archives. 212/3, Gamble House. 213l, Greene & Greene Archives. 213r, Richard Bryant/Arcaid. 214, Ezra Stoller/Esto Photographics. 215, Robert Holmes. 216, Norton Simon Museum, Pasadena. 217, Norton Simon Collection, Pasadena, CA, USA/Bridgeman Art Library. 219, Robert Holmes. 220, Pacific Asia Museum. 221, California Institute of Technology. 222, Frank Balthis. 223, Frank Balthis. 225, James Davis Worldwide. 227, Kathleen Norris Cook. 228/9, Disney Enterprises, Inc. 230, Frank Balthis. 231, Alex Webb/Magnum Photos. 232, Kathleen Norris Cook. 233, Kathleen Norris Cook. 235, Robert McGilloway/Robert Holmes.

CREDITS

Published by the National Geographic Society
John M. Fahey, Jr., *President and Chief Executive Officer*
Gilbert M. Grosvenor, *Chairman of the Board*
Nina D. Hoffman, *Senior Vice President*
William R. Gray, *Vice President and Director, Book Division*
Elizabeth L. Newhouse, *Director of Travel Publishing*
Cinda Rose, *Art Director*
Barbara A. Noe, *Associate Editor*
Caroline Hickey, *Senior Researcher*
Jane Sunderland, *Editorial Researcher*
Carl Mehler, *Director of Maps*
Joseph F. Ochlak, *Map Coordinator*
Gary Colbert, *Production Director*
Richard S. Wain, *Production Project Manager*
Angela George, *Staff Assistant*

Edited and designed by AA Publishing (a trading name of Automobile Association Developments Limited, whose registered office is Norfolk House, Priestley Road, Basingstoke, Hampshire, England RG24 9NY. Registered number: 1878835).
Rachel Alder, *Project Manager*
David Austin, *Senior Art Editor*
Allen Stidwill, *Senior Editor*
Keith Russell, *Designer*
Inna Nogeste, *Senior Cartographic Editor*
Richard Firth, *Production Director*
Steve Gilchrist, *Prepress Production Controller*
Cartography by AA Cartographic Production
Picture Research by Zooid Pictures Ltd.
Drive maps drawn by Chris Orr Associates, Southampton, England
Cutaway illustrations drawn by Maltings Partnership, Derby, England

Library of Congress Cataloging-in-Publication Data
Johnson Marael
    The National Geographic Traveler: Los Angeles / Marael Johnson
            p   cm
        Includes index.
        ISBN 0-7922-7947-6
        1. Los Angeles (Calif.)—Guidebooks. I. Title: Los Angeles.
        II. Title
        F869.L83 J65 2000
        917.94'940454—dc21   00-061306
                                                         CIP

Printed and bound by R.R. Donnelley & Sons, Willard, Ohio.
Color separations by Leo Reprographic Ltd., Hong Kong.
Cover separations by L.C. Repro, Aldermaston, U.K.
Cover printed by Miken Inc., Cheektowaga, New York.

Visit the Society's Web site at http://www.nationalgeographic.com

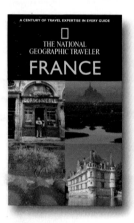
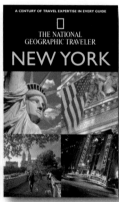
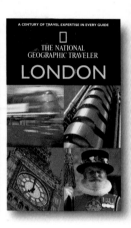